Confronting Catastrophe

A GIS HANDBOOK

R.W. Greene

ESRI PRESS

REDLANDS, CALIFORNIA

ESRI Press, 380 New York Street, Redlands, California 92373-8100

Printed in the United States of America

Library of Congress Cataloging-in-Publication Data
Greene, R. W.
Confronting catastrophe : a GIS handbook / R. W. Greene.
    p.   cm.
  ISBN 1-58948-040-6 (pbk.)
    1. Emergency management—Data processing. 2. Disaster relief—Data processing.
  3. Geographic information systems. I. Title.
  HV551.2 .G74   2002
  363.34'8'0285—dc21   2002008728

ISBN-13: 978-1-58948-040-7
ISBN-10: 1-58948-040-6

Ask for ESRI Press titles at your local bookstore or order by calling 1-800-447-9778. You
can also shop online at www.esri.com/esripress. Outside the United States, contact your local
ESRI distributor.

ESRI Press titles are distributed to the trade by the following:

In North America, South America, Asia,
and Australia:
Independent Publishers Group (IPG)
Telephone (United States): 1-800-888-4741
Telephone (international): 312-337-0747
E-mail: frontdesk@ipgbook.com

In the United Kingdom, Europe,
and the Middle East:
Transatlantic Publishers Group Ltd.
Telephone: 44 20 7373 2515
Fax: 44 20 7244 1018
E-mail: richard@tpgltd.co.uk

Book design and production by Michael J. Hyatt
Cover design by Doug Huibregtse
Image editing by Jennifer Galloway
Printing coordination by Cliff Crabbe

Acknowledgments and credits

M ANY highly skilled men and women contributed their insights and knowledge so that this book could get written; all of them deserve a much heartier round of applause than can be generated by ink on paper here. I thank them all again for their generous contributions of time and energy, and for their support of the goals of this book.

In particular, several people who contributed much valuable GIS work to the nation in the weeks after September 11 also played important roles in this project. David Kerhlein, GIS Manager of the State of California Governor's Office of Emergency Services, served as *eminence grise;* without the hours he spent relating how GIS gets done when buildings lie smashed and fires rage, this book probably could not have been done. In a similar capacity, Tim Walsh, Fire Captain Specialist with the Marin County Fire Department, contributed several hours of patient explanation about good GIS technique and methodology. Also providing much invaluable insight and patient tutoring were Ron Langhelm, GIS Coordinator for Response and Recovery with FEMA's Region X, and Christopher Schielein and Susan Harwood of ESRI's New York City satellite office. Alan Leidner of the New York City Department of Information Technology and Telecommunications (DoITT) provided several hours of insight and inspiration.

Thanks also to K. Adams Manion of URS Corporation, Wendy Dorf of the New York City Department of Environmental Protection, and Marina Havan-Orumieh of PlanGraphics, Inc., for allowing the reprint in chapter 4 of their detailed and affecting account of the Deep Infrastructure Project work at Ground Zero.

Much thanks as well to Roy Price; John Heller of the Wyoming Emergency Management Agency; Catherine Potts of Dewberry & Davis, LLC; Eric Mosher of the U.S. Coast Guard Seventh District; Eric Householder,

Jude Denick-Turner, and Karen Volarich of the South Florida Water Management District; Dick Andrews and Neil C. Blais of ABS Consulting; Richard Knudson and Doug Wilder of the Florida Fish and Wildlife Conservation Commission; Michael Fené of Science Applications International Corp.; Barbara Schauer of the National Institute of Building Sciences; Bruce Cahan of Urban Logic, Inc.; Jay Sadler of Michelle's AAA Equipment Rentals, Inc.; James Wood of Dialogic Communications Corp.; Kurt Olmsted of the Mecklenburg County Department of Property Assessment and Land Records Management; Linda Gerull of Pierce County, Washington; Scott McAfee of FEMA; Daniel Dubno of CBS News; Soheila Ajabshir, Karen Grassi, Chuck Lanza, and Bill Johnson of Miami-Dade County; Brian Pierce of the Florida Department of Agriculture and Consumer Services; James Hall of PlanGraphics, Inc.; Mary Beth Fletcher of Arlington County, Virginia; Lisa Flax and Russell Jackson of the NOAA Coastal Services Center; Stewart Gary of the Livermore-Pleasanton Fire Department; and Twyla McDermott of the City of Charlotte, North Carolina.

At ESRI, thanks to Dave LaShell, Russ Johnson, Kris Goodfellow, Brenda Martinez, Caroline Staab, Robert Hofmann, Patrick Fowler, Chris Cappelli, Chris Wayne, Dale Loberger, Jaime Crawford, Jason Brouillette, Jeff Garland, John Calkins, Jon Harrison, Lori Shienvold, Craig Devine, Mike Tait, Paul Hartwell, Shelly Sommer, Caroline Chen, Tom Pederson, Rob Della Marna, Michael Zeiler, Judy Boyd, Nick Frunzi, and Jack Dangermond.

At ESRI Press, David Boyles edited the text. Michael J. Hyatt designed, produced, and copyedited the book. Jennifer Johnston contributed to the design and did the image editing. Edith Punt provided deft cartographic and title advice. Steve Hegle tackled administrative issues. Christian Harder led this able team. Thanks to all.

CREDITS

The Deep Infrastructure Project reprint originally appeared in slightly different form on *GeoWorld* magazine's Web site, geoplace.com/gr/groundzero. Thanks to *GeoWorld* Integrated Content Editor, Matt Ball, for permission to reproduce it here.

Screen captures from the Community Vulnerability Assessment Tool are by permission of the NOAA Coastal Services Center.

EarthData, Inc., helped provide several aerial images for chapter 4. Thanks to Linda Harrington Baker, EarthData director of Marketing and Communications, for her assistance.

Other maps and images related to the World Trade Center disaster response were obtained from the Pier 92 Emergency Mapping and Data Center of the Mayor's Office of Emergency Management, and from the California Governor's Office of Emergency Services.

Data for the 3-D image of New York City on the cover is courtesy of Vexcel Corp.

Contents

Acknowledgments and credits   v

Introduction   ix

chapter 1   **Identification and planning**   1

chapter 2   **Mitigation**   15

chapter 3   **Preparedness**   27

chapter 4   **Response**   41

chapter 5   **Recovery**   71

appendix A   **Challenges for GIS in Emergency Preparedness and Response**   80

appendix B   **Spatial data layers**   111

appendix C   **Five-year general strategies matrix of the FIRESCOPE Geographic Information Systems and Spatial Information Technology Group (GISSIT)**   121

Introduction

O NE afternoon in October 2001, Alan Leidner took a quick break
from his work and sat down to talk about using GIS in disaster
management. In the space of a few weeks, he'd become an expert
on the issue. As director of Citywide GIS for the New York City
Department of Information Technology and Telecommunications
(DOITT), Leidner and dozens of others had been doing nothing but
GIS and disaster management since September 11—working fifteen-,
eighteen-, and twenty-hour days at the Emergency Mapping and
Data Center on Pier 92. Leidner explained how he and teams from
city agencies, consulting firms, and hardware and software vendors
had been rebuilding the GIS system right there in the cavernous pier
building on the Hudson River—rebuilding it because much of it had
been destroyed when terrorists assaulted the World Trade Center
only a few miles south.

Since that day, the GIS teams had been working relentlessly, scroung-
ing backup data sets from everywhere, administering databases,
geocoding buildings, creating three-dimensional models of the Ground
Zero debris pile, reconstructing the underground geography of lower
Manhattan—not to mention making hundreds of maps for anyone
who asked for one—from the world-famous mayor on down the line.

Leidner is a soft-spoken man, but there is no mistaking his commitment to GIS, or his pride in what the teams were able to accomplish
with the technology. There had been some, however, who had ques-
tioned whether all these maps, however pretty they looked, really did
all that much good.

Leidner searched in the air for a second for the words he needed to
respond to that point of view.

"This stuff," he said, "saves lives."

GIS INTEGRAL TO DISASTER MANAGEMENT

Leidner's belief is the premise of this book also: that now, as never before, GIS technology has become integral to any comprehensive disaster management plan—as essential for dealing with a catastrophic event as bandages and radios.

That premise has taken on new validity after the events of September 2001. GIS was a key tool for those responding to the terrorist destruction in New York City and at the Pentagon—or, to put it another way, there was never any consideration given to *not* using GIS in those response and recovery efforts.

And as the United States begins to focus its disaster management efforts on a new goal—defending against future attacks under the banner of homeland security—the need for GIS will become even more clear.

This premise has been enunciated by a growing number of figures in the field of emergency and disaster management.

The assessment of Roy C. Price, past president of the National Emergency Management Association, is representative: "Geographical Information Systems provide the best method to efficiently support emergency management information needs. Emergency crisis events will impact more than people and facilities; they have an impact on the environment, agricultural crops, livestock, ocean food stocks, and economic dislocation of communities. GIS provides the means for widely diverse organizational and governmental agencies to participate in the full range of emergency management activities at all levels of government."

VISUALIZING DATA

No other technology allows for the visualization of an emergency or disaster situation as effectively as GIS. By placing the accurate physical geography of a disaster event on a computer monitor, and then aligning other relevant features, events, conditions, or threats with that geography, GIS lets police, fire, medical, and managerial personnel make decisions based on data they can see and judge for themselves. This visualized information can be of critical relevance to a disaster manager: the size and direction of wildfire perimeters, the location of broken levees or of hazardous chemical spill release points, or the whereabouts of surviving victims inside a bombed building.

It is difficult to understate the innate connections in the brain that this kind of visualization creates; a spatial or geography-based method presents necessary information in a way far more real than any other.

Leidner says it is sometimes easier for skeptics to understand this concept if they think of GIS in a different way—as a tool that visualizes data, any kind of data.

GIS is also a data consolidator. Decision makers, whether in the state capitol or at the scene of a toxic chemical spill, are almost always faced with much more information than they can deal with. GIS brings many information sources into one focus, helping clarify which elements in a disaster need immediate attention, which can wait, and which can be delegated. These are the kinds of choices and compromises—for it is a sad reality in a disaster that you can't save everything—that are intrinsic to disaster management. GIS allows them to be seen with new clarity.

With the right data and the right GIS, understanding of where help is needed becomes instantaneous. And in a disaster, instantaneous is the speed at which responders want to be moving.

PURPOSE

This book is designed for several different audiences, each with a stake in disaster management but each with different interests and point of view. It is not intended to be a comprehensive enumeration of all GIS disaster-management applications in the United States, nor a technical or policy manual. It is more in the nature of a survey—synthesizing some of the lessons that have been learned so far, showing a glimpse of what a few of the experts are doing around the county, and, it is hoped, giving the reader a firm enough footing to investigate whether a particular application or piece of advice may have local relevance.

For GIS professionals and managers, articulating the underlying premise of the book is preaching to the choir. They already understand the power of GIS to convey information.

However, they may not be fully aware of how making maps and doing GIS analysis in a disaster response situation—where seconds count—can be a far different experience from daily GIS tasks such as analyzing watersheds or mapping new property tax boundaries. The point is succinctly made by David Kehrlein, head of GIS operations for the California Governor's Office of Emergency Services.

"It's one thing to say, 'make me a map'," Kehrlein says. "It's a lot different to stick a gun to your head and say, 'make me a map'."

Among the goals of this book is to show those in the GIS community ways that some of their colleagues have learned to make maps and to do GIS analysis under gunpoint conditions.

EMERGENCY MANAGERS

Another audience is the men and women who are already quite familiar with what it is like to make split-second decisions affecting human life while the chaos of disaster rages around them.

Within this community, however, promoting the use of new technologies has sometimes been uphill work. It is not hard to understand why: the tradition-rich task of responding to disaster, of saving lives and property, is a basic kind of labor, one that doesn't require a lot in the way of high-tech. You don't create a fire line, for example, by equipping a squad of firefighters with notebook computers; you equip them with a no-nonsense, axe-like tool known as a Pulaski.

Moreover, being the first on the scene of some soul-wrenching panorama of human devastation, such as the one that took place on September 11, requires qualities from human beings that often make machines and software seem entirely irrelevant.

But it is equally true that there is more to disaster management than the first, adrenaline-filled, on-scene response to it. Knowing *where* to respond, which is what GIS lets you do, is a critical piece of knowledge for everyone at a disaster scene. And knowing well ahead of time the location of the most dangerous areas (when GIS is used in a planning and preparation context) can only benefit those on the front lines, not hinder them.

DECISION MAKERS

It is also hoped this book will help legislators and managers in government who are eager, in the wake of September 11, to learn new ways to protect their communities and constituents. While this volume is not intended to be a definitive handbook on homeland security, many lessons from implementing GIS in a disaster management context can easily be transferred to the homeland security arena.

These decision makers may in fact already be ahead of the game: if they look around their own public agencies, they will probably find GIS being used in some capacity easily turned to a disaster management purpose. A property-tax database, for example, usually contains names and phone numbers of homeowners, information that can be imported into an emergency notification application.

STOVEPIPES OF DATA

Managers and decision makers may find that their data holdings put them ahead of the game, but it is also quite possible they will find that data in disarray. That leads to another premise for this book: the key to an effective GIS-based disaster management operation is the freely flowing interchange of data among every organization that needs it.

In many communities and states in the United States at present, data relevant to disaster management is scattered across the enterprise, and often in incompatible formats. "Data stovepipes" are common—data created or purchased by one department or agency for its own GIS applications, and not shared with other departments and agencies. Indeed, another agency may not even know of the existence of that data, even though it may contain information directly relevant to its own mission. In many cases, bureaucratic turf wars and a perceived need to "protect" data from "outside" agencies form another barrier, preventing the effective use of geographic data for all constituents.

Indeed, one important factor in the workload of those laboring in the Mapping and Data Center on Pier 92 was the effort involved in getting access to relevant, complete, and compatible data for the myriad layers of New York City—much of which was held by departments and agencies that had no history of data-sharing, or even of carrying on effective communication. One salutary effect of the tragedy was that it helped to start bringing down those barriers.

To create an effective GIS-based disaster management plan and an effective homeland security plan, such stovepipes and barriers must be eliminated. The beginnings of a solution are being seen in such initiatives as the National Spatial Data Infrastructure (NSDI), created by executive order in 1994 to encourage geospatial data acquisition and access. The order specifically enumerates emergency response efforts as one of the areas where the initiative should be targeted, and it seems likely the events of September 11 may bring additional energy to the NSDI goals.

DATA CHALLENGES

As with any application of a GIS, data is the key to its most effective use—its accessibility, its quality, and its compatibility with other formats and systems. The principles of good data management, such as laying a solid foundation with thorough, current metadata, are even more of an imperative in the disaster context. So is backing up the data itself, at two or three remote locations.

The most effective disaster management systems are those built on an enterprise, or centralized, basis.

An enterprise GIS solution—in which all agencies have access to a centralized base of geographic data layers—leverages the public's already considerable investment in data by reducing redundancies in both data and processing. An enterprise-based system allows disaster and emergency management agencies to access any data layer that might be most useful to them during a time of crisis. Because it can never be predicted which data layer that might be, accessing the entire system allows for more flexibility than one in which disaster managers access only a previously selected, compartmentalized set of data layers.

INTERNET

The effects of the Internet and of mobile, wireless applications are impacting disaster management GIS even as this book is being written. GIS applications such as ESRI® ArcPad™, deployed on personal digital assistants (PDAs), are now allowing for field-level assessments of conditions at a disaster scene in real time, which can then be transmitted back to emergency operations centers. The same kind of immediacy is also available through the Internet, also enhancing disaster decision making; interactive mapping applications such as the GEOMAC system for monitoring wildfires (geomac.usgs.gov) are allowing for real-time assessment of rapidly changing disaster conditions from anywhere in the country.

STAGES OF DISASTER MANAGEMENT

The book is organized to follow roughly the accepted methodology of disaster management (although some authorities consolidate some stages and use slightly different names). These are: planning and identification; mitigation; preparedness; response; and finally, recovery. The first three stages deal with tasks that an organization or community can take before a disaster event, while the latter two focus on postdisaster efforts.

In general, GIS applications in disaster management have been integrated unevenly across these five stages in the United States, depending on the amount of experience, the area, and the size of budget.

Disaster management agencies in California, Florida, and North Carolina have developed more robust systems than have those in other parts of the country, and so receive more attention here. Having been hit with many hurricanes, floods, earthquakes, and wildfires over many decades, they have by necessity gained much experience at confronting catastrophe, with GIS.

chapter 1   **Identification and planning**

Mitigation

Preparedness

Response

Recovery

"WHAT IS THERE TO BURN?"

That simple question is an effective, if blunt, way to begin thinking about using GIS in the identification and planning stage of disaster management.

A question that comes originally from the world of firefighters, its purpose is straightforward: to identify the physical, human, and other assets in a community most in danger from a natural or man-made disaster. Only when you know what it is you and your city or community value the most can you begin to plan for ways to protect those assets, and to move on to the next stage of disaster management, mitigation.

"What is there to burn?" is an obvious oversimplification; you are looking for much more than some buildings that might catch fire. You are doing the broadest possible assessment of assets at risk from any kind of man-made or natural disaster.

That requires answering a related question, along the lines of "What kinds of fires are burning?" This is the other half of the planning equation, the one requiring an assessment of the hazards, or threats, to those assets you've identified. And because it also involves calculations of risk and probability, it can be a considerably more complex question to answer.

ASSESSMENT CRITERIA

These assessments will be in some sense ideals, since no assessment can anticipate every eventuality; nor is such an assessment ever really finished, since hazard conditions change daily, sometimes hourly. And while these inventories should be as precise as possible, they should not be too technical; an inventory should have the attribute of being easily communicated, not only to responders, but also to the public—if for no other reason that in the wake of a disaster, decisions to protect one group of assets at the expense of another will have to be defended.

WHY GIS?

The spatial display and analysis tools of GIS are ideal for satisfying the myriad answers these two questions will give rise to. GIS can display the location, size, value, and significance of assets. It can show the kinds of environmental, atmospheric, and other conditions that give rise to particular kinds of natural disasters. GIS can juxtapose a particular kind of asset—beachfront hotel properties, for example—with specific hazardous conditions—storm surge caused by hurricane—over a wide geographic area, allowing a precise calculation of potential loss in the immediate area.

When this kind of graphic depiction is drawn, the choices about what to do and where to do it are appreciably clarified for those who have to make those choices.

ASSETS FOR DISASTER MODELING

A prodigious inventory of assets and hazard risks is a basic ingredient of disaster-modeling software applications. The two best-known, publicly available software packages—known by their acronyms CATS and HAZUS—both use GIS (ArcView® and ArcGIS®) for a user interface. They include extensive national data sets of assets that can be customized for local use, and include both obvious candidates, such as hospitals and nuclear plants, and not-so-obvious ones, such as pharmacies, which can be mapped in GIS. They also perform complex calculations of hazard risk and probability for a variety of disaster events, from floods to toxic spills. They then return extremely accurate estimates of human casualties, building damage, infrastructure loss, and other consequences.

And each is available at no cost to communities that want them.

ASSESSING HAZARDS AND HAZARD RISKS

GIS can help at the beginning of a hazard and hazard risk assessment by mapping the history of hazards in a particular area: seismic activity or tropical storms, for example. Conditions that make an area more susceptible to disaster can also be mapped: the location of known active earthquake faults (as differentiated from historical seismic activity), or El Niño conditions at a certain time of year, or precipitation and snowpack information.

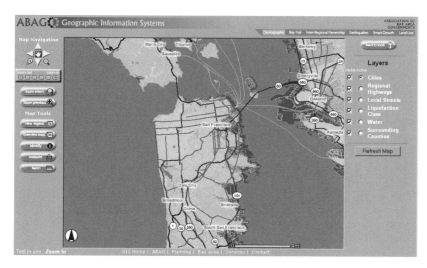

The Association of Bay Area Governments (gis.abag.ca.gov) provides some of the most comprehensive online earthquake identification and planning tools, including this ArcIMS®-based interactive map for identifying liquefaction zones.

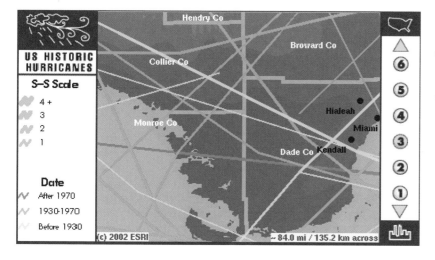

Online hazard maps from ESRI and the Federal Emergency Management Agency (FEMA), available at esri.com/hazards/index.html, show historical disaster patterns in different parts of the country.

ASSESSING ASSETS

Just what constitutes a valuable asset in a community is a qualitative, and therefore political, question for the community and its leaders. GIS can help answer it simply by displaying for decision makers the kinds of geographic patterns these assets form—clustered uncomfortably close to a floodplain, or near an earthquake fault.

Some asset data sets will be obvious: law enforcement facilities, fire and other emergency services, hospitals, schools, government buildings, communication systems, major highways and rail links, airports, nuclear and other kinds of power-generating plants, and military facilities are among those that clearly need to be mapped. But others will require more research, and more imagination.

GASB 34: A NEW IMPERATIVE

A significant change in the way state and local governments do their financial reporting adds a new impetus for doing a GIS-based inventory of assets. In June 1999, the Governmental Accounting Standards Board (GASB), which lays out the financial reporting rules for state and local governments, adopted "Statement No. 34: Basic Financial Statements – and Management's Discussion and Analysis – for State and Local Governments." Statement 34 mandated a wholesale revision in the way local governments' financial reports should be done and published. Among these mandates are those affecting the way the assets of an organization's infrastructure are accounted for and reported. Infrastructure is considered to be things like roads, bridges, and utility systems. Although a complete discussion is not possible here, it is expected that the new rules will tend to encourage governments to spend more for maintenance over the life of an infrastructure asset, thus extending its life and usefulness to the public.

The new rules require that governments keep track of these assets much more closely than they ever have had to before, not only at the beginning of their switch over to the new rules, but for the succeeding years.

Especially for infrastructure assets, GIS is an ideal system by which to perform these inventories, because location is, of course, one of their most important attributes.

DATA: THE MORE SOONER, THE BETTER

To state a point that will be made often, obtaining complete and up-to-date data about both assets and hazards should be an overriding concern in the early planning stages of any GIS-focused disaster management program.

Just what data sets will be relevant will challenge the imagination of all stakeholders. Since the exact size, form, and timing of a disaster cannot be predicted (and in the case of earthquakes or terrorism, little to no prediction can be done at all), the worst course would be to place limitations on the data that a GIS team might need. There is no way to know that a data set that now seems to have no connection to a disaster response—the location of veterinary clinics, for instance—may become crucially important later.

Obtaining data will require learning what local data sets are available from other sources, other local agencies, relevant federal and state agencies, and important private enterprises, such as utilities. The GIS user network, which easily crosses agency boundaries, will be an obvious place to start; it will also know where other data sets have been buried.

Good data can be found in many places other than the conventional ones—another reason for all participants in disaster management to think imaginatively. For example, while the Census Bureau continues to be an excellent source for population data, much additional data about world and U.S. populations can also be found at the Center for International Earth Science Information Network at Columbia University (ciesin.org/index.html). Other research and nonprofit institutions can provide complementary or enhanced data sets of a variety of disaster information.

DATA-SHARING AGREEMENTS

Finding data will also necessarily mean sitting down with other agencies to work out data-sharing arrangements. Such negotiations may be protracted, especially if they are with reluctant data holders who contend that their data is proprietary and cannot be disclosed, even for life-saving purposes.

The reasons for such a point of view vary—fear of litigation, fear of losing bureaucratic turf or administrative authority—but the effect in a disaster context is uniform: an organization's ability to save lives and property will be degraded.

In the face of this certainty—especially when the new paradigm of homeland security is driving many new disaster management efforts—holding data hostage to advance administrative or commercial goals is hardly a credible position.

The time to hold difficult data-sharing negotiations is well before the data is actually needed. There will be little or no time after a disaster actually hits; even the ability to communicate at a basic level is likely to be compromised.

Interagency agreements that will guarantee access to sensitive, password-protected data, but only in a disaster situation, may be a viable alternative. The details of such arrangements could be problematic, however: if you give sensitive data to an agency that they can't get to until you give them the password, a communication network breakdown—highly likely in many a disaster—will render the whole arrangement useless.

CONSIDER ALL THE ASSETS

In inventorying assets, the GIS-aware disaster manager should consider many other, less obvious assets whose destruction or disablement might have repercussions beyond the immediate. For example, an asset inventory cannot be focused solely on public property. Even though disaster management for the purposes of this handbook is considered a public function, the private sector's asset losses in a disaster must also be considered by those on the public side; not only will privately owned businesses expect public emergency services, their physical plants may contain additional, hidden hazards that can multiply the impact on public services. Manufacturing plants and distribution centers, for example, will likely contain hazardous chemicals and other substances. Even large retail stores that sell items as mundane as sofas and candy bars also have large inventories of significant hazards to the community, such as pesticides or compressed gas tanks. In most states, these will be in a database somewhere. Finding that database is the mission of the GIS team at this stage.

COOPERATION, NOT COMPETITION

Many forward-thinking businesses have their own disaster contingency plans; in fact, disaster-recovery and business-continuity services are a booming niche industry. That fact, however, may tend to foster the greatest danger to effective disaster management, failure to communicate. Public and private worlds in a community cannot plan for disaster independently.

SYMBOLIC TARGETS

In the new homeland security paradigm, it is worth noting that potential assets at risk now include buildings or assets that may not appear to have specific value either militarily or economically. They may, however, be symbolic of a nation's culture or values. The World Trade Center's Twin Towers were not only centers of commerce, they were symbols of American capitalism. While there are few other symbols of that magnitude in other parts of the country, a thorough inventory should not neglect such potential targets.

NATIONAL ASSETS AT HOME

Some communities will have within their boundaries facilities that seem to have minimal local impact, but which actually have national importance.

For example, in the cities of Livermore and Pleasanton, east of San Francisco, Fire Chief Stewart Gary does his disaster management and homeland security planning with the knowledge that within his area of responsibility is the Lawrence Livermore National Laboratory, a premier center of research on physics and other sciences. A national intellectual resource of immense value, the lab's destruction or disablement could have profound effects on national research and development policy over the long term. While the Livermore lab has its own extensive security measures, it would still need some local response resources in the event of a disaster. Moreover, Gary must also consider the lab's human assets—the disproportionate number of engineers and scientists, some of them working at Nobel Prize altitudes, who also happen to eat and sleep on the ground, and do so well within the range of Livermore-Pleasanton's fire apparatus.

NEW HANOVER COUNTY COMMUNITY VULNERABILITY ASSESSMENT

One of the most thorough and easily accessible examples of the identification and planning process can be found in work done in New Hanover County, North Carolina, in 1998 and 1999.

New Hanover was one of seven pilot areas selected by the Federal Emergency Management Agency (FEMA) to participate in Project Impact. This was a national program to help communities reduce their vulnerability to natural and man-made disasters, preferably through innovative uses of technology, and preferably through collaboration between private and public sectors. The end result of the collaboration between New Hanover, FEMA, and the Coastal Services Center of the National Oceanic and Atmospheric Administration (NOAA) was the Community Vulnerability Assessment Tool (CVAT), which consists of GIS software, data, and related methodologies and tutorials on CD. (The package is available online at csc.noaa.gov/products/nchaz/startup.htm. The free CD can also be ordered by anyone from this site.) Nearly four thousand of the CDs have been distributed, and many state and local governments have used it as a model for their own hazard identification and mitigation efforts and projects.

As a coastal community, New Hanover County and its largest city, Wilmington, have suffered numerous assaults from nature over the previous century, including hurricanes, flooding, and wind and lightning damage. The CVAT used New Hanover as a case study for a GIS-based solution to find ways to reduce the damage nature was constantly wreaking on the area.

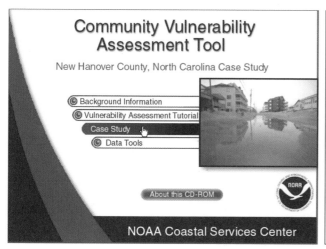

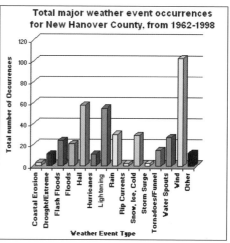

The opening screen of the Community Vulnerability Assessment Tool contains hyperlinks to background materials such as the chart, above right, showing the broad array of natural hazards that have hit the county over the years.

COMBINING ASSETS AND HAZARDS

With the CVAT, relevant hazard and asset data sets for the New Hanover area are included on the CD and can be viewed and analyzed using ArcView or ArcExplorer™ software. Hazards and assets can be combined to show which areas of New Hanover are most at risk—and therefore, where mitigation efforts might take place.

The data layers for the hazard assessment half of the equation are diverse—but also easy to get. Hazard data on the CVAT is all publicly available, to demonstrate how the process can be duplicated with minimal costs for data or labor, anywhere. The hazard data was first based on historical events and then prioritized further based on frequency, magnitude, and area of impact of the hazard. Specific data sets include earthquakes, erosion, floods, hazardous materials spills, storm surge, tornadoes, toxic releases, wildfire, wind, and a final category known as summary hazard. All these data sets were created as shapefiles, although they are also available in ArcInfo™ export format (.e00) and Spatial Data Transfer Standard (SDTS) format.

The likelihood of earthquake risk and tornadoes in New Hanover is considered small; the area faces the most frequent danger from flooding. So the CVAT uses its most sophisticated tools to measure flood risk. Among the tools it uses to do this are complex modeling programs such as SLOSH (Sea, Lake and Overland Surges from Hurricanes) from the National Hurricane Center. Data about local soils, beach erosion, and floodplains are also incorporated into the flooding calculations.

The high-risk areas from this analysis are further refined and assigned a risk level, based on flood probability and historic flooding data.

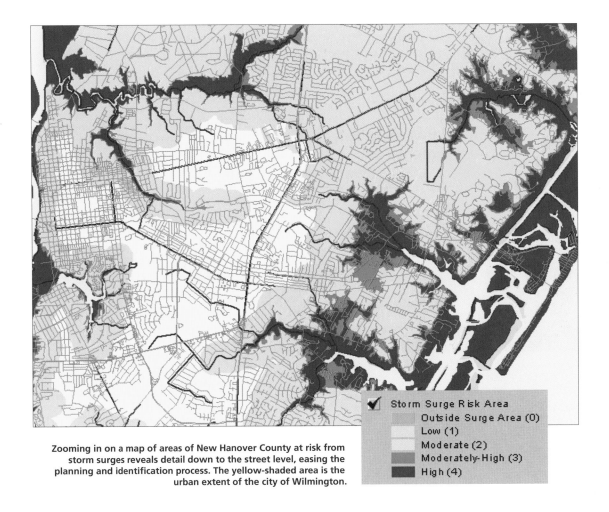

Storm Surge Risk Area
☑
Outside Surge Area (0)
Low (1)
Moderate (2)
Moderately-High (3)
High (4)

Zooming in on a map of areas of New Hanover County at risk from storm surges reveals detail down to the street level, easing the planning and identification process. The yellow-shaded area is the urban extent of the city of Wilmington.

NEW HANOVER ASSETS: OBVIOUS AND NOT-SO-OBVIOUS

On the other side of the equation are assets vulnerable to damage, including critically important facilities in the community, and other vulnerable social, economic, and environmental elements. New Hanover's first level of assets, "critical facilities," includes structures and buildings used for communication; fire and rescue; government; hospital and nursing care; police; schools and day care; shelter; transportation; and utility services.

Also included are assets on another, less obvious level that require more careful consideration—for example, facilities and structures whose destruction would have consequences beyond the loss of their own intrinsic value. These include marinas or known hazardous material storage sites—because damage to them could release additional hazards into the surrounding environment. Another asset class in this category is economic: manufacturers or other large employers whose loss would be magnified in the community because of unemployment, loss of revenue, and even permanent shutdown.

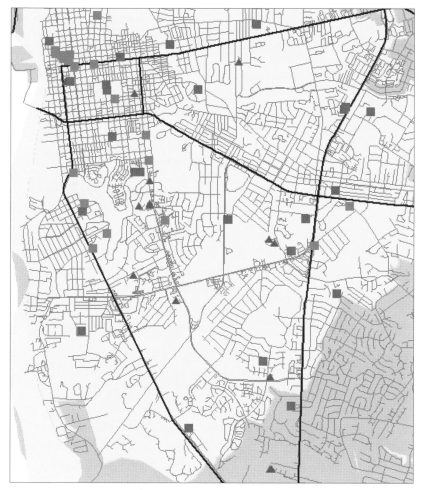

Fire & Rescue
●

Police
●

Communication
■

Transportation
■

Hospital & Nursing Home
▲

Government
■

School
■

**This detail from the CVAT
shows the location of assets
critical to the functioning
of the community, with
government offices and
schools predominant. If any
of these critical assets also
lie in high-risk areas, it will
be clear where mitigation
efforts could be focused.**

Some of this kind of asset data was extrapolated from other sources, typifying the kinds of creative thinking that are often needed for good disaster management. One asset class, vulnerable populations, measures societal vulnerability. Census Bureau demographic categories do not specifically encompass populations by such names. However, from areas where a higher proportion of the elderly live you can infer that evacuation may be more difficult and time consuming because the people who live there won't be as mobile and may need specialized medical attention—thus, this is a more vulnerable class of assets.

Similarly, areas more densely populated with members of an ethnic minority may not be able to understand instructions given to them in English. Areas with a large population of rental units are more likely to be ones that are uninsured or underinsured. Areas with a greater proportion of people who didn't finish high school may mean that written evacuation instructions won't reach as wide an audience as they would in other areas.

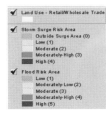

Maps created with CVAT data, using ArcView 3.1, show how GIS can pinpoint the effects of disaster on a community's economy. The top map shows retail land-use areas clustered along major roads. Most are out of danger from flood and storm surges—areas colored red and dark red. Service economy business areas, however, are not so fortunate, as the bottom map shows, with several of these located in areas of high risk from flood and storm surge.

High-Need Block Group

Storm Surge Risk Area
   Outside Surge Area (0)
   Low (1)
   Moderate (2)
   Moderately-High (3)
   High (4)

Flood Risk Area
   Low (1)
   Moderately-Low (2)
   Moderate (3)
   Moderately-High (4)
   High (5)

GIS can also help in planning disaster response efforts in this CVAT display. Areas with concentrations of people with high need for outside assistance, derived from census data, are shown.

MODELING THE DANGER: HAZUS

The HAZUS disaster-modeling software package also grew out of a FEMA initiative to help communities plan and prepare for the worst, and like the CVAT, is free to any community that wants it. The HAZUS (Hazards U.S.) package is a sophisticated, robust, loss-estimation modeling program whose methodology is based on, and tested against, rigorous national standards. Using an extensive database of national assets from federal sources—which can and should be localized with the appropriate data—it allows its users to forecast the most probable physical and economic damage that a community will suffer in a disaster, and to do so in striking detail.

First offered only as an earthquake-modeling program, the HAZUS release in 2003 adds flood modeling, as well as a limited wind-modeling (i.e., hurricane) component. Later releases are planned that will incorporate the full wind component, and later still, the entire spectrum of disaster events. The earthquake HAZUS 99 SR2 runs on ArcView software; beginning with the 2003 release, HAZUS will run on ArcGIS exclusively; the flood-modeling HAZUS will require the ArcView Spatial Analyst extension.

MODELING THE WORST

Despite its sophistication, the GIS platform makes it fairly easy to begin using HAZUS, with at least a crude estimation of the kinds of damage that are likely to occur in the event of an earthquake in a certain area; this is known as a Level 1 analysis. Much more sophisticated and exact Level 2 and Level 3 analyses can also be prepared if more detailed, localized data sets, such as soils, buildings, highway bridges, and transportation systems, are used. More detailed parameters about the earthquake event will also increase the detail of the effects analysis. FEMA offers a HAZUS training course for those wanting to take full advantage of the software's capabilities.

First, a geographic area of the United States is selected, as is the epicenter of an earthquake. (Recent seismic research has tended to show that the relationship between an epicenter and the area of greatest damage is not as direct as popular conception has it.) Such an epicenter can be completely arbitrary, or based on historical patterns. The user then selects an earthquake magnitude and earthquake type—or simply lets the software pick these and other parameters.

HAZUS then runs the model, calculating estimates of a wide array of damages and probable recovery needs and costs. These include human casualties; direct economic losses; immediate shelter needs; the amount of damage to structures (residential, industrial, and commercial), as well as to essential facilities such as airports, schools, hospitals, and utilities; location and extent of fires that might be expected; the amount of debris that the earthquake event would generate; and indirect economic losses to the area for the subsequent several years.

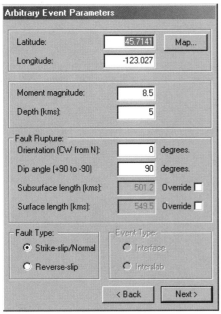
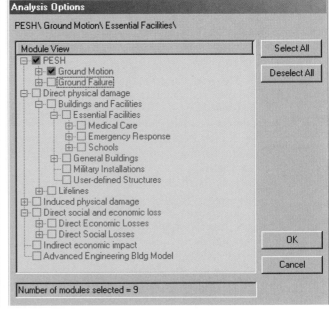

Dialog boxes from the HAZUS earthquake-modeling software package show how much customization of a disaster scenario can be done. Users can pinpoint an exact location, size, and type of earthquake, at left, and then request a wide array of damage assessments, right.

CALCULATING CULTURAL PARAMETERS

The HAZUS analyses encompass not only these more conventional physical parameters, adjusting damage according to building type, for example, but also social and cultural parameters.

For instance, in calculating what emergency shelter requirements might be necessary after an earthquake, the user can include an ethnic population factor. Social scientists have found that populations with a high concentration of immigrants from Central America, fearing after-shock effects, will tend to shun covered buildings in a postearthquake environment, preferring instead to take shelter in parks and other open spaces. This effect may reduce the number of shelters required after an event; it would also allow law-enforcement and social services departments to deploy personnel more precisely.

High-income areas may also skew the calculation of shelter requirements because their residents will tend to seek refuge with friends and family, or in hotels, rather than in shelters.

Although the HAZUS package is bundled with federal data sets, and loss-estimation modeling can be done with them alone, customizing the application with as much local data as possible is strongly encouraged for more accurate Level 2 and Level 3 results. In fact, for many scenarios, using the national data sets at the regional or local level may be most useful for pinpointing where better local data would be called for.

The HAZUS creators acknowledge that coaxing some of this localized data from reluctant organizations may require considerable extra effort. They do not, however, include a scenario for having the software do this coaxing—that will be up to you.

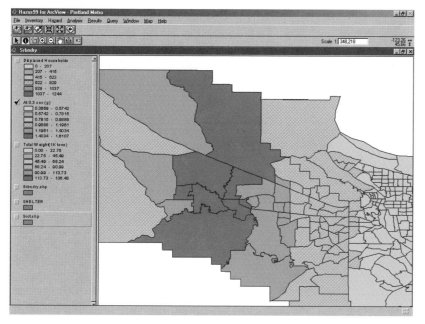

Three thematic damage-estimation maps in a HAZUS-generated scenario of an 8.5 earthquake hitting census tracts in the Portland, Oregon, area (Multnomah, Clackamas, and Washington counties) show, here and on the next page, the variations in the way an earthquake can affect an area. The first map shows where the greatest amount of ground shaking would be felt .3 seconds after the quake, measured in percentage of gravity. Since the epicenter, not shown, is on the western side of the affected area, the most violent shaking is felt there.

The second HAZUS map shows high numbers of displaced persons in only a few of the same tracts. The third map estimates the amount of debris, in thousands of tons, that would be generated by this event, and indicates that most of the debris would be generated in tracts away from those in the first two maps.

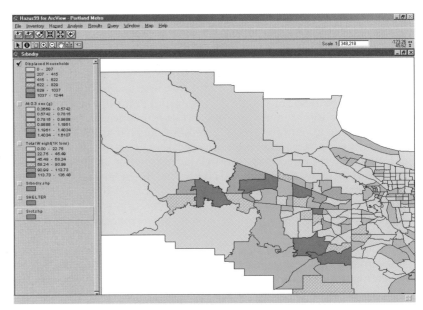

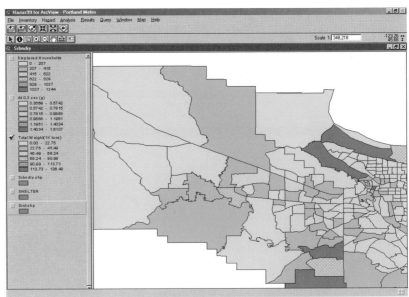

Identification and planning

chapter 2   **Mitigation**

Preparedness

Response

Recovery

PRECISION is key to reducing or eliminating those hazards identified in the planning and identification stage. One reason: all but the smallest mitigation measures will require getting people to do things they haven't done before, or to change the way they are used to doing things. Inertia like this often requires considerable force to dislodge, so the more precisely you can define what mitigation measures should be taken, and where, the better luck you will have at getting things moving.

This is especially true when those mitigation measures involve cranking up the machinery of government, which, some contend, is especially prone to inertia.

Moreover, if government action is needed to promote mitigation efforts through actions such as zoning changes, code enforcement, or inspections, precision will be required to draft appropriate rules or regulations.

Mitigation measures are also most effective when they have support from the greatest number of people across a broad spectrum of the community.

GIS products and spatial analyses help satisfy both these criteria, for precision and for garnering broad community understanding, by mapping where hazards exist with enough precision to satisfy administrative requirements, and, through visualization, communicating what needs to be done to the broadest array of people.

WHAT CAN WE KEEP FROM BURNING?

A prime example of the exacting analysis that can be done to assess both hazard location and asset risk is found in the California county of Marin, where the fire department uses GIS precision to map the location of the most dangerous, wildfire-prone areas within the 200,000 acres of its jurisdiction, and then uses that information to give the public ideas about the best places for mitigation measures to take place.

Mitigation actions can be as simple as cutting back brush—but if it is not done in the right location and at the right time, such precautions are a waste of time and money. Done correctly, they can save lives and millions of dollars in property values.

Despite its proximity to the San Francisco Bay area, directly across the Golden Gate Bridge, Marin County is more rural than urban. Within its heavily forested boundaries, it houses some of the most expensive residential real estate in the country.

The Fire Plan of the Marin County Fire Department is organized in much the same way that the New Hanover CVAT is—using GIS to combine areas of high risk with areas where many high-value assets are found. The intersection of these two layers indicates where the search for mitigation measures can begin.

A thematic map of the San Francisco Bay area, created with ArcGIS, shows median housing values by census tract.

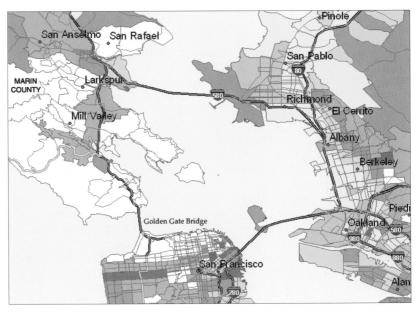

ASSEMBLING MARIN DATA

Accurate, up-to-date data is as important to the mitigation stage of disaster management as it is to any other stage. It so happens that Marin County is as rich in data resources as it is in other ways. One reason is that much of its land is owned by either the state or federal government, by the county itself, by other public agencies, or by public-interest organizations. It is also a place that is the target of much study by specialized agencies, such as the USGS's Bay Area Regional Database (bard.wr.usgs.gov). These entities are interested in sharing information for the public good, not in keeping it to themselves.

This good fortune presents its own problems for Fire Captain Specialist Tim Walsh, the department's GIS expert, however, because myriad data sources meant he had to do much preliminary conversion work in order to make the data usable. The time and energy needed for this kind of data preparation should not be underestimated in any GIS-based disaster management plan.

ASSEMBLING HAZARD AND HAZARD RISK DATA

Walsh's data preparation work included reprojecting several raster data sets into the UTM coordinate system. He used 10-meter digital elevation models (DEMs) for much of his work, as well as the ArcView Spatial Analyst extensions for ArcView and ArcGIS. This is because calculations about the behavior of fire are heavily dependent on variations in terrain that only DEMs and ArcView Spatial Analyst can measure well.

To arrive at a comprehensive assessment of the fire risk facing Marin County, Walsh created four different analyses: one known as Level of Service, another measuring fire weather, another assessing the kinds of vegetative fuels that fire feeds on, and a fourth showing all of the things available, called "assets," for a fire to burn.

Walsh's basic design for map creation is based on the California Fire Plan, which divides the state into 450-acre cells, each known as a Quad 81st.

HAZARD RISK

Level of Service, the most complex of the four analyses, is a kind of economic damage assessment map, designed to calculate the probability that a bad wildfire would cause unacceptably high dollar-value losses, and would cost an excessive amount of money to contain and extinguish.

This kind of assessment encompasses more than just a geographic analysis of potential disaster threats; it also attempts to measure the probability that a threat will cause significant damage. While no risk analysis of this kind can ever predict the future, it can help planners make better, more educated guesses about where best to focus mitigation efforts.

Walsh used a number of geographic components to measure and to put a value on Level of Service. Inaccessibility was one—the farther from a fire station, the more risk. In the Level of Service calculation, the center of a cell more than ten minutes from fire equipment response was determined to be a high-risk cell, and given the highest score of 4.

High residential density was another criterion. Walsh overlaid Marin County parcel data on the Quad 81st and mapped the residential density. A cell with more than five hundred residences was considered to be in the highest category and given a 4 score.

Still another assessment of risk on the Level of Service map was the history of fire ignitions in the county in general, and in individual cells.

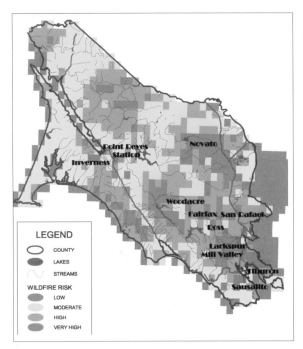

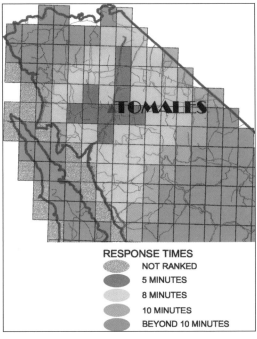

The Level of Service map, left, that resulted after combining different factors to calculate the likelihood that a serious wildfire in Marin County would cause an excessive amount of damage and expense to extinguish. Factors included response times, housing density, a fire's resistance to efforts to fight it, and ignition probability. At right, a close-up of response-time cells around a fire station.

Walsh mapped 880 total fire ignitions during a six-and-a-half-year period; those cells that had had eleven or more fires were given a high 4 score.

Walsh also calculated a criterion he called Resistance of Control. Different from the accessibility factor, this measured the difficulty that fighting a fire in a particular cell would present to Marin County fire-fighters. Calculating this factor required measuring several others: the likely speed, size, and intensity of a fire, based on the vegetation in that cell and on industry-standard fire behavior models; he also considered the distance from a road (which in some instances would tend to delay the arrival of fire equipment); and finally, slope. Land with a grade of more than 40 percent can slow down fire fighting in a number of ways: fire equipment can't move on slopes that steep, and steep slopes also slow down the building of fire lines while increasing the rate of burn. These four factors made up the resistance-of-control criterion; cells that had more than half their area meeting that criterion were given the highest score, 4.

WEATHER: EXACERBATING RISK

Creating the Fire Weather map also required that Walsh isolate individual factors, rank and combine them, and then rank them on a final summary map. There were fewer factors to consider in this calculation than in the Level of Service map, but that is not to say it reduced its overall complexity.

Walsh considered first what he labeled the inversion component. Because the county is on the Pacific shoreline, many areas find themselves under a layer of cool, moist air, and thus at reduced risk for fire.

This inversion layer sits at about 1,100 feet above sea level, so areas above that elevation in Marin County do not enjoy that reduced risk.

These areas Walsh mapped and assigned a value of 2 to their cells. Those cells at lower elevations received a 0 score.

Next, five fire weather reporting stations for different areas in the county have microclimate patterns associated with them; their impact on fire risk was given a rank from moderate to very high.

Another weather criterion came from measuring the degree of protection afforded by tree canopies. Tree canopies can have a dramatic impact on fire risk because they keep soil and vegetation moist, and shield an area from wind. Tree-canopied areas and noncanopied areas were assigned scores of −1 and 0, respectively.

Lastly, for the weather map, Walsh calculated hillside aspect, or the direction that slopes face. In the Northern Hemisphere, south aspects tend to burn faster, and north ones more slowly. Flat spaces were assigned a 0 score, south aspects a 3.

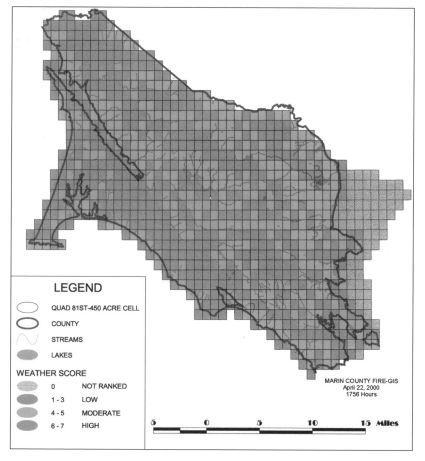

LEGEND

⬭ QUAD 81ST-450 ACRE CELL

⬭ COUNTY

〰 STREAMS

⬬ LAKES

WEATHER SCORE

⬬ 0 — NOT RANKED

⬬ 1 - 3 — LOW

⬬ 4 - 5 — MODERATE

⬬ 6 - 7 — HIGH

MARIN COUNTY FIRE-GIS
April 22, 2000
1756 Hours

5   0   5   10   15 Miles

Weather is critically important in calculating wildfire risk, but this weather-ranking map incorporates outside factors as well, including inversion layers, microclimates at different locations, the impact of tree canopies on vegetation flammability, and the effect of hillside aspect.

PINPOINTING DANGER

The last set of calculations for hazard risk takes into account the actual burning capability of different kinds of vegetation in Marin County. Fire experts have long known which particular trees and bushes might burn more quickly and hotter than others. This knowledge is encapsulated in such fire-modeling software packages as BEHAVE, the Fire Behavior Prediction System (FBPS), and FARSITE, which also runs on a GIS platform.

Walsh obtained vegetation maps of the county and reclassified them in ArcView Spatial Analyst as fuel ranks. He then wrote a query that assigned a numerical value to each cell based on the majority fuel model vegetation in the cell, combined with slope factors.

When finished, Walsh had a map that showed where to find the fiercest- and fastest-burning fuels growing in Marin County.

FUEL MODELS

ANNUAL
GRASS FUEL
MODEL 1

OAKS WITH GRASS
UNDERSTORY FUEL MODEL
2

MATURE CHAPARRAL
FUEL MODEL 4

COASTAL SHRUB
FUEL MODEL 5

OAK-BAY-MADRONE FOREST
FUEL MODEL 8

MODERATE CONIFER FUEL
MODEL 9

HEAVY CONIFER FUEL
MODEL 10

URBAN FUEL MODEL 28

AGRICULTURE
FUEL MODEL 97

WATER FUEL MODEL 98

BARREN FUEL MODEL 99

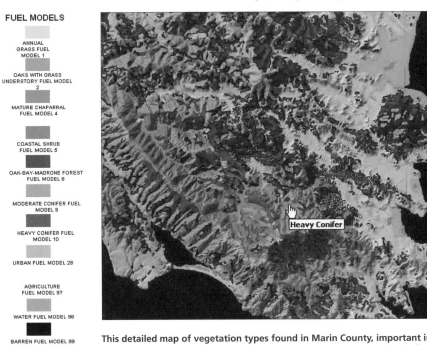

This detailed map of vegetation types found in Marin County, important in calculating fire risk, is available at the county Web site (co.marin.ca.us/depts/FR/main/firedept/fuelmap/ index.html). Vegetation types are revealed by rolling the cursor over them on the screen.

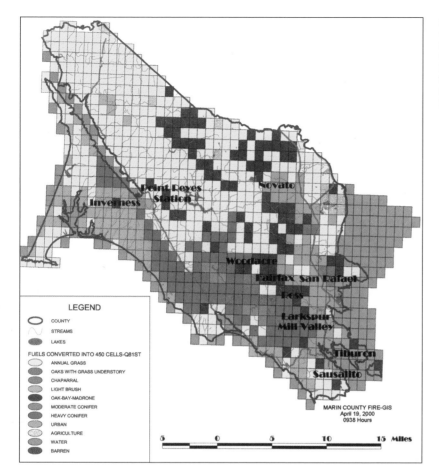

On this fuel model map, each cell was given a fuel model value based on the majority of the vegetation type found in that cell. In cells where two fuels combined to create a higher risk, the cell was given that higher value.

WHAT NEEDS PROTECTION?

The identification of assets that would be at risk of destruction from these now-identified hazards was similar to the way it was done in North Carolina, although the actual types of assets differed, as they would in any unique community.

There were maps of obvious assets, such as residential density and population density. (Despite its per-capita wealth, Marin's high real-estate values never figure into any of the Fire Plan calculations.)

There were also some not-so-obvious assets: the presence of nongame wildlife, of rangeland, and of water supply and storage facilities.

Additionally, Walsh created maps to show fire's longer-term effects, such as soil erosion, and the increased risk of flooding that erosion brings.

All these assets were summarized in the Fire Plan's Total Asset Rank map.

Total assets at risk in each cell covering the county were combined to create this map. All relevant assets were included in this calculation, such as residential density and presence or absence of nongame wildlife.

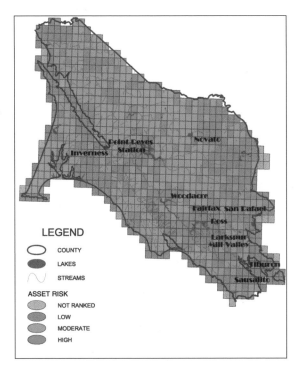

The final Total Ranking Map was calculated by adding scores from the earlier hazard maps of Hazardous Fuels, Level of Service, and Fire Weather, with the Asset totals.

The Total Ranking Map, the culmination of all the other map calculations, combined both assets and hazard risks. For decision makers and responders alike, it focused attention on the areas in the county of most concern, and where mitigation efforts would be most needed.

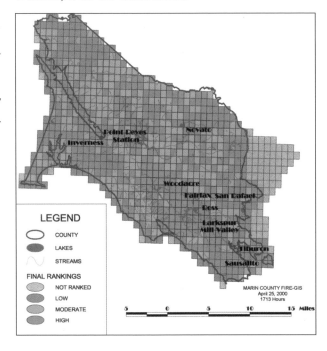

TARGETED CLEAN-UP

With the most dangerous areas of the county now precisely defined, it is that much easier for mitigation measures to be targeted at the areas where they will do the most good.

Just what these measures will consist of, and to what extent they will be carried out, are decisions to be made according to the wishes of the community and its leaders. GIS, by creating the kinds of analysis that Walsh did, helps clarify the choices to be made. For public education, or as a tool for public discussion and consensus building, the Total Ranking Map shows plainly where public concern should be focused.

In Marin, identification of high-hazard areas allowed for mitigation measures that included land closures during particularly dangerous times of the year; posting road signs for residents using farm equipment to check spark arrestors; and building and maintaining fire breaks and fire roads.

Other fire mitigation measures included public education, examining new housing plans to ensure that homes are built with fire-safe materials, and encouraging residents to clear brush from around their houses. In Marinview, a residential development of 252 homes, the department's forester, Kent Julin, took Walsh's data and created a map to lay out precisely where such brush clearance ought to take place. The development is located within an urban–wildland interface and many residences are built with wood sidings, decks, and roofs, making brush clearance imperative.

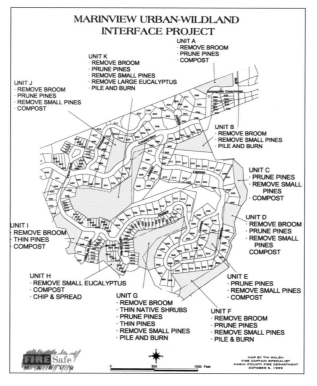

Marin County Forester Kent Julin created this mitigation map from Tim Walsh's data, laying out an exact set of instructions for how to reduce fire danger in this residential area.

WHERE NOT TO BUILD

Mitigation can be done for both the short term and the long term, and GIS can help with both.

In North Carolina, long-term mitigation plans were developed for New Hanover County with information developed with the Community Vulnerability Assessment Tool (CVAT). As shown earlier, high-hazard

A CVAT zoning map of a portion of New Hanover County, with a partial legend, shows mainly light manufacturing and industrial districts. Below, those same zoning areas—with high-risk (crosshatched) areas overlaid—shows where mitigation efforts could be concentrated. The legislative language defining these zoned areas could be modified to require that additional measures be taken to defend against flooding damage.

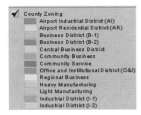

zones and high-value asset zones can be compared to show areas where the highest danger lies.

But these high-hazard zones can also be compared with other kinds of land classification, so that a map reader can better visualize the context in which the hazards exist.

An obvious long-term strategy for avoiding damage to homes and businesses from a disaster is not to build homes and business in disaster-prone areas. When GIS is used, as was done in New Hanover, determining precisely where these areas are is much simplified. In turn, this graphic representation gives decision makers and the community a chance to deliberate with better information before development permits are granted.

In the alternative, if development should not be or cannot be restricted in higher-risk areas, GIS can show where development standards can be beefed up. These could mean requiring reinforcement for certain buildings in earthquake-prone areas, or in flood-prone areas, increased setbacks and minimum floor heights in new construction. Such tougher standards, restrictive as they might seem to some property owners, also protect those property owners—not to mention taxpayers.

BEING MORE PRECISE WITH HELP

When combined with different data, CVAT shows locations where specific programs for disaster mitigation can be targeted more precisely.

The National Flood Insurance Program (NFIP) is one, helping to make flood insurance available to homeowners in more than nineteen thousand communities in the United States. Participation in the flood program is required for some kinds of mortgage-lending activity. The advantages to participating in the NFIP are clear, according to FEMA,

CVAT shows where National Flood Insurance Program policies are in place in the community, allowing for more focused public awareness and education efforts about the usefulness of the program.

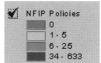

NFIP Policies
0
1 - 5
6 - 25
34 - 633

which runs the program: buildings constructed in compliance with NFIP building standards suffer approximately 80 percent less damage annually than those not built in compliance.

By examining the distribution of NFIP claims and policies in a high-risk flood area, administrators can easily spot where to target outreach and public education programs on the importance of maintaining adequate flood insurance, and of taking measures that reduce the impact of flooding. These could include using fewer impervious surfaces on the ground, such as asphalt and concrete, that impede drainage, and also elevating hot-water heaters and air-conditioning units.

GIS can also pinpoint building construction that might be more susceptible to damage from flood, such as mobile homes or older homes; this information is available from the Census Bureau or local property-tax databases.

High rates of repetitive claims for flood damage under the NFIP are indicated by red areas. These may be areas that officials want to consider for more drastic mitigation actions, such as buying out property owners entirely and demolishing the homes.

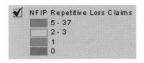

Identification and planning

Mitigation

chapter 3   **Preparedness**

Response

Recovery

THE distinction between the identification-and-planning stage of disaster management and the preparedness stage is mainly one of time:
preparedness is loosely considered to encompass short-term tasks to be
done to prepare for an imminent disaster, whereas planning tasks tend
to be longer-term. (Even this definition has its limitations, since some
disasters cannot, by definition, be "imminent"—terrorist acts and earthquakes, to mention two.)

In any case, experts recommend that all predisaster activities be
treated as part of a dynamic process, not as a series of static stages.
In such a paradigm, contingency plans are continually updated, not
left on a shelf to grow obsolete, and exercises are conducted regularly
to test plans and response capabilities. If you're heeding that advice,
the stages of planning, mitigation, and preparedness will all tend to
become part of the same predisaster preparation process.

In a GIS context, one of the most important preparedness activities
is anticipating and planning for the likely mapping and spatial analysis needs of those who are responding to a disaster, those who are
assisting the response, and those affected in some way by it—in other
words, just about everyone.

MAPS: A HIGH-DEMAND ITEM

When disaster hits, there will be enormous demand for spatial information, on paper and online. Depending on the seriousness of the event, the demand for maps of a disaster area can be enormous, once people know they're available: decision makers will want them, the media will want them, incident commanders will want them, people in affected neighborhoods will want them, responders will want them, and emergency responders and managers from other jurisdictions will want them. So a reliable system for disseminating hard-copy and online maps is imperative.

Those who have been through such events say the reasons for this kind of demand are not hard to understand.

For the public, when daily life is turned to shambles by a disaster, a geographic, spatial view of reality can provide a mechanism for reorientation and stabilization.

For responders and emergency personnel, one of the greatest problems in a disaster situation is lack of information—about the location of events, of resources, of transportation and emergency networks, and myriad other items that never get considered until events are upon them. But maps are pure information—in a familiar form that is versatile enough to be customized for whatever arena a responder is working in.

Failures of communication are another common issue in disaster response. Not only do communication devices break down because of power-supply or other problems; the communication systems among people and agencies also have a tendency to fail. Problems arise because key personnel are missing; strangers who have differing priorities are thrown together with a mandate to solve major problems, without any previously established relationship to start from. But a spatial visualization of the common area of concern can help establish that base of communication. A map can provide a common language for people who might otherwise have no way of communicating well.

TIME TO GET SPECIFIC

Ideas about specific data sets and map products should be solicited from as wide a group of potential customers as possible. If other agencies see that the GIS team is working to create products that help them, the less resistance there will be to the idea of contributing data or other support. Many of the needed data sets will be obvious and require little debate; for example, street centerline data sets to make accurate street maps will be necessary as basemaps in most urban and suburban environments.

But some additional thought should be given to how these can be customized for a particular situation. For example, consider how street map products might be configured so they don't simply end at the county line: if you are delineating evacuation routes, it's very likely the evacuation will continue into the adjacent jurisdiction. In a flood-prone area, shoreline data sets would be obvious components of a basemap, or if the event is inland, the location of streams and flood canals would be a priority. In a wildfire situation, property ownership data and DEMs would be more obvious candidates for basemap data.

ONE SIZE DOESN'T FIT ALL

There may be no more than a half-dozen of these basic, almost generic maps prepared. But basic and simple as they may be, care should be taken with the selection and display of features on them.

Because many responders to a local disaster may be from out of town, and because street signs themselves may be damaged or missing, it will be important to clearly relate streets on the maps to visible landmarks, such as parks, rivers or streams, bridges, hills or other areas of high elevation, or high landmarks such as tall buildings, cell towers, and water tanks.

However, these should not overload a map display: a first responder unfamiliar with an urban area will not need information on every downtown building, but rather, just enough information to get oriented. Good cartographic design should prevail on such maps: consistent, understandable labeling of features, sufficient white space, no confusion in the legend.

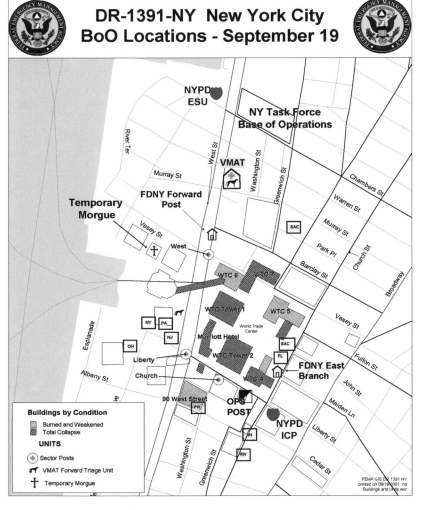

A basic FEMA Base of Operations (BoO) map of the area at the World Trade Center shows responders from around the country the locations of key command posts in relation to damaged buildings. Uncomplicated cartographic designs like this help responders by not overwhelming them with information they do not need at that moment.

EDUCATING SPATIAL DATA CONSUMERS

Part of the job of preparedness also includes educating other departments in a public agency as to how maps and spatial data can aid their disaster response. How this education is accomplished will vary from one agency to another, and will depend on how well existing lines of communication are working. They could be as simple as e-mailing appropriate department heads, or organizing Microsoft® PowerPoint® seminars on GIS applications and capabilities.

It will be useful, in such efforts, to discuss the broad range of geographic information that can be relevant to any disaster management plan. A short list could demonstrate that data needs can cross many administrative boundaries, and even departments that can imagine no connection to GIS or disaster management do in fact possess relevant data.

A short, random list of likely map products is likely to require data resources from some not-very-obvious sources:

- Staging and triage areas (police, building department, property tax department)
- Helicopter landing zones (Federal Aviation Administration)
- Hospitals, hospital emergency access routes, potential medical triage areas (local health authorities)
- Command posts and danger zones (police, fire and emergency services)
- Power generation assets (local utilities)
- Shelters (school district, social services agency)
- Nursing homes, assisted-living facilities, and board-and-care homes (local office on aging, state licensing agency)
- Freeway and highway areas under construction (state or local transportation agency)

FAR-FETCHED DATA?

There will also be a need for data that in calmer times seems odd, and irrelevant at best. Consider domestic animals. Emergency personnel may overlook the importance that residents place on their pets, but in times of crisis, some residents will refuse to go to shelters or to evacuate an area without their household pets. If no provision has been made for animals, the job of persuading people to evacuate may be made more difficult. As a step toward a solution, creating a standard basemap of pet shelter locations would help. (If there aren't any such shelters, then perhaps that provision needs to be considered at a higher level.)

The response to the events of September 11 in New York City was instructive on the point about seemingly unrelated data or requests for irrelevant maps. One unexpected request at the Pier 92 Mapping and Data Center in New York City was for a map product that showed all vacant lots in lower Manhattan, for potential use as parking lots, because the emergency response had filled the city with many new vehicles in a city already choking on them.

Another, more chilling request for the lower Manhattan area—a map of all the concrete-slab buildings that had at least 10,000 square feet of clear space, for use as temporary morgues.

STANDARD PRODUCTS

Anticipating mapping needs means understanding that inevitably there will be points of failure. Data and equipment will break, be lost, or be unusable for the most arcane, unexpected reasons. You will not, for example, be able to assume that your connection to your geographic data server—or to the backup server, if you are farsighted enough to have one—will be working, or will stay working.

Thus, the GIS team should prepare data and templates of standard map products well ahead of time. The exact data and geographic areas represented on these will depend naturally on local conditions, local hazard risks, and substantially on the preferences and needs that local responders and others express when you consult with them on this issue. The relevant data should be kept on CDs in agreed-on formats, and in agreed-on locations, with many copies in many different places. Whatever normal data backup and update systems are already in place should be modified to encompass these disaster response CDs.

THE MIAMI-DADE SOLUTIONS

In Miami-Dade County, Florida, the solution to the problem of making GIS data available to disaster managers is simple—they have access to all of it, more than one hundred coverages and shapefiles that make up the Miami-Dade enterprise GIS system. These are listed in appendix B.

The Miami-Dade Office of Emergency Management, in fact, simply mirrors the central county government databases because it is understood that a disaster may require that the office operate on a stand-alone basis.

Because of this accessibility, the Miami-Dade OEM can access any layer needed to create any map necessary. This includes highly detailed digital orthophotos, which are updated every two years.

GIS FOR MODELING AND TRAINING

GIS is at the core of several disaster-modeling applications that can be invaluable for preparedness training.

One of these is the well-known Consequences Assessment Tool Set, or CATS. Created by Science Applications International Corporation (SAIC) of San Diego under contract to the federal government, CATS estimates damage and probable casualty figures for a broad range of natural and man-made disasters anywhere in the forty-eight contiguous states, using real-time climate conditions and 150 national data sets. Operating from ArcView and ArcGIS, CATS can model and predict the outcome of a variety of man-made and natural disasters, including earthquakes, hurricanes, and toxic substance releases. It can be operated in the field, letting responders model possible outcomes of a disaster being played out in front of them. It also lets them download real-time weather information from sources such as the National Hurricane Center in Florida.

Because it was developed under contract to the federal government for disaster management purposes, it is freely available to local governments through ESRI.

The layers of national asset data that come with the CATS software in both raster and vector formats can serve as a template for local agencies looking to begin assembling their own, more detailed and customized asset database. The complete list is given in appendix B, but even a few examples here may provide some inspiration: railroad lines, oil refineries, FBI offices, hardware stores, immigration offices, dams, hospitals, prisons, Superfund sites, coal mines, drugstores, and even lawyers.

Why lawyers? The rationale is the possibility that in the event of a disaster, an incident commander may have an urgent need to commit some clearly illegal but necessary act, such as breaking into a pharmacy to obtain medical supplies. Since it is unlikely that the IC will have an assistant attorney general standing right next to him, local legal counsel of any kind would be the next best thing.

If this seems like a farfetched data set to have available, it is worth remembering that farfetched is exactly the territory that disasters inhabit; the events of September 11 all seemed farfetched on September 10. In planning for the data you may need in a disaster, the data that seems most farfetched may turn out to be the data that saves you.

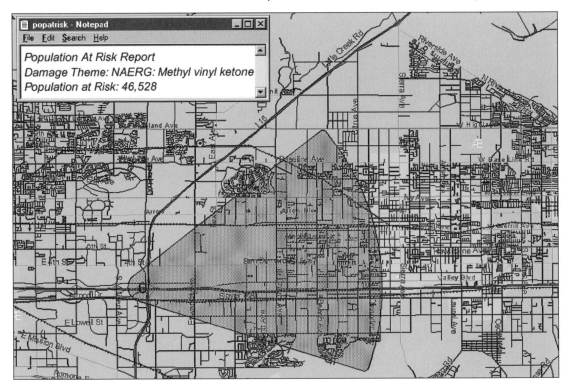

This sample CATS scenario predicts damage and an evacuation area for the release of a highly toxic chemical, methyl vinyl ketone, at the intersection of two busy Southern California freeways, Interstates 15 and 10, using real weather conditions on a January morning. The blue area indicates the direction and extent of the toxic cloud that would form, based on the amount of chemical spilled, the dispersal properties of the chemical, and wind direction and force present at that time. Census data forms the basis of an estimate of the population of the nearby city of Fontana that might need to be evacuated. The scenario also suggests optimal locations for roadblocks, to keep the unsuspecting from driving into the area of the toxic plume. Using laptops, responders in the field could update weather conditions from a mobile Internet connection and redeploy as conditions change.

THE FLORIDA SOLUTION: A COMPLETE PREPAREDNESS PACKAGE ON CD

Several agencies collaborated in Florida to come up with a product that might serve as a model for using GIS for in-the-field disaster response. Developed by the Florida Marine Research Institute (FMRI) of the Florida Fish and Wildlife Conservation Commission (FWC), under contract to the 7th U.S. Coast Guard District Marine Safety Office, the idea behind the digital Area Contingency Plan (ACP) is to incorporate not only the official written plan for all agencies responding to a hazardous-waste spill—a 642-page document—but also the digital geographic data necessary to implement all the procedures required by the plan—and the software to use that data. Using the ACP CD, a team responding to an oil spill emergency with no previous knowledge of the area, and no knowledge of the plan, could get to work immediately with minimal outside direction.

The South Florida ACP CD incorporates several elements of critical importance to responders and to good disaster management in general:

• *Breadth of data*
Data for both basemap purposes and for the specific purposes of environmental emergency response, in shapefile and tabular form, is both voluminous and detailed. Examples of data sets include geographic coordinates for positioning oil skimmer boats and oil containment booms; locations and phone numbers of local salvage companies available for ship rescues; locations and phone numbers of cleanup contractors; locations of sensitive ecological areas; detailed shoreline bathymetry data; boat ramps and dock locations; fueling locations; names and phone numbers of marine pilots; digitized nautical charts from the National Oceanic and Atmospheric Administration (NOAA); and Florida land data including highways, cities, airports and heliports, police stations, and hospitals.

• *Software*
An installed version of ArcView 3.x is required to do a full analysis of the data on the CD, but it can also be viewed with ArcExplorer 2.0, ESRI's free data viewer. This software is included on the CD, allowing anyone with basic computer skills to take advantage of the GIS data.

In addition, several other free software programs specific to oil-spill and marine emergencies can be loaded onto a notebook or desktop PC from the CD. Developed jointly by NOAA and the Environmental Protection Agency, they include Spill Tools, a package of applications that measure the dispersal and burn rates of various substances; ADIOS (Automated Data Inquiry for Oil Spills), which integrates cleanup models with chemical data on more than a thousand different kinds of oil; CAMEO (Computer Aided Management of Emergency Operations); ALOHA (Aereal Locations of Hazardous Atmospheres), a gas-dispersion modeling software; and MARPLOT, a simple mapping application.

ArcExplorer 2.0 is bundled on the ACP CD, allowing novice GIS users to view detailed maps, such as this one, outlining some of the environmentally sensitive areas of the Florida coastline.

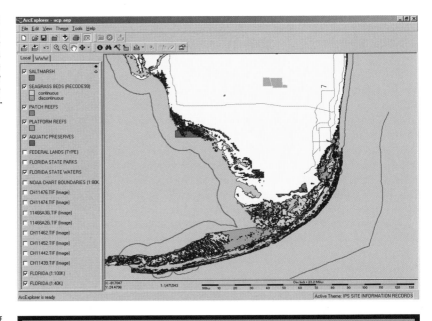

A number of hazardous-material software applications are available from the South Florida digital ACP, and can be launched from this screen.

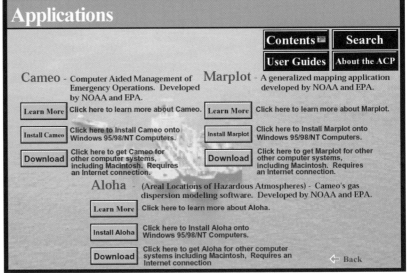

• *Metadata*

This is an important component in GIS-based disaster management, one often overlooked in a disaster situation because time is short and there are so many other priorities. But responders and decision makers must have confidence in the spatial data being presented to them. When different GIS users are working different shifts in different locations, they should all know the pedigree of the data they are using.

The metadata for all the layers on the South Florida ACP is included on the CD in PDF format—including summaries of its origin, update schedules, and contact numbers for data librarians.

- *Response and supporting documentation*

Response and emergency plans that would—and do—take up several feet of bookshelf space have been loaded onto the CD in PDF format. These documents include the Contingency Plan itself, which contains procedures, responsibilities, statutory authorities, and related material for South Florida coastal emergency response; Inlet Protection Strategy (instructions and maps) for every water inlet on the Florida coast; Incident Command System procedures and forms, which can be printed out for hard-copy use, or in online form; Incident Command System Training procedures; detailed maps and orthophotos of the ports of Miami, Everglades, and Palm Beach; detailed coastal navigation information for marine pilots; specialized information for such sensitive areas as the Turkey Point Nuclear Plant; and hyperlinks to relevant Web sites.

All told, the documentation included on the CD would take up more than two thousand printed pages.

> The water always becomes milky following windy weather. The usual color of the water on the reefs is bluish green, and the shoal patches show dark, shading through brown to yellow as they approach the surface. The shoal sand patches show as a bright green. At depths of 10 to 15 feet grass patches on the bottom look quite similar to rocks. When piloting in this area choose a time so that the Sun will be astern, conning the vessel from aloft or from an elevated position forward, for then the line of demarcation between deep water and edges of the shoal will be indicated with surprising clarity.
>
> —*From United States Coast Pilot 4, Atlantic Coast, Cape Henry to Key West, included on the South Florida ACP CD.*

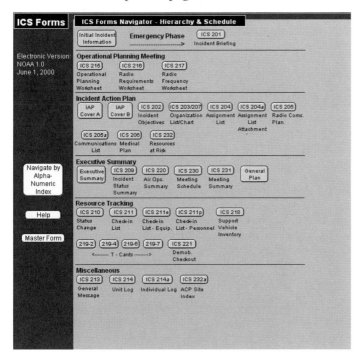

The Incident Command System, with its complex array of forms to be filled out, is a standard organizational tool in disaster management. The South Florida ACP package eases its usage by making ICS forms available right from the CD, in both online and printable format.

By including the entire written, detailed Area Contingency Plan on the CD, disaster managers in South Florida save paper, but more importantly, can be assured that responders new to the area will know exactly what procedures to follow no matter where they are doing their work.

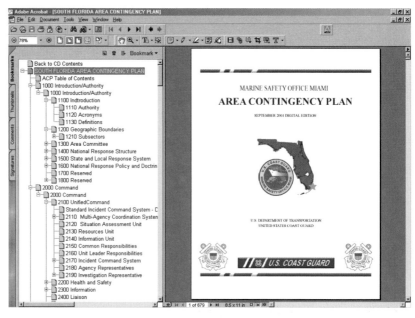

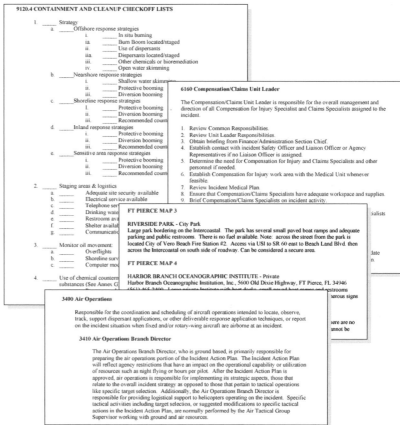

- *Collaboration*

The ACP CD program came about through cooperation among several agencies, most notably the Florida Department of Environmental Protection, FMRI, FWC, and the U.S. Coast Guard. While these are agencies with seemingly vastly different missions, these missions merge when it comes to protecting Florida's shorelines.

The Coast Guard's 7th Marine Safety Office has federal responsibility for environmental protection along the Florida (and several other states') coastline, and has jurisdiction over all ships—including those that might cause oil spills, collisions, or other environmentally unfriendly conditions.

FWC is mandated to respond, track, and analyze any hazardous substance spills that occur in Florida's coastal waters, and to assess which resources are at risk. The commission takes those responsibilities very seriously, given the size of that coastline, the importance that it has on the Florida economy, and the amount of commercial shipping that steams in, out, and around it. Florida's DEP takes its mission of protecting the Florida environment equally seriously.

FROM ALASKA TO FLORIDA

The ACP development began after the Exxon Valdez disaster in Alaska in 1989. Even though that event was far distant from Florida, it nonetheless made both state and federal legislators acutely sensitive to the possible effects of a similar spill on other states' coastal waters, and led to the passage of the federal Oil Protection Act of 1990.

In the early 1990s, the Florida agencies began using Environmental Sensitivity Index (ESI) atlases developed by Research and Planning, Inc. Now incorporated into GIS, the indexes detail the shoreline habitat, biological resources, and human-use resources along all the nation's coastlines. FMRI incorporated ESI into its Florida Marine Spill Analysis System (FMSAS), a sophisticated ArcInfo-based hazardous-substance-response software package later transferred to the ArcView platform. The FMSAS development team was motivated to come up with a software application that not only helped the cleanup, but also helped the cleanup get done in an environmentally friendly fashion. A great deal of damage had been done to the Alaskan environment by the out-of-state volunteers who came north to help clean up oil, trampling much of the pristine coastal ecosystem in their haste to rescue wildlife.

With its long history of gathering information, and with the FMSAS software package, the FWC knew more about Florida's marine life and coastlines than probably anyone else. So the Coast Guard contracted with FWC to do hazardous spill cleanups in Florida waters, and then, in 1999, to come up with a GIS-based disaster response package that resulted in the digital ACP. The South Florida version is the second of what is expected to be a series of digital ACPs for major ports in the Southeast.

A TOOL FOR INFORMATION MANAGEMENT

For the Coast Guard Marine Safety Office, the ACP model fulfills not only a need for a compact, self-contained disaster response tool, it also begins to fill the need for information management during disaster response, a need it shares with every other response agency.

In the view of many experienced disaster managers, only a portion of the response work that is done at an emergency operations center is the actual labor of responding. The majority of the labor is focused on information management—finding out what's happening where, who's doing it and how, who needs what, where is it needed and when—and then conveying the answers to all those questions to decision makers, usually far away in some state capital or in Washington, D.C.

The digital ACP and its companion Web sites, driven by ArcIMS® software, reduce those information-management tasks considerably—either by giving decision makers a digital map that gives them much more information in a glance than they could get from many minutes of staring at a spreadsheet—or by allowing them to do GIS analysis themselves. If they have control of the information they need and want, that frees an emergency operations center to do other work—such as protecting property and saving lives.

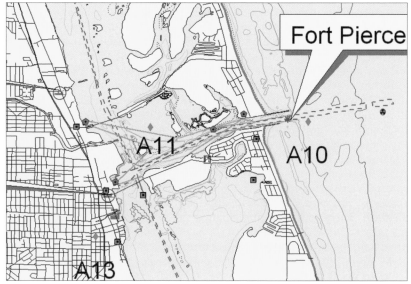

Detailed plans for protecting tidal inlets are included on the digital ACP in several formats. The South Florida ACP ArcView 3.2 project included on the CD shows here the Ft. Pierce harbor area with a basic map and some of the relevant layers for oil spill response turned on. Detailed written instructions for response are provided and made accessible from the project either as hotlinks or tables, next page.

INLET SUMMARY SHEET

SITE: Fort Pierce Inlet, St. Lucie County, Florida

DATE AND TIME SURVEYED (TIDE):   25 June 1994; 1815   [Low @ 1618 (-0.7);
                                                             Fort Pierce Inlet,
                                                             south jetty]

RANKING (DEGREE OF DIFFICULTY):   (see ranking scale)

B.

PRINCIPAL RESOURCES AT RISK:

Mangroves. Manatees present. Atlantic green turtles, Atlantic leatherback turtles, and Atlantic loggerhead turtles nest on the outer beaches. Shorebirds; wading birds, including the Great blue heron, Little blue heron, Louisiana yellow-crowned night heron, and Black-crowned night heron, the Great egret, Snowy egret, and Cattle egret, and the White ibis on the spoil islands in the Indian River Lagoon; and seabirds, including the Brown pelican, Anhinga, and Double-crested cormorant. Mounds of the Eastern oyster occur on the flats in the Indian River Lagoon. Marina facilities, boats, and seawalls, revetments, docks, etc. along the Indian River.

PRELIMINARY PROTECTION STRATEGY:

Use a Christmas tree configuration of deflection boom to divert oil out of the main channel and to the inlet shorelines. The north limb will divert oil to a sandy collection point adjacent to the north jetty (CP1) and the south limb to a sand beach along the developed shoreline on the south side of the main channel. Deploy protection boom in front of Coon Island to prevent oil from entering the tidal channels and fouling the mangroves and tidal flats, and also across the entrance to the small embayment adjacent to the Coast Guard station to prevent the tidal flats from becoming contaminated. Use deflection boom to divert oil to a collection point at the Coast Guard station (CP3).

Shape	Point
Inlet Name	Fort Pierce Inlet
File_name	FtPierce3
Site Type	mechanical/staging
Site Name	USCG Base Fort Pierce Collection Site #3
Contact Name	Hazmat Specialist
Contact Agency	USCG Base
Phone	(407)464-6100
Secondary Contact	
Relative Location	One mile west of Inlet on south of Inlet
Location Address	900 Seaway Drive
City	Ft. Pierce
Latitude (Decimal Min.)	27.470000
Longitude (Decimal Min.)	-80.301667
Water Depth	3-4' @ 50'
Current Information	1-2 knots current alongshore, 4-5 knots offshore
Shoreline Type	concrete bulkhead
Site Access Information	paved to waters' edge
Supporting Information	(2) 41', 1 RHIB, 1 Mako, gas, diesel, docks, 1 acre light paved parking lot
Site Survey Comments	Local boat ramp 1/2 mile west

Identification and planning

Mitigation

Preparedness

chapter 4 **Response**

Recovery

AFTER the first shock of a catastrophic event—a hurricane flattening hundreds of homes, an earthquake severing freeway arteries, or jetliners slamming into skyscrapers—the focus of everyone even remotely connected to the disaster will be on one thing: understanding all that has happened.

Of all the tasks of disaster management, it is this one at which GIS excels. Its visualization and data consolidation capabilities allow GIS to convey large amounts of information to a large number of people in a short period of time—exactly what is needed in the immediate aftermath of disaster.

As that fact has been better understood over the last decade, GIS has been increasingly integrated into disaster response capabilities along two tracks.

One of these has seen GIS becoming more and more part of the standard operating procedure of traditional disaster response, in which a dedicated GIS support unit is sent to the scene of a disaster as a matter of routine.

In some jurisdictions, in fact, a GIS response is now all but mandated. California's FIRESCOPE program, for example, which is charged with finding ways to promote interagency cooperation and technological innovation in California's emergency response, has long incorporated GIS as a core element of recommendations for best disaster management practices. The program also trains GIS disaster response specialists, and its legal authority specifically mentions mapping as a discipline necessary for ongoing research and development efforts. In addition, each of the twenty state and federal National Interagency Incident Management Teams based in California now deploy to disasters with a GIS specialist on board.

The GIS response to the events of September 2001 starkly demonstrated the validity of incorporating GIS routinely into disaster response.

SEPTEMBER 11

The days and weeks after September 11 saw perhaps the most intense GIS disaster response effort since the Northridge earthquake more than seven years earlier, on the other side of the country. Within hours of the terrorist attacks on the east coast, GIS specialists from around the country began rushing to New York City and Washington, D.C., to lend mapping and spatial analysis support. At the same time, New York's own GIS specialists and managers, such as Alan Leidner, were scrambling to find a place to set up shop to provide their own response support—because the city's Emergency Management Center had been located in the World Trade Center complex. That meant that suddenly, all of the hardware, software, and geographic data that the city would normally use for its own GIS response to a major disaster had been destroyed.

The GIS efforts in New York in the wake of the terrorist attacks comprised a concentrated, yet also protracted, version of what might best be termed "combat GIS." GIS personnel from a variety of agencies and backgrounds all converged on Manhattan, where they had to work with data sets most of them had never seen before, under conditions they could never have imagined—laboring in buildings where soldiers with loaded M-16s guarded the entrances, for example. They managed nonetheless to keep rescuers, recovery teams, city officials, and the public extremely well informed about virtually every geographic aspect of the tragic events.

Generally, there were two distinct GIS support operations in the city; one, based at the Jacob Javits Convention Center and on Pier 90, focused on mapping Ground Zero, while the other, based at the new Emergency Operations Center on Pier 92, focused on mapping for the rest of the city. In reality, of course, every group did a lot of everything, and data flowed freely back and forth among them.

Ground Zero

GIS operations at Ground Zero, under the direction of the Federal Emergency Management Agency and the New York City Fire Department, focused first on mapping the immediate devastation there, to help guide rescuers and recovery teams confronted with piles of smoking rubble five stories high.

The FEMA and NYFD GIS efforts first needed an accurate basemap to begin to make sense of the devastation. Fortunately, the city had a good one. Known as NYCMap, it consisted of high-resolution orthophotography only a few years old, with some standard vector data sets, such as street centerlines, registered to it; because NYCMap was still a relatively new product, many city departments had not yet had much opportunity to incorporate their data with it. Although most copies of the basemap had been destroyed or were inaccessible, enough copies surfaced in the first days that work could begin on registering more vector files to it. From those, accurate map products could be created.

Despite its limitations, without the NYCMap basemap the work would have been far more difficult than it already was.

Another critically important data set included was floor plans and engineering plans for the vast underground city beneath the Trade Center complex. Although this was in digital form, it was also in CAD format, and had to be processed and reformatted before it could be used in a GIS.

Left, a detail from the building plans of One World Trade Center that were used by disaster GIS personnel to map recovery efforts at Ground Zero. Below, a map showing the search status of one of the underground levels of the World Trade Center complex.

Once these two data sets were combined, the Ground Zero GIS teams could begin producing accurate map products for Urban Search and Rescue (USAR) teams, showing the accurate locations of hazards, such as fuel tanks and elevator shafts, as well as likely spaces where survivors might more likely be found.

A third data set of critical importance was orthophotography and other remotely sensed data of the Ground Zero complex, so that recovery teams could see how best to deploy their forces. Overflights of the complex by EarthData Inc. of Maryland began on September 14 and continued every day for several weeks. The specially outfitted Piper Navajo Chieftain also captured thermal and LIDAR (light detection and ranging) data—the latter allowing for extremely accurate 3-D imaging of the debris pile. The planes flew from Manhattan on to a processing center in Albany set up by the New York State Office for Technology. Technicians processed the imagery and other data, then transmitted it to the city, and also gave copies on CD to New York state troopers, who drove it back at high speed.

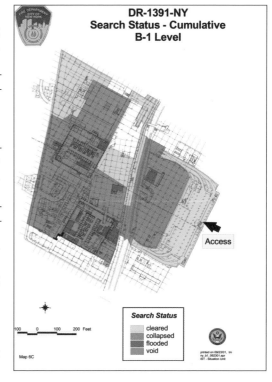

DR-1391-NY
Search Status - Cumulative
B-1 Level

Access

Search Status
- cleared
- collapsed
- flooded
- void

Orthophotographs such as this one, with street sign labels to orient the viewer, are essential in a major disaster response to show personnel the full extent of damage from a perspective they cannot get from ground level.

Another critically important use of orthophotography was to show recovery and debris-removal crews the areas of danger within the massive debris pile, such as the locations of crane booms and of hanging debris.

Experience gained in using GIS in an earlier terrorist attack helped the September 11 efforts. As was done in Oklahoma City six years earlier, when a bomb had also obliterated recognizable landmarks, the Ground Zero area was given its own coordinate system. A grid of cells was laid on an orthophotograph of the area. In Oklahoma City, the grids were 10 feet square; in New York they were 75 feet. The grid gave USAR and other teams a way to coordinate their searches. It also provided a way to categorize the results of all the other Ground Zero activity, including evidence collection, environmental monitoring, and debris removal.

Infrared and LIDAR data produced some very detailed 3-D images of the massive debris pile and highly accurate location information about fires that were still burning within it.

Of the many lessons that can be taken from the September 11 GIS experience, one was not to underestimate the high value that disaster response teams and the public place on orthophotos; even those who distrust maps will be drawn to a detailed, accurate orthophoto of a disaster area, especially when it is joined with street centerline or building footprint data. GIS response teams in other disasters should expect a high demand for this product.

But experts recommend laying the groundwork for obtaining remote sensing data of a disaster scene well before the event. That may mean executing contracts and agreements with vendors and government agencies well ahead of time, so that planes can be in the air, gathering this highly valuable data, with no more than a phone call or two.

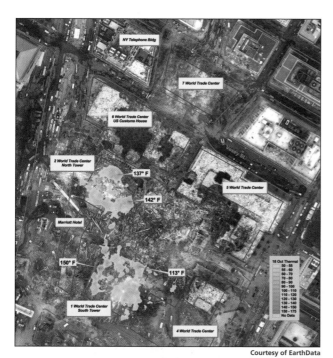

Left, a thermal imagery map showed high temperatures where fires still smoldered in the debris at Ground Zero. These maps showed not only areas of danger, but also the potential locations of flashovers, where two fires might jump the space between them and become one large and very dangerous fire.

Courtesy of EarthData

Courtesy of EarthData

Light Detection and Ranging (LIDAR) data allowed technicians to construct detailed 3-D maps of the Ground Zero area, showing the comparative heights of both buildings and debris.

The GIS teams at Ground Zero also produced basic field operations maps, simple in design and invaluable for orienting the thousands of men and women who had descended on the site with different missions and motives. They were also valuable for organizations' off-site support teams, who needed to know exactly where their people were supposed to go, and for suppliers needing to know where to send equipment.

Courtesy of EarthData

A section of the grid overlaid on an orthophoto of Ground Zero and used as the coordinate system for response and recovery operations. A similar kind of grid was used at the Oklahoma City bombing. Combat GIS experts say such a local coordinate system is essential for major urban disaster operations.

Pier 92

The GIS operation at Pier 92, under the direction of the City of New York, had a broader mandate. Its map product customers included dozens of federal and state agencies who had set up shop in the cavernous pier building, as well as every New York City agency affected in any way by the event. In addition, the Mayor's Office was a major customer, needing geographic information and maps to brief local, state, and federal leaders, to inform the public and the media, and to show visiting dignitaries.

Because of the demise of the Emergency Operations Center, the Pier 92 GIS teams had to put together a disaster GIS system virtually from scratch. This they managed to do by reconstituting data sets such as NYCMap from a variety of sources, including GIS vendors; other city, state, and federal agencies; and educational institutions.

With donated hardware and ArcGIS as its principal software platform, the GIS teams set up shop under a banner that read Emergency Mapping Center.

There was little interest in what they were doing for the first hours until two things happened: Alan Leidner changed the name of the sign to read Emergency Mapping and Data Center—adding the additional phrase in keeping with his conception of GIS as a data visualization tool. In addition, GIS team members hung some large-format sample map products on the walls, and then began an educational process—showing personnel from the disparate agencies just how GIS could create individualized maps, customized to show exactly the map features and attributes relevant to a user's task.

Once their educational efforts for this core concept caught hold, the GIS teams were inundated with map requests. Within days, it was clear certain map products were more popular than others, and so

Personnel in the New York City Emergency Mapping and Data Center on Pier 92, above, responded to requests for hundreds of standard and customized map products in the days and weeks after September 11. Left, one of the most popular standard map products, updated constantly, showed areas and types of restricted zones around Ground Zero.

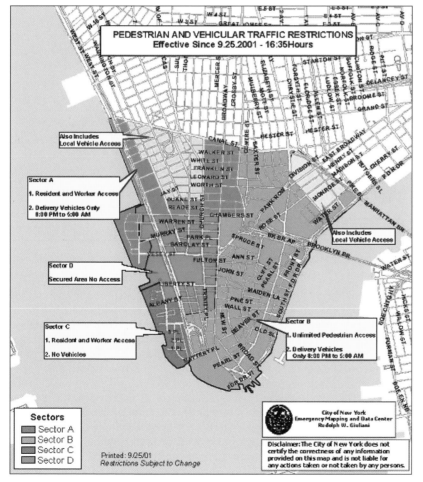

the team came up with standard maps and templates to satisfy the demand for them, while still creating custom maps for special needs.

Among the most popular of the standards were maps showing restricted zones in the city; locations of command posts and other response-related resources; utility outages and transportation restrictions; building-status maps; and street maps over orthophotos of the city.

The demand for hard-copy maps became so great that it required that a number of organizational changes be made in order to keep the operation running smoothly.

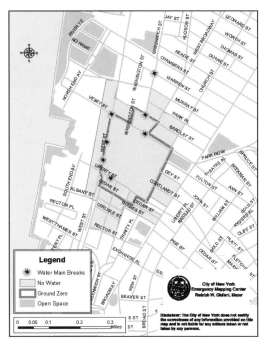

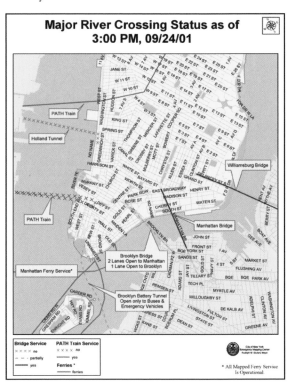

Two standard map products from the Emergency Mapping and Data Center conveyed needed information to city officials and the public.

ArcSDE

In the early days, the GIS team simply filled requests for maps as they came in. But this ad hoc system quickly became unwieldy. One problem was that customers would often come in with new geographic data—a change to a street closure, for example—and ask for a new map based on this new data. A GIS team member would call up the appropriate shapefile, make changes to it based on the new information, and generate the map. With a dozen or more mapmakers, and scores of customers, shapefiles could undergo several changes in a day, without it being clear who made the changes, how reliable the new information was, and which version of the new map should be used for what purpose. Mapmakers were also creating certain kinds of products over and over again.

The team instituted a new system using ArcSDE™ software, which works as a bridge between desktop-mapping products such as ArcGIS and a relational database of geographic data such as SQL Server™. With the help of ArcSDE, GIS team leaders were able to bring some order to the system. Rules were set for who would be authorized to make changes to a data layer, how those changes would be made, where data and map products would be located within the database, and so on. A GIS administrator was assigned authority over the system for each shift. In this new system, when a map request came in with new data attached to it, a map team member would enter the data into a temporary version of the data layer to which nobody else had access. After the new map's accuracy was verified with the original map requester, the GIS administrator reviewed the updated version, then approved its use by everybody.

These and other efficiencies streamlined the workload greatly, but implementing it was made extremely difficult because the work of mapmaking, using the same data that was being reorganized, still had to continue. There was no time to take a break so that the new system could be put in place and tested—another aspect of combat GIS conditions.

Archived data for recovery

The ArcSDE implementation had another benefit in that it allowed a reliable history of maps and therefore data to be built. Such histories are critical for the kinds of longer-term recovery efforts that must take place in the wake of a disaster response, especially for one as big as September 11.

In the heat of the moment, it may seem important only to create the most up-to-date map, do it quickly, and then discard anything outdated. But in fact, disaster response data and map products create a disaster history that can be crucially important for reasons unforeseen at the time of the response.

In Manhattan, for example, keeping old data was important for environmental protection purposes at Ground Zero. Because it was still unknown at that time what kinds of hazardous substances might be at the Ground Zero site, vehicles that came into and left the site were washed down at decontamination stations. These stations were moved several times, each time presumably leaving behind a residue of all the stuff, possibly hazardous, that had been washed off the trucks. Knowing the history of these moves was important. For a complete decontamination of the site to be done months later, cleanup crews would have to know where all of the decontamination stations had been, not just the ones that happened to be on the most recent maps. Certain contaminants, if necessary, might also have to be traced back to specific locations for further investigation and, possibly, litigation.

Online map requests

Another innovation implemented at Pier 92 was an online system for requesting map products. Although the initial paper system worked well, the online system worked better: it allowed the GIS team to customize the kinds of information that map requesters submitted, and also let them get to the requests faster.

The GIS team also developed plans to extend this online system to allow for online publishing of the completed maps with Web browsers, using ArcIMS. This would have allowed users to create customized maps on their own desktops, panning and zooming at will to create maps of locations, extents, and features they need. (The Emergency Mapping and Data Center operation generated an enormous amount of paper, much put to good use, but also much wasted, and much taken home as mementos of the tragedy.) ArcIMS is deployed perhaps most notably in a disaster context at the Geomac wildfire site (geomac.usgs.gov), where people can observe the progress of any wildfire in the country in real time.

The online map request system invented at the Emergency Mapping and Data Center made the entire operation more efficient, allowing GIS administrators to see exactly who was making what maps, and for whom.

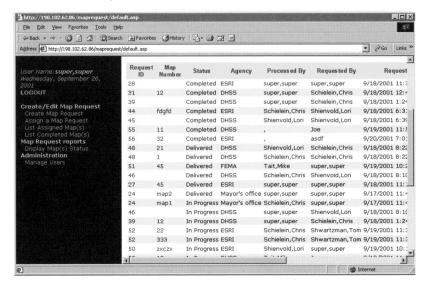

COMBAT GIS CONSIDERATIONS

As the work in New York City demonstrates, the mission and particular needs of a rapid-deployment, combat GIS operation are distinctly different from more normal, day-to-day GIS operations. Its pace is faster and far more intense, and its work products are put to immediate use for concrete, highly visible purposes.

Some of the experts at this specialized work have compiled a thick playbook of recommendations.

Speed

One of the most notable differences between a regular GIS operation and the combat GIS version is how much faster it is, the experts say. This is not a consideration that should be underestimated. The speed and pace of a combat GIS operation will probably astonish those coming from a more leisurely paced GIS operation; it will nevertheless be the most in-your-face aspect of the reality there: on-scene commanders will want geographic information, maps, and analysis immediately—and then they will want it all over again, because the situation at the disaster scene may have changed from twenty minutes before. There may be a great deal of different kinds of data at different locations to collect and keep track of, as floodwaters and brushfires expand and contract at various places on the ground, seemingly quiet one minute, but threatening lives and structures the next.

Moreover, the command post or emergency operations center will itself constitute a major distraction from focused geographic analysis and mapmaking, because it will be noisy, chaotic, and crowded. Emotions will run raw. This kind of pace and situation will demand quick thinking from GIS team members, at a time when there will be a great deal to think about.

Experience will be the best preparation for this reality, and disaster response exercises should try to reflect it. Accurate anticipation of the probable data and map needs of the operations center—and good preparation toward meeting those needs—will help reduce the stress.

Culture

The organization of a disaster response will in all likelihood follow the nationally recognized Incident Command System, or some variation thereof. Familiarity with this system ahead of time will help smooth the transition. A disaster response organization and its hierarchy may be quite unlike any encountered by GIS personnel before. Its authority figures may come from military or law-enforcement backgrounds where lines of authority are unambiguous. While they may appreciate the value that maps and spatial analysis can bring to the operation, they may not always be interested in the technical constraints and requirements that bring those products to reality. They will simply ask for what they need from the GIS team and expect to receive it quickly—especially if life and property are at stake, and time is short.

Hardware and system design

The details will vary with each organization and each response incident, but in general, the equipment and system architecture of the GIS response team should reflect the needs of the mission: mobility, flexibility, and interconnectivity will count the most.

Above all, the system should avoid what Dave Kehrlein of California's Governor's Office of Emergency Services calls "single points of failure"—a comparatively minor vulnerability that can render the entire system inoperable. Passwords are one example of this. If they must be used at all, they should be accessible in an emergency by several members of the team. In a disaster, nothing ever works as smoothly as it was intended to. This means that it is entirely possible that the system administrator who knows the passwords may become stranded—or worse—and this absence could make the entire system inaccessible to the rest of the team and therefore useless to the entire response operation.

Data access is another example of a potential point of failure. All necessary basemap data for a particular region—decided on well in advance, of course—should be on CD, with many copies easily accessible. Although the GIS team may have access to a centralized, enterprise GIS that may contain more complete data sets, the team cannot depend on having any communication available to connect to those databases; CDs of previously consolidated data are a far more reliable option.

Workstations will need to have fast processors and, obviously, large amounts of storage space and RAM—this is especially the case with the growing pervasiveness of remotely sensed data. They and any notebook computers should be configured to be easily networked into small LANs, which should themselves have the ability to link to larger networks (if they happen to be available). Keep in mind that new equipment may not have had all the bugs worked out, and team members will not have had the chance to become familiar with the individual idiosyncrasies of a particular piece of hardware. Older equipment that has been used in exercises, whose condition and quirks are well known, are a better bet.

A similar situation will apply to printers and plotters, which will see a lot of hard use during a response operation. Printers and plotters should have the most current drivers installed, with copies of driver and firmware files in several easily accessible locations. Battery backups for everything are a must.

Directory structure

Clearly laid-out directory structures and file organization are of critical importance because of the stability they can provide. In a disaster response, everything outside the operations center will seem to be in chaos, and everything inside will be in a state of flux as well—most noticeably, personnel will be moving in and out, with many people handling different assignments throughout the course of a response. This kind of turnover—among those both making maps and those needing them—will quickly turn the mapmaking process into disarray if the digital workspace is not clearly laid out.

Folders and directories should use logical, not arbitrary, names. Naming conventions learned in software training classes over many years—where a training folder or workspace is identified by student name, perhaps—should be discarded in favor of simple and descriptive labels that clarify, not obscure, the contents of a directory.

Physical space

An easily overlooked item, physical room in which to work, is something the GIS team needs to be assured of. Although notebook computers and workstations may have small footprints, large monitors, plotters, and printers do not. Nor do large-format hard-copy maps, necessary for briefings of large groups of people, but which require large flat surfaces or walls—and some way to attach them—so they can be studied clearly. The storage or shelving system used to store these hard-copy map products will also require extra space, especially because these products will accumulate rapidly.

Interdependencies and communication

Combat GIS is not done in a vacuum. Disaster response situations involve a great deal of interagency communications, since disasters ignore administrative boundaries. Contact names, current mobile telephone numbers, and e-mail addresses of GIS personnel at other relevant local and state agencies should be obtained well ahead of time. Up-to-date FEMA contacts will also be important to have close at hand.

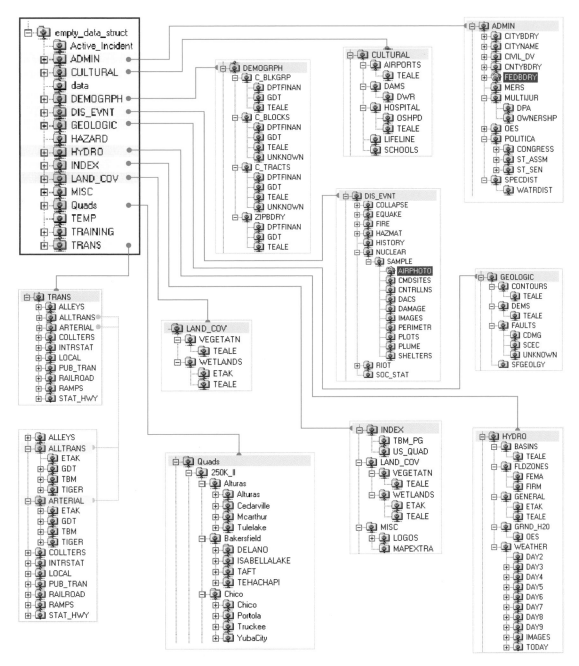

The central disaster incident GIS data structure used by the California Governor's Office of Emergency Services at its Sacramento headquarters and regional offices. It represents the OES view of the most useful GIS data sets to have readily available during a disaster, and the most logical arrangement of them within a directory structure. Smaller, more compact versions are derived from this structure for use by OES teams in the field.

Disaster operations centers have their own unique communications dynamic, which GIS teams will need to adjust to. Because there are so many different tasks and missions going on, information flows in the operations center exist on many levels. Those personnel coming from the world of public agencies may be used to a more linear communication tradition, usually up and down an organizational hierarchy. But such a flow will not work in an overheated disaster response situation; cross-jurisdictional communication will be the norm, not the exception.

Those coming from a public agency hierarchy will also be used to fairly rigid reporting requirements, where information is not considered valid unless it has been approved at some higher level. But this kind of thinking may hinder real communication in a disaster operations center. The reporting of information is not always synonymous with communicating it.

Standardized map and data products

In the preresponse phase, exercises and discussions with other stakeholders will have shown which data and map products are likely to be most in demand. Because the exact location of a disaster event can't be known, it will be possible to assemble data only for the most likely areas where problems might be expected.

It will be critical to consult with the experts in a particular agency on which data they will most urgently need in a disaster.

Perhaps no more than six or seven likely map products will result from this discussion, but that will be sufficient to begin assembling the appropriate data sets.

For example, on the operational side, if wildfires have historically been seen in a certain park system that is hundreds of thousands of acres in size, then the relevant DEMs can be obtained and stored close at hand. Also in the wildfire context, property ownership data for large chunks of uninhabited land will be important when it comes time to send out bills for services. Similarly, the imminent arrival of floods will mean that data sets of levees and flood canals, with accurate latitude and longitude coordinates attached, should be made part of the CD set, after having been checked for accuracy.

On the logistics side, a likely data cache to have on hand for quick mapping would be the locations of fuel for motor vehicles—diesel as well as gasoline.

There will be hundreds of possibilities for such data sets, depending on regional history and location. These should be thoroughly explored well beforehand.

Map templates

Predefined templates of map documents can save a great deal of time, even if the exact data sets that will be needed are not yet known. Experts say these can and should include the layers that might possibly be used, organized into a layout that would be most helpful cartographically. Symbology and label styles can be predefined and standardized, as can equally important elements such as the map title, disclaimers, organization identification, some legend information, and a time and date stamp.

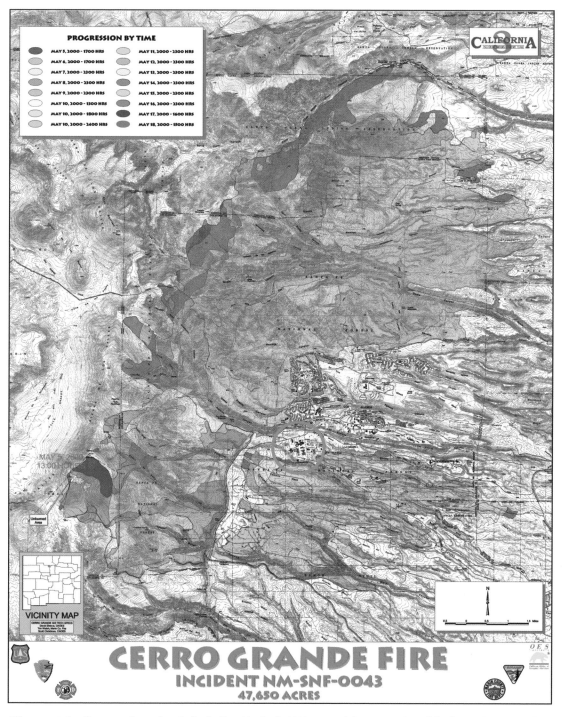

PROGRESSION BY TIME

MAY 5, 2000 - 1700 HRS	MAY 11, 2000 - 2300 HRS
MAY 6, 2000 - 1700 HRS	MAY 12, 2000 - 2300 HRS
MAY 7, 2000 - 2300 HRS	MAY 13, 2000 - 2300 HRS
MAY 8, 2000 - 2300 HRS	MAY 14, 2000 - 2300 HRS
MAY 9, 2000 - 2300 HRS	MAY 15, 2000 - 2300 HRS
MAY 10, 2000 - 1300 HRS	MAY 16, 2000 - 2300 HRS
MAY 10, 2000 - 1800 HRS	MAY 17, 2000 - 1600 HRS
MAY 10, 2000 - 2400 HRS	MAY 18, 2000 - 1500 HRS

VICINITY MAP

CERRO GRANDE FIRE
INCIDENT NM-SNF-0043
47,650 ACRES

GIS crews at the disastrous Cerro Grande fire in New Mexico in 2000 mapped the progression of the fire as thousands of firefighters fought the blaze. At its conclusion, they produced this map showing the progression from beginning to end. Within the locator circle is the headquarters of the Los Alamos National Laboratory, a national resource.

Staffing

Viewed realistically, staffing will be largely driven by budgets, not by what is best in a disaster response. How GIS personnel are deployed varies with each jurisdiction and with the type of situation. In Miami-Dade County, for instance, where the Office of Emergency Management has one full-time GIS person, a significant disaster would trigger a call-up of all GIS-skilled personnel from every other department. In California, the basic Office of Emergency Services configuration calls for a three-person GIS response team, a manager, a lead, and a technician.

Experienced GIS responders say that such teams should include specialists in programming, in handling remotely sensed data, and in working with hard-copy map production on printers and plotters.

When there is an extreme need for personnel with GIS skills, informal networks will prove useful. This occurred in New York City at the Emergency Mapping and Data Center, where a call for volunteers went out over a GIS Internet mailing list whose subscribers included virtually anyone with an interest in or connection to GIS in the New York metropolitan area. The call was answered by many volunteers from college GIS programs and other sources, such as people who could not go to work because their employers were located within a restricted zone. Other organizations may want to consider establishing similar disaster GIS volunteer lists. However, outside volunteer personnel will require allocating time and energy to training—orienting volunteers to the current system, configuration, and situation, and even providing on-the-job software instruction. The return on this kind of investment may not be worth it for some organizations.

A decision to use volunteer help may mean that a list be compiled ahead of time, and that volunteers be asked to participate in predisaster exercises, planning, and training.

Media

The media will also be an important consumer of map products during a disaster and the aftermath. In an age when several cable networks run virtually nothing but news twenty-four hours a day, and online sites by the hundreds compete with them, the media's appetite for information will be prodigious. Ignore this reality at your peril. In the absence of facts, rumors and half-truths tend to fester, and in the end it will mean more work for the disaster response team, not less.

Leaving aside any philosophical disagreements with modern media behavior in a disaster, keep in mind that the media will often be an emergency operation center's best conduit to getting information out to the public—whether simply updating a situation, reporting evacuation orders, or warning the public to stay clear of certain areas.

Keep in mind also that maps make great graphics for the media. Experienced editors and producers know a graphic message will usually grab their readers' and viewers' attention better than a long string of text, or an announcer talking. When it comes to informing the public about the location of evacuation routes, fire lines, or no-go areas, maps will do it better than anything else.

Whatever public information plan is in place at a particular response, the GIS team should make it a point to educate those doing public information of the great amount of information that a map can put into a small compact package. One necessary preparation for this will be to discuss with incident commanders which data can be widely disseminated (such as the path and speed of fire perimeters or flood-waters) and which may need to be held more closely (such as the exact location of the ignition point of a suspected arson-caused fire).

On a technical level, thought should be given to some kind of direct link, or URL, that will allow map products to be transmitted directly to media organizations with the greatest clarity. If possible, a GIS staffer could be assigned to answer specific questions about map products from media organizations' graphic specialists, who can make those products look very good.

GIS RESPONSE INNOVATIONS

Another trend in GIS response has seen many organizations moving beyond basic mapping tasks, into customizing GIS applications for particular, innovative uses. Several involve integrating Internet and wireless capabilities, stretching the distance at which GIS can be an effective yet still timely tool.

A COMPLETE ONLINE EMERGENCY SYSTEM

In Pierce County in the state of Washington, GIS mapping and analysis capabilities play a central role in the county's innovative online disaster response system. Built as the internal Web site for the Pierce County Emergency Operations Center, the Pierce Incident Management System (PIMS) incorporates into a common interface all the information-gathering and mapping needs of the EOC, including command, communications, operations, logistics, finance, and even public information functions.

In an emergency or disaster (designated in terms of seriousness as Level 1, 2, or 3), telephone call takers and other PIMS users enter addresses and other pertinent information about an ongoing crisis— such as damage reports after an earthquake, or power outages after a storm—into the system on standardized HTML forms. The data from the form is stored in an SQL database.

The call-taker forms can then be called up by an EOC or operations manager for further action, such as a return phone call for further information, assignment to someone inside or outside the EOC, or locating the incident on a digital map.

If a particular report appears to warrant further investigation, the manager brings up an ArcIMS application from within PIMS to map the address recorded by the call taker. The manager can do address geocoding to find the precise location of the report—reducing the chances of an erroneous address given mistakenly by a distraught caller. The recorded address is automatically sent to the map and a list of possible address matches can be retrieved, using a button on the interface. When the manager clicks on an address, the system zooms to that location and labels the address. At that point, the address can be saved to the database.

Two examples of the kinds of custom online mapping the PIMS system in Pierce County lets emergency managers do. These maps, showing a buffer around a school and a flooded area, can be used internally or put on a public Web site.

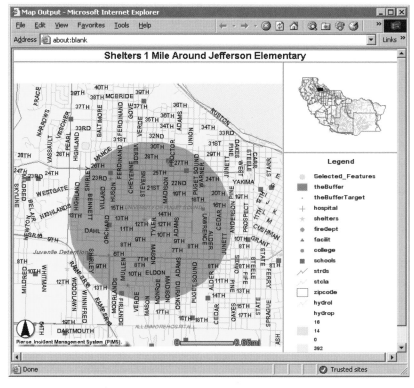

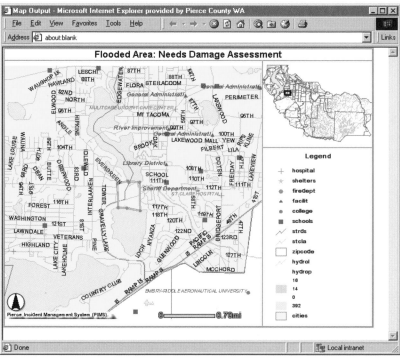

When a manager wants to look for geographic patterns, or to perform some analysis among the reported incidents, the ArcIMS application allows for many standard GIS functions: zooming and panning, querying, distance measurement, identification, and buffering, using a variety of data sets selected specifically from Pierce County's enterprise GIS for disaster applications. Specific disaster management mapping functions can also be accomplished, such as querying for specific events within a particular time frame, or locating areas in need of special assistance or resources.

CITIZEN NOTIFICATION WITH GIS

In North Carolina, one county is using a GIS-based application, coupled with an automated telephone-dialing system, to warn citizens about impending or ongoing disasters. The GeoNotify™ system from Dialogic Communications Corp. and Bradshaw Consulting Services allows police and others in Mecklenburg County to order thousands of citizens to evacuate their homes, or to alert them to dangerous conditions such as oncoming floodwaters or hazardous chemical releases.

Created with MapObjects® 2 and Microsoft Visual Basic®, GeoNotify presents users with a GIS map interface and prompts them to select a layer. This can be any layer that an agency has available, including street centerlines and orthophotos, that have been geocoded. In early 2002, that included more than 228,000 listed residential phone numbers in the Mecklenburg County area, and more than 31,000 businesses.

From the layer, the user can then simply draw a shape around the affected area. These can be conventional shapefiles, user-defined ones, such as a floodplains, or specialized—a triangle for example, useful for an area downwind of a toxic substance release, or a doughnut shape, for situations in which you want a small crisis area isolated.

A GeoNotify screen shows the user has created a doughnut polygon around a point. Residences within the doughnut will receive automated telephone calls informing them of an emergency in their area.

Once the area is defined, the list of phone numbers within that area is displayed, along with a dialog box for choosing which messages will be broadcast. These messages can also be customized on the spot, useful when a disaster situation is changing rapidly.

Press another button, and an automatic calling application known as The Communicator!, also from Dialogic, kicks in. Depending on the number of phone lines dedicated to the job, the application can call thousands of people an hour. Calling options can be customized as well, allowing the operator to specify that calling will continue for a specified number of attempts, or to leave a message on an answering machine.

MAPPING FLOODWATERS IN FLORIDA

With widespread use, wireless, mobile GIS services may revolutionize the way disaster response is carried out. A foreshadowing of the myriad benefits in efficiency and flexibility of these new services can be seen in southern Florida.

The South Florida Water Management District has responsibility for water resource protection and flood control planning for all of South Florida, an immense and diverse geographic area, encompassing both the urban sprawl of Miami-Dade County and the fragile ecosystems of the Everglades.

Flooding is a frequent problem in the low-lying South Florida area, and after storms and hurricanes, it can cause hundreds and millions of dollars in damage.

Figuring out just how much damage is the task of the district's Secondary Assessment Teams. These teams slog out into flooded communities even before the rains have stopped, to see which communities have been hit and how hard. The district operates a network of flood canals, floodgates, and other mechanisms that can be adjusted to reduce the amount of floodwater in a given area, and the teams' assessments are a critical part of that decision-making process.

Until recently, the teams ventured out with little more than paper maps and pens, trying to draw flood boundaries by hand in areas where street signs had been blown down—and trying to do it all as wind and rain raged around them.

The resulting maps, driven back to headquarters for inputting into the GIS for formulating response plans, were less than ideal. Often, in fact, they were little more than soggy wads of ink-blotched paper. When they were legible, the time-consuming labor of digitizing the field teams' hand-drawn maps of flood boundaries into the GIS system consumed valuable time and manpower.

But advances in mobile GIS technology now let the water district's assessment teams draw shapefiles of the boundaries of floodwaters directly into a GIS application right in the field. This can be done with ArcPad, GIS software that can be used on a personal digital assistant (PDA) running Microsoft Windows® CE, or on a notebook computer operating inside the (warm) cab of a pickup truck.

The system will bring the district some notable improvements over the soggy-paper method.

First, it will give the water district assessment teams more and better information to work with, before they even arrive at the flooded zones.

This South Florida Water Management District ArcPad screen shows a polygon delineating an area of flooding drawn over an orthophoto. Transmitted back to the operations center, this information will allow flood emergency managers to make adjustments much sooner and more efficiently than before.

A previously created street or topographic map or orthophoto of the relevant area, for use as a reference basemap, can be loaded onto the laptop or PDA before the teams leave headquarters. Then, once the assessment teams are in place, ArcPad lets them create a new shapefile of the actual flood boundaries, as team members stand beside or drive around them. ArcPad also allows for the calculation of flood boundary distances and area.

Positional accuracy can also be enhanced when a GPS unit is used in conjunction with ArcPad.

With a wireless modem, water district teams will also be able to transmit their new field data immediately to the district's emergency operations center, allowing for even speedier response to changing conditions. At the operations center, the new data will be updated in an SDE® layer with an ArcObjects™ script and then displayed in ArcIMS for the emergency operations staff. Because ArcPad is easily customizable for different skill levels, training times can be reduced. Forms can be created to enable field workers to enter only attributes that apply to a particular incident, using value ranges appropriate for the task and the particular incident.

STATEWIDE DISASTER COORDINATION IN PENNSYLVANIA

While some kind of on-scene response will always be a requirement for most disasters, the Internet and online map services are beginning to extend significantly the range of the support that GIS can give. Nowhere is this better demonstrated than in Pennsylvania, where GIS forms the core of a new online, statewide, interagency response system. Its remote capabilities permit not just long-distance monitoring of disaster situations from anywhere, but also facilitate communication among agencies.

Each of several agencies with potential lead disaster response responsibilities access the Pennsylvania Incident Response System (PAIRS). The pilot program roster includes the Pennsylvania Emergency Management Agency, the Department of Environmental Protection, and the Department of Agriculture; other state agency access is planned for the future.

When users enter the site, they can access a variety of informational and data-entry Active Server Page screens. These are similar in appearance but customized for each agency—and customized for the kinds of incidents for which the agency would most likely lead a response. For example, the Department of Health screens provide human health-related forms that the Department of Agriculture might not need.

The PAIRS input screen drop-down list shows the wide array of disaster incidents the system is designed to handle.

The incident-entry screen includes buttons to allow the user to share the information with a variety of others—including the state director of homeland security—or to use it only for internal agency use.

The common point of reference, the glue that links all these agencies, is the common geographical point of reference they all have. When the incident information is entered—by any employee, regardless of technical expertise—its location is automatically recorded in the database, along with the relevant attribute information.

The record of the incident, which each agency can access from a screen that allows them to search incidents by county, agency, data, type of incident, or incident status, has a hyperlink to an online map. Clicking the hyperlink brings the user directly to the incident location on the map. A variety of functions can be performed from the online map screen, including zooming, panning, distance measurement, and identification of any incident or map layer feature.

The incident-entry screen also contains geographic parameters, not only to locate the incident within the online state map, but also to more precisely define its effects on the environment—when the operator enters the incident's location by address, intersection, or latitude and longitude, for example, the application automatically places that incident in the correct county and municipality, and also in the relevant watershed.

The incident data is stored in an Oracle® database, from which ArcSDE retrieves and serves it to the interface screens.

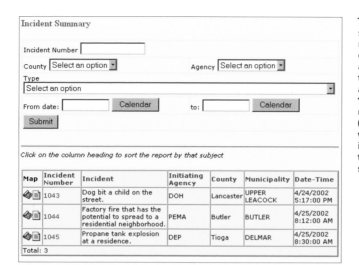

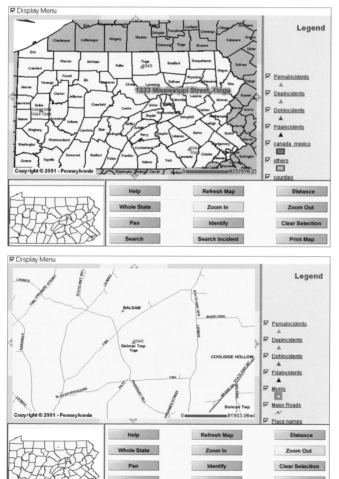

The PAIRS incident summary screen (top) shows a list of recent incidents of potential concern, and relevant associated information. Clicking on the hyperlinked "Map" column at the far left, on Incident 1045, brings the user automatically to a locator map (middle), showing the incident within Pennsylvania. Zooming in further brings the user to street-level detail (bottom), still within the same interface.

GIS ON WHEELS

Go to the scene of a wildfire of any size in the western United States and you are likely to see the large red trucks of Michelle's AAA Equipment Rentals, Inc., of Perris, California, parked nearby. Called simply "Michelle's" by fire response personnel, the company offers disaster support services on wheels, including water trucks, generators, medical support trucks, and mobile operations centers—and GIS support services.

These mobile GIS units, operated by both public and private organizations, have been appearing at disaster events with increasing frequency in recent years. Michelle's was a pioneer in the business.

Michelle's "Situation Analysis Mapping" 35-foot-long truck is outfitted with eleven PCs and servers, each with at least 100 GB of hard-drive space and ArcGIS software. There are also top-of-the-line printers and plotters, and the trucks are completely networked, with network and phone jacks flush with the exterior walls.

The trucks see heavy use during a disaster event, says Jay Sadler, who oversees operations, with plotters sometimes going twenty-four hours a day printing large-format maps delineating fire lines and other information for incident commanders and others.

The truck comes equipped with complete data on the topography and fire fuels for all of the state of California. That works fine inside the state, but when it moves out of state, data access is more problematic. Often, local jurisdictions in rural areas have little more than property maps or street maps to offer. Sometime, the data isn't in digital format, and that's a bigger problem, because as big as the trucks are, they aren't big enough to allow for the scanning of maps or digitizing on the scene.

That is one reason why Michelle's latest investment in mobile GIS capabilities is in satellite technology. This will allow for high-speed wireless data communication that will all but eliminate problems with data unavailability. With the satellite equipment, the Situation Analysis Mapping truck, even when parked in the most remote forest, will still be able to download relevant geographic data right down to the scene of the disaster.

Compassion, urgency, and science

By K. Adams Manion, URS Corporation; Wendy Dorf, New York City Department of Environmental Protection; Marina Havan-Orumieh, PlanGraphics, Inc.

Shortly after the September 11 tragedy, the Deep Infrastructure Group was formed to support the Emergency Mapping and Data Center for the New York City Mayor's Office of Emergency Management (OEM) at the newly constructed Emergency Operations Center (EOC) located at Pier 92 on Manhattan's midtown west side. Wendy Dorf, GIS director at the New York City Department of Environmental Protection (NYCDEP) and project manager of the acclaimed NYC-wide Water Main Mapping and GIS projects, was directed by OEM to lead the Deep Infrastructure Group, focusing initially on supporting rescue operations being conducted by the Fire Department of the City of New York (FDNY). Dorf assembled a technical staff and began developing a data structure of underground infrastructure to support the rescue operation at Ground Zero.

The Deep Infrastructure Group developed a three-phased approach to meet the city's underground utility needs for disaster relief.

Phase I consisted of identifying and collecting pertinent data sets from both city and private companies specializing in utilities. Data collection efforts were focused on water, sewer, gas, electric, steam, telecommunications, and transportation, as well as engineering floor plans of the subsurface levels of the World Trade Center (WTC) complex. Contact began with the New York City Department of Design and Construction (NYCDDC), the New York City Department of Transportation (NYCDOT), the New York City Department of Environmental Protection (NYCDEP), the state Department of Health, the Port Authority of New York and New Jersey, the Federal Emergency Management Agency (FEMA), the Metropolitan Transportation Authority (MTA) Triborough Bridge and Tunnel Authority, New York City Transit (NYCT), Consolidated Edison (Con Ed), Empire City Subway (ECS), and Verizon. Participants elaborated on their available data sets, data format, and distribution restrictions.

Phase II involved registering the data sets to the city's standard cartographic basemap, NYCMAP. K. Adams Manion, a senior GIS engineer with URS Corporation and project manager for the Deep Infrastructure Group, tapped into the resources already established at the EOC for GIS support. Data registration began with an inventory of the data and an evaluation of formats. Data sets varied in format from hard-copy paper to digital, on several CAD and GIS platforms. Content, standards, and accuracy also varied greatly among data sets. With support from GIS staff working at the Emergency Mapping and Data Center, including representatives from ESRI and PlanGraphics, the collected data sets were registered to the NYCMAP and customized to allow data distribution to authorized parties.

Because time was critical in the wake of September 11, data sets were divided among group specialists. Ms. Manion focused on engineered utility data sets, such as water and sewer from NYCDEP, and Marina Havan-Orumieh, executive consultant with PlanGraphics, concentrated her efforts and years of experience on gas, electric, and steam utilities. Products were created for distribution from approved requestors.

As data was collected, multiple initiatives were pursued during meetings that took place continuously at the Emergency Mapping and Data Center. New technologies were introduced and evaluated for potential enhancement to the Deep Infrastructure data structure, and, more significantly, to facilitate the rescue and recovery operation. There were also continuous security and legal discussions concerning protection of the infrastructure data. Participants addressed data security issues quickly, to ensure the rapid exchange of data among city agencies and private companies, to protect the rescue workers, and to eliminate fears of inappropriate data leakage.

CONTINUED

Data security and legal issues

The security of utility data is of utmost importance. The sensitive content of Deep Infrastructure data sets could provide terror attack "hot spots," locations at high risk for human injury. For protection, all data sets were made confidential. To obtain maps and data in hard-copy or digital format, approval was required from the data originator/owner through the Emergency Mapping and Data Center manager and would not be released without approval at the highest levels of the OEM.

The Mapping and Data Center provided a secure data service, along with access and privilege rights. Paper maps were held at the EOC podium in a secured area until digital images were produced and cataloged, then hard-copy versions were destroyed. All digital data sets were cataloged and tagged with metadata, including appropriate use and distribution restrictions. Additionally, data security policy was expanded to include nondisclosure agreements. A legal nondisclosure agreement was written for the private utilities that readily provided their data to the city.

Coordination efforts

Immediately after the formation of the Deep Infrastructure Group, Wendy Dorf scheduled a GIS infrastructure meeting at the EOC, inviting the entire GIS infrastructure community, including public and private utilities and technology vendors. With representation from most entities involved in GIS, the Deep Infrastructure Group described the project, the contribution required of the various entities, and the time frame required. The Emergency Mapping and Data Center needed data from the various entities to map Ground Zero, to help the FDNY to accomplish its rescue and recovery operation. A team that was expert at registering varied data formats to the NYCMAP, using ESRI software, had been assembled. Each agency and utility was asked to compile its data digitally or otherwise, with or without the help of vendors, at its own location, and then to submit the paper or digitized products to the EOC as soon as possible.

It was fortuitous and critical that the New York City GIS community had been established for many years before this tragic event; this provided the operation with knowledgeable people who were not only skilled mappers, but also participants in the formation of citywide GIS policy. Rapid mobilization and quick response to the infrastructure team's requests were helped by the GIS and Mapping Organization (GISMO), a grassroots organization of GIS advocates established by Jack Eichenbaum of the Department of Finance, and by the Citywide GIS Steering Committee, originally established in the Mayor's Office, and chaired, among others, by Alan Leidner. Because of the existence of this community, volunteers and data began streaming into the Emergency Mapping and Data Center soon after the attack.

Federal and state GIS databases also were developed more fully at the EOC during the emergency. In particular, FEMA used GPS and LIDAR technologies at the WTC site to identify and locate features and to help its Urban Search and Rescue operations. Upon completion of this mission, FEMA turned its data over to the Deep Infrastructure Group. Additional data was provided by the U.S. Army Corps of Engineers based at the EOC, and from their New York office.

The data

The following sections provide a more detailed description of the infrastructure and data sets used in spatial data operations for the WTC disaster:

Water and sewer

NYCDEP provided water and sewer coverage for lower Manhattan. Efforts to compile data for the search and rescue efforts were greatly aided by the ongoing GIS focus within NYCDEP. Instead of having to sort through detailed distribution maps and associated field cards, water coverage was already compiled in a centralized CAD system. Two data sets were made available from this resource. The first was an extracted version, imported into AutoCAD® drawings. These drawings were registered to the NYCMAP. Pipe segments were grouped into sizes and assigned appropriate line styles. The second version was an Adobe® Acrobat® PDF, which was routinely used for asbestos-monitoring locations.

Sewer Infiltration and Inflow (I/I) maps were made available in image format. The images were scanned and registered to the NYCMAP. Streets fit closely, due to the schematic nature of the I/I maps—that is, most sewer mains were drafted in the center street line area, and the overlay accuracy was acceptable. From the registered, scanned image, screen digitizing was conducted to include pipe dimensions and to maintain flow direction. Sewer pipes, manholes, and regulators were graphically created, along with attributes such as pipe dimension, size, and shape. These two data sets, water and sewer, were customized to create an overview of the WTC infrastructure conditions.

Gas, steam, electric, and telecommunication

Con Ed provides gas, steam, and electric services to Manhattan. Initially, Con Ed provided composite coverage in CAD format. The data was used to map zones of power outages, which were posted on the city's Emergency Management Online Locator System (EMOLS) Internet site, where the public could also gather information about pedestrian and vehicular restrictions. Fortunately for the relief effort, many NYC agencies and private utility leaders, such as Con Ed, have dedicated resources to the GIS effort.

Empire City Subway (ECS) provides conduit distribution for phone and cable systems for almost all of Manhattan. ECS provided raster images for WTC's Liberty Street section. This data was used for a pilot project to provide an estimate of work effort to integrate ECS and OEM data sets in case of future emergencies.

Transportation

Additional data sets were requested and integrated as they were made available from MTA Bridges and Tunnels and NYCT. Basic data sets were used to increase geographic awareness for volunteers who came from all regions of the nation to support the relief effort.

WTC sublevel infrastructure

As fires raged at Ground Zero, more comprehensive data sets were needed to help direct rescue and recovery efforts. What was feeding these fires? Where should efforts be focused to contain and eventually extinguish these hazards? How could search crews be better directed to more promising recovery areas? Digital images of subsurface floor plans were registered to the NYCMAP and integrated with other data sources to provide search, rescue, and recovery grids for FDNY, Urban Search and Rescue, and for structural integrity assessment by NYCDDC engineering consultants.

CONTINUED

Ongoing support

Phase III of the project is ongoing—providing GIS to support new NYC policies for disaster relief and terrorism. As new data sets are created or uncovered, the Deep Infrastructure Group sets about the task of assessing the technical issues, compiling the data, and customizing the product into a universal commodity to best serve the city. The transition from raw data to product is driven by critical time frames and tasks, from saving lives to protecting residents, to reducing the risk of future incidents.

In mid-October, the Deep Infrastructure Group turned its attention to using GIS in response to bioterrorism against the city. In accordance with a memo from the federal Office of Homeland Security, local agencies were asked to compile secure, standardized databases to be made available in bioterrorism emergencies. For this, the Deep Infrastructure Group evaluated the location and availability of building data. Specifically, the group explored the availability of building floor plans to locate features that might be vulnerable to an attack. A preliminary meeting was held in November with representatives of the Department of Buildings (DOB), at which DOB representatives committed to sharing data. Since then, a pilot project was initiated to integrate DOB's data sets into OEM's integrated GIS. The primary function of the project is to build a data collection workflow and an institutional framework for monitoring the availability, completeness, and accessibility of information in emergencies.

Another aspect of the strategy to prepare for potential bioterrorism was to explore NYCT mapping data and drawings for infrastructure features vulnerable to an attack. This information would be useful for better securing the transit system. This data is being developed for Ground Zero and may serve as a model for other locations.

Lessons learned

The New York City GIS community has long supported the concept of an infrastructure data structure registered to the NYCMAP. The September 11 events magnified the need for and value of a central repository of compiled infrastructure data as a tool for responding more efficiently to an emergency. The compilation of data at Ground Zero proved to be of great use in the rescue and recovery operations. The event highlighted the need to have data compiled prior to an emergency and available immediately. It would be appropriate to consider expanding the infrastructure model already developed at Ground Zero, along with the planned building model that is to be developed.

Personal accounts
K. Adams Manion
Before September 11, I would have never envisioned a project assignment that would involve an armed escort.

As fires were still raging at Ground Zero, engineers and scientists were pooling resources to assist in the search-and-rescue mission. Accurate data sets were at a premium. It was especially important to ascertain the fuel source that fed the fires. Soon we had a breakthrough. Engineering floor plans with hazardous material tanks were located and hand-delivered to the Deep Infrastructure Group. Immediately, I found myself surrounded by armed agents, led to a sheriff's secure vehicle, and sped downtown to the Duane Street photocopy shop across from the FDNY Command Post, where a document reproduction facility had been made available for the relief efforts. Shortly after, I found myself back at the Command Center, helping to register images and produce products to better guide relief efforts and protect those who bravely continued the search.

Never have I imagined the importance of GIS as a life-saving, life-protecting tool. To apply the skills one has learned—bridging compassion, urgency, and science—is very rewarding.

On a personal level, the September 11 tragedy stunned many of us into bouts of paralyzing sadness. At these moments, waves of emotion could become so overpowering that many sought refuge in lending their talents to the relief effort. The strength and endurance of the FDNY firefighters will always remain within my heart. Their valor, in the face of so much adversity, will be an example for me for the rest of my years.

Wendy Dorf
I was grateful to be working on this critical mission, because it helped me cope with the pain of the tragedy. Being among all the people who worked day in and day out, despite their grief—specifically the firefighters—provided us with the strength to contribute. Working with people in the GIS community was an honor, in that everyone gave it their all, and responded to whatever requests were made of them. The camaraderie and bonding among members of the community during these difficult days heightened my awareness of the special nature of the work we perform.

Marina Haven-Orumieh
I never thought GIS would be used for finding people. Two firemen were directed to the Deep Infrastructure Group to get floor plans for the WTC's North Tower. In talking to them to find out what they really needed, they told me that they had lost six of their members. They found the bodies of three in a staircase, and that took an entire day. When they went back the next day to try to locate the others, they couldn't find the staircase. So I used the latest orthophotography as a base to give them a bearing, and overlaid the plaza floor plans for both the towers. I added and highlighted all column numbers and stairway numbers available to us. Then I overlaid the FDNY grid on top of the base, and then generated two plots for them. They picked up the plots and were off. Later, they came back with a "thank you" in the form of T-shirts for us that bore their squad emblem.

Up to that time, I was well composed and dealt with the issues on technical terms. It wasn't until then that I fully recognized what I was doing and totally lost it.

The Deep Infrastructure team continues to identify data sets, prevent duplication, and establish itself as the central repository for deep infrastructure data in New York City.

Identification and planning

Mitigation

Preparedness

Response

chapter 5 **Recovery**

I F the first, most urgent question asked at the moment of a disaster is, "What has happened?" the second, equally urgent question is usually, "How can I help?"

In the same way that GIS helps clarify the answers to the first question, so too can it help refine the answers to the second—because the third obvious question in the series is "Where is help needed?"

TARGETING HELP

In the aftermath of disaster, GIS can map patterns of destruction, letting those bringing aid to the task of rebuilding—whether the Red Cross, FEMA, or an insurance carrier—target their reconstruction efforts with precision.

This is not an inconsequential consideration: recovery from disasters costs a lot of money. According to FEMA statistics, the agency spent more than $25.4 billion for disaster relief between 1990 and 1999, about $6.3 billion for temporary housing and related housing grants to families, and $14.8 billion allocated to state and local governments. The worst disasters can surpass $1 billion in FEMA costs alone: Hurricane Georges in 1998 came to $2.3 billion, Hurricane Andrew totaled $1.8 billion in 1992, and the Northridge earthquake in 1994 cost about $7 billion.

Dollar figures at this level usually mean lots of accountants, to keep a close eye on how the government's money is being spent. GIS can make a significant difference in this critical area.

Generally, the more precisely a community can document exactly where money is most needed, and for whom, the less delay there will be in getting those funds from federal sources to the people who need them.

While this may seem a function far removed from mainstream GIS activities, it is no less beneficial for being so. When people are in severe distress in the wake of a catastrophic event, the last thing they want to do is to scramble around in a house—or what's left of it—looking for paperwork that proves they qualify for help that they already know they're entitled to. By showing precisely the extent and nature of the destruction that occurred in a geographic area, GIS can considerably reduce additional, and unneeded, stress on the families in a community.

EARTHQUAKE INTENSITY AND ASSISTANCE

The ability of GIS to provide critical help in this way was demonstrated clearly in the days and weeks after Southern California's Northridge earthquake of 1994—accomplished with hardware and software that would be considered hopelessly underpowered by today's standards. Many of these early efforts laid the groundwork for more sophisticated work later.

At the heart of the GIS recovery effort in Northridge was an exhaustively detailed mapping of damage locations. Only until this was done could other, more sophisticated, analyses be accomplished, allowing other recovery efforts to move forward. Of course, damage assessments will have already begun during the response phase of a disaster event—another instance in which the dividing line between one phase of disaster management and another gets blurred. However, damage assessments made for recovery and rebuilding efforts will continue long after the first responders have left.

In most cases, data for damage assessments will be collected from the field, either through direct observation by emergency workers or through indirect reports, such as 911 calls.

Northridge was unusual in that its initial damage assessment and first recovery efforts were based on damage models—that is, software extrapolation of a small amount of real data to a much larger area of predicted damage. In the case of Northridge, the model took data about the size of the quake (6.7 on the Richter scale), its epicenter (Northridge), the type of seismic event involved (blind thrust fault), and detailed data about Southern California geology to estimate damages for the entire San Fernando Valley and surrounding region. The models performed well, predicting types and degrees of damage in locations that later field observation proved accurate.

From their output, GIS teams from the Governor's Office of Emergency Services created shaking intensity maps, showing gradations of physical damage and physical sensation in affected areas. This damage and sensation are measured on the Mercalli scale of intensity. Level VI on the Mercalli, for example, is described as "Felt by all. Many frightened and run outdoors. Persons walk unsteadily. Windows, dishes, glassware broken, knickknacks, books, etc., off shelves. Pictures off walls. Furniture moved or overturned. Weak plaster and masonry D cracked. Small bells ring (church, school). Trees, bushes shaken (visibly or heard to rustle)."

These maps are now known as ShakeMaps and created by the TriNet Project, a joint venture of the U.S. Geological Survey, the California

Institute of Technology, and the California Division of Mines and Geology. They are based no longer on models, but on real data from hundreds of ground sensors distributed throughout the region.

In Northridge, the teams overlaid ZIP Codes on the shaking intensity maps. Trusting both the integrity of the models and the maps, those in charge of the recovery operation decided that anyone who lived within ZIP Codes that suffered Mercalli intensities above Level VIII ("Steering of motor vehicles affected . . . fall of stucco and some masonry walls.") would be given temporary housing funding, almost automatically.

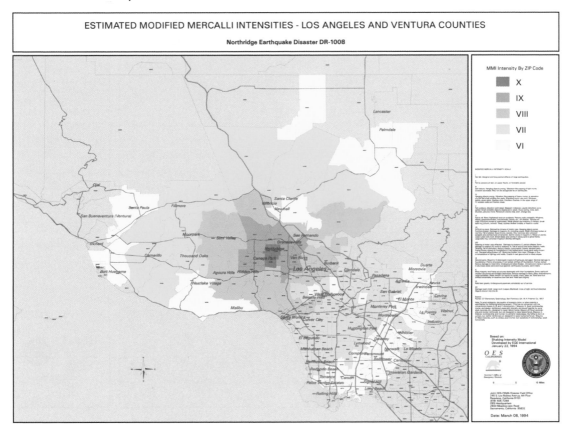

The ZIP Code shake map created from the model that was used to expedite applications for housing assistance. Those whose residences were located in ZIP Code areas with a Mercalli index of VIII or above who applied for assistance were put on a fast track for application approval.

LOCATING ASSISTANCE CENTERS

Another significant map product helped decision makers in the establishment of assistance centers where residents of the affected areas could go for longer-term help on a variety of problems they might be suffering. For various reasons, landing such a center in a particular community or legislative jurisdiction became a competitive process. Again, the GIS teams helped those who had to make these decisions by supplying damage density maps that showed how a center needed to be in a location equally accessible to the greatest number of affected people—criteria both rational and defensible.

INDIVIDUAL ASSISTANCE APPLICATIONS, EARTHQUAKE SERVICE CENTERS AND TARGET AREAS AS OF APRIL 22, 1994
Northridge Earthquake Disaster DR-1008

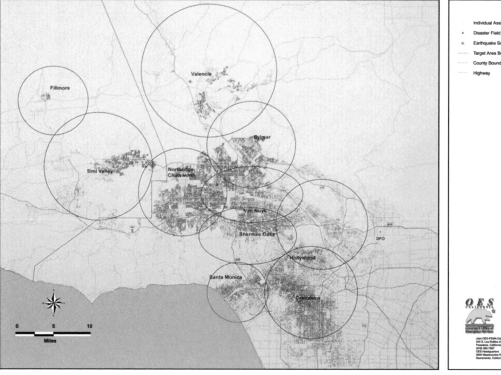

Assistance service centers were placed near the center of target areas.

DISASTER IN ANY LANGUAGE

Good demographic data can go a long way toward pinpointing the kinds of services that are needed in particular areas of a devastated region. Social service providers can make use of the technology to refine where they provide assistance. This is especially important when different languages are involved, as was the case in the Northridge earthquake. To help disseminate information about the kinds of assistance available to the widest number of people, GIS teams developed maps of locations of the many different languages spoken in the affected areas, so that social service teams would know where to send interpreters and information in the appropriate language concerning assistance that was available.

There had been precedent—and startling results—for this kind of cultural and linguistic mapping in a disaster context, less than two years earlier, also in Southern California. GIS teams from the California OES were working in the wake of civil unrest that had convulsed a large portion of Los Angeles County in the wake of the Rodney King verdicts. That unrest caused death, injuries, and millions of dollars in property damage—a disaster, only this one caused by humans instead of nature.

As people streamed into local assistance centers to apply for emergency help, the GIS teams from OES mapped areas of destruction and of economic assistance applications. They noticed a strange phenomenon: Korean applicants weren't going to the nearest assistance center, but rather, traveling miles out of their way to distant centers, for no readily apparent reason.

Investigation revealed that several of the assistance centers that would have been most logical for Korean applicants to visit happened to be in neighborhoods that were predominantly African-American. Although the civil unrest was not sparked by tension between these two groups, it surfaced during the rioting.

The GIS recovery mapping showed that the Koreans were deliberately avoiding African-American areas, even if that was where the nearest assistance center was located, and even if it meant going many miles away to apply for assistance.

New assistance centers were set up in Korean neighborhoods. The long-detour travel patterns stopped. This inequity in recovery assistance might have remained hidden without the GIS teams.

BROAD-BASED MAPPING

These are the kinds of issues that decision makers will have to consider before agencies, of any kind, set up shop and offer recovery services to communities. Demographic, cultural, and linguistic factors, critical to the success of full recovery for the entire community, can be revealed with GIS.

The GIS teams in the Northridge recovery also created map products to help the temporarily homeless to find housing, and products to help with economic analyses so that assistance could be targeted to businesses.

As field data came in over subsequent weeks, the GIS team took the opportunity to understand just how much GIS could do. Along the way they compiled map products of virtually everything: freeway closures, hospital damage, power outages, and extremely detailed data sets of building damage, including a map of damage to chimneys—175,000 separate points of data.

GIS personnel from the California Governor's Office of Emergency Services created exhaustively detailed maps like this one of building damage in relation to other factors, such as ground shaking as shown here.

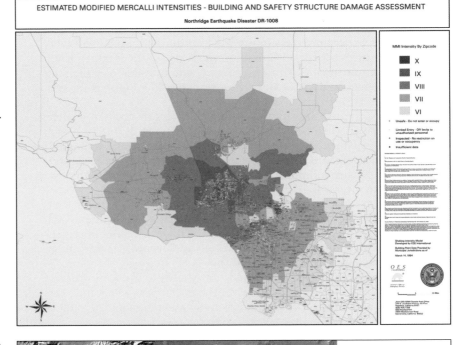

Mapping the expenditure of assistance dollars showed a high correlation with areas that experienced the most severe damage.

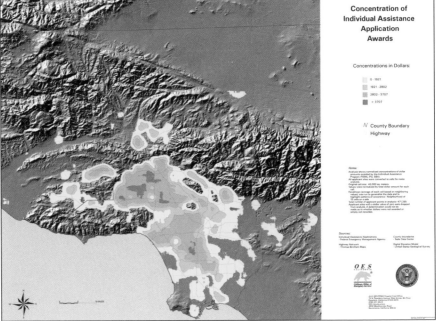

KEEPING THE COMMUNITY INFORMED

GIS managers should seriously consider using the Internet and interactive mapping applications such as ArcIMS to keep the community informed of recovery progress in the wake of disaster. There will be a deep hunger for this information, but hard-copy paper map products in many instances may be an impractical way to satisfy it. Moreover, events can change quickly in this environment, and such changes can be made far more quickly in an online context.

CLEANING UP THE MESS

Clearly, human and social recovery are the priorities in a postdisaster setting. From a fiscal standpoint, however, cleaning up debris—although rarely making headlines—is likely to be one of the most costly expenses for government agencies and the private sector alike. Little can get accomplished in the way of recovery in any context until the streets are cleared of fallen trees, building materials, and all other kinds of miscellaneous detritus. But none of that will get cleared way until those who write the checks are given at least an idea—and preferably, much more than an idea—of exactly how much stuff has to be picked up, so they know who will be writing the checks, and for how much.

In GIS, an increasing number of organizations are finding a useful tool to help them accurately calculate their cleanup needs and, therefore, costs.

As noted earlier, the HAZUS software package, available from FEMA and the National Institute of Building Sciences, can predict with some certainty the type and amount of debris that will be generated by an earthquake. This estimate will be considerably more accurate the more local, detailed data is used.

Considerable work on debris removal after hurricanes has also been done by the U.S. Army Corps of Engineers, which has produced a model it says will be accurate to within 30 percent. The model generates estimates of debris in cubic yards based on a calculation that includes population, household density, storm strength, vegetation density, commercial density, and precipitation associated with a storm; it then generates estimated debris produced by the storm in cubic yards—usually, millions of cubic yards.

The engineering firm of Dewberry and Davis, LLC, of Fairfax, Virginia, has incorporated the Corps of Engineers model into GIS debris-estimation applications in use by the city of Houston and by the Palm Beach County Solid Waste Authority in Florida.

The Palm Beach GIS Debris Prediction Model, built on MapObjects, divides the county into twelve debris management zones. Users can calculate the debris for a zone or draw a polygon of any area within the county. After the user defines some parameters, such as the size of the storm and the type of housing in the area, the application will output the exact amount of debris that can be expected from that area.

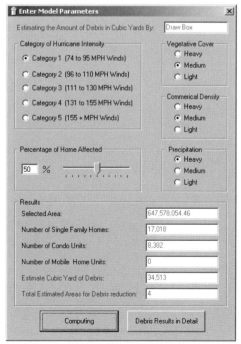

The Palm Beach County debris model lets users select from several variables that will affect the amount and type of debris generated from a disaster.

The Houston application performs the same functions—although it does not have to account for as many condominiums as the Palm Beach application—and then takes the process one step further, showing the degree of debris clearance. Field data about whether roads have been cleared of debris or not is entered into a spreadsheet. The spreadsheet is then used to created a street segment layer in the application to show at a glance which streets are passable, and which will require a detour.

The twelve debris management zones in the Palm Beach application. Users can also create their own polygons and calculate debris generated.

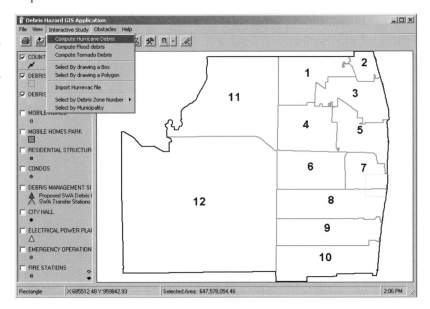

The Houston debris model takes the application one step further, showing users which roads are still blocked by debris and which have been cleared.

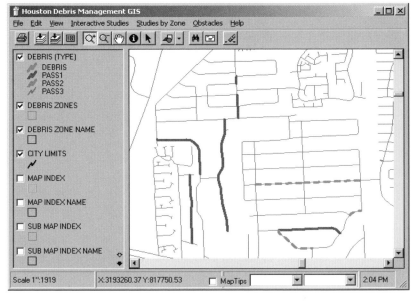

Appendixes

The material in this section provides readers additional details on different aspects of GIS disaster management applications. Appendix A contains an ESRI White Paper published in May 2000, "Challenges for GIS in Emergency Preparedness and Response." It explores some theoretical issues involved in disaster management GIS, and contains an excellent bibliography. Appendix B contains two data sets, which readers may want to peruse for ideas on the kinds of data for use in their own disaster management programs. The first is the list of data layers of Miami-Dade County, Florida. Emergency operations personnel there may access any of these for disaster management. The second list is data layers supplied with CATS modeling software, discussed in chapter 3. Appendix C is a matrix of strategies to strengthen GIS applications, utility, and awareness within California's FIRESCOPE program, discussed in chapter 4. It was put together by disaster management GIS specialists in the Geographic Information Systems and Spatial Information Technology group (GISSIT) of FIRESCOPE.

appendix A **Challenges for GIS in Emergency Preparedness and Response**

An ESRI White Paper

May 2000

Challenges for GIS in Emergency Preparedness and Response

An ESRI White Paper

Contents   **Page**

The Application Challenge—Emergency Preparedness and Response.   1

A Paradigm for Geographic Information Science's Contribution to
   Emergency Preparedness and Response   2

Geographic Information Science Contributions to Advance the
   Discussion   2

Natural Disasters That Impact Humans   3
     Earthquakes   3
     Volcanoes   4
     Tsunamis...   6
     Landslides..   6
     Fires..   7
     Floods..   8
     Tornadoes...   9
     Hurricanes   9

Human-Induced Disasters That Impact Humans and Environs...........   10
     Health-Related Epidemics   10
     Social Unrest—War...   11
     Toxic Spills, Explosions, and Fires (Accidental or Otherwise)   12

Research Challenges   12
     Spatial Data Acquisition and Integration.......................   12
     Distributed Computing..   14

Contents   **Page**

Extensions to Geographic Representations 15
Cognition of Geographic Information 15
Interoperability of Geographic Information 16
Scale 16
Spatial Analysis in a GIS Environment 17
The Future of Spatial Information Infrastructure 18
Uncertainty in Geographic Data and GIS-Based Analyses 18
GIS and Society 18

Linkages to Education Priorities 19
Emerging Technologies for Delivering Geographic Information
    Science Education 20
Supporting Infrastructure 20
Access and Equity 20
Alternative Designs for Curriculum Content and Evaluation 20
Professional GIS Education Programs 21
Research-Based Graduate GIS Education 21
Learning with GIS 21
Accreditation and Certification 21

Policy Implications 21

Conclusion 22

References 22

Glossary 28

Challenges for GIS in Emergency Preparedness and Response

John Radke, Tom Cova, Michael F. Sheridan, Austin Troy, Lan Mu, Russ Johnson

Understanding geographic information is critical if we are to build and maintain livable communities. Since computing has become almost ubiquitous in planning and managing our communities, it is probable that advances in geographic information science will play a founding role in smarter decision making. This paper examines the challenges that occur between humans and their environment under conditions thought to be hazardous to life and habitat. Emergency preparedness and response are reviewed, and recommended priorities for research, educational, and policy contributions to emergency preparedness and response are documented.

The Application Challenge— Emergency Preparedness and Response

The emergency preparedness and response application challenge is mainly concerned with the interaction between humans and their environment under conditions thought to be hazardous either to life or habitat. This application challenge is not only multifaceted as its title implies but also covers a wide range of disasters, many with fundamentally different underlying processes (such as earthquakes, hurricanes, and wildfires). Even though the processes that generate the disaster might be fundamentally different, techniques to assess risk, evaluate preparedness, and assist response appear to have much in common and can share and benefit from advances in geographic information science (such as data acquisition and integration; data ownership, access, and liability issues; and interoperability).

Natural hazards and most human-generated hazards do not recognize political boundaries, yet policy must be generated in order to mitigate effectively against disaster, manage rescue and response operations, or organize and deliver relief, and this policy is usually administered within politically defined boundaries. Geographic information and the systems within which it is collected and managed have particular utility in modeling and analysis, which transcend political boundaries while providing the necessary structure for assisting the implementation of policy within administrative areas.

In a similar vein, while hazards do not often differentiate between land uses, the recovery and the cost and impact on society are often greatly affected by this land use differentiation. In some circumstances, the hazard itself is modified and often magnified by heterogeneous landscapes and land use, such as those found where humans interact with nature. These boundary conditions are difficult to map and virtually impossible to model without the use of concepts, tools, and technologies that are evolving within geographic information science. In order to assess and mitigate risk to human life and property, and in order to respond effectively, we must develop predictive and operational models that are embedded within geographic information system (GIS) software.

A postdisaster statement might conclude that if we knew then what we know now, we could prevent or at least reduce the risk, damage, and loss and shorten the recovery period. Since GIS and related technologies provide an operational forum for realizing this statement, the effort here begins the process of answering the question, What are the challenges for geographic information science arising from disaster management?

A Paradigm for Geographic Information Science's Contribution to Emergency Preparedness and Response

The contribution of geographic information science to emergency preparedness and response might best be navigated within a paradigm that at the very least might be represented as a three-dimensional grid but will more likely be depicted as a graph with three axes as illustrated in Figure 1. One axis represents the hazards as we commonly refer to them: (1) natural hazards such as earthquakes, volcanoes, tsunamis, landslides, fires, floods, tornadoes, hurricanes, droughts, and freeze; and (2) human-induced hazards such as health-related epidemics, social unrest, war, infrastructure failure and collapse, toxic spills, explosions, and fires (accidental or otherwise). Along a second axis we represent time, which can characterize actions taken such as pre-event (proactive–risk assessed), during the event (reactive–response), and post-event (reactive–recover). The third axis encodes action taken or response sought by the application of geographic information science to assessment, emergency preparedness, and response such as prevention, discovery, planning, mitigation, management, insurance settlement, and policy.

Figure 1
A Paradigm for Geographic Information Science's Contribution to
Emergency Preparedness and Response

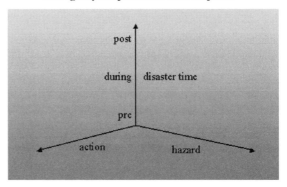

Geographic Information Science Contributions to Advance the Discussion

Geographic information science and related technologies have already contributed in many areas encoded within the paradigm. There are numerous examples of ongoing projects to predict hazards, assess the risk to human life and property, assist response during an emergency, discover and recover from damage, manage ongoing hazardous conditions, plan and mitigate for future hazards, and impact policy and decision making. To navigate a small sample of these will not only serve to point out where geographic information science is already contributing to emergency preparedness and response, but it will also help us understand the future geographic information challenges for this application area.

Although the following list of hazards is not all inclusive, it is an appropriate list to begin the discussion for emergency preparedness and response. In the interests of brevity and breadth of coverage, each hazard is not addressed in great detail, but rather is reviewed for the role geographic information has played, which includes predicting, responding to, managing, and recovering from these disasters.

As with any hazard, in order to reduce the loss of life and damage to property, public safety officials, policy decision makers, and the general public must be aware of potentially hazardous conditions well in advance. In many past disasters the general public would have been able to themselves respond in a crisis if they had knowledge of existing conditions. Geographic information science in its research and education initiatives appears to be able to offer concrete support here.

Natural Disasters That Impact Humans

In most of the cases examined, a major part of the effort relating to natural hazards was a focus on mapping. This is not surprising as most solutions involving GIS are data poor until they become part of an accepted set of procedures. However, the mapping procedures and how information is being displayed appear to have been impacted by the advancing of technologies within geographic information science. Simply encoding where some single variable existed is being replaced by maps depicting combinations of variables and their contribution to and potential for failure in hazardous conditions.

The data and information are being made more available to the general public due to advances in and the acceptance of World Wide Web technology. It is likely that advances in Web technology that have greatly impacted emergency preparedness and response mirror the rate and potential impact of advances in geographic information science to this application area. Rather than look too far into the future, we choose to respond to existing conditions as we discuss emergency preparedness and response challenges. In the first section of the paper, we examine the nature of the event and role of geographic information for earthquakes, volcanoes, tsunamis, landslides, fires, floods, tornadoes, hurricanes, epidemics, social unrest, war, toxic spills, explosions, and fires.

Earthquakes

Earthquakes can destroy human infrastructure and habitat, killing and impacting large populations, especially in urban areas. Although the 1989 Loma Prieta earthquake was considered by some to be a wake-up call, it certainly reminded others that proactive mitigation efforts pay off as damage and loss of life were minimal for such a large earthquake in such a populated area.

Major earthquakes of the recent past, including Adana-Ceyhan, Turkey (1998); Izmit, western Turkey (1999); Taiwan (1999); and Hector Mines–Joshua Tree, California (1999), demonstrate the wide range of human impact that can result from events of similar magnitudes. Earthquakes can affect any area within a broad zone and may pose great risk to human life and infrastructure, depending on settlement distribution and densities, in addition to building materials, engineering standards, and the like. Unlike hurricanes and often volcanoes, predicting when an earthquake will happen still eludes us; however, where they will occur is well mapped by existing fault lines.

Of the many seismic digital mapping projects that have been undertaken, one of the most notable state projects stems from the 1990 California Seismic Hazards Mapping Act, which requires the California Department of Conservation, Division of Mines and Geology (DOC/DMG) to map seismic hazard zones and identify *areas of risk* that are subject to potential ground failure. The purpose of these maps is to help cities and counties regulate development in hazardous areas to indicate areas requiring mitigation and to assist in making disclosures for the California Natural Hazard Disclosure Act (AB 1995). These maps show amplified shaking hazards zones, which are defined as areas where historic amplified ground shaking has occurred or local geological and geotechnical conditions indicate a potential for ground shaking to be amplified to a level such that mitigation would be required. They also depict areas of past or potential liquefaction (ground displacements) and past or potential earthquake-induced landslides. Urbanized areas have the highest priority for mapping, and to date DOC/DMG has mapped most parts of Alameda, Los Angeles, Orange, San Francisco, Santa Clara, and Ventura counties at a 1:24,000 scale. There are plans to release and distribute these maps to the public on the Web in a variety of data formats to likely include GIF, PDF, and various other formats that would be compatible with the most popular GIS software.

At the federal level, the United States Geological Survey (USGS) has produced the National Seismic Hazard Maps, which were made available on the Web in 1996. These maps, which cover the conterminous United States, depict probabilistic ground motion and spectral response with return times of approximately 500, 1,000 and 2,500 years. The nation is divided into two regions (central east and west) that use separate calculations for attenuation relations. For the western portion, the maps use a grid spacing of 0.1 degrees (for the east it is 0.2°). For grid cells with historic seismic events, seismic hazard is determined based on the number of events greater than the minimum magnitude. For areas with little historic seismicity, "background zones" were created based on discussions at regional workshops (Frankel, 1996). Also, at the federal level, FEMA's predictions (using GIS to assist) brought unprecedented efficiency to the process of speeding relief to victims of natural disaster. After the Northridge earthquake in northern California on January 17, 1994, FEMA said that 560,000 households would be affected; the agency received about 600,000 applications for help.

A notable local or regional organization in the area of seismic hazard mapping is the Association of Bay Area Government (ABAG). With the help of the USGS and the National Science Foundation, ABAG has been using GIS technology since 1975 to produce seismic hazard maps for the Bay Area. The maps, which include designations of fault study zones, ground shaking intensity fault traces, and tsunami inundation zones, are easily combined with other data sources, such as the United States Bureau of the Census TIGER street and boundary files, to help local planners in land use decisions and mitigation planning.

Volcanoes

Volcanic phenomena can destroy vast areas of productive land and human structures destroying and killing the population of entire cities. Major eruptions of the recent past include Mount St. Helens (1980), El Chichon (1982), Nevado del Ruiz (1985), Unzen (1991), and Pinatubo (1994). Mount Rainier currently has a potential to threaten the cities of Tacoma and Seattle, and Popocatepetl menaces an area near Puebla and Mexico City, home to more than ten million people. Hazardous volcanic phenomena range from passive gas emission and slow effusion of lava to volcanic explosions accompanied by the development of a stratospheric plume with associated dense descending currents of incandescent volcanic ash and rocks that race at high speeds along the surface away from the volcano (nuée ardante). Mass movement of surficial materials takes the form of rock falls and avalanches or even the sudden collapse of large sectors of the volcanic edifice. These phenomena and their associated water-saturated debris flows are extremely dangerous geologic events and have caused tens of thousands of deaths during the past two decades. In many cases the loss of life could have been reduced if public safety officials and the general population were aware of the potential effect of the phenomena on their local environment.

The management of hazards related to volcanoes in the United States is administered by the USGS. The eruption of Mount St. Helens, which began in 1980, killed seventy-nine people, and disrupted the area for several years, is the worst case in the United States. Long Valley, California, experienced several crises in the past three decades and is potentially dangerous. Mount Rainier (and other Cascade Range volcanoes) presents a risk to a very large population and infrastructure. Hazard maps at various scales exist for most of the potentially active volcanoes of the United States. In contrast, most dangerous volcanoes in developing countries lack adequate hazard assessment and map coverage.

The use of GIS in volcanic hazards studies is very modest. The first papers appeared in the late 1980s, and about two papers per year have been published during this decade. About half of the topics addressed have been mass movements (landslides and debris flows), and the remainder treated general topics. Sophisticated themes, such as distributed computing, visualization, use of large data sets, and interactive modeling and analysis, are lacking.

Volcanoes usually present a known source area of threat, in contrast to earthquakes that could affect any area within a broad zone. This makes them particularly appropriate for GIS analysis. In the United States the geologic histories of most volcanoes are sufficiently understood to forecast the types of phenomena to be anticipated. The relative magnitude and frequency of future events are harder to predict. A complicating factor for volcanoes is that the repose time since the previous event may be very long. The inhabitants surrounding the volcano may have a belief that even if there were eruptions in the past, nothing will happen in their lifetime. At any rate, they are willing to take a chance that they will be safe.

The last decade of the twentieth century witnessed the development of several forms of computerized models for volcanic eruptions and their associated hazards. Unfortunately, these have not often been linked to interactive GIS systems. Computation, communication, and information technologies during this period advanced at a faster rate than the development, testing, and utilization of controlled scientific models. In general, posters, still images, or video scenes of events at other volcanoes were the main methods used to explain the phenomena to the public safety officials and to illustrate potential events at a volcano in crisis to the local inhabitants. Only in a few cases were advanced technologies or computer models used in the development of volcanic hazard maps.

Tsunamis

Tsunamis, like earthquakes, are difficult to predict, but their inundation zone along the coastline can be mapped and early warnings can result. A National Tsunami Hazard Mitigation Program was initiated in July 1994 when the Senate Appropriations Committee directed the National Oceanic and Atmospheric Administration (NOAA) to formulate a plan for reducing the tsunami risks to coastal residents. The program is designed to reduce the impact of tsunamis through hazard assessment, warning guidance, and mitigation. The first step in producing Tsunami Inundation Maps is essential to assess the tsunami hazard. The Center for Tsunami Inundation Mapping Efforts (TIME) within the Pacific Marine Environmental Laboratory of NOAA (NOAA R/PMEL) (Bobbitt, 1999) was created for the purpose of development, maintenance, and upgrade of maps that identify areas of potential tsunami flooding.

The Pacific Marine Environmental Laboratory maintains large databases related to the research and exploration of hydrothermal vent processes and applies GIS to integrating multidisciplinary data sets to create both a map gallery and an Internet site. The states involved in the PMEL Tsunami Program are Hawaii, California, Oregon, Washington, and Alaska, and they seek to mitigate tsunami hazards by focusing development on improved tsunami inundation maps, hazard assessment tools, and advanced technology to increase the speed and accuracy of tsunami forecasts and warnings (Trudeau, 1998).

Landslides

Although landslides can destroy human infrastructure and potentially be deadly, except for a few famous incidents, their impact is generally localized and predictable. The USGS has been extremely active in mapping landslide hazards and in developing new methods and models for assessing and analyzing these hazards. In anticipation of the heavy El Niño rains in 1997–98, scientists from the USGS San Francisco Bay Landslide Team (SFBLT) created landslide hazard maps of the Bay region. Following the rains, the San Francisco Bay Area Region Project and their Landslide Hazards Program, both of the USGS, conducted inventories of landslides in the Bay Area, which were then used to develop digital landslide distribution databases, computer landslide models, and landslide hazard maps. The SFBLT created digital maps that depict areas of potential slides (slumps and translational slides), earth flows (flows of clayey earth), and debris flows (rapidly moving slides). The map layers include topography in shaded relief, road networks, hydrography, mapped distributions of slides and earth flows, rainfall thresholds for debris flows, and likely debris flow areas. Most of the data is mapped at 1:125,000 scale (for local emergency planning) and 1:275,000 scale (for regional planning). These maps are part of an overall strategy to help planners mitigate and respond to disasters (Pikei, 1997).

Additionally, the California Department of Conservation (1999) DOC/DMG has been active in mapping landslide hazards in the State. They produce six types of maps that depict landslide hazards. Among them are Landslide Hazard Identification Maps, 1:24,000-scale maps showing landslide features, landslide susceptibility, and debris flow susceptibility. They were produced from 1986 to 1995 under the now-repealed Landslide Hazard Mapping Act. Watershed Maps are 1:24,000-scale maps that include landslide features to assist in timber harvest planning and water quality protection. They were produced in concert with the California Department of Forestry. Four categories of active and dormant landslides are depicted including debris flows, debris slides, translation slides, earth flows, and torrent tracks. These maps cover parts of Mendocino, Humboldt, and Del Norte counties.

Fires

In the landscape, fire is frequently a naturally occurring phenomenon and in the long run is often considered more beneficial than hazardous. However, Philadelphia's most famous citizen, Benjamin Franklin, understood the hazards of fire when it intrudes upon human habitat and wrote on the need to regulate urban growth in order to decrease fire and environmental hazards. Although wildfire is often considered a natural hazard, the extent of the hazard can be mitigated with sound land use practices and management. Today, the practice of fire suppression in both rural and urban environments mostly does not follow sound vegetation management plans and has created potential catastrophic conditions for fires. A fire hazard exists to a greater or lesser extent across the North American continent, but nowhere in the United States is the hazard greater than in California. The Mediterranean climate, the rugged topography, a shifting urban–wildland interface, and the recent practice of fire suppression all collaborate to create catastrophic conditions. In the hills east of the San Francisco Bay alone, 5,298 structures have been lost in dozens of fires since 1920, with the majority of them occurring in the last decade (Radke, 1995).

Geographic information science plays a critical role in mapping and documenting fire, then subsequently predicting its course, analyzing alternative fire-fighting strategies, and directing tactics and strategies in the field. The California Department of Forestry (CDF) began an intensive program of mapping fire in response to legislation in the early 1980s. This legislation required CDF to map different classifications of fire hazards with State Responsibility Areas (SRAs), or areas of State fire prevention responsibility (i.e., outside of large, incorporated cities). As a result of the catastrophic Oakland Hills fire, the Bates Bill (AB 337) was passed in the California legislature in 1992. This bill required the CDF to work with local fire authorities to map fire hazard severity zones within Local Responsibility Areas (LRAs), generally referring to areas subject to wildfire hazard that are within incorporated city boundaries. These maps are intended for purposes of enforcing roofing and vegetative clearance requirements, in addition to serving as the basis for disclosure statements in real estate transactions under AB 1195. For both types of maps, fire hazard is determined on the basis of fuel loading, fire weather, and slope, among other criteria. Vectorized fire hazard zones were overlaid on USGS topographic maps at 1:24,000, 1:62,500, and 1:100,000 scales (Irby, 1997).

Nationwide, the U.S. Forest Service has implemented the Wildland Fire Assessment System (WFAS), based out of the Forest Service's Rocky Mountain Research Station. Unlike CDF's mapping efforts, this is not designed for long-term hazard assessment as much as for short-term fire danger warning. This system constantly generates maps of fire weather and fire danger components of the National Fire Danger Rating System (NFDRS) based on daily observations from 1,500 weather stations throughout the United States. Because each station is merely a sampling point, values between stations are estimated with an inverse distance squared technique using 10-km grids. The Fire Danger Rating Maps that result are based on current and antecedent weather, fuel types, and the state of live and dead fuel moisture. Fuel models to be used generally are decided upon by local managers. Weather forecasts are based on data from the National Weather Service. Live fuel moisture is generated from greenness maps, derived on a weekly basis from Normalized Difference Vegetative Index (NDVI) data from satellite imagery. Dead fuel moisture is available on digital maps showing ten-hour, 100-hour, and 1,000-hour fuels. Additionally, drought maps and lower atmosphere stability index maps are used.

At the local or neighborhood scale, mapping and modeling topography and fuel load based on vegetation and structures is gaining in popularity due to advances in geographic information technology. The 1991 Oakland Hills fire resulted in a local study integrating fire models and data inputs within a GIS to map potential *firestorm* risk (Radke, 1995). Although much of this input data was encoded by hand, many more GIS-encoded databases have since become available with Web delivery. This simple advance has not only led to more modeling, it has also stimulated the development and use of new fire models embedded within GIS. FARSITE, a stand-alone fire growth simulation model, is a good example of such a model. It runs within several GIS software programs (ArcInfo™, ArcView® GIS, or GRASS) and is used to simulate wildland fire growth and behavior under complex conditions of terrain, fuels, and weather.

Floods

Flood zones can be mapped and floods can be predicted with some degree of accuracy. The widest-scale and most systematic mapping of flood hazards comes from the Federal Emergency Management Agency (FEMA). FEMA produces flood insurance rate maps (FIRMs) for the purposes of determining whether properties lie within the floodway of a river system or the 100-year floodplain. These maps form the basis of FEMA's policy under the 1969 National Flood Insurance Act (and later amendments). These policies call for restriction of development in the floodway and require purchase of flood insurance and/or flood proofing for structures within the 100-year flood zone. FEMA has worked in recent years to make these maps digitally available.

As part of a Map Modernization Program, Digital Q3 Flood data was developed by scanning FIRM hard copies and vectorizing flood zones as a thematic overlay including the 100- and 500-year floodplains (i.e., 1 percent and .2 percent annual probability of flooding). Q3 data does not contain all information from the FIRM and is not as accurate. Rather, Q3 data is intended to support regional-scale uses such as planning activities, insurance marketing, and mortgage portfolio reviews. For more precise parcel-based queries or for engineering analysis, the more detailed digital FIRMs (DFIRMs) or paper FIRMs are more appropriate. DFIRMs include all of the information required to create a hard-copy FIRM in digital form. This includes basemap information, graphics, text, shading, and all other geographic data necessary to meet the standards and specifications set for FIRMs. This data provides the basis for the digital line graph (DLG) of flood risks, known as DFIRM-DLG.

Another very different application of flood mapping technology was used to help emergency managers in North Carolina to evacuate flood-prone areas prior to Hurricane Fran in 1996. Before this hurricane, the North Carolina Center for Geographic Information and Analysis had used the Sea, Lake, and Overland Surges from Hurricane (SLOSH) model to prepare several Hurricane Storm Surge Inundation Area Maps for coastal areas of the State, showing the historic extent of hurricane storm surge inundation. The model was used to produce maps showing flood extent under conditions of slow- and fast-velocity hurricanes. These flood extents were then overlaid on 1;24,000-scale USGS topographic maps. Based on the SLOSH model, Hurricane Evacuation Restudy Maps were prepared that were used to guide the evacuation of residents from low-lying and coastal areas. These maps were also used by other agencies, such as the Division of Forest Resources, that performed overlays of these maps with forest cover layers to predict the amount of forest damage (Dymon, 1999).

The Office of Emergency Services (OES) of California has produced digital flood maps depicting areas at risk from dam failure. These maps are intended to be used by local and State officials in devising emergency procedures under the Emergency Services Act (Section 8589.5 of CA Government Code) and in making natural hazards disclosure statements under the California Natural Hazard Disclosure Act (AB 1195). The inundation maps produced by OES represent the best estimate of where water would flow if a dam failed suddenly and completely under full capacity conditions, recognizing that later downstream land use changes may affect the extent and intensity of inundation. These digital maps were produced by scanning paper blue-line copies of the original maps and are organized by county and are available from the OES Web site as PDF files.

Tornadoes
Tornadoes are one of nature's most violent storms. In an average year, 800 tornadoes are reported across the United States, resulting in eighty deaths and over 1,500 injuries, which is the most severe of any country in the world (Edgetech, 1999). These violently rotating columns of air extend from a thunderstorm to the ground and are capable of tremendous destruction with wind speeds of 250 miles per hour or more. Damage paths can be in excess of one mile wide and fifty miles long. Tornado strength is measured on the F-scale, ranging from F0 through F5 for the most powerful storms.

Although GIS is employed to map and summarize the events of tornadoes, in a growing number of communities it is used in real time on the front line. On the evening of May 3, 1999, the National Weather Service (NWS) issued a tornado warning for southeastern Sedgwick County, Kansas (DeYoe, 1999). Though not officially part of the emergency response personnel, the Sedgwick County GIS Department (SCGIS) produced more than 300 maps for the Emergency Operations Center (EOC) to get initial locations of damage reports and identify the actual properties. SCGIS provided the EOC with a probable path and damage map and estimated values based on the damage reports received up to that time.

Hurricanes
Hurricanes can destroy human infrastructure and habitat, killing and impacting large populations across vast territory. We only have to refer to a few—Agnes (1972), Hugo (1989), Andrew (1992), and Floyd (1999)—to illustrate the damage and loss to society.

After the devastation of Hurricane Andrew, FEMA upgraded its pre- and postdisaster planning and response capabilities. The GIS-based system, called the Consequences Assessment Tool Set (CATS), developed by Science Applications International Corporation (SAIC), enables FEMA to predict the effect of impending disasters, such as hurricanes, and quickly mobilize a well-coordinated and directed response (Corbley, 1999 and Kehlet, 1998). This allows FEMA to pinpoint critical evacuation areas as well as make accurate damage predictions for phenomena such as storm surge and wind damage that facilitates a quick recovery (Trudeau, 1998).

As disaster strikes, CATS, using combined government, business, and demographic databases, produces reports and graphics that provide emergency managers and the national media with timely information. Known damage is reported along with mapped estimates of the extent of damage and affected population. Suitable mobilization sites are identified along with nearby airstrips, empty warehouse space, and information about federal and local sources for disaster relief. When Hurricane Eduardo (1996) was threatening to endanger the U.S. coastline, FEMA identified areas of potential water contamination and quickly moved freshwater supplies to those sites ahead of the storm.

In the aftermath of Hurricane Mitch, the USGS's Center for Integration of Natural Disaster Information (CINDI) created a digital atlas containing more than sixty different types of geospatial information. These new maps showed the locations of landslides and floods; damage to roads, bridges, and other infrastructure; precipitation information; and impacts on agricultural lands. The information used to create these maps came from remote sensors as well as existing ancillary databases such as geologic maps, aerial photos, and dozens of other digital and paper sources. The maps, which are available at the CINDI Web site (http://cindi.usgs.gov/), serve as a critical resource for allocating resources in short-term relief efforts, for understanding the disaster's long-term impact on ecosystems, and for planning the region's economic recovery and reconstruction.

Human-Induced Disasters That Impact Humans and Environs

Unlike many natural hazards, most human-induced hazards could be prevented, reducing or even eliminating loss of life and damage to property. With a better understanding of the underlying forces that induce disasters, we can work toward mitigation and possibly elimination of some of them.

Health-Related Epidemics

Epidemiologists use maps to log locations, encode associations, and study the spread of disease (Clarke et al., 1999). Add to the map the ability to undertake spatial analysis through advances in geographic information tools, and the result is a technology that is well suited to track disease. Studies that quantify lead hazards (Tempalski, 1994), model exposure to electromagnetic fields (Wartenberg, 1992), and monitor air- and water-borne diseases all benefit from the development of technologies in geographic information science.

GIS was used to identify and locate environmental risk factors associated with Lyme disease in Baltimore County, Maryland (Glass et al., 1995). Watershed, land use, soil type, geology, and forest distribution data was collected at the residences of Lyme disease patients and combined with data collected at randomly selected addresses to fuel a model detecting the most probable locations where Lyme disease might occur. With GIS it is much easier to combine epidemiology data and ecological data to model and predict disease spread and transmission. This data integration is essential if we hope to mitigate epidemics through better health policy planning.

At a national level, GIS has been used to help design a surveillance system for the monitoring and control of malaria in Israel (Wood et al., 1994). The GIS-based surveillance system located breeding sites of Anopheles mosquitoes, imported malaria cases, and population centers in an effort to better respond in the cases of outbreaks.

On a global scale, the National Aeronautics and Space Administration (NASA) established the Global Monitoring and Disease Prediction Program at Ames Research Center to identify environmental factors that affect the patterns of disease risk and transmission (Ahearn and De Rooy, 1996). The program developed predictive models of vector population dynamics and disease transmission risk using remotely sensed data and GIS technologies and applied them to malaria surveillance and control (Beck et al., 1994).

Social Unrest—War

Although one could argue that war is a good candidate for a health-related epidemic via germ warfare, the use of geographic information technologies by the military has been more proactive than simply monitoring and surveillance.

The National Imagery and Mapping Agency (NIMA) (NIMA, 1999b), a major combat support agency of the Department of Defense and a member of the intelligence community, was established in 1996 to provide accurate imagery, imagery intelligence, and geospatial information in support of the nation. For example, during the 1995 Bosnia peace accord, the Defense Mapping Agency (now NIMA) employed technology called Powerscene, developed by Cambridge Research Associates, to recalculate the territorial balance between rival factions as the borders were modified and adjusted based on landscape and political conditions. This interactive process was undertaken at Wright–Patterson Air Force Base in Dayton, Ohio, where orthorectified imagery and digital terrain elevation data was integrated to produce a Terrain Visualization Manuevering Support system (NIMA, 1999a). This system enabled NATO commanders and peace negotiators to tour the 650-mile cease-fire border and any disputed territory without endangering lives on the ground.

GIS is also used as a tracking tool for troops in training and combat, and as a planning and negotiation tool for peacemakers. A prototype terrain visualization system was installed at the National Military Command Center in the Pentagon in 1994 to help support national command-level missions such as locating downed aircraft (Scott O'Grady's F-16) and troop withdrawals (from Somalia) (NIMA, 1999b). To serve such technology better, NASA's Shuttle Radar Topography Mission (SRTM) collected vital, high-resolution elevation data during February 2000. The mission, a partnership between NASA and NIMA, will use the SRTM data to generate digital elevation models and three-dimensional pictures of the earth's surface. Besides scientists using the data to study flooding, erosion, landslide hazards, earthquakes, ecological zones, weather forecasts, and climate change, the military will use it to plan and rehearse missions, improve weapon accuracy, and for modeling and simulation purposes.

Geographic information technology is also being used for environmental monitoring and cleanup at several Navy installations as part of the Navy's comprehensive, long-term environmental action (CLEAN) program and at the Rocky Flats Nuclear Weapons Complex (Bromley, 1995).

Toxic Spills, Explosions, and Fires (Accidental or Otherwise)

Man-made crises are extreme events that can be accidental, such as toxic spills, or premeditated such as bombings by terrorists. No matter what their origin, many of these human-induced disasters could be lessened or even prevented by integrating geographic information technologies. For example, in a case of toxic release, population data, residential locations, wind speed, and direction could populate a model to map the extent of the disaster and suggest evacuation strategies.

All crises require an immediate and well-coordinated response where data handling and system interoperability are critical. Besides the political and technical challenges of fusing data from mixed sources, proprietary data formats often impede interoperability. Commonalities, such as coordinate systems and the representation of locations, boundaries, and aerial features, must transcend a broad community of users and tool vendors. Metadata is crucial for identifying and managing the quality of data, while access protocols and retrieval parameters will determine the speed of extracting data from a digital archive or library. During a crisis, such as the Oklahoma City bombing, data access speed is paramount for rescue workers, and advances in robust indexing mechanisms, such as geographic footprints (Goodchild, 1996), will prove invaluable. Although many successful initiatives are already underway at both the local and national levels, they could greatly benefit from advances in geographic information science.

The City of Winston–Salem, North Carolina, built an Integrated Network Fire Operations (I.N.F.O.) system that is designed to reduce the time it takes for firefighters to respond to emergency (911) calls and to provide information about the address of an incident to aid firefighters in making better informed decisions and plan the fire fighting effort while en route (Chakraborty and Armstrong, 1996). I.N.F.O. automatically uses the address of an incident to search for any prefire and HazMat planning information that might be available (e.g., building floor plans, hazardous waste information, occupants).

FEMA developed HAZUS, a natural hazard loss estimation methodology software program that is useful for earthquake-related mitigation, emergency preparedness, response and recovery planning, and disaster response operations and that is implemented within PC-based GIS software.

Research Challenges

The research of hazards illustrates how geographic information is being integrated into solutions and the important role the Web now plays in communication and disseminating information to the public for mitigation, management, and recovery from a disaster. Although much of the information on the Web might be represented as a document, the results are often displayed in map and graphic form, which is clearly the result of applying geographic information technologies to the problem. In some instances, it is clear that geographic information technology has advanced the information from simple data display to output from an advanced modeling effort.

Spatial Data Acquisition and Integration

Data acquisition and integration may be the single-largest contribution area needed for emergency preparedness and response. Although models can be developed for handling disasters, making them operational on a day-to-day basis means huge investments in data acquisition and integration.

There are essentially three parties that have spatial information needs in an emergency management arena. These include public sector authorities, such as emergency managers and government agencies, private citizens, and researchers. Also, as discussed above, the disaster cycle can be divided into the temporal stages of before, during, and after a disaster. Using these two dimensions, a matrix can be defined where each cell represents a given party's spatial information requirements at each stage in the disaster cycle.

Table 1
Spatial Information Needs

Interested Parties	Disaster Cycle		
	before	during	after
public sector personnel			
private citizens			
researchers			

This matrix can be used to examine the information needs of various parties at various stages in the disaster cycle. For example, if we focus on the cells in the diagonal of the matrix, the cell in the upper-left corner of the matrix would represent the public sector's spatial information needs before a disaster. This would include risk mapping, emergency simulation, and any other activities that involve spatial information in emergency planning or analysis. The cell in the center of the matrix represents the spatial information needs of private citizens during a disaster. This would include evacuation orders and routing, information about the spatial extent of the hazard, and any other information that citizens might require during a disaster. Finally, the cell in the lower right-hand corner would represent the spatial information needs of researchers after a disaster. This might include data on the processes that led to the disaster, the routes taken by evacuees, or any other spatial information that researchers might want to know about a particular event. It should be noted that there is a significant amount of overlap in the information needs of these parties during the various cycles of a disaster. However, the matrix supports the notion that the information needs of these parties are not identical.

A significant challenge in emergency management is delivering the appropriate information to the proper party at the appropriate place and time in a useful form. "Useful form" in this context refers to the scale, accuracy, and detail of the delivered information. Spatial data acquisition and integration should focus on research associated with questions and problems related to acquiring and integrating spatial information to meet the various needs of the parties listed in the table above for the given time periods.

As an example, assume that an engine company from county A has been instructed to respond to an emergency call in county B. The problem is to provide the company with the nature of the incident and the needs of the parties in distress, the location of the incident, and, ideally, the best route to the site. This information must be delivered in a timely manner in an appropriate form, where errors in the information may have serious consequences. The fact that the information must also be delivered in a timely manner puts unique demands on any system designed to deliver this information. It implies that there is a time window within which the information must be delivered to have value.

The overall research challenge in spatial data acquisition and integration for emergency management can be viewed as one of delivering accurate, appropriate information to all the parties involved in a disaster at the proper stages of the disaster in a timely manner. There are a number of research questions that can be generated from this overarching research challenge.

- What information needs to be provided to what parties at what times during an emergency?

- What sources of data are available for meeting these information needs?

- What data needs to be collected during an actual emergency?

- What problems arise in integrating sources of spatial information with various levels of accuracy and detail to meet the unique needs of each party at various points in the disaster cycle?

- What amount of uncertainty can various parties tolerate when receiving information provided to them at various stages in the disaster cycle?

Distributed Computing

Modern computer simulations of complex natural phenomena, such as rapid forest fire growth or development of a volcanic plume, require supercomputer facilities with distributed simultaneous computing on many processors. Linked to geographic information systems, these models for predisaster planning, crisis management, and postdisaster recovery could become extremely valuable mitigation and response tools.

Although this level of analysis is not possible today, during a crisis such a system could be highly interactive, allowing real-time communication between parties and aiding in the execution of models that could be viewed remotely. This would allow scientists and civil protection agencies to apply results immediately to the current extremely dangerous conditions. Here the data must be output in various levels of format complexity, allowing images and animation of various scenarios to be viewed by scientists, decision makers, and the general public (with the approval of the appropriate public safety and government officials).

It is important that any new data systems be developed on a platform that is widely compatible with those of existing data users. It is also important that these systems be designed to run on thin clients, as in an emergency it is likely portable, wireless computers will be the communication tool in the field.

Extensions to
Geographic
Representations

A key area to pursue is the dynamic representation of physical and human processes in emergency preparedness and response. Geographic information systems have not traditionally been designed to represent dynamic phenomena, but this is critical in assessing and responding to emergencies. Very little research has been conducted in this area, despite the obvious consequences of making critical decisions with inaccurate or incomplete information.

There is a need to improve the representation of risk and human vulnerability. The computational representation of human vulnerability has lagged behind the theoretical advancements in this area. As such, GIS is not representing the depth and richness of the theoretical frameworks, and empirical research on human vulnerability to environmental hazards remains incomplete. Risk and human vulnerability are much more dynamic than the representations that are now being used in GIS. There is a need to be able to rapidly model and summarize alternative scenarios, especially when the future is uncertain (e.g., tornado, hurricane, fire).

Before proceeding to extending representations, we must make sure that the representations we have are up to date. There are many cases where the data that emergency managers are relying on is simply out of date. As an example, during the recent tornado season in Oklahoma, the 1997 TIGER files did not have many of the schools included in the database. We need to progress to hazard, risk, and vulnerability classification systems that include multiple hazards. An example of this approach is the Community Vulnerability Assessment Tool for New Hanover County in North Carolina, developed by the NOAA Coastal Services Center. However, most research in this area has focused on single-hazard scenarios (i.e., classifying based on just one hazard). Finally, there is a need to develop representations of past disasters and events, both static and dynamic, including what factors led to a particular disaster, where the event occurred, what development has taken place since the last disaster, and how many hazardous events have occurred at a particular location.

Cognition of
Geographic
Information

The scientific domain of the cognition of geographic information includes humans, computers, and the earth. Research in this area centers on questions related to human conceptualizations of geographic spaces, computer representations of geographic space, and human perceptions of computer representations of geographic space. During a crisis, the emergency worker has the added pressure of time to deal with, and the representation and depiction of complex spatiotemporal information can easily be overwhelming. Uncertainty increases when decision making is data starved, the process of extracting support information is flawed, or communicating information accurately and effectively is impeded. Mistakes can serve to magnify the crisis or even propagate false hope or false fear, leading to even greater disasters resulting from evacuation. A balance between sufficient information and inducing panic and overreaction is critical.

The trend toward digital information foreshadows potential data saturation where emergency workers would be overwhelmed by vast influxes of digital data from a variety of sources such as HazMat, police, transportation, weather, demographics, and social welfare. Automated or robotic processes will be necessary to cull and mine this data into a manageable and worthwhile emergency assist tool. Algorithms will replace humans at the firing line, where geographic information is synthesized for modeling and decision making purposes. Getting this right is critical in healing rather than exacerbating disasters. Emergency preparedness is heavily influenced by social decision making processes, which depend in part on how information is understood by and communicated between participants in groups. Improvement in representations, operations, and modeling of spatial data is needed and is very real.

Interoperability of Geographic Information

The technical problem of interoperability arises from the need to share data, algorithms, and models (DAMs). What DAMs need to be shared in emergency management arenas? Institutions must know about DAMs that exist elsewhere before the need to share data arises. International attempts are in progress in the area of sharing geographic information for emergency management purposes. The Global Disaster Information Network (GDIN) is a prominent example.

GDIN is an interagency program undertaken at the initiative of Vice President Gore to assist fire and emergency management personnel. GDIN has two proposed components: (1) a national disaster information network and (2) a global system. GDIN will operate on the Internet and possibly Guardnet (National Guard Network) during disasters to broadcast and integrate disaster management information from all sources and provide it rapidly and readily. GDIN will also promote training and communication in the areas of emergency preparedness and mitigation. It is expected to produce many benefits that include saving lives and minimizing costs, enhancing coordination and sharing of compatible capabilities, facilitating the leveraging of existing resources, and assisting in validating and verifying information. To date, completed projects include the State of Florida Hurricane Simulation Exercise and the State of Alaska Information Process Flow Report. In addition, a regional, theme-based disaster information network is being developed to promote collaborative activities between the United States and Canada. The Red River Basin Disaster Information Network was established in response to the 1997 flood-affected portions of North Dakota, Minnesota, and Manitoba.

Experience has shown that a top-down approach to data sharing in disaster management is not entirely effective. The problem of interoperability in emergency preparedness and response must be approached by first assessing users' needs such as What geographic information needs to be shared? What information needs to be acquired? What information exists in other agencies, institutions, and companies? Data sharing and interoperability of geographic information must occur under tremendous time constraints in emergency preparedness and response. There are incompatibilities between physically based forecast models and the data stored in geographic databases. This is the data integration, or coupling, problem in all its forms.

Scale

Digital elevation model (DEM) resolution is not adequate for many applications in risk mitigation. Until the February 2000 shuttle radar topography mission (SRTM), we had better DEM data for Mars and Venus than for earth, and it may be many years before seafloor and subice surfaces are acquired at similar resolution. Even now, the SRTM data will move more rapidly into the military domain than into civilian use. Present applications use simplified flow models that display results in two dimensions as data files or images. Such small data sets are easy to use on PCs or workstations, and computational nodes for models are widely spaced. For example, standard DEM data sets have thirty meter spacing of nodes, and working files are on the order of megabytes.

Although this data makes very large files for ordinary computers, the detail is insufficient for realistic prediction of many natural phenomena for which small differences in topography or other parameters could have a large effect on the spatial pattern of the result. A more suitable grid spacing could be meter scale, and the data sets could be as large as one or two gigabytes. Development of such large data sets on a supercomputer could provide a valuable source that could be distributed for use at various remote GIS sites.

Current risk simulation codes work on small areas with large grids and are slow. Future codes should operate on fine grids of data sets that include the entire area of risk surrounding, for example, a volcano. For optimal use the data will be a high-density grid of topographic points (x,y,z data) at a horizontal spacing of ten to thirty meters and at vertical increments of one to ten meters. The areas encompassed by a single network may be as large as 50-km x 50-km grids. Such a large computational grid is too large for a single-processor computer; hence supercomputers are necessary for computation and visualization. Even finer resolution data will be required for cities to model the movement of fire, chemical, or biochemical plumes through complex urban canyons. Currently, such data is being acquired by laser devices and other new technologies.

Spatial Analysis in a GIS Environment

Computer simulations linked to GIS systems could permit analysis of loss of life and disruption of infrastructure that is not possible today with the current set of available tools. Sophisticated visualization systems allow public safety officials, scientists, and the general population to understand the effect of the various phenomena in their areas of interest and to design appropriate mitigation plans. A three-dimensional visualization system could provide an animated illustration of the areas threatened by volcanic phenomena at several scales.

Perspective views of the phenomena could be interactively manipulated to include a spectrum of possibilities ranging from individual rivers, streets, and buildings to entire disaster scenes. Overlays of images on topographic grids would create a realistic three-dimensional appearance of the phenomena that will move in real time with data moving in and out of the system dynamically. The GIS interface could allow query and manipulation at various levels and between multiple viewers at different sites. The use of CAVE (Pape et al., 1996) or even holograph technology could create realistic simulations necessary for training and prevention missions as well as for coordinated, distributed simulations for coordination of multiple factors in disaster response.

It is important that scientists involved in the GIS analysis can interact in several different ways. Multiple windows on their computer desktops could allow the interaction via the Internet. Such interaction allows them to send explicit equations or mathematical expressions at the time of the crisis. This facility could permit scientists to continuously update parameters and expressions that represent the current scientific state of the lava flow, for example. These changes could then filter through all others areas of the system infrastructure, providing scientists the ability to see the effects immediately. Another window displays a representation of the volcano or area around it, whether it is an actual picture or graphic or some other visual representation. Another window could control some general functionality of the other windows (e.g., automatic refreshing of all information and what files are viewed). At any time a scientist could change this setup.

If the scientist wants multiple graphic windows and no equation interface, this can be easily done. This type of interface should focus on communicating the nature of the disaster including the magnitude, extent, and uncertainty of the event. A very important element is to ascertain the risk of making a wrong decision.

The Future of Spatial Information Infrastructure

Emergency managers rely on a system for managing emergencies called an incident control system (ICS). An ICS specifies exactly which party (e.g., police, fire, highway patrol, mayor) is to do what during an emergency and precisely how communication, authority, and many other critical facets of the emergency management process are to take place. It is nationwide at local and state levels. Is there an equivalent institutional protocol, procedure, or approach for agencies to determine exactly who will collect and share geographic information before, during, and after an emergency? A global disaster information network could be central in developing and disseminating model data sharing procedures that address the institutional and technical issues associated with geographic information data sharing in emergency preparedness and response; an "ICS for geographic information," if you will. This might exist in the form of information sources, flows, and ultimately applications. There is also the need to develop foundation data models for sharing geographic information that is multidimensional, multiscale, and multisource in nature.

Uncertainty in Geographic Data and GIS-Based Analyses

As methods and models of GIS analysis become more sophisticated, the quality of data increases in importance. Many data sets undergo temporal adjustments, which add uncertainty to the analysis. For example, using one- or two-day-old data in volcano forecasting at the time of the crisis would lead to a faulty conclusion. The same is true of other disasters where geopolitical or natural conditions change from moment to moment. We must be able to analyze and incorporate such temporal uncertainty in the analysis and forecast that we make.

We must be able to quantify the uncertainty in the data (and the analysis) and express this in a satisfactory mode. A major problem exists in how we report uncertainty in GIS. For example, what significance do we place on the lines on various maps and diagrams? How do we address this issue? A case in point would be designing a hazard map for flooding on an alluvial fan where there is no defined channel and the flood has different probabilities of spreading in various directions. Another major problem is the propagation of uncertainty through the data set as we combine several sets of data of different levels of confidence and even potentially different types. Research on this topic should help to resolve this problem.

GIS and Society

GIS is the new thing in society, and new things often arrive with added baggage. Questions arise about rates of adoption and participation across society. Is there equity of access? Is there equity of the distribution of the costs and benefits? Access to GIS can simultaneously marginalize and empower different groups in society. The adoption of geographic technologies to emergency preparedness and response can fall prey to this equity of access issue where some groups are kept safe at the expense of those that cannot afford the technology.

Risk assessment and subsequent mitigation actions can impact a community and have a wide range of consequences. Incomplete data can lead to unwarranted fears, restrictive and costly regulation, and even serve to affect property values. These can all lead to increases in disaster insurance, bias in the allocation of emergency resources, and the attachment of stigma to a neighborhood. There is a strong need for public participation both in developing the GIS for emergency preparedness and for gaining access to it during a disaster. This participation and ownership has implications for empowerment within community and grassroots groups who are often relied upon during emergency response.

Defining potential barriers between GIS technology and different segments of society will aid in delivering critical information during a crisis. Often, information usually considered private becomes invaluable in managing a disaster but its use also raises legal and ethical questions about intrusion into private lives. What role, responsibilities, ethics, and motivations in disseminating geographic information for warning, preparedness, and response does the media play? How are new technologies, such as pagers, handheld devices, and other electronic innovations, affecting equity, vulnerability, and the perception of risk? How are issues like socioeconomics, insurance, race, and other issues related to the application of geographic information in emergency preparedness and response? Much research addressing GIS and society is needed.

Linkages to Education Priorities

The search of hazards to determine application challenges for emergency preparedness and response illustrated the important role the Web now plays in communication and disseminating information to the public. It appears that an informed population is more prone to accept and even embrace mitigation, respond and participate in the management of a hazard or emergency, and be better equipped to assist and appreciate recovery from a disaster. Much of the information on the Web is commonly represented as a document, yet images, maps, and graphics illustrating the results of some analysis are slowly finding their way onto emergency preparedness and response-related Web sites.

The most important educational needs or components that surface when one looks at individual hazards, either natural or human induced, focus on issues of certification of specialists to undertake response and settlement, public education and awareness of response during a disaster, the development of a model curriculum to develop geographic information science experts for emergency preparedness and response, and the development of simulators to train rescue workers and settlement specialists. It is clear that only a few people that work within this area will require in-depth education in geographic information science, while most others will benefit by training on installed GIS-related technology. However, training needs to be presented within the context of the profession with appropriate amounts of spatial literacy and integrated with other technologies common to the profession.

To best illustrate emergency preparedness and response needs, some discussion is undertaken here.

Emerging Technologies for Delivering Geographic Information Science Education

Technology is playing a central role in education at the college and university levels. In some instances, it serves to lower the cost of education, while in others it enhances and even makes possible some opportunities never before imagined. Distance learning taught by domain experts, Web-based programs, and simulators to create better and cheaper technology, are all served by these emerging technologies.

Emerging technologies make it possible to educate more people and are even more effective for training. It is now relatively common to find Web-based training courses in which one can enroll and conveniently become well versed in GIS. However, unlike the rigors of the college classroom, quality, accreditation, and assurance are not clearly defined and regulated. Assessing liability and assuring accountability in a disaster may call for the regulation of emerging technologies as they are applied to education.

Supporting Infrastructure

As training and modeling in GIS become more the status quo for personnel in emergency preparedness and response, demands on technology classrooms and Internet portals will rapidly increase. Who will bear the cost of such infrastructure in the short run, and will this persist and set a trend? Emergency preparedness and response support is recognized during a disaster when many groups step forward to lend a helping hand, but what is being done over the long haul to help mitigate and be prepared if a disaster strikes?

Access and Equity

The geographic information science community must ensure access to the technologies and data to disadvantaged groups and impaired individuals so that they may also be effective in emergency preparedness and response in their communities. The first goal of this education priority is to ensure access and determine what is the necessary "spatial literacy" to effectively use GIS. However, in an emergency, access and equity issues quickly shift from "How effective is the trained emergency worker?" to questions such as, "Under what circumstances should rescue workers have access to private information?" and "Under what circumstances may a community breach ownership rights in order to acquire and access data?" In the heat of a disaster, is it impossible to even address some of these issues let alone come up with solutions.

Alternative Designs for Curriculum Content and Evaluation

Although the basic geographic information science concepts might be the same, as you cross domains specific concepts vary. Likewise, in emergency preparedness and response, the level of geographic information knowledge necessary for emergency workers to carry out their jobs varies. At one end of the spectrum a worker may need to be able to read a map, while at the other end a sophisticated understanding of spatial statistics might be in order. Delivering education under such extreme needs calls for a scalable curriculum to increase the likelihood that GIS will be deployed properly and effectively in the emergency preparedness and response area.

Adopting these technologies and employing them in the field to save lives and property do not come easy. The emergency worker must not only have faith in the technology, but must also have confidence in the data. Building this confidence starts with a sound education where the student participates in data collection so that ownership and a stake in the data buys into its use in emergency preparedness and response.

Professional GIS Education Programs	The majority of emergency preparedness and response workers need training on how to use the technology to extract information about infrastructure, follow guidelines in assessing risk, navigate and follow procedures during a crisis, and assess damage after a disaster. It is likely the majority of workers in this area will not have been widely exposed to geospatial technologies, and professional training will play a key role in filling this gap.
Research-Based Graduate GIS Education	To advance the state of any science, researchers must be educated so that they may lead on the frontiers of research and then train and collaborate with those emerging researchers to push those frontiers forward.

Learning with GIS

Learning with GIS in emergency preparedness and response employs a curriculum that emphasizes emergency preparedness and response-specific topics and uses geographic information to study them. Since most disasters can be mapped, a GIS can provide a very effective navigation tool for dissecting problems and learning the steps necessary to deliver an effective response.

Proactive approaches to disasters lead to practice sessions where geographic information-fueled simulators play out a variety of disaster scenarios. These simulators will play a critical role in educating the emergency preparedness and response community and its response strategies during an emergency.

Accreditation and Certification

Although accreditation and certification may carry with it problems associated with licensing, for emergency preparedness and response workers liability is a serious issue and accreditation and certification are most often embraced. Just as emergency response workers must be certified on their search-and-rescue techniques and technologies, certification on how to properly use geographic information data is a necessary component if quality control and assurance is to be taken seriously.

Policy Implications

Both natural and human-generated hazards usually transcend political boundaries that are effective for defining regions used to effectively mitigate against disaster, manage rescue and response operations, or to organize and deliver relief. Since policy is most often generated and administered within politically defined boundaries, we must develop new policies that emulate hazards rather than human administrative structures.

Policy and regulation are commonly applied on the landscape as a function of form. For example, brush must be cleared to create a specific size protective buffer zone around homes in an urban–wildland intermix region. Although the specific buffer zone, represented here as a form, can easily be complied to and administered, it is naive and unrealistic to assume the impact of this buffer zone will be uniform over space. Advances in geographic information science will bring about a shift where policy and regulation can become a function of the underlying process rather than relying on an easily administered but limited form-based policy. The greater our confidence in data and models, the more likely policy will be process- rather than form-based.

There are three primary policy arenas.

■   Science policy

- Information policy (ownership, privacy, access, liability)
- Public policy

Within these arenas, several questions arise with respect to emergency preparedness and response.

- If you have confidence in data and models, can policy then be process based rather than regulation based?

- Should there be different disaster access policies depending on pre-, during, or postdisaster? Is there a general policy to cover all possibilities? Can one design a policy that is generalized across disasters?

- What information policies result in the most effective use of geographic information in emergency response situations? (For example, comparative studies are necessary where one examines the experiences of city A with city B). Is there a need to distinguish between pre-, during, and post-situations? Is there a need to compare unpredictable versus more predictable events (those that are time dependent)?

Conclusion

Research and education in emergency preparedness and response is crucial as we search for conditions thought to be hazardous to life and habitat, undertake mitigation efforts, respond during emergencies to reduce loss of life and property, and settle and restore a damaged environment. In some instances, we found that early warning systems need to be built, while in other instances we need to change more fundamental elements such as land use and lifestyle. In almost all instances, large databases that contain information on humans, their activities, and their habitat are necessary. We need to ensure that this data is accessible to assess risk, prepare to engage disaster, and aid in effective response and settlement. Although the tools must be engineered to effectively assist emergency workers, we must also ensure privacy of the individual so exploitation cannot occur.

The question is whether advances in research and education priorities might contribute to needs within the application of emergency preparedness and response. By identifying and recommending priorities for research, education, and policy contributions to emergency management, a focus for geographic information science for this application challenge can be identified. The interaction between humans and their environment under conditions thought to be hazardous to life and habitat can be facilitated through advances in geographic information science.

Through emergency preparedness and response we will be able to realize shifts where policy can be more directly linked to underlying processes rather than simply the form that appears during and as a result of a disaster.

References

Ahearn, S.C., and C. De Rooy. 1996. A Temporal Analysis of Tillage Area in Kwara, Nigeria, Using Remote Sensing. *International Journal of Remote Sensing.* 17(5), 917–929.

Applied Environmental Geographic Information Science, Eastbay Hills Vegetation Survey and Fire Hazard Assessment GIS Project. http://www5.ced.berkeley.edu:8005/aegis/home/nfprojects/eastbay/.

Association of Bay Area Governments. www.abag.ca.gov.

Barnes, S. and A. Peck. 1994. Mapping the Future of Health Care: GIS Applications in Health Care Analysis. *Geo Info Systems.* 4(4), 31–33.

Beck, L.R., M.H. Rodrigues, S.W. Dister, A.D. Rodrigues, E. Rejmankova, A. Ulloa, et al. 1994. Remote Sensing as a Landscape Epidemiologic Tool to Identify Villages at High Risk for Malaria Transmission. *The American Journal of Tropical Medicine and Hygiene.* (51), 271–80.

Beer, T. 1990. The Australian National Bushfire Model Project. *Mathematical Computer Modeling.* 13(12), 49–56.

Bobbitt, A. 1999. VENTS Data and Interactive Maps. http://newport.pmel.noaa.gov/gis/data.html.

Braddock M., G. Lapidus, E.R. Cromley, G. Burke, and L. Branco. 1994. Using a Geographic Information System to Understand Child Pedestrian Injury. *American Journal of Public Health.* 84, 1158–61.

Brainard, J., A. Lovett, and J. Parfitt. 1996. Assessing Hazardous Waste Transport Risks Using a GIS. *International Journal of Geographical Information Systems.* 10(7), 831–849.

Brantley, S. R. Volcanoes of the United States. http://pubs.usgs.gov/gip/volcus/titlepage.html.

Bromley, M. 1995. A Sampling of PRC's GIS Contracts for the Defense Community. www.esri.com/library/userconf/proc95/to300/p283.html.

California Environmental Resources Evaluation Systems (CERESa) Natural Hazard Disclosure Statement. http://ceres.ca.gov/planning/nhd/ (maps used in enforcing AB 1195).

California Environmental Resources Evaluation Systems (CERESb) Natural Hazard Disclosure Statement Wildland Fire Areas. http://ceres.ca.gov/planning/nhd/wild_fire.html.

California Environmental Resources Evaluation Systems (CERESc) Natural Hazard Disclosure Statement, Wildland Fire Areas (State Responsibility Areas). http://ceres.ca.gov/planning/nhd/fire_sev.html.

California Governor's Office of Emergency Services. Important Notice Regarding Posted Maps. www.oes.ca.gov/dim.nsf/web+pages/home.

Catchpole, E.A., W.R. Catchpole, and R.C. Rothermel. 1993. Fire Behavior Experiments in Mixed Fuel Complexes. *International Journal of Wildland Fire.* 3(1), 45–57.

Center for Tsunami Inundation Mapping Efforts. 1999. http://newport.pmel.noaa.gov/time/home.html.

Chakraborty, J., and M.P. Armstrong. 1996. Using Geographic Plume Analysis to Assess City of Winston–Salem Integrated Network Fire Operations Project. www.ci.winston-salem.nc.us/fire/infoproj.

Chou, Y.H. 1992. Management of Wildfires with a Geographical Information System. *International Journal of Geographical Information Systems.* 6(2), 123–140.

Clarke, K.C., S.L. McLafferty, and J.T. Barbara. 1996. On Epidemiology and Geographic Information Systems: A Review and Discussion of Future Directions. *Emerging Infectious Diseases.* 2(2), 85–92. www.cdc.gov/ncidod/EID/vol2no2/clarke.htm.

Community Vulnerability Assessment Tool. http://www.csc.noaa.gov/newsletter/back_issues/novdec99/cvat.html.

Community Vulnerability Assessment Tool, New Hanover County, North Carolina. http://www.modernag.com/Common/currentissues/Dec99/nancy.htm.

Community Vulnerability to Hazardous Accidents. *Computers, Environment, and Urban Systems.* 19(5–6), 341–356.

Corbley, K.P. 1999. Fleeing from Floyd: Internet GIS in the Eye of the Storm. *Geo Info Systems.* 9(10), 28–35.

Coverage Description. ftp://ftp.ca.gov/pub/gis/nhdf/wildland.txt.

Department of Conservation. 1999. Landslide Maps Available from the California Department of Conservation's Division of Mines and Geology. www.consrv.ca.gov/dmg/geohaz/ls_maps.htm.

Department of Conservation, Seismic Hazards Evaluation and Zoning Program. www.consrv.ca.gov/dmg/shezp.

DeYoe, C.D. 1999. ArcView GIS Worked Extensively During Storm Emergency Response, GIS on the Front Lines. *ArcNews Online.* www.esri.com/news/arcnews/fall99articles/28-gisonfront.html.

Dymon, U. 1999. Effectiveness of Geographic Information Systems (GIS) Applications in Flood Management During and After Hurricane Fran. *Quick Response Report #114.* University of Colorado at Boulder, Natural Hazards Center. www.colorado.edu/UCB/Research/IBS/hazards/qr/qr114.html.

Edgetech America, Inc. 1999. Tornado Hits (1950–1996). www.edgetech-us.com/Map/MapTornado.htm.

Federal Emergency Management Agency, Map Service Center. www.fema.gov/msc.

Federal Emergency Management Agency. Natural Hazard Loss Estimation Methodology (HAZUS). www.fema.gov/hazus/index.htm.

Fire Area Simulator (FARSITE). http://farsite.org.

Frankel, A. 1996. National Seismic-Hazard Maps: Documentation. *USGS Open-File Report.* 96–532.

Glass G.E., B.S. Schwartz, J.M. III Morgan, D.T. Johnson, P.M. Noy, and E. Israel. 1995. Environmental Risk Factors for Lyme Disease Identified with Geographic Information Systems. *American Journal of Public Health.* 85(7), 944–948.

The Global Disaster Information Network. www.state.gov/www/issues/relief/gdin.html.

Goodchild, M.F. 1996. Directions in GIS. Proceedings, Third International Conference/Workshop on Integrating GIS and Environmental Modeling, Santa Fe, New Mexico (Santa Barbara, CA: National Center for Geographic Information and Analysis), January 21–26, 1996. www.ncgia.ucsb.edu/conf/SANTA_FE_CD-ROM/sf_papers/goodchild_michael/good.html.

Hinton, C. 1997. North Carolina City Saves Time, Lives, and Money with Award-Winning GIS. *Weathering Natural Hazards with Information Technology.* 7(9), 35–37.

Irby, B. 1997. "Hazard zoning." *California's I Zone: Urban–Wildland Fire Prevention and Mitigation.* Slaughter, R. (Ed.). California Department of Forestry, State of California. 46–55.

Kehlet, R. 1998. FEMA Speeds Up Disaster Relief with GIS. *ArcNews.* Spring 1998. www.esri.com/news/arcnews/spring98articles/22-fema_speedsup.html.

Kessel, S.R. 1990. Australian geographical information and modeling system for natural area management. *International Journal of Geographical Information Systems.* 4(3), 333–362.

Marquez, L.O., and S. Maheepala. 1996. An Object-Oriented Approach to the Integrated Planning of Urban Development and Utility Services. *Computers, Environment, and Urban Systems.* 20(4–5), 303–312.

McRae, R.H.D. 1990. Use of Digital Terrain Data for Calculating Fire Rates of Spread with the Preplan Computer System. *Mathematical Computer Modeling.* 13(12), 37–48.

Mount St. Helens National Monument. http://volcano.und.nodak.edu/vwdocs/msh/msh.html.

National Hurricane Center. www.nhc.noaa.gov/.

National Imagery and Mapping Agency. 1999a. Terrain Visualization Fact Sheet. http://164.214.2.59:80/general/factsheets/pwrscn.html.

National Imagery and Mapping Agency. 1999b. The Shuttle Radar Topography Mission. www.nima.mil.

National Oceanic and Atmospheric Administration. www.outlook.noaa.gov/tornadoes/.

NOAA Coastal Services Center. www.csc.noaa.gov/.

Pape, D., C. Cruz–Neira, and M. Czernuszenko. 1996. CAVE User's Guide. www.evl.uic.edu/pape/CAVE/prog/CAVEGuide.html#description.

Pikei, R. 1997. Index to Detailed Maps of Landslide in the San Francisco Bay Region. *USGS Open-File Report.* 97-745-D.

Popocatepetl Volcano, Central Mexico. www.geo.mtu.edu/volcanoes/popocatepetl/.

Preparedness, Training, and Exercises Committee Meeting, National Emergency Management Association Conference. 1999. www.fema.gov/pte/gosspch79.htm.

Radke, J. 1995. Modeling Urban/Wildland Interface Fire Hazards Within a Geographic Information System. *Geographic Information Sciences.* 1(1), 1–14.

Richards, F.O., Jr. 1993. Use of Geographic Information Systems in Control Programs for Onchocerciasis in Guatemala. *Bulletin of the Pan American Health Organization.* 27(1), 52–55.

San Francisco Bay Landslide Mapping Team. 1997. Introduction to the San Francisco Bay Region, California, Landslide Folio. *USGS Open File Report.* 97–745-A.

Sheridan, M.F. Dr. Sheridan's Home Page. www.eng.buffalo.edu/~mfs/.

Shu-Quiang, W., and D.J. Unwin. 1992. Modelling Landslide Distribution on Loess Soils in China: an Investigation. *International Journal of Geographical Information Systems.* 6(5), 391–405.

Sitar, N., and K. Bijan. 1999. Landsliding in Native Ground: A GIS Application to Seismic Slope Stability. The Geological Society of America Cordilleran Section, University of California Berkeley, California. June 2–4, 1999. 31(6). www2.ced.berkeley.edu:8002/.

Tempalski B.J. 1994. The Case of Guinea Worm: GIS as a Tool for the Analysis of Disease Control Policy. *Geo Info Systems.* 4(4), 32–8.

Trudeau, M. 1998. Weathering Natural Hazards with Information Technology. *Geo Info Systems.* 8(10), 10.

Tsunami Research Program. www.pmel.noaa.gov/tsunami.

USDA Forest Service, Rocky Mountain Research Station, Fire Sciences Laboratory, Fire Behavior Research Work Unit, Missoula, Montana, Wildland Fire Assessment System. www.fs.fed.us/land/wfas.

University Consortium for Geographic Information Science Research Priorities. www.ncgia.ucsb.edu/other/ucgis/CAGIS.html.

United States Fire Administration Hazardous Materials Guide for First Responders. www.usfa.fema.gov/hazmat/.

U.S. Department of Interior. Fact Sheet: DOI Science Helping Honduras Recover from Hurricane. *U.S. Department of Interior News.* http://cindi.usgs.gov/events/mitch/DOInews.html.

U.S. Geological Survey (USGSa). Earthquake Hazards and Preparedness. http://quake.wr.usgs.gov/hazprep/#Hazards.

U.S. Geological Survey (USGSb). Landslide Research by the San Francisco Bay Region Project. http://sfgeo.wr.usgs.gov/sfbay/slides.html.

U.S. Geological Survey (USGSc). San Francisco Bay Region Landslides Folio Home Page. http://wrgis.wr.usgs.gov/open-file/of97-745.

Wadge, G. 1988. The potential of GIS modeling of gravity flows and slope instabilities. *International Journal of Geographical Information Systems.* 2(2), 143–152.

Wartenberg D. 1992. Screening for Lead Exposure Using a Geographic Information System. *Environmental Research.* 59(2), 310–317.

Wartenberg D., M. Greenberg, and R. Lathrop. 1993. Identification and Characterization of Populations Living near High-voltage Transmission Lines: a Pilot Study. *Environmental Health Perspectives.* 101, 626–632.

Wood B.L., L.R. Beck, S.W. Dister, and M.A. Spanner. 1994. Global Monitoring and Disease Prediction Program. *Sistema Terra.* 3(1), 42.

Yeh, A.G., and M.H. Chow. 1996. An Integrated GIS and Location–Allocation Approach to Public Facilities Planning—An Example of Open Space Planning. *Computers, Environment, and Urban Systems.* 20(4–5), 339–350.

Young, W., and D. Bowyer. 1996. Modeling the Environmental Impact of Changes in Urban Structure. *Computers, Environment, and Urban Systems.* 20(4–5), 313–326.

Glossary

Disaster
: Disasters are characterized by the scope of an emergency. An emergency becomes a disaster when it exceeds the capability of the local resources to manage it. Disasters often result in great damage, loss, or destruction.

Emergency
: An emergency is a deviation from planned or expected behavior or course of events that endangers or adversely affects people, property, or the environment.

Hazard
: Hazard refers generally to physical characteristics that may cause an emergency (for example, earthquake faults, active volcanoes, flood zones, and highly flammable brush fields are all hazards).

Risk
: Risk is the potential or likelihood of an emergency to occur. For example, the risk of damage to a structure from an earthquake is high if it is built upon, or adjacent to, an active earthquake fault. The risk of damage to a structure where no earthquake faults exist is low.

appendix B **Spatial data layers used by Miami-Dade County government, available for use in disaster management applications**

Spatial data layers used in Consequences Assessment Tool Set (CATS) software
Science Application International Corporation

Miami-Dade County GIS production layers

Layer name	Description of layer www.co.miami-dade.fl.us/itd/spatialdata.htm	Last update	Update schedule
	Single Tile Library Layers		
abusrout	Miami-Dade County Bus Routes	Apr-01	As needed
acanals	Miami-Dade County Canals	Oct-95	As needed
acccl	Miami-Dade County Coastal Construction Control Line	Jul-97	As needed
aconduit	Miami-Dade County Conduits	Apr-89	
acontour	Miami-Dade County Contour	Sep-89	
adade	Miami-Dade County Street Network	Jan-99	Weekly
adebremr	Miami-Dade Hurricane Debris Removal Routes	Sep-96	As needed
aeop	Miami-Dade County Edge of Pavement - Derivative	Jan-91	Not updated
aeopcl	Miami-Dade County Edge of Pavement Centerlines - Copyrighted	Jan-91	Not updated
ahighway	Miami-Dade County Main Highways	May-98	As needed
ahydro	Miami-Dade County Hydrology (Water Features)	Feb-90	As needed
alakes	Miami-Dade County Lakes	Jun-90	As needed
amajor	Miami-Dade County Major Streets & Highways	Sep-99	Quarterly
ammover	Miami-Dade County Mover Transit System	Aug-00	As needed
amrail	Miami-Dade County Rail Transit System	Aug-00	As needed
arail	Miami-Dade County Railroads - Copyrighted	Jan-91	Not updated
ashoreln	Miami-Dade County Shoreline	Feb-91	As needed
astreams	Miami-Dade County Streams	Sep-90	
atrirail	Tri-rail System	Aug-00	As needed
auia	Miami-Dade 1998 Urban Infill Area	Jun-98	As needed
aurb2000	Urban Area according to Miami-Dade comprehensive Master Plan for year 2005	Jun-95	
aurb2010	Urban Expansion Area according to Miami-Dade comprehensive Master plan for year 2015	Dec-96	
lbusstop	Miami-Dade County BusStops	Jul-92	As needed
lcollege	Miami-Dade County Colleges and Universities	Mar-94	Yearly
lcontrol	Miami-Dade County Control Points	Aug-94	
lcourts	Miami-Dade County Courts	Jun-01	As needed
ldclease	Miami-Dade Leased Properties	Aug-96	As needed
ldcown	Miami-Dade Owned Properties	Aug-96	As needed
ldumps	Solid Waste Management Sites, including: Landfill, Trash/Recycling Centers	Feb-95	As needed
lfiremun	Municipal Fire Stations	May-98	As needed
lfirest	Miami-Dade Fire Stations	Apr-00	As needed
lhrsaclf	Miami-Dade County DCF Adult Congregated Living Facilities	Jun-98	Bi-yearly
lhrsafch	Miami-Dade County DCF	Apr-96	
lhrsdycr	Miami-Dade County DayCare Centers	Aug-01	Yearly
lhrsfacl	Miami-Dade County DCF Facilities	Mar-96	As needed
lhrshdst	Miami-Dade County DCF Headstart Projects	Mar-96	As needed
lhrshlth	Miami-Dade County DCF Health Department Locations	Mar-96	As needed
lhrshosp	Miami-Dade County Hospitals	Jun-99	Yearly
lhrsnrhm	Miami-Dade County DCF Nursing Homes	Jun-98	Yearly
lhrswicc	Miami-Dade County DCF Women, Infant & Children Centers	Mar-96	As needed
lhrswicv	Miami-Dade County DCF Women, Infant & Children Vendors	Mar-96	As needed
lhurshel	Miami-Dade Hurricane Shelters	Jun-01	Yearly
llibrary	Miami-Dade County Public Libraries (includes municipalites)	Apr-00	Yearly

Layer name	Description of layer	Last update	Update schedule
lmdpdcty	Miami-Dade Police Stations	Feb-99	Yearly
lmmovrst	Miami-Dade County Mover Stations	Jun-95	As needed
lmobhome	Miami-Dade Mobile Home Parks	Jun-01	Yearly
lmrailst	Miami-Dade Rail Stations	Aug-00	As needed
lparks	Miami-Dade County Parks	Jul-00	Quarterly
lpolimun	Municipal Police Stations	Jun-01	Yearly
lpolls	Miami-Dade Voters Polling Places	Sep-92	As needed
lprop	Miami-Dade County Property Location- Derivative	May-99	Bi-weekly
lsbuild	Miami-Dade County Small Buildings - Copyrighted	Dec-93	Not planned
lschlpvt	Miami-Dade County Private Schools	Aug-01	As needed
lschools	Miami-Dade County Public Schools	Jul-01	As needed
lsigs	Miami-Dade County Traffic Signals	Aug-99	Bi-Yearly
ltcomste	Miami-Dade Telecommunication Sites	Jun-01	As needed
ltelphne	Miami-Dade County Owned Telephone Systems	Jul-99	As needed
ltmetro	Miami-Dade Team Metro Regional Offices	Aug-00	As needed
lwpawell	Miami-Dade WellField Locations	Oct-93	
pallneig	Property Appraiser Major Neighborhoods Boundaries	Apr-97	As needed
pblkgrp	Miami-Dade County Census Block Groups / Not aligned	Jul-91	
pcablesa	Miami-Dade County Cable Television Company Service Areas	Oct-00	As needed
pcb2000	Miami-Dade County Census 2000 Blocks	Apr-01	Every 10 yrs
pcbg2000	Miami-Dade County Census 2000 Block Groups	Apr-01	Every 10 yrs
pcdp2000	Miami-Dade County Census 2000 Designated Places	Apr-01	Every 10 yrs
pcenblk	Miami-Dade County Census Blocks / Not Aligned / Original	Jul-90	
pcenpla	Miami-Dade County Census Places / Not Aligned	Oct-90	
pcommiss	Miami-Dade County Commission Districts	Apr-01	As needed
pct2000	Miami-Dade County Census 2000 Tracts	Apr-01	Every 10 yrs
pcouncil	Miami-Dade Community Council	Feb-01	As needed
pdadeblk	Miami-Dade County Census Block created from Street Network	Apr-98	
pdadebnd	Outer Boundary of Miami-Dade County	Jun-98	Not Planned
pdadesol	Miami-Dade County Soil Conversion Map	Aug-95	As needed
pdevsite	Miami-Dade County 1998 Developable Sites	Jan-99	As needed
pempzbnd	Miami-Dade County 1998 Empowerment Zones	Jan-99	As needed
pempzcen	Miami-Dade County 1998 Empowerment Zones with Census Tracts	Jun-98	As needed
pestwdho	Miami-Dade County 1998 EastWard Ho!	Jun-98	As needed
pfdgrid	Miami-Dade County Fire Department Grid	Jun-96	As needed
pfemapnl	FEMA Panels (flood zones)	Apr-92	
pfiredis	Miami-Dade County Fire Board District	May-98	As needed
pfireres	Miami-Dade County Fire Rescue Response Service Areas	Apr-00	As needed
pfiresro	Miami-Dade County Fire & Rescue Station Response Order	Apr-00	As needed
pfiresta	Miami-Dade County Fire Station Response Service Areas	Apr-00	As needed
pfiresup	Miami-Dade County Fire Station Suppression Response Service Areas	Apr-00	As needed
pfloodzn	FEMA Flood Hazard Zones	May-98	As needed
pfocusar	Miami-Dade County Focus Area	May-98	Not planned
photoind	Miami-Dade County Digital Orthophotography Index	Mar-00	Not planned
phrsacsc	Miami-Dade County DCF Areas of Critical and Social Concerns	Mar-96	As needed
phrsprcr	Miami-Dade County DCF Primary Care Centers	Mar-96	As needed

Miami-Dade County GIS production layers (continued)

Layer name	Description of layer	Last update	Update schedule
phurevac	Miami-Dade County Hurricane Evacuation Zones	May-97	Yearly
pindxdml	Index coverage for DML library - Derivative	Apr-00	As needed
pindxstl	Index coverage for STL library	Sep-95	Not planned
planduse	Miami-Dade County Landuse layer 1998 - Derivative	Feb-00	As needed
pmdpdgrd	Miami-Dade County Police Grids	Jan-01	As needed
pmrailst	Miami-Dade County Rail Stations with 50 Feet Buffer	Apr-98	Not planned
pmunic	Municipal Boundaries (out to the water)	Aug-01	As needed
pmunicwt	Municipal Boundaries (up to the coastline)	Aug-01	As Needed
poutline	Miami-Dade County Outline Boundary	Sep-96	Not planned
pparkdst	Miami-Dade County Parks Districts	Oct-95	
pparks	Miami-Dade County Parks - Derivative	May-97	
ppatrold	Miami-Dade County Police Patrol Areas	Jan-01	As needed
ppoldist	Miami-Dade County Police Districts	Jan-01	As needed
pprecinc	Miami-Dade County Precincts	Oct-00	As needed
prdimpct	Miami-Dade Road Impact Fee Districts	Oct-99	As needed
psection	Miami-Dade County Section Boundaries - Derivative	Feb-99	As needed
psenate	Miami-Dade County State Senate Districts 1993	Apr-98	As needed
pshouse	Miami-Dade County State House Districts 1993	Apr-98	As needed
pstszon	Miami-Dade Special Transportation Services (Bus fare zones)	Apr-98	As needed
psubarea	Miami-Dade Subareas of Community Council	Aug-01	As needed
ptad1992	Miami-Dade County Traffic Analysis Districts	Dec-98	Not planned
ptaz1992	Miami-Dade County Traffic Analysis Zones	Sep-95	
ptaz2000	Miami-Dade County, 2000 Traffic Analysis Zones	Jul-01	Every 10 yrs
ptiger	1990 Original Census Tiger file for Miami-Dade County	Jun-91	
ptk90ful	Miami-Dade County Census tracks / Not Aligned / Original	Jul-90	
ptk90lnd	Miami-Dade County Census tracks / Not aligned / Uses coastline	Oct-90	
ptmcdbg	Miami-Dade Team Metro Commission District Block Groups	Oct-00	As needed
ptmcriwa	Miami-Dade Team Metro Crime Watch Area	Jan-01	As needed
ptmetro	Miami-Dade Team Metro Boundaries	Mar-01	As needed
ptmhoa	Miami-Dade Team Metro Home Owners Association	May-01	As needed
ptminhse	Miami-Dade Team Metro Minimum Housing	Oct-00	As needed
ptmnco	Miami-Dade Team Metro Neighborhood Code Officers	Oct-00	As needed
ptmoutrc	Miami-Dade Team Metro Out-Reach	Oct-00	As needed
ptmpaint	Miami-Dade Team Metro Painters Territory Boundaries	Oct-00	As needed
ptownshp	Miami-Dade County Townships - Derivative	Dec-98	Not planned
ptpevac	Miami-Dade County Turkey Point Evacuation Zones	Aug-93	
ptpradii	Miami-Dade County Turkey Point 5/10 miles Radius Rings	Apr-98	Not planned
ptpzones	Miami-Dade County Turkey Point Plume Exposure Pathway Evacuation Zone	Oct-95	
ptract	Miami-Dade County Census Tracts / Aligned / Uses Coastline	Jun-97	Not planned
ptractf	Miami-Dade County Census Tracts / Not Aligned / Full Boundary	Jul-97	
ptua	Miami-Dade County Targeted Urban Areas	Apr-98	Not planned
pusgsdde	Miami-Dade County Quads	Jul-90	
pusgsqad	USGS 7.5 minute Quad Sheet	Sep-90	
pushouse	Miami-Dade County United States House of Representatives	Apr-98	As needed
pwasdsa	Miami-Dade County Water & Sewer Department Service Area	Dec-98	As needed
pwater	Canals, Lakes, Streams and Coastline as defined by water line in Aerial Photography - Copyrighted	Mar-00	Not planned

Layer name	Description of layer	Last update	Update schedule
pwpa	Miami-Dade County WellFields Protection Areas May-98		As needed
pwstrte	Miami-Dade Solid Waste Management Garbage Pickup Routes Boundaries Sep-90		
pzipcode	Miami-Dade County Zipcode Boundaries..Apr-99		As needed

Square Mile/ Level 2 Layers

Layer name	Description of layer	Last update	Update schedule
EASE	Large Utility Easements, Road and Lot Closings as drafted on the Engineering Section Sheets - Copyrighted..Daily		
EOP	Edge of Pavement captured from aerial photography - Derivative..............................1999		Biennially
EOP_CL	Edge of Pavement Center Line derived from Edge of pavement layer - Copyrighted...1991		Not planned
FH	Fire Hydrants in the WASD service area (Library not completely populated - work in progress) ....Daily		
GRID	Aliquot parts of a Public Lands Survey System down to ten acre parts. Each polygon has an attribute to enable use ....Not planned		
INDEX	Index layer for the Digital Map Library - Derivative...Not planned		
LBUILD	Large building footprint as captured from aerial photography - Derivative 1999		Biennially
LOT	Platted land derived by digitizing the Engineering Section Sheets for most of the county & digitizing the City Atlas S ....Daily		
LANDUSE	Land Use - Derivative..As needed		
PROP	Ownership boundaries as defined by legal description - Copyrighted ....Daily		
PVTSYS	Private Sewer Systems in the WASD service area (Library not completely populated - work in progress - Derivat ....Daily		
RAIL	Miami-Dade County Railroads 1999		Biennially
RES	Miami-Dade County Commissioner's resolutions derived from the Buildings' Zoning paper maps used by the BN..Daily		
SBUILD	Small building symbols as captured from aerial photography. Included single family homes and mobile homes - 1991		Not planned
SUBD	Subdivision boundaries derived by digitizing marked copies of the Engineering Section Sheets - Copyrighted. ....Daily		
SEW	Sewer lines in the WASD service area (Library not completely populated - work in progress) ....Daily		
WAT	Water lines in the WASD service area (Library not completely populated - work in progress) ....Daily		
WATER	Canals, lakes, streams, and edge of coast as defined by water line in aerial photography- Copyrighted..1999		Biennially
WSANNO	WASD Annotation layer in the WASD service area (Library not completely populated - work in progress) - Deriv..Daily		
ZONE	Miami-Dade County buildings' zoning derived from the Buildings' Zoning paper maps used by the BNZ Departme..Daily		

Digital Aerial Ortho Rectified Images (TIFF format)

Image Resolution		
1 ft per pixel	1168 images covering Miami-Dade County at +/- 2ft horizontal accuracy. ....Biennially
2 ft per pixel	323 images covering Miami-Dade County..Biennially
4 ft per pixel	93 images covering Miami-Dade County..Biennially
8 ft per pixel	30 images covering Miami-Dade County..Biennially
16 ft per pixel	11 images covering Miami-Dade County..Biennially
32 ft per pixel	4 images covering Miami-Dade County...Biennially
64 ft per pixel	1 image covering Miami-Dade County ....Biennially

Note: Available in the Alpha 8200 processors (UNIX) and in the Windows NT servers.

Miami-Dade County GIS production layers (continued)

Layer name	Description of layer	Last update	Update schedule
	Digital Ortho Images (Mr. Sid format)		
Compression ratio			
20:01	1 file covering the entire Miami-Dade County (File size = 1.4Gb)		Biennially
10:01	5 files covering the entire Miami-Dade County (File size= Less than 650 Mb each)		Biennially
	Note: This format is only available for Windows NT.		
	Spatial Engine Database (SDE)		
landuse	Land Use - Derivative		Weekly
lot	Platted land derived by digitizing the Engineering Section Sheets for most of the county & digitizing the City Atlas S		Weekly
prop_ptx	Contains fields from prop and data from the mainframe ptx application - Derivative		Weekly
subd	Subdivision boundaries derived by digitizing marked copies of the Engineering Section Sheets - Copyrighted.		Weekly
tmcase	Case number from the TMETRO application		Daily
zone	Miami-Dade County buildings' zoning derived from the Buildings' Zoning paper maps used by the BNZ Departme		Weekly

CATS database listing

NAME	ORIGIN	DATE
1990 HOUSING BY ZIP CODE	FEMA MASTER	1992
AIR FLIGHT SERVICE STATIONS	FEMA MASTER	1992
AIR NAVIGATIONAL AIDS	FEMA MASTER	1992
AIRPORTS	FEMA MASTER	1995
AIRPORTS - AIR FORCE AIRPORTS	FEMA MASTER	1992
AIRPORTS - ARMY AIR AIRPORTS	FEMA MASTER	1992
AIRPORTS - NAVAL AIR BASES	FEMA MASTER	1992
AIRPORTS - PRIVATE AIRPORTS	FEMA MASTER	1992
AIRPORTS - PUBLIC AIRPORTS	FEMA MASTER	1992
AIRPORTS (US & TERRITORIES)	FEMA MASTER	1992
AIRPORTS (WORLD)	DCW (ESRI)	1992
AIRPORTS <= 5000 FT	FEMA MASTER	1992
ALL RAIL SITES	FEMA MASTER	1992
AMTRAK	FEMA MASTER	1992
ATCHISON, TOPEKA AND SANTA FE	FEMA MASTER	1992
ATF	FEMA MASTER	1992
ATTORNEYS	FEMA MASTER	1992
BALTIMORE AND OHIO	FEMA MASTER	1992
BORDERS & SHORELINE	DCW (ESRI)	1992
BORDERS & SHORELINE (WORLD)	DCW (ESRI)	1992
BURLINGTON NORTHERN	FEMA MASTER	1992
CANADIAN PACIFIC	FEMA MASTER	1992
CHEMICAL PLANTS	FEMA MASTER	1992
CHESAPEAKE AND OHIO	FEMA MASTER	1992
CHICAGO & NORTHWESTERN	FEMA MASTER	1992
COAL MINE	FEMA MASTER	1992
COAST GUARD	FEMA MASTER	1992
COKE PLANTS	FEMA MASTER	1992
COMUNICATIONS NODES	FEMA MASTER	1992
CONRAIL	FEMA MASTER	1992
CONSTRUCTION MATERIALS	FEMA RRS	1995
COUNTRY NAME	DCW (ESRI)	1992
COUNTY LOCATIONS (centroids)	FEMA MASTER	1992
DEA	FEMA MASTER	1992
DEEP WATER LOCKS & DAMS	FEMA MASTER	1992
DEPARTMENT STORES	FEMA RRS	1995
DEPT OF JUSTICE	FEMA MASTER	1992
DRUGS	FEMA RRS DMAT	1995
EBS AM-FM-TV EMP	FEMA MASTER	1992
ELECTRIC PWR PLANTS	FEMA MASTER	1992
ELECTRICAL APPLIANCES	FEMA RRS	1995
ELECTRO MEDICAL EQUIPMENT	FEMA RRS DMAT	1995
ELECTRONIC PARTS	FEMA RRS	1995

CATS database listing (continued)

NAME	ORIGIN	DATE
ENERGY IMPORT FACILITIES	FEMA MASTER	1992
ESRI STREETMAP	FEMA MASTER	1992
FABRIC MILLS	FEMA RRS	1995
FBI	FEMA MASTER	1992
FEMA PERSONEL	FEMA MASTER	1992
FEMA REGIONAL CENTERS	FEMA MASTER	1992
FEMA REGIONS & STATES	FEMA MASTER	1992
FIRE DEPARTMENT	FEMA RRS	1995
FURNITURE STORES	FEMA RRS	1995
GRAND TRUNK (ME & NH)	FEMA MASTER	1992
HAND TOOLS	FEMA RRS	1995
HARDWARE	FEMA RRS	1995
HELICOPTER PAD	FEMA MASTER	1992
HOSPITALS	FEMA RRS DMAT	1995
HUD FIELD OFFICE	FEMA MASTER	1992
ICE MANUFACTURER	FEMA RRS	1995
ILLINOIS CENTRAL GULF	FEMA MASTER	1992
IMMIGRATION	FEMA MASTER	1992
INDUSTRIAL MACHINERY	FEMA RRS	1995
INLAND WATERWAYS LOCKS & DAMS	FEMA MASTER	1992
INTERSTATE STRUCTURES	FEMA MASTER	1992
IRRIGATION DAMS	FEMA MASTER	1992
LAKES	DCW (ESRI)	1992
LAND MASSES & OCEAN	DCW (ESRI)	1992
LAND MASSES & OCEAN (WORLD)	DCW (ESRI)	1992
LAWLEGAL	FEMA MASTER	1992
LIVESTOCK INVENTORY	FEMA MASTER	1992
LOCAL EOCS	FEMA MASTER	1992
LONG ISLAND	FEMA MASTER	1992
LOUISVILLE-NASHVILLE	FEMA MASTER	1992
LUMBER BUILDING MATERIALS	FEMA RRS	1995
LUMBER PLYWOOD	FEMA RRS	1995
MAJOR POSTAL SITES	FEMA MASTER	1992
MEDICAL HOSPITAL SUPPLY	FEMA RRS DMAT	1995
MEDICAL PERSONNEL	FEMA MASTER	1992
MILWAUKEE	FEMA MASTER	1992
MISCELLANEOUS COMPANIES	FEMA MASTER	1992
MISSOURI PACIFIC	FEMA MASTER	1992
MOTORS GENERATORS	FEMA RRS	1995
NATURAL GAS PLANTS	FEMA MASTER	1992
NATURAL GAS STORAGE	FEMA MASTER	1992
NETWORK	FEMA MASTER	1992
NIGHT TIME POPULATION	1990 Census Data (Block Group)	1992

NAME	ORIGIN	DATE
NORFOLK & WESTERN	FEMA MASTER	1992
NUCLEAR POWER PLANTS	FEMA MASTER	1992
NUCLEAR REACTORS	HPAC Reactor Data File	1994
OIL REFINERIES	FEMA MASTER	1992
OPTHALMIC GOODS	FEMA RRS DMAT	1995
PBS AM-FM,TV ALL	FEMA MASTER	1992
PHARMACEUTICAL PREPS	FEMA RRS DMAT	1995
PITTSBURGH-LAKE ERIE	FEMA MASTER	1992
PLASTIC BOTTLES	FEMA RRS	1995
POLICE DEPARTMENTS	FEMA RRS	1995
POPULATED PLACES	DCW (ESRI)	1992
PORTS - EAST COAST	FEMA MASTER	1992
PORTS - INLAND WATERWAYS & TERMI	FEMA MASTER	1992
PORTS - WEST COAST	FEMA MASTER	1992
POPULATION (World, GRID)	LANDSCAN	1998
POPULATION (USA, TRACT POLYGONS)	1990 Census Data (Tract)	1997
POPULATION (USA, BLOCK GROUP POLYGONS by	1990 Census Block Group Data; 49 States	1990
PRIMARY FACTORIES	FEMA MASTER	1992
PRISONS	FEMA MASTER	1992
PWS	FEMA MASTER	1992
RADIO TELEPHONE EQUIPMENT	FEMA RRS	1995
RADIO TV COMMUNICATIONS	FEMA RRS	1995
RAILROAD BRIDGES	FEMA MASTER	1992
RAILROAD COMPUTERS	FEMA MASTER	1992
RAILROAD CONTROLS	FEMA MASTER	1992
RAILROAD INTERFACES	FEMA MASTER	1992
RAILROAD INTERLOCKINGS	FEMA MASTER	1992
RAILROAD MISCELLANEOUS SITES	FEMA MASTER	1992
RAILROAD REPAIR SHOPS	FEMA MASTER	1992
RAILROAD TUNNELS	FEMA MASTER	1992
RAILROAD YARDS	FEMA MASTER	1992
RAILROADS	DCW (ESRI)	1992
RAILROADS (WORLD	DCW (ESRI)	1992
REACTORS	FEMA MASTER	1992
RICHMOND-FREDRICKSBURG-POTOMAC	FEMA MASTER	1992
RIVERS	DCW (ESRI)	1992
RIVERS (WORLD)	DCW (ESRI)	1992
ROADS	DCW (ESRI)	1992
ROADS (WORLD)	DCW (ESRI)	1992
ROCK ISLAND	FEMA MASTER	1992
RRS AIRPORTS	NTAB	1995
RRS MOBILITY SITES	FEMA MASTER	1992
RRS RUNWAYS	FEMA MASTER	1992

CATS database listing (continued)

NAME	ORIGIN	DATE
SANITARY PAPER PRODUCTS	FEMA RRS	1995
SEABOARD COAST LINE	FEMA MASTER	1992
SEWAGE TREATMENT PLANTS	FEMA MASTER	1992
SHADED RELIEF	Chaulk Butte, Inc.	
SHADED RELIEF (WORLD)	Chaulk Butte, Inc.	
SOAP DETERGENTS	FEMA RRS	1995
SOFTDRINKS	FEMA RRS	1995
SOUTHERN PACIFIC	FEMA MASTER	1992
SOUTHERN RAILWAY COMPANY	FEMA MASTER	1992
SPORTING GOODS	FEMA RRS	1995
STATE EOCS (PRI & ALT)	FEMA MASTER	1992
STOCKPIL	FEMA MASTER	1992
STRATEGIC RESERVE	FEMA MASTER	1992
SUPERFUND SITES	FEMA MASTER	1992
SURGICAL APPLIANCES	FEMA RRS DMAT	1995
SURGICAL MEDICAL	FEMA RRS DMAT	1995
TANK FARMS	FEMA MASTER	1992
UNION PACIFIC	FEMA MASTER	1992
Urban Areas	DCW (ESRI)	1992
Urban Areas	DCW (ESRI)	1992
US CUSTOMS	FEMA MASTER	1992
US MARSHALS	FEMA MASTER	1992
US POSTAL VEHICLE MAINTENANCE	FEMA MASTER	1992
US SECRET SERVICE	FEMA MASTER	1992
VA CEMETARY SITES	FEMA MASTER	1992
VA HOSPITAL STAFF	FEMA MASTER	1992
VA HOSPITALS	FEMA RRS DMAT	1995
WATER SUPPLY	FEMA RRS	1995
WATER SUPPLY DAMS	FEMA MASTER	1992
WEATHER STATIONS	FEMA MASTER	1992
WHOLESALE GROCERY	FEMA RRS	1995
XRAY APPARATUS	FEMA RRS DMAT	1995

appendix C **Five-year general strategies matrix of the FIRESCOPE Geographic Information Systems and Spatial Information Technology Group (GISSIT)**

FIRESCOPE Geographic Information Systems (GIS) Specialist Group

General Strategies

Executive Summary

The use of GIS for the emergency management community is at a turning point. The FIRESCOPE Geographic Information Systems (GIS) Specialist Group (FIRESCOPE-GIS) mission statement states we will champion the role of geospatial solutions in emergency management and make recommendations to the FIRESCOPE Board on data requirements, processes for sharing data, tools required and standard operating procedures. The following General Strategies are a matrix of the goals, objectives and tasks outlined in order to direct our efforts and measure the success of our mission.

General Strategies

1. Set standards.
2. Meet user's needs.
3. Educate and train the users and management.
4. Improve data development and accessibility.
5. Increase organizational effectiveness.

General Strategy: Set Standards

Summary: In supporting the emergency management community, GIS specialists will be expected to provide the best available information using appropriate technologies, often within very short time frames. To meet these expectations, the FIRESCOPE Geographic Information Systems (GIS) Specialist Group has identified the following five-year-goals for standards. These standards will facilitate the development of seamless statewide data layers, promote consistency in the information provided to incident command teams, and ensure the efficient generation of standard products on scene.

Goals for the Next Five Years:
1. Develop standards for data development and sharing.
2. Develop standards for metadata.
3. Develop standard products and symbology.
4. Develop standard operating procedures and tools.
5. Develop guidelines for appropriate equipment configuration.

1998	1999	2000	2001	2002	GOAL
Develop standards for fire data layers & associated attributes	Update standards for fire data layers & associated attributes	→	→	→	1
	Develop standards for flood, EQ & nuclear data layers & associated attributes	Update standards for flood, EQ & nuclear data layers & associated attributes	→	→	
		Develop standards for other event data layers & associated attributes	Update standards for other event data layers & associated attributes	→	
			Develop standards for all event data layers & associated attributes	Update standards for all event data layers & associated attributes	
Temporarily standardize on a few projections	Verify ESRI has developed a "project on the fly" tool/extension				
Develop naming conventions for incident data layers	Incorporate users' suggestions into naming conventions	→	→	→	
Research existing data sharing procedures & import methods	→	→	→	→	
• **Standards for fire & aviation data documented** • **Teale projection for Quads & Lat/Long projection for base data accepted** • **Procedures & methods for sharing datasets**	• **Standards for flood, nuclear & EQ data documented** • **Data sharing are standardized across agencies** • **Projections are no longer an issue**	• **Standards for other event data documented** • **Data sharing procedures are updated & standardized across agencies**	• **Standards for all event data documented**		**Success Factors**
Develop metadata standards	Incorporate users' suggestions into metadata standards	→	→	→	2
• **Metadata standards are documented & accepted**	• **Updated metadata standards are documented & accepted**	→	→	→	**Success Factors**

3

Phase 1	Phase 2	Phase 3	Phase 4	Phase 5
Develop standard directory structure	Incorporate users' suggestions into standard directory structure			
Develop standard symbology for fire & aviation	Develop standard symbology for flood, nuclear & EQ	Develop standard symbology for other events	Develop standard symbology for all events	Update standard symbology for all events
Develop a "cookbook" of standard GIS products for fire management	Incorporate users' suggestions for improvement, disseminate new standard product samples & guidelines	Incorporate users' suggestions for improvement, disseminate new standard product samples & guidelines	Incorporate users' suggestions for improvement, disseminate new standard product samples & guidelines	
Develop standard analyses & reports for fire management	Incorporate users' suggestions for improvement of standard analyses & reports for fire management	Incorporate users' suggestions for improvement standard analyses & reports		
	Develop a "cookbook" of standard GIS products for flood, nuclear & EQ	Develop a "cookbook" of standard GIS products for other events	Develop a "cookbook" of standard GIS products for all events	
	Develop standard analyses & reports for flood, nuclear & EQ	Develop standard analyses & reports for other events		
			Incorporate users' suggestions for improvement standard analyses & reports for other events	Incorporate users' suggestions for improvement, disseminate new standard product samples & guidelines
			Develop standard analyses & reports for all events	Incorporate users' suggestions for improvement standard analyses & reports for other events

Success Factors

Phase 1
- Identified products are used to support fire incidents
- Standard directory structure is adopted
- Fire & aviation hazards symbology is standard in ArcView
- Fire & aviation symbology is adopted by FIRESCOPE
- Fire management "Cookbook" is distributed

Phase 2
- Standard products & analyses are routine & part of the fire incident mapping
- Updated directory structure is adopted
- Flood, nuclear & EQ symbology is standard in ArcView
- Flood, nuclear & EQ symbology is adopted by FIRESCOPE
- Flood, nuclear & EQ "Cookbook" is distributed

Phase 3
- Standard products & analyses are routine & part of the fire, flood, nuclear & EQ incident mapping
- Other emergency management symbology is standard in ArcView
- Other emergency management symbology is adopted by FIRESCOPE
- Other incident "Cookbook" is distributed

Phase 4
- Standard products & analyses are routine & part of all emergency management mapping
- All emergency management symbology is represented in an "Emergency Management Cookbook" & adopted by FIRESCOPE

Phase 5
- Updated products & analysis with standard symbology are adopted by the emergency management community

			4		**5**	
Develop a set of application tools to produce fire "cookbook" maps, reports & analysis	→	→	→		→	
	Develop a set of application tools to produce flood, nuclear & EQ "cookbook" maps, reports & analysis	Develop a set of application tools to produce other incident "cookbook" maps, reports & analysis	Develop a set of application tools to produce all incident "cookbook" maps, reports & analysis		→	
	Update application tools to keep pace with users' suggestions for improvement	Update application tools to keep pace with users' suggestions for improvement	Update application tools to keep pace with users' suggestions for improvement		Update application tools to keep pace with users' suggestions for improvement	
Identify procedures for capturing data for a fire incident	→	→	→		→	
	Identify additional procedures for & update data captures procedures for a fire incident		Identify additional procedures for & update data captures procedures for other incidents		Identify additional procedures for & update data captures procedures for all emergency management	
	Identify additional procedures for capturing data at a flood, nuclear & EQ incident	Identify additional procedures for capturing data at other incidents	Identify additional procedures for capturing for all emergency incidents		→	
• Application tools are developed & used on incidents **• Data capture procedures are written up**	**• Application tools is expanded & used on fire, flood, nuclear & EQ incidents** **• Additional data capture procedures are incorporated into application tool**	**• Application tools is expanded & used on all emergency management incidents**	→	**• Application tools is updated & successfully used on all emergency management incidents**		**Success Factors**
Identify appropriate equipment configuration	→	→	→		→	
• Guidelines are written up & shared with users	→	→	→	**Success Factors**	→	**Success Factors**

General Strategy: Meet User Needs

Summary: In order to be successful, an organization must be responsive to its constituency and look forward to the future. In the case of the FIRESCOPE Geographic Information Systems (GIS) Specialist Group, success will be measured not only by those individuals who use and develop the tools and techniques for incident mapping support, but by the people requesting spatial information and the recipients of those analytic and cartographic products. Therefore, the term, "user" refers to all those individuals and organizations, which are the direct beneficiaries of the mapping support effort and meeting their needs refers to a dynamic process of anticipation, review and action.

Goals for the Next Five Years:

1. Develop a mechanism for providing standard products and services to the users.
2. Develop a mechanism for inviting and collecting feedback, addressing criticism and user's suggestions for improving the services rendered.
3. Periodically evaluate all aspects of incident mapping support and services in order to correctly modify current practices and better anticipate future needs.

1998	1999	2000	2001	2002	GOAL
Create task book for fire response GIS	Create task book for flood, nuclear & EQ response GIS	Create task book for other incident response GIS	Create task book for all incident response GIS	Update task books as necessary	**1**
	Publish Web page &/or newsletter	Improve Web page to offer links to data	→	→	
	Establish the minimum needed equipment/data caches	Establish the appropriate needed equipment/data caches	Maintain the appropriate needed equipment/data caches		
• Task book is created	• **Task book is updated** • **Web page &/or Newsletter published** • **Minimum equipment/data caches established**	• **Task book is updated** • **Web page improved** • **The appropriate amount of equipment/data caches are established**	• **Task book is updated** • **Web page improved** • **Equipment/data caches are maintained**	→	**Success Factors**
stablish a user list and profile	Update the user list and profile	→	→	→	**2**
Create user evaluation checklist to document service process	Review user evaluation check list data & make recommendations	→	→	→	
Develop, distribute & review a questionnaire	Improve questionnaire, distribute & review	→	→	→	
Present products & poster session at conferences	Presentations at Team Meetings	Expand presentations to other ICS groups & classes	Expand presentations to organizations worldwide	Host user's group meeting	
Support the "Info. Tech. In Fire Mgt." Conference	Establish contacts with emergency management groups & plan for user's group meeting in 2000	Host user's group meeting (linked with "Info. Tech. In Fire (Emergency) Mgt." Conference	Host user's group meeting	Host user's group meeting	
• **User list and profile is completed** • **User checklist is distributed** • **Report on results of questionnaire to the Standards group** • **Products displayed at conferences** • **Conference supported**	• **User list and profile is updated** • **Updated Checklist is distributed** • **Report on results of updated questionnaire to the Standards group** • **Team meeting presentations are given** • **Contacts are established & meeting in place**	• **User list and profile is updated** • **Updated Checklist is distributed** • **Report on results of updated questionnaire to the Standards group** • **Presentations to other ICS groups & classes are done** • **User's group meeting held in conjunction with the conference.**	• **Locate & furnish products to groups from other countries** • **Host user's group meeting**	• **Host user's group meeting**	**Success Factors**
	Evaluate of new products & methods	Evaluate & implement new products & methods	→	→	**3**
	• **Report on new products & methods to the Standards group**	→	→	→	**Success Factors**

General Strategy: Train and Educate the Users and Managers

Summary: The future success of GIS use for Emergency Management depends on our resourceful preparedness and planning. This can be achieved by recruiting skilled GIS candidates, preparing them through training and mentoring, and providing them with solid leadership. Presenting our challenges and success with the GIS community allows us to reach potential candidates, learn of new tools that would benefit Response GIS, and potentially solve any shortcomings we might encounter. By reaching out to the emergency management community, we have the opportunity to educate them on how they can use GIS as an effective management tool.

Goals for the Next Five Years:

1. Recruit qualified GIS personnel for incident response and other emergency management responsibilities.
2. Provide leadership and training of emergency management GIS personnel.
3. Educate the emergency management community in the capabilities of GIS.

GOAL	1998	1999	2000	2001	2002
1	• Recruit GIS staff for fire emergency management GIS	Recruit GIS staff for fire, flood, nuclear & EQ emergency management GIS	Recruit GIS staff for fire, flood, nuclear, EQ & other emergency management GIS	Recruit GIS staff for all emergency management GIS	↑
Success Factors	• **Adequate GIS staffing to support all Type 1 Management Teams**	**Adequate GIS staffing to support all Type 1 & 2 Management Teams**	**Adequate GIS staffing to support all Type 1 & 2 Management Teams & USAR Teams**	↑	↑
2	Develop training regimen	Review & revise training regimens & adjust as needed	↑	↑	↑
	Develop training manual for fire mapping & analysis	Review & revise training manual to include all incident mapping & analysis	↑	↑	↑
	Mentor recruits in the field	↑	↑	↑	↑
		Develop unique mock fire scenarios for practice drills before every fire season	↑	↑	↑
		Develop exercise manual	Review & revise exercise manual	↑	↑
		Provide fire exercises for trained GIS staff	Provide flood exercises for trained GIS staff	Provide EQ exercises for trained GIS staff	Provide other exercises for trained GIS staff
		Create a web site for GIS staff to use for problem-solving	Maintain a web site to use for problem-solving	↑	↑
		Provide "train-the-trainers" workshop for GIS managers & training staff			
	Train new recruits in fire mapping & analysis procedures	Train new recruits in fire, flood, nuclear & EQ mapping & analysis procedures	Train new recruits in fire, flood, nuclear, EQ & other mapping & analysis procedures	Train new recruits all mapping & analysis procedures	↑
Success Factors	• **Training manual is distributed** • **FIRESCOPE GIS Incident Fire Mapping Workshop is held in the North & the South**	• **Fire exercise manual is distributed** • **Web site is established** • **"Train-the-trainers" workshop is held** • **FIRESCOPE GIS Incident Fire Mapping Workshop is held in the North & the South**	• **Flood exercise manual is distributed** • **Wider informational & skilled resources for problem solving** • **FIRESCOPE GIS Incident Fire Mapping Workshop is held in the North & the South**	• **EQ exercise manual is distributed** • **FIRESCOPE GIS Incident Fire Mapping Workshop is held in the North & the South**	• **General exercise manual is distributed** • **FIRESCOPE GIS Incident Fire Mapping Workshop is held in the North & the South**

3

	Develop Sit Stat GIS training manual for fires	Develop Sit Stat GIS training manual for flood, nuclear & EQ incidents	Develop Sit Stat GIS training manual for other incidents	Develop Sit Stat GIS training manual for all incidents
Make presentations to Sit Stat Classes	Make presentations to Sit Stat Classes & Type 1 & 2 Management Teams	→	→	→
Write articles in GIS, emergency management, fire, & government publications	→	→	→	→
Develop a fire season packet to give to Sit Stat	→	→	→	→
	Develop a fire season annual update packet to give to GIS personnel			
• GIS used as an effective management tool • Articles are published • Fire season packet distributed to Sit Stat • Presentations to Sit Stat Classes are done	• Fire season annual update packet distributed to GIS personnel • Presentations to Sit Stat Classes & Type 1 & 2 Management Teams • Sit Stat GIS training manual for fires is distributed	• Sit Stat GIS training manual for flood, nuclear & EQ are distributed • GIS module for Sit Stat class is approved by FIRESCOPE	• Sit Stat GIS training manual for other incidents is distributed	• Sit Stat GIS training manual for all incidents are distributed

Success Factors

General Strategy: Data Development and Access

Summary: Developing and maintaining a complete, consistent, and accurate state-wide spatial data layer library will be critical to establishing GIS as an integral tool for emergency management. Based on a preliminary analysis, for the top 50 priority data layers, 21 are completed, 23 are only partially completed in terms of geographic extent and/or data content, and 6 are virtually non-existent. In addition to data availability, there are numerous problems that must be addressed:

- Emergency management data needs are not clearly defined;
- Existing data layers are often not consistent across jurisdictional boundaries;
- Existing data layers often require significant enhancements in order to be useful for emergency management;
- There are barriers that limit sharing of existing data;
- Some existing data are becoming outdated due to lack of a viable maintenance mechanism; and
- There is no system that allows users to quickly locate and access available data.

Goals for the Next Five Years:

1. Analyze emergency management data needs, and then inventory and evaluate existing data sources.
2. Address known critical data needs by implementing data development projects and data maintenance mechanisms.
3. Identify and remove barriers that limit data sharing.
4. Implement a system that allows all FIRESCOPE participants to locate and access priority data.

1998	1999	2000	2001	2002	GOAL
Identify data needs	Monitor/update needs	→	→	→	1
Inventory existing data sources, evaluate based on GISSIT standards	Monitor data sources	→	→	→	
Develop prioritization data/methods (fire hazard, flood risk, etc)	Monitor prioritization data & methods, adjust priority areas as needed	→	→	→	
• Data list: needs, availability, status	• Revised data list	→	→	→	Success Factors

Data Layer	Phase 1	Phase 2	Phase 3	Success Factors
Framework data[1]: inventory data development & enhancement efforts	Support existing/create new cooperative data development & enhancement efforts	→	Complete framework data development efforts	
Roads: evaluate sources, develop strategy for enhancing existing roads data	Implement roads strategy	→	Evaluate 911 mandate performance	
Structures: pilot test data capture methods	Identify priority areas. Develop data capture strategy	Implement strategy	→	
"Flood elevation" data: evaluate mapping methods	Identify priority areas. Develop data capture strategy	Implement strategy	→	
Fuels: create statewide fuels from existing vegetation data. Pilot test fuels mapping methods. Explore partnerships.	Develop strategy to capture & maintain fuels	Implement strategy	→	
Site summary data[2]: develop capture & maintenance strategy	Implement strategy	→	→	
Other fire data: develop capture and maintenance strategy	Site specific data[3]: Develop capture & maintenance strategy	Implement strategy	→	
Other emergency management data: scope non-fire emergency mgmt data	Develop capture & maintenance strategy	Implement strategy	→	
Test Computer Aided Dispatch (CAD) data maintenance capabilities. Assess requirements/methods for field validation	Expand CAD testing for maintaining dispatch related data. Pilot test field data validation. Develop data maintenance strategy.	Implement strategy	Field validation, CAD maintenance fully operational statewide	
• Proposed standards • Minimum data needs to support 1998 fires • Proposed strategies	**• Pilot CAD Test Results Report • Statewide prelim fuels data • Proposed strategies • Framework projects initiated**	**• Statewide prelim roads • Strategies implemented**	**• Statewide framework data • Improved ability to meet data needs for '01 fires • Improved ability to meet non-fire data needs • Meet 911 mandate**	**• Completion of 90% geographic coverage of 90% of the priority data layers statewide • 90% completion for critical areas for flood elevation, site specific, structures • Successful maintenance strategies in place**

2

[1] Data layers as defined by the Federal Geographic Data Committee: geodetic control, ortho imagery, elevation, transportation, hydrography, governmental units and cadastral information. These data layers will involve interests beyond FIRESCOPE.
[2] Location and general information (contact name, phone number, capacity, facilities) on specific important sites such as potential base camps, hospitals, campgrounds, etc.
[3] Location and detailed information (hazmat, evacuation plan, floor plan) on specific important sites

					Success Factors
Identify data sharing barriers & develop strategy for there removal	Implement strategy	→	→	→	**3**
	Barriers to data sharing lessened	**Barriers not a major issue**			**Success Factors**
Develop short term access strategy for '98 fire season	Implement data access system	→	→	→	**4**
Scope potential data access systems for longer term, develop strategy					
Identify "linked" systems with priority data (e.g. lightning, weather)	Automate access to linked systems	Automate linkage to new systems	→	→	
• **Adequate support for 1998 fires** • **Data access strategy**	• **Improved support for 1999 fires** • **Ability to access linked systems**	• **Data access system has the capacity to meet needs of FIRESCOPE participants for all types of emergency management situations**	• **FIRESCOPE participants utilize data access system**	• **All developed data layers available through the data access systems**	**Success Factors**

General Strategy: Increasing Organizational Effectiveness

Summary: This set of goals is focused on improving how organizations involved in emergency management GIS work together, and provide support and funding for both programs and individuals. Barriers restricting coordination between organizations must be identified and remedied through a combination of internal change and the establishment of partnerships. Opportunities for organizations to better support and fund GIS programs involved in mutual aid need to be identified and implemented. Individuals participating in emergency management GIS must have a career path that rewards their effort in order to insure an adequate cadre of qualified, motivated individuals.

Goals for the Next Five Years:
1. Develop a budget strategy.
2. Fully integrate emergency management GIS into ICS.
3. Reduce interagency barriers and promote partnerships.
4. Publicize and reward success.

1998	1999	2000	2001	2002	GOAL
Develop a budget strategy	Review & revise budget strategy	→	→	→	**1**
Research grant & alternative funding opportunities	Research grant & alternative funding opportunities & apply for appropriate grants	→	→	→	
Budget strategy report Report on funding opportunities	• **Establish budget strategy** • **Do grant applications** • **Research BCP's & legislation**	• **Continue to review & revise budget strategy** • **Continue to apply for appropriate grants** • **Continue to review & revise BCP's & legislation**	→	→	**Success Factors**
Develop ICS positions & prepare GIS entry for Mobilization Guide	Prepare GIS entry for Field Operations Guide for ICS commanders/ dispatch centers	Review & revise GIS entry in FOG manual	→	→	**2**
Prepare GIS call up protocols for dispatch centers	Review & revise GIS protocols	→	→	→	
• ICS positions & protocols developed • Addendum re: GIS is distributed for the 1998 Mobilization Guide	• **GIS entry for FOG manual developed** • **Revised ICS positions & protocols approved by FIRESCOPE** • **GIS is a permanent entry in the 1999 Mobilization Guide**	• **Revised ICS FOG manual approved by FIRESCOPE**	→		**Success Factors**

3

Phase 1	Phase 2	Phase 3	Success Factors
Obtain necessary agency support for GISSIT participants	Explore proposal for co-locating for multi-agency GIS	Report on proposal for co-locating multi-agency GIS	Review & revise the proposal as needed
Examine inter-agency barriers	Develop agreements to reduce/eliminate interagency barriers	Implement recommendations for reducing interagency barriers	
Identify pilot projects to establish partnerships	Examine the GISSIT Group & identify needed participants	Types of needed GISSIT participant are identified	
Build partnerships with other agencies to provide GIS staff & resources for fires	Build partnerships with other agencies to provide GIS staff & resources for fires, nuclear & EQ	Establish projects & create partnerships	Build partnerships with other agencies to provide GIS staff & resources for fires, floods, nuclear, EQ & other incidents	**Build partnerships with other agencies to provide GIS staff & resources for all incidents**
		New partnerships are created to provide GIS staff & resources for fire	• **New partnerships are created to provide GIS staff & resources for fires, floods, nuclear, EQ & other incidents**	• **New partnerships are created to provide GIS staff & resources for all incidents**

4

Phase 1	Phase 2	Phase 3	Success Factors
Create & give effective presentations	Review, redevelop & give effective presentations		
Establish webpage(s)	Expand website		
Publish articles			
Research awards offered by public & private sector	Apply for awards	Promote awards among emergency management GIS personnel & management	Promote establishment of new awards & advertise current winners
Start career path development analysis	Identify opportunities to enhance career path based on emergency management GIS participation	Implement strategies to enhance career path opportunities	Insure that qualified candidates are aware of the benefits of emergency management GIS participation
• **Distribute presentation module**	• **Distribute updated presentation module**	• **Greater career path opportunities**	
• **Create webpage(s)**	• **Review & revise website**		
• **Publish articles**	• **Publish articles**		
• **Report on Awards**	• **Find awards applications**		
	• **Report on career path opportunities**		

FIRESCOPE Geographic Information Systems (GIS) Specialist Group

Appendix

Vision Statement for the Year 2003

Geospatial information is recognized as an integral part of emergency planning, preparedness, response and recovery. All jurisdictions within California at all levels have developed, openly share, and maintain priority data in a seamless information system. Standardized tools and procedures are used in all phases of emergency management.

Mission Statement

Champion the role of geospatial solutions in emergency management.
Make recommendations to the FIRESCOPE Board on:
- Data requirements
- Processes for sharing data
- Tools required
- Standard operating procedures

FIRESCOPE Geographic Information Systems (GIS) Specialist Group

Appendix

FIRESCOPE-GIS Executive Staff

Chair: Jim Kniss, Manager, Mapping Services, Ventura County Fire Department
Vice Chair: Lee Weber, Captain, Los Angeles City Fire Department
Logistics: Alfie Blanch, GIS Research Analyst, California Office of Emergency Services

FIRESCOPE-GIS Primary Members

Dorothy Albright, Fire GIS Program Manager, US Forest Service
Joe Appleton, Fire Engineer, Mapping Technician, Kern County Fire Department
John Craney, Division Chief, Mapping and Staffing, California Department of Forestry
Dave Eden, Fire Engineer, Mapping Technician, Santa Barbara County Fire Department
Chris English, GIS Coordinator, Bureau of Indian Affairs
John Fisher, Firefighter, San Diego Fire Department
David Kehrlein, GIS Research Manager, California Office of Emergency Services
Jim Kniss, Manager, Mapping Services, Ventura County Fire Department
Christine Lampe, GIS Mapping, Orange County Fire Authority
Karen Folger, Fire GIS Specialist, Sequoia & Kings Canyon National Parks
Ros Schenck, Senior Survey Mapping Technician, Los Angeles County Fire Department
Victoria Smith, Fire GIS Specialist, Bureau of Land Management
Lee Weber, Captain, Los Angeles City Fire Department

Advanced Spatial Analysis: The CASA Book of GIS *1-58948-073-2*
ArcGIS and the Digital City: A Hands-on Approach for Local Government *1-58948-074-0*
ArcView GIS Means Business *1-879102-51-X*
A System for Survival: GIS and Sustainable Development *1-58948-052-X*
Beyond Maps: GIS and Decision Making in Local Government *1-879102-79-X*
Cartographica Extraordinaire: The Historical Map Transformed *1-58948-044-9*
Cartographies of Disease: Maps, Mapping, and Medicine *1-58948-120-8*
Children Map the World: Selections from the Barbara Petchenik Children's World Map Competition *1-58948-125-9*
Community Geography: GIS in Action *1-58948-023-6*
Community Geography: GIS in Action Teacher's Guide *1-58948-051-1*
Confronting Catastrophe: A GIS Handbook *1-58948-040-6*
Connecting Our World: GIS Web Services *1-58948-075-9*
Conservation Geography: Case Studies in GIS, Computer Mapping, and Activism *1-58948-024-4*
Designing Better Maps: A Guide for GIS Users *1-58948-089-9*
Designing Geodatabases: Case Studies in GIS Data Modeling *1-58948-021-X*
Disaster Response: GIS for Public Safety *1-879102-88-9*
Enterprise GIS for Energy Companies *1-879102-48-X*
Extending ArcView GIS (version 3.x edition) *1-879102-05-6*
Fun with GPS *1-58948-087-2*
Getting to Know ArcGIS Desktop, Second Edition Updated for ArcGIS 9 *1-58948-083-X*
Getting to Know ArcObjects: Programming ArcGIS with VBA *1-58948-018-X*
Getting to Know ArcView GIS (version 3.x edition) *1-879102-46-3*
GIS and Land Records: The ArcGIS Parcel Data Model *1-58948-077-5*
GIS for Everyone, Third Edition *1-58948-056-2*
GIS for Health Organizations *1-879102-65-X*
GIS for Landscape Architects *1-879102-64-1*
GIS for the Urban Environment *1-58948-082-1*
GIS for Water Management in Europe *1-58948-076-7*
GIS in Public Policy: Using Geographic Information for More Effective Government *1-879102-66-8*
GIS in Schools *1-879102-85-4*
GIS in Telecommunications *1-879102-86-2*
GIS Means Business, Volume II *1-58948-033-3*
GIS Tutorial: Workbook for ArcView 9 *1-58948-127-5*
GIS, Spatial Analysis, and Modeling *1-58948-130-5*
GIS Worlds: Creating Spatial Data Infrastructures *1-58948-122-4*
Hydrologic and Hydraulic Modeling Support with Geographic Information Systems *1-879102-80-3*
Integrating GIS and the Global Positioning System *1-879102-81-1*
Making Community Connections: The Orton Family Foundation Community Mapping Program *1-58948-071-6*
Managing Natural Resources with GIS *1-879102-53-6*
Mapping Census 2000: The Geography of U.S. Diversity *1-58948-014-7*
Mapping Our World: GIS Lessons for Educators, ArcView GIS 3.x Edition *1-58948-022-8*
Mapping Our World: GIS Lessons for Educators, ArcGIS Desktop Edition *1-58948-121-6*
Mapping the Future of America's National Parks: Stewardship through Geographic Information Systems *1-58948-080-5*
Mapping the News: Case Studies in GIS and Journalism *1-58948-072-4*
Marine Geography: GIS for the Oceans and Seas *1-58948-045-7*
Measuring Up: The Business Case for GIS *1-58948-088-0*
Modeling Our World: The ESRI Guide to Geodatabase Design *1-879102-62-5*
Past Time, Past Place: GIS for History *1-58948-032-5*

Continued on next page

Books from ESRI Press (continued)

Planning Support Systems: Integrating Geographic Information Systems, Models, and Visualization Tools *1-58948-011-2*
Remote Sensing for GIS Managers *1-58948-081-3*
Salton Sea Atlas *1-58948-043-0*
Spatial Portals: Gateways to Geographic Information *1-58948-131-3*
The ESRI Guide to GIS Analysis, Volume 1: Geographic Patterns and Relationships *1-879102-06-4*
The ESRI Guide to GIS Analysis, Volume 2: Spatial Measurements and Statistics *1-58948-116-X*
Think Globally, Act Regionally: GIS and Data Visualization for Social Science and Public Policy Research *1-58948-124-0*
Thinking About GIS: Geographic Information System Planning for Managers (paperback edition) *1-58948-119-4*
Transportation GIS *1-879102-47-1*
Undersea with GIS *1-58948-016-3*
Unlocking the Census with GIS *1-58948-113-5*
Zeroing In: Geographic Information Systems at Work in the Community *1-879102-50-1*

Forthcoming titles from ESRI Press

A to Z GIS: An Illustrated Dictionary of Geographic Information Systems *1-58948-140-2*
Charting the Unknown: How Computer Mapping at Harvard Became GIS *1-58948-118-6*
GIS for Environmental Management *1-58948-142-9*
GIS for the Urban Environment *1-58948-082-1*
Mapping Global Cities: GIS Methods in Urban Analysis *1-58948-143-7*

Ask for ESRI Press titles at your local bookstore or order by calling 1-800-447-9778. You can also shop online at www.esri.com/esripress. Outside the United States, contact your local ESRI distributor.

ESRI Press titles are distributed to the trade by the following:

In North America, South America, Asia, and Australia:
Independent Publishers Group (IPG)
Telephone (United States): 1-800-888-4741 • Telephone (international): 312-337-0747
E-mail: frontdesk@ipgbook.com

In the United Kingdom, Europe, and the Middle East:
Transatlantic Publishers Group Ltd.
Telephone: 44 20 8849 8013 • Fax: 44 20 8849 5556 • E-mail: transatlantic.publishers@regusnet.com

ESRI Press • 380 New York Street • Redlands, California 92373-8100 • www.esri.com/esripress

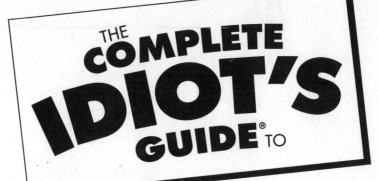

Success as a Real Estate Agent

Second Edition

by Marilyn Sullivan

ALPHA

A member of Penguin Group (USA) Inc.

ALPHA BOOKS

Published by the Penguin Group

Penguin Group (USA) Inc., 375 Hudson Street, New York, New York 10014, U.S.A.

Penguin Group (Canada), 10 Alcorn Avenue, Toronto, Ontario, Canada M4V 3B2 (a division of Pearson Penguin Canada Inc.)

Penguin Books Ltd, 80 Strand, London WC2R 0RL, England

Penguin Ireland, 25 St Stephen's Green, Dublin 2, Ireland (a division of Penguin Books Ltd)

Penguin Group (Australia), 250 Camberwell Road, Camberwell, Victoria 3124, Australia (a division of Pearson Australia Group Pty Ltd)

Penguin Books India Pvt Ltd, 11 Community Centre, Panchsheel Park, New Delhi—110 017, India

Penguin Group (NZ), cnr Airborne and Rosedale Roads, Albany, Auckland 1310, New Zealand (a division of Pearson New Zealand Ltd)

Penguin Books (South Africa) (Pty) Ltd, 24 Sturdee Avenue, Rosebank, Johannesburg 2196, South Africa

Penguin Books Ltd, Registered Offices: 80 Strand, London WC2R 0RL, England

Most Alpha books are available at special quantity discounts for bulk purchases for sales promotions, premiums, fund-raising, or educational use. Special books, or book excerpts, can also be created to fit specific needs.

For details, write: Special Markets, Alpha Books, 375 Hudson Street, New York, NY 10014.

Publisher: *Marie Butler-Knight*
Editorial Director/Acquiring Editor: *Mike Sanders*
Managing Editor: *Billy Fields*
Development Editor: *Ginny Bess Munroe*
Production Editor: *Megan Douglass*
Copy Editor: *Ross Patty*

Cartoonist: *Chris Eliopoulos*
Cover Designer: *Bill Thomas*
Book Designers: *Trina Wurst/Kurt Owens*
Indexer: *Heather McNeill*
Layout: *Chad Dressler*
Proofreader: *Aaron Black*

Part 4:   **Putting It All Together**   **213**

14   A Master of Organization   215
Take the technology and business plan you have built and put
them together. You will be able to work from anywhere and
everywhere, at your home, in your vehicle, or in the middle
of the woods. Transaction management software helps you cal-
endar your sales more efficiently.

15   Building a Referral Stream System   229
Through populating your contact database with information
about everyone you meet, this input-output system delivers
marketing products according to preset categories, resulting in
a continuous stream of referrals.

16   The New Ideal   245
The New Ideal shows you how to render quality professional
services to your clients while you satisfy your fiduciary obliga-
tion to them. It discards outdated high-pressure sales models.
We also extend The New Ideal to the way we treat fellow
agents.

17   A Winning Listing Presentation   257
Qualify the seller prospect. What makes your presentation a
winner so that the seller chooses you as his agent? It's not a
Hollywood show; it's a careful, deliberate process of preparing
a listing package and presenting it. Now you can set up a web
site just for their listing and use it to get the listing.

Part 5:   **The Parts of a Transaction**   **269**

18   Representing the Seller   271
Staging the property for sale, listing it on the MLS, and han-
dling the broker's open house and the open house are your first
steps in representing the seller. Responding to offers and han-
dling multiple offers lead your listing to its closing. Dealing
with the stale listing is covered, too.

19   Representing the Buyer   285
Representing the buyer begins with qualification of your
prospect and covers making an offer, dealing with title issues,
handing the loan and physical inspection contingencies, and
finally, acting as a dual agent.

20 Using the Transaction Documents 303

Review the important terms of the agency disclosures, listing agreement, and purchase agreement. Understand those confounding physical inspection and home replacement and sale contingencies using a transaction management program.

Part 6: **Becoming a Top Dog** **315**

21 Cutting-Edge Top Dogs 317

Top Dogs build lead generating websites rich with promotional content and valuable tools, and set their business up for rapid response to e-mail inquiries. They receive specialized training and obtain professional designations.

22 Giving and Getting Support 329

Top Dogs obtain administrative and technological support to catapult their businesses to the next level. They enhance their personal and professional power with humanitarian values and spiritual competence.

23 Staging Your Listings 347

Top Dogs pay for staging of their listings as a business development tool and a valuable way of increasing listing price and marketability. The elements of staging from adding curb appeal to interior staging are examined in a step-by-step sequence.

24 Future Income Streams 357

Top Dogs develop an entrepreneurial state of mind as they plan for future income streams, seeing real estate as a long-term investment instead of a short-term source of income. They treat their business as a conduit for investments, always on the lookout for future income streams.

Glossary 371

Index 381

Contents

Part 1: First Things First   1

1 The Attraction of Real Estate   3

The Satisfaction of the Job 4
Qualifications for the Job...5
The Call to Real Estate..6
Real Estate Has No Hierarchy 7
Financial Reward...8

2 The Spectrum of Careers   11

An Overview of Career Choices 12
Personality Profiling..12
Extroverts and Introverts...*13*
Sensors and Intuitives *14*
Thinkers or Feelers *14*
Judgers or Perceivers...*15*
Residential Sales 16
Commercial Sales 18
Mortgage Brokers..19
Property Managers 20
Appraisers 21
Take Your Time...22
Research the Field..23
What's Your Passion? 24
Carving a Niche 25

3 A Day in the Life   27

Residential Sales 28
Julie's Background *28*
Why Julie Chose Her Career *28*
Julie's Career..*29*
The Appeal of Julie's Career *30*
A Day in the Life of Julie *31*
Julie's Journal Entry for a Day..*31*
Julie's Opinion of Residential Sales...*33*
Commercial Sales 34
Jim's Background...*34*

Why Jim Chose His Career *34*
The Appeal of Jim's Career *35*
A Day in the Life of Jim *35*
Jim's Opinion of Commercial Sales *36*
Mortgage Broker 37
Jeff's Background *37*
Why Jeff Chose His Career *37*
The Appeal of Jeff's Career *37*
A Day in the Life of Jeff *38*
Jeff's Opinion of Being a Mortgage Broker *38*
Property Management 39
Melissa's Background *39*
Why Melissa Chose this Career and the Appeal of It *39*
A Day in the Life of Melissa *39*
Melissa's Opinion of Being a Property Manager *40*
The Appraiser 40
Paul's Background *41*
Why Paul Chose this Career and the Appeal of It *41*
A Day in the Life of Paul *41*
Paul's Opinion of Being an Appraiser *41*

4 Your Prelicensing Education   43
The Terminology 44
Requirement Exceptions 44
Prelicensing Course Procedures 45
Determine Your State's Requirements..............................46
Prelicensing Courses 46
Timing and Surviving 47
Real Estate Principles...48
Nature of Real Property and Ownership *48*
Valuation of Property *53*
Financing of Real Estate *53*
Transfer of Ownership *54*
Closing Procedures *55*
Real Estate Brokerage *55*
Course Challenges..58

5 Preparing for and Taking the Exam   59
A Checklist of Exam-Preparation Tasks 60
Apply to Take the Exam..60

Determine Exam Procedures 61
Gather Information on Exam Content 62
Take an Exam-Preparation Course...64
Simulate the Exam Conditions 65
    Pencil and Paper or Computer Terminal *65*
    The Simulation Process *65*
Master Exam-Taking Strategies...66
Adopt the Right Attitude 67
    Shore Up Your Confidence..*67*
    Sleep Well and Feel Good *67*
    Look at the Worst-Case Scenario *68*
    Look at the Best-Case Scenario *68*
    Have a Positive Attitude *68*
Implement Good Exam-Taking Policies....................................69

Part 2:   Getting Started   71

6   Choosing Your Office   73
Socializing with the Real Estate Country Club 74
Don't Believe All Agents 75
Understanding the Relationship 75
Supporting the Fable...77
Choosing the Right Office...78
    Company Ideals..*78*
    Training and Support *79*
    Sizing Up the Company Reputation *81*
    Sizing Up Financial Considerations *82*
    Sizing Up the Office Manager..*82*
    Getting Leads from the Company.......................................*83*
    Office Spirit and Agent Support...*83*
    Sizing Up Your Work Space *84*
    Getting Recognition *84*
Interviewing Firms 85
Regrets of New Agents 86

7   Building Your Business   89
A Dose of Reality Training 90
Obtain Office Training and Support 91
Make Lead Generation Your First Priority Every Day 92
Participate with Your Realtor Associations 93

Know the Market 94
    Check Out the Multiple Listing Service 94
    Tour Houses 96
    Get to Know Your Local Neighborhoods 97
Upgrade Your Image 97
    How You Look 98
    Your Car is Your Calling Card 98
    Make Your Office an Inviting Space 99
    Create a 30 Second Spiel 99
    Create Professional Marketing Materials 100
Manage Your Own Business 100
    Incorporate Technology Fully 100
    Include Web Technology 101
    Open Your Bank Accounts 101
    Prepare for Tax Time 101
    Deduct Most of Your Expenses 102
    Set Up Your Retirement Accounts 104
    Package Your Business 105
    Check Your Insurance Coverage 106
Take Construction and Architecture Courses 106
Take Continuing Education and Specialty Training 107

8   Building Personal and Professional Power   109

The Seven Principles of Power 110
Principle 1: See Your Work as Your Passion 111
Principle 2: Develop a Burning Desire to Succeed 112
Principle 3: Be an Independent Thinker 114
Principle 4: Have a Positive Attitude 115
Principle 5: Be Self-Disciplined 116
Principle 6: Be Ethical 118
Principle 7: Have Good People Skills 119
The Sum of the Parts 120

9   Building Your Power Team   121

Choosing Your Power Team Members 122
Partnering with Another Agent 123
Arranging the Partnership 124
Using a Professional Stager 125
Finding Power Team Members 125
Qualifying Power Team Members 126

Commitment to a Power Team Plan.............................127
Availability...127
Quality of Services..128
Personal and Professional Power.........................128
Good People Skills..129
High Integrity..129
Team Motivation..129
Transaction and Quality Control...........................130

Part 3: Building an Unbeatable System   131

10 Building A Lead Generating Machine   133

Are You a Social Butterfly? 134
Potential Markets Swirl Around You......................134
Generating Leads for Survival 135
Where Do You Get Leads?.....................................136
The Master Marketing Model 137
Tap Your Sphere of Influence 138
Making Markets Through Networking 139
Adopt a Positive Networking Style 140
Do More of What You Like 141
Market to Your Neighborhood...............................141
Have Your Own Website 142
Promote Your Listings on the Internet 144
Planning Your Website 144
Remind Past Clients..145
Give Free Seminars 145
Advertise Wisely...146
Prospect for Gold..147
The Philosophy That Works 147
Dealing with FSBOs 148
Dealing with Expired Listings.............................149
Specialize 150

11 Managing the Time Demon   153

Use Your Time Well 154
Don't Be a 24/7 Person 154
Being On-Call for Your Clients 155
Beware of High-Maintenance People 155
Peer Pressure...156
Hire a Helper 157

Partnering with Another Agent 158
The Loan and Inspection Contingencies 159
The Title Contingency 159
Work with the Closing Professional 160

12   Technology   163

No More Excuses 164
Your High-Tech System 165
The Hardware You Will Need 165
   Laptop *166*
   Laptop Field Requirements *167*
   Cell Phone *168*
   Personal Data Assistant (a.k.a. PDA) *169*
   Digital Camera *169*
   Printer, Copier, and Fax *170*
   Becoming Paperless *171*
The Software You Will Need 171
   An Office Suite *172*
   Contact Management Options *173*
   Consider Web-Based Contact Management *174*
   Accounting and Check Writing *175*
   Transaction Management *176*
   Mastering Computer Attachments *177*
   Scanning and Editing Software *178*
   Photo Management Software *178*
   Internet Access *178*
   Multiple Listing Service *179*
   Security (Backups and Virus Protection) *179*
Connectivity 180
Synchronization 181
Obtaining Computer Training 181
Stay in Touch with NAR 182

13   A Multimedia Lead Generation System   185

The New Agent's Quandary 186
Even Top Dogs Need Technology Upgrades 187
How the System Works 187
The Master Marketing Model Defined 188
   The Secret to the Master Marketing Model *188*
The Master Marketing Model in the Flesh 189

Adopt a Master Marketing Mindset................................*189*
The High-Tech Component *190*
A 24/7 Self-Generating Model *191*
Having Your Own Website................................*192*
Don't Reinvent the Website Wheel *193*
Adding a Comprehensive Search Feature to Your Website *193*
Contacts Database with Campaign Capability..........................*194*
Web Based Pager *195*
800 Line Call Capture System *195*
The Low-Tech Component of the Model 197
Magazine Advertising *197*
Networking *198*
Newsletters *199*
The Lead Projector.................................200
How Many Leads Will Do It?.................................*200*
Commission Splits and Median Home Price..........................*201*
The Results of the Lead Projector 201
Setting Net Income Desired.................................*203*
Finding Gross Income Required.................................*203*
Identifying Expenses.................................*203*
Finding Gross Commissions Required *206*
Finding Gross Sales Required.................................*206*
Find Closed Escrows Required *206*
Finding Listings Required.................................*207*
Finding Listing Appointments Required *207*
Finding Leads Required *207*
Working Your Lead Projector 208
Listings or Buyer Sales? 209
Converting Your Leads 210

Part 4: Putting It All Together **213**

14 A Master of Organization **215**
Make Your Computer Your Business Partner 216
Wean Yourself off Paper *216*
Become a Computer Multitasker *217*
Bring Your Database Everywhere You Go..........................*218*
Multitasking in the Field *218*
Becoming a Calendar Wizard.................................219
Keep Track of Your Tasks.................................*220*

Print Out Your Calendar the Day Before 220
Organizing Your Computer Files 221
   Maintaining Your Paper Files 222
Synchronizing and Backing Up Data 222
Establishing Your Home Office 223
   Transforming Your Home Office 224
   Commercial Transformation 225
Setting Up a Vehicle Office 227
Working Anywhere in the Field 227

15   Building a Referral Stream System   229

Meeting People and Keeping Their Information 230
Keeping Organized and Caretaking 231
Step 1—Setup 232
   Snail and E-Mail Newsletters 232
   Newsletter Choices 233
   Frequency of Newsletter Transmittal 234
   Evaluate Snail Mail Newsletter Costs 234
   Personalize Your Newsletters 235
   Gift Certificates for Referrals 235
   Buyer Gifts 236
   Seller Gifts 236
   Nice to Have Met You Cards (NTHMYs) 236
   Holiday Cards 237
   Birthday Greetings 238
Step 2—Input 238
Step 3—Processing 240
   The Gift Department 240
   The Snail Mail Department 240
Reviewing the Referral Stream 241
Examining the Philosophy 242
Tips on Making the System Work 243

16   The New Ideal   245

The Times They Are A-Changin' 246
Performing Your Fiduciary Duty 246
Recognizing the Sales Scripts 247
Participating in the Transformation 248
   Dropping the Hard Sell 249
   Demand for Agent Services 250
   Appreciating the Client's Decisions 250

Supporting Clients 253
Replacing the Scripts 253
Relating to the Competition 254
Predicting the Result 256

17   A Winning Listing Presentation   257

Qualifying Sellers 258
Listing Presentations 259
Your Listing Package 260
Provide a Current Market Trends Page and Marketing Plan 261
Prepare Your Bio and Mission Statement 262
Include Your Newsletter in the Listing Presentation Package 263
Comparative Market Analysis 263
Prepare the Sample Net Sheet 264
Include a Transaction Management Sample 264
Listen to Your Clients 264
Include Your Agency Disclosure and a Listing Agreement 265
Utilizing Technology to Instill Trust 266
Allow for Rejection 266

Part 5:   The Parts of a Transaction   269

18   Representing the Seller   271

Professional Staging 272
Evaluating Property Problems 272
Listing on the MLS 274
Hosting the Broker's Open House 274
Holding the Open House for the Public 275
Your Open House Checklist 276
Greeting Buyers 278
Responding to the Offer 279
Handling Multiple Offers 280
Facilitating the Transaction to Closing 281
Dealing with a Stale Listing 282
Reporting to Your Clients 283

19   Representing the Buyer   285

Qualifying the Buyer 286
Presenting to the Buyer 287
Review a Sample Listing 288
Review Their Loan Approval Status 288

Include Your Bio and Mission Statement..................................289
Include Your Newsletter 289
List of Transaction Steps and Standards.............................289
Include a Transaction Management Sample..........................290
Listen to the Buyer..290
Touring Buyers 291
Reporting to Your Client 291
Preparing the Offer 292
Offer Presentation 293
The Transaction Timeline and Steps 293
Opening Escrow..293
Obtaining the Title Report..294
Dealing with All-Important Contingencies 298
The Physical Inspection Contingency..................................298
The Loan Contingency 300
Closing...301

20   Using the Transaction Documents   303
A Transaction Management Model 304
The Primary Documents 304
The Listing Agreement...304
Listing Price 305
Listing Term...305
Commission 306
Agency Disclosures...306
Whose Agent Are You? 307
Dreaded Dual Agency 308
The Purchase Agreement..308
Understanding the Terms..309
Dealing with Legal Terminology 310
The Terms of the Purchase Agreement.................................311
Seller Disclosures 313
Agent Inspection and Disclosures.....................................313
The Settlement Statement 314

Part 6:   Becoming a Top Dog   315

21   Cutting-Edge Top Dogs   317
The Top Dog's Motivation 318
Lead Generation Is the Top Priority.................................318

Destination Websites..319
    Catering to Internet Clients....................................319
    Defining a Specialty that Caters to Keyword Search.................321
    Using Your Site as a Destination Point..........................322
E-Mail Productivity and Professionalism...............................323
Specialized Training and Professional Designations................324
    Broker Licensing..324
    Specialty Training..324
    Obtaining Professional Designations.............................325
Reasons for Success—Community Leadership.......................327
The Rest of the Reasons...328

22 Giving and Getting Support   329
The Top Dog Plan..330
Hiring a Business Coach...330
Monitoring Personal and Professional Power.........................331
Obtaining Technology Support.......................................333
    Monitor Your Level of Personal Service..........................334
    Monitor Your Website Performance...............................335
Administrative Assistance..336
    Part-Time or Full-Time?...336
    Licensed, Unlicensed, and Experienced?.........................337
    In Office or Out of Office?.....................................337
    Specific Skills...339
    How to Find an Assistant..340
    Money and Benefits..341
Obtaining Virtual Assistance...342
Virtual Assistance Versus Live Assistance............................343
Receiving Spiritual Support..343
Giving Support Through Mentorship.................................344

23 Staging Your Listings   347
The Stage for Home Staging..348
Staging Is Finally Taking Hold.......................................348
Convincing Clients to Stage..349
What Is Staging?...350
    Adding Curb Appeal...350
    Interior Staging..352
Staging Is an Investment...354

24 Future Income Streams   357

Creating Future Income Streams 358
The *Rich Dad* Books 358
Investing in Real Estate Continually 359
Take Commissions as Equity Interests 360
Facilitating Stock Market Investor Transition 361
   Create Diversification Opportunities.....................................*362*
   Your Business Plan...*363*
   The More the Merrier *363*
   Use of a Business Entity *364*
   Qualified Retirement Fund Investment *364*
Selling Your Business 366
   They Are Your Clients..*366*
   Be Entrepreneurial-Minded *367*
   Your Business Opportunity Checklist.......................................*368*

Glossary   371

Index   381

Foreword

If you are in the real estate business or considering making real estate sales your career, you need to read this book. Marilyn Sullivan brings a new and refreshing perspective to the real estate profession. As a past president of the National Association of Realtors, I can attest to the fact that the real estate industry is experiencing phenomenal change in the way we do business from the ground floor up. As a result, there is a need for a kind of refurbishing of the way real estate professionals represent and communicate with their clients. Marilyn Sullivan is able to address these issues from many vantage points through her expertise as a real estate broker, lawyer, author, and entrepreneur over the past 25 years.

Marilyn's legal background gives her the tools to define the job of the real estate agent as more of a professional client advocate instead of a salesperson geared toward selling a client on a product. As a broker and lawyer who has analyzed the legal obligation of the real estate agent to her client from both perspectives, she is able to introduce you to *The New Ideal* in the way real estate professionals represent their clients. This important book tutors you in this updated and upgraded model of providing ethics-based, client-first service to clientele. The New Ideal as presented in this book is an about-face from salesperson mentality to professional real estate practitioner as the image of the real estate agent evolves with its changing marketplace.

The real estate industry is both rewarded and challenged by technological innovation. The handshake of yesteryear has turned into high-tech methods of conducting business. The business of real estate sales has become so directly linked to the Internet and to a well-organized contacts database, by virtue of its endless stream of people, that technology must be the mainstay of your business. This book shows you how to stay in step with technology and to incorporate it fully into your business, yet still retain the personal touch, which is so important in the real estate business.

Real estate professionals are entrepreneurs in every sense of the word. We work under a company's logo, but we are the owners and operators of our own small businesses. If you come to real estate with an entrepreneurial state of mind, you will have the best chance to achieve maximum success, personal fulfillment, and optimum profit. In this excellent new book, Marilyn coaches you to set your limits high and reach them. Her approach is both practical and philosophical, incorporating high ideals, creative thinking, and practical solutions.

As an innovator of deal-making strategies, Marilyn mentors you to sharpen your creative mindset for forging your own specialties and making deals happen. Home staging is emphasized as a valuable way to advance your listing package and increase the market for residential listings. She also shows you a method of reverse farming whereby your market finds you 24/7 through scrupulous building and indexing of your website.

Marilyn also shares her proven technology-based marketing technique called the referral stream system to help you build a business that is entirely referral-based. Her future income stream strategies will cause you to view your earnings as long-term investments instead of short-term sources of income, transforming you into a profit-earning investor. You will be motivated to adopt an investor state of mind as you are tutored to become a Top Dog in your field.

While many other books have been written about how to achieve success as a real estate agent, this book is a treatise on how to practice real estate in a more productive, professional manner. Let me say it one more time; if you are in the real estate business or considering making real estate sales your career, you need to read this book.

Richard Mendenhall

2001 President of the National Association of Realtors

Introduction

Careers in real estate are appealing to a wider group of people now that the real estate market has earned its reputation as a powerful and reliable sector of our economy. With the real estate market's enviable long-term appreciation and favored tax treatment, real estate as an investment has become enormously attractive. Compared with the stock market's dismal performance, the real estate market has claimed a leadership position.

The market is not the only aspect of real estate that has experienced influential change. Its workforce has undergone a dramatic shift. Not so long ago, a career in real estate sales was the second profession of the homemaker or teacher. In recent years, with the downsizing of corporate America, real estate professionals now include upper management and technology professionals. More and more people are recognizing that the independence afforded the real estate sales professional coupled with the potential for unlimited income make a career in real estate sales quite attractive.

The real estate market's consumer has also transformed as investors move funds between the stock market and the real estate market depending on where the gains are found. The weary stock market investor has found that he can wear both hats, gaining ground as either a real estate or stock market investor. Market jumping has become more common as real estate has gained its leadership position in our economy and as investors gain real estate expertise. This is where we agents confer a professionalism and proficiency required by an industry that has claimed market share.

These revolutionary changes mark an important crossroads in the real estate industry. No longer do economic trends and statistics remain solely within the purview of the financial planner. A more savvy real estate consumer now requires that real estate agents have this important data at their fingertips. No longer do agents write offers on the hoods of cars and bait their clients with sales pitches. Today's agent serves an entirely different consumer and is expected to work faster, smarter, and more efficiently. Mobile technology has replaced the hood of the car, and a more professional client relationship has replaced the old sales routine. Outdated mailers and cold calls no longer create markets, having been replaced by 24/7 web technology and agent specialization. This book addresses the many changes occurring within the real estate industry, and bridges the gap between the real estate industry of yesteryear and the one that is before us now.

In this new edition of this book I have featured two new innovative products that may change the face of real estate marketing. Chapter 13 features a high-tech, automated multimedia Master Marketing Model that will generate leads without you. I have also featured a program called the Lead Projector that tells each agent exactly how many leads they require to meet their income needs. Just input your unique information and your bottom line lead requirements are set for you. Without exception, the state-of-the-art strategies I have developed and shared in this book make it possible for you to gain unparalleled momentum no matter where you are in your real estate career.

What You Will Learn in This Book

The Complete Idiot's Guide To Success as a Real Estate Agent, Second Edition, is written in six parts. Each one addresses a different aspect of the real estate business.

Part 1, "First Things First," answers your question, "Is real estate for me?" It explores why the real estate profession is luring more and more people through its doors. Although the residential real estate agent is featured throughout this book, the many other career opportunities available to the licensed agent are described with a day in the life of each. This part concludes with a primer on the educational requirements you will need to fulfill prior to obtaining your license, and, finally, taking the real estate licensing exam itself.

Part 2, "Getting Started," coaches you on making the right choices from the moment you obtain your license. Choosing your first office is a crucial decision since this is where you will develop your style of real estate practice. And although you will be working under a broker's supervision, you are actually about to become the CEO of your own small business. The business model from which to launch your successful real estate practice includes formulating a concrete small business plan as well as incorporating basic principles of personal and professional power. In this book, you will be coached to adopt an entrepreneurial vision through finding your passion in your work, cultivating and sustaining independent thinking, and honing self-discipline as the force that puts it all together. The final step in the small business plan is to build a Power Team that sustains your business and your clientele throughout the rest of your career.

Part 3, "Building an Unbeatable System," provides the stability and competence to give your business a strong foundation. In the real estate world, that means consistent lead generation, managing your time, and using technology to the maximum. The many faces of market making are examined, from the old-school handshake to high-tech, web-based protocols. Computer technology is introduced as a peak platform for your business to serve you and your clients in a powerful way. Online transaction management is introduced. A multimedia Master Marketing Model gives you a powerful array of products to lead generate for you automatically.

Part 4, "Putting It All Together," delivers a new way of practicing real estate through two success-building strategies, the referral stream system and The New Ideal. While the referral stream system generates your client base and turns your business into a referral-based operation, The New Ideal delivers an upgraded, more professional quality of client service. One system brings clients in the door while the other keeps them after they enter. This part also presents a new perspective on what makes up a winning listing presentation. If any part of this book is the most essential to the creation of your success, this is it.

Part 5, "The Parts of a Transaction," is a primer on real estate practices and principles. It presents the residential real estate transaction from every conceivable perspective: representing the seller or the buyer and preparing and analyzing the transaction documents. Chapters 18 and 19 examine your client relationships from the beginning of a transaction to the very end. The important transaction documents are reviewed from the author's legal-oriented perspective. This part will provide you with a valuable legal resource for the rest of your career.

Part 6, "Becoming a Top Dog," presents the tools and strategies highly successful agents use to move their careers into high gear. These peak performers adopt cutting-edge approaches as they dominate the market through entrepreneurial planning, specialization, and web-based technology. The importance of staging your listings is discussed, beginning at the curb and flowing throughout the home. Top Dogs develop an entrepreneurial state of mind as they plan for future income streams by seeing real estate as a long-term investment instead of a short-term source of income. The Top Dog takes on the role of a profit-earning investor in lieu of a commission-earning salesperson.

Extras

With the hope of making this book easy to read and conveniently organized for finding what you need to succeed as a real estate agent, there are four different types of sidebars that provide additional information. These are explained here.

FYI!
Statistics and other information amplifying important points to give you extra tools and resources.

def•i•ni•tion
Definitions of words or terms for the real estate Top Dog's dictionary, which can also be found in the Glossary.

Agent to Agent
Insider tips and statistics for use in your career.

Cave!
Heads up so you can avoid stumbling blocks others have encountered!

Acknowledgments

My special thanks to my agents Bob Diforio and Marilyn Allen for making the writing of this book possible; to Mike Sanders, my acquisitions editor, for having faith in my abilities; to Ginny Bess, my development editor, for wise navigation through the manuscript and for her encouragement and support; to Grant Munroe for his technical review; to Michael Blue, Ken Orgill, Paul Sheng and Anita Hatfield for their valuable input; to the great Spirit above for the creative resources you continually instill in me; to Richard Page for his love and emotional support; to Penguin-Putnam for developing *The Complete Idiot's Guides* as a series of excellent reference books; to Paul and Barbara Tiegers for profiling the personality type for real estate professionals for Chapter 2; to the many Top Dogs who shared their insights and experiences, including Paul Lehman, Melissa Prandi, Maureen McGettigan, Jeff Drawdy, Paul James, Eric Fishbein, and James McKenney, Esq.; to Jim Edmondson for his wisdom; and last but not least, my special thanks to Al Bianchi, Esq., for the many ways in which he has contributed to my success in real estate.

Special Thanks to the Technical Reviewer

The Complete Idiot's Guide to Success as a Real Estate Agent, Second Edition, was reviewed by an expert to help me ensure that this book gives you everything you need to know about succeeding as a real estate agent. Special thanks are extended to real estate trainer, Layne Kulwin.

Trademarks

All terms mentioned in this book that are known to be or are suspected of being trademarks or service marks have been appropriately capitalized. Alpha Books and Penguin Group (USA) Inc. cannot attest to the accuracy of this information. Use of a term in this book should not be regarded as affecting the validity of any trademark or service mark.

Part 1

First Things First

This book begins with the novice and ends with the top notch producer. Part 1 discusses the reasons why real estate is particularly attractive to people looking for career satisfaction and why so many people have walked through its doors recently.

The real estate field gives its agents a diverse array of specialties from which to make a career choice. The spectrum of careers is featured along with personality profiles that were created just for this book. You will then review a day in the life of each career, so you can take your own personality profile and match it to the real estate career best suited to you. Once you decide that real estate is for you, this part guides you through satisfying the prelicensing educational requirements and taking and passing the licensing exam.

The Attraction of Real Estate

In This Chapter

- ◆ The real estate agent is an entrepreneur
- ◆ A long list of job satisfactions
- ◆ The many roles the agent plays
- ◆ Independence and flexibility mark the real estate profession
- ◆ A potential for great financial reward

Real estate agents are a sneaky bunch. They know they've found utopia, but you'd never know it by speaking with them. People ask, "How do you like what you do?" The agent grimaces, "It's a lot of hard work. There's no rest for the real estate agent." As she walks away, proud to have guarded her secret and her market once again, a smile washes back over her. The truth is the real estate profession confers a bundle of rewards that its members jealously guard.

One reason real estate agents are smiling is that they have discovered a profession that calls to the entrepreneur. It is, so to speak, outside of the traditional career box. Where other careers set very specific criteria for its members, real estate has few. College education? Not required. High school diploma? Not really. Nine to five, five days a week? Nope. Suit and tie? Not for a second. Starter salary with little incremental increases along the way? Definitely not. A boss and the typical working-class hierarchy? Absolutely not. Act a certain way, portray a certain image? No, just be who you are. Respected professional? Yes, especially if you practice according to *The New Ideal* presented in this book. Yes, it can be utopia, but don't let anyone know.

FYI!

Are you too old to make real estate your profession? The average age of real estate agents has increased from age 42 in 1978 to age 52. Almost a third of brokers (as opposed to agents) are 60 years old, and 16 percent of brokers are over 60. Only 12 percent of sales agents are under the age of 35.

Despite the agent's vow to secrecy, real estate has become the number one profession people turn to when their careers prove less than fulfilling. This chapter speaks to the reasons why the real estate profession has emerged as the favored arena for people changing careers. Although the many career options available to the agent are described in Chapter 2, residential sales is featured throughout this book because 80 percent of agents choose to practice in this field.

The Satisfaction of the Job

Now let's take a look at exactly why it is that real estate sales draws people in droves and rewards them so well when they arrive. The factors described at the beginning of this chapter sound like reason enough. No set hours, no boss, and the potential for unlimited pay sound like a terrific offer. The truth is that these are the perks that draw people to the profession, but it's not the factors that keep them. Agents find that there is something more satisfying that lurks behind those big checks at the close of each escrow.

We find that the greatest reward of all is making a difference in our clients' lives. We come to find that our jobs are far more than that of a salesman pitching his product. When we encounter our clients, they are often faced with major life transitions like buying a first home, relocating, getting married, divorcing, starting a business, coping with the death of a loved one, or retiring.

We seem to join their lives in an effort to help them define and obtain property to give them shelter, fill their needs, and provide investment return. No little job, indeed. When it comes right down to it, we discover that our job is to help clients define their most basic core needs and convert them into real estate answers.

It sounds like an impossible job, but we translate our client's needs into rooms and gardens and communities. We help with financial deliberations and transform those assessments into real estate investments. Our role turns out to be one of assisting clients with key life decisions and doing everything possible to make the process seamless, meaningful, and rewarding.

That's why many of us who enter the door of real estate, especially sales, have been through many of our own life transitions and other career portals. We have lived a lot of life and want to mentor others through the process in our work. We usually have a good deal of experience in the belly of life. Although education in its traditional sense isn't required to become an agent, life's extended curriculum of varied experience *is* important if you want to become a successful real estate agent.

> **Agent to Agent**
>
> The typical agent is a 52-year-old married female, although there is nearly an equal gender split between males and females.

Qualifications for the Job

One of the best advantages of a career in real estate is that it is not bound by the rigid traditional structures that shroud other careers. Real estate is outside of the traditional box, both in terms of its educational requirements and in terms of the practice of the profession itself. Because of these aspects, the real estate career is made for those with an entrepreneurial state of mind.

To qualify for the real estate exam, you are required to complete a certain number of real estate courses. It generally takes two to six months to complete the courses. If you have a college degree or are licensed in a related profession, this time frame is much shorter. Often the real estate licensee does not even require you to have a high school diploma.

> **FYI!**
>
> To determine your state's licensing requirements, go to your state regulatory board's website. An Internet search for "(name of your state) real estate commission" or "(name of your state) real estate department" should bring you to the site. Apprenticeship requirements to be eligible for a broker's license also vary by state.

The facts show, however, that nearly half of agents have Bachelor's degrees or advanced degrees, 7 percent have no college education, and the rest have some college education. In other words, although the licensing boards do not have high educational standards, agents tend to be well educated.

In most states there are two levels of real estate agents. The first is an agent or broker associate; the second is a broker. Most people first take the agent's exam and apprentice as an agent for a year or two before taking the broker's exam. Broker licensing is optional, but it is required if you want to work for yourself or employ others. Chapters 4 and 5 describe prelicensing requirements and the licensing exam itself.

The Call to Real Estate

Many real estate agents spend years in training or obtaining educational degrees in one career only to find their way into real estate when boredom sets in. Some people want to do more than the same job everyday in a highly structured environment, and others feel they are ignoring aspects of themselves, such as their interpersonal skills, a passion for their job, and use of their more creative talents. Others find that as they get older, regular jobs carry income ceilings while in real estate income seems to rise with age.

In fact, many agents come to real estate as a second, third, or even fifth profession. A recent survey by the National Association of Realtors revealed that real estate was a first career for only 7 percent of agents. That means that 93 percent of agents came from other professions.

In my case, I obtained my law degree, practiced law, and found my passion in real estate after spending years cultivating just one facet of my professional side. Real estate gave me the key to unlock the diversity of my talents and unleash a multifaceted, far more authentic persona.

> **FYI!**
>
> Real estate encourages you to draw on your life experiences as you mentor your clients through theirs. The person who chooses the field of real estate understands that you can make a living and do what makes you feel good at the same time. In fact, you are almost guaranteed to earn a better living if you enjoy what you do.

The same is true of many other professionals dissatisfied with their career choices. Real estate acts like a magnet to those in career transition. The divergent spectrum of roles offered by the real estate career and its liberal working environment make real estate the choice for those who have felt restricted in other professions. Its financial reward is also a factor because the potential money you can make in the real estate field is staggering.

The successful agent finds that he or she often plays the role of decorator, coach, architect, therapist, financial advisor, lawyer, and friend. Real estate is the only profession where you can tap into all aspects of who you are and do it for a living.

The practice of real estate also escapes the traditional working class structure. While the traditional professions are engaged in structured working schedules, real estate has no set hours of operation. Real estate is listed, sold, exchanged, and managed at all times. The *for sale* sign is always out. Your schedule is earmarked by autonomy and flexibility in determining how and when to render your services.

Real Estate Has No Hierarchy

Real estate professionals are not bound by the traditional choice between self-employment and working for a company. In real estate, you can do both. You join an office within which you work for yourself at your own pace. The office already has a foundation for building your career in place. You just step into the framework and carve out your own niche. Incorporating *floor time* and office meetings is the basis of your schedule, but other than that your schedule is up to your own making.

Real estate also steers clear of the corporate structure that governs most other professions. In a hierarchical structure, centralized power often inhibits creativity in its professionals. The last thing you're supposed to be is your creative, passionate self. The traditional chain of command regulates and instructs its workers. If you step too far from your box, you are pushed back into its confines.

In real estate there are guides, not rules. Office management has very little hold on you because you're making money for them, not the other way around. The result is a far more relaxed environment where there is no real gap between economics and creativity. In real estate, making money and being creative go hand in hand.

Because of these characteristics, people with an entrepreneurial mindset thrive in the real estate industry. Your expertise is derived more from having lived a full life than from years of traditional academia. This high

def•i•ni•tion

Floor time is the rotation of agents to respond to inquiries that come from advertisements and signs. These agents get the walk-in traffic and phone calls to the office where no agent in particular is requested. Now that most agents have direct lines, floor time is fast becoming something of the past.

Cave!

Always remember, you make money for your office, not the other way around. New agents often find that they did not stockpile enough funds to get them through their first year in their new career. You should aim at starting your new real estate career with six months of living expenses on hand.

degree of flexibility and autonomy makes real estate the ideal profession for people with an entrepreneurial spirit seeking the ultimate in independence. It also presents the biggest challenge for the undisciplined person.

Financial Reward

Another aspect of real estate that attracts consumers and agents alike is its self-sustaining nature. As a natural resource, it is perpetual in its ability to nurture itself under the loving care of Mother Nature. In addition, its consistent appreciation and long-term and short-term tax benefits make it a highly respected commodity and the symbol of the American dream and the icon of intergenerational inheritance.

As agents, we act as its caretaker in our roles as its transfer agents. Our job is to safeguard its tender between purveyors as it travels the chain of supply and demand. When we perform our job, sustainability is built into our profession just as it is built into the earth itself. Its appreciation not only serves our clients, it rewards us with higher commissions and our own personal investments.

Agent to Agent

National median appreciation for 2005 was 13.2 percent. California's appreciation was 19.3 percent.

Agent to Agent

The National Association of Realtors reports that the average time agents spent per transaction is 20 hours. For an average home price of $215,000 and a commission of 3 percent for just one side of the transaction, the agent's time was worth $323.00 an hour.

Because of these inherent factors, real estate rewards its caretakers' social ability, organization, and determination with the potential for immense financial abundance. When you join the ranks of the real estate entrepreneur, there is no limit to how much you can earn in both money and personal fulfillment. The doors are open, ready for you to reap the limits of your own personal capacity.

Few professions can provide similar rewards without presenting a litany of rules regulating its members' behavior. You can enter the real estate door with just a few months of study, pass the real estate exam, and earn a hardy commission, all in less than six months. There are few other careers where you can net six figures the first year working for yourself and have no set hours and no college degree.

It is not just the commission you earn that marks your success. The financial expertise you gain as an agent is a valuable asset. Not only are you learning how to handle high-stakes deals, but you also learn the tax significance and mathematics of buying and selling properties.

Because of this exposure to a market that continually offers investment opportunities, real estate can become a primary choice of investment, allowing you to personally take advantage of its profit potential. Real estate becomes your own thoroughfare to personal and financial abundance, as it sets you up for income streams that will sustain you for the rest of your life. It is no longer just your clients that prosper from your acquired acumen. You step into an investor state of mind as you learn to treat real estate as a profitable, long-term investment instead of a short-term source of commission income.

Although this chapter highlights why real estate attracts a wide array of professionals, we will concentrate on the many challenges that face the agent throughout the rest of this book. The profession is not without its downside, but with the concepts presented in this book you will be prepared to encounter them in a confident, empowered manner.

> **Agent to Agent**
>
> Read any of the *Rich Dad, Poor Dad* books by Robert Kiyosaki. These books will lead you to adopt an investor state of mind through looking for long-term investment as opposed to short-term return.

The Least You Need to Know

- Real estate is an ideal field for someone who wants to be independent, have a flexible schedule, and enjoy an unlimited income potential.

- Your career in real estate gives you the ability to become an entrepreneur, develop rewarding client relationships, and ensure future income streams.

- It can take as little as three months of study to get a real estate agent license.

- Helping clients with their real estate decisions can be very rewarding in terms of personal satisfaction and financial reward.

Chapter 2

The Spectrum of Careers

In This Chapter

- ◆ Examining the diversity of careers within real estate
- ◆ Profiling your personality
- ◆ Taking your time and determining your passions when choosing a field
- ◆ Dreaming about the niche you can create in real estate

The real estate field gives its licensees a diverse array of specialties from which to make a career choice. For the agent, there is a career for every personality type, from the extreme introvert to the extrovert, and everywhere in between. Like any other career, real estate has its share of distinctive personality traits that mark the successful professionals in each of these specialties.

Chapter 1 looked at real estate from more of an intuitive standpoint. What is it about real estate that gives it its glamour and appeal? This chapter describes the spectrum of careers available to you once you are licensed, and the personality type best suited to each career. In the next chapter, you will look at a day in the life of each career professional so that you can see for yourself which field is most attractive to you.

An Overview of Career Choices

Your real estate license allows you to work as …

- A residential sales agent.

- A commercial sales agent.

- A mortgage broker.

- A property manager.

- An appraiser.

Later in this chapter, a description of each career is presented along with the ideal personality profile for each. But first, let's profile your personality so you can identify the real estate agent career that fits you best.

Personality Profiling

The material presented here is based on the excellent work of Paul Tieger and Barbara Barron-Tieger, authors of *Do What You Are: Discover the Perfect Career for You Through the Secrets of Personality Type*. The Personality Type model, which was created by Carl Jung and Isabel Myers, describes four key aspects of personality. The four aspects of Personality Type identify people as being primarily (but not exclusively) either:

- Extroverts or Introverts

- Sensors or Intuitives

- Thinkers or Feelers

- Judgers or Perceivers

Each person has natural, inborn *preferences* for some processes and characteristics over others. Everyone has the ability to use different parts of their personalities, but their *preferences* reflect their greatest natural strengths and talents. Because Personality Type is clearly linked to career choice, it is possible to predict which types are likely to be more satisfied and successful in different careers.

FYI!
According to the Tiegers, who wrote *Do What You Are*, the secret of career satisfaction lies in doing what you enjoy most. They say, "A few lucky people discover this secret early in life, but most of us are caught in a kind of psychological wrestling match, torn between what we think we can do and what we (or others) feel we ought to do, and what we think we want to do. Our advice? Concentrate instead on who you are, and the rest will fall into place."

To identify your type, review the brief lists below and try to determine which one sounds most like you. After you decide on personality characteristics that describe you, look at the profiles based on the same characteristics. This should help you decide which career path is most closely aligned with your personality profile.

Extroverts and Introverts

Extroverts and introverts represent the two different ways people receive and direct their energy.

Extroverts (E) show these characteristics:

- They are energized by being with people.
- They often like being the center of attention.
- They tend to act first, and then think.
- They talk more than listen.
- They enjoy a fast pace and lots of variety.

Introverts (I) show these characteristics:

- They need time alone to "recharge their batteries."
- They avoid being the center of attention.
- They think about things before acting.
- They listen more than talk.
- They like to focus on one thing at a time.

Are you more of an extrovert or an introvert? _____

def•i•ni•tion _____

An **extrovert** is a person who directs much of his or her energy to the outer world of people and things. An overwhelming number of real estate sales agents fall into this category.

An **introvert** is a person who focuses his or her energy on the world inside of themselves. They enjoy spending time alone and need this time to "recharge their batteries."

Sensors and Intuitives

Sensors and intuitives describe how people take in information.

Sensors (S) show these characteristics:

- ◆ They pay attention to facts and details.
- ◆ They trust what they experience through their five senses.
- ◆ They like new ideas only if they have practical utility.
- ◆ They are realistic and value common sense.
- ◆ They present information in a step-by-step manner.

Intuitives (N) show these characteristics:

- ◆ They pay attention to the big picture.
- ◆ They like possibilities and new ideas.
- ◆ They value imagination and innovation.
- ◆ They like to learn new skills and they get bored quickly.
- ◆ They present information in a roundabout manner.

Are you more of a sensor or an intuitive? _____

Thinkers or Feelers

Thinkers and feelers represent the ways that people make decisions.

Thinkers (T) show these characteristics:

- ◆ They tend to analyze things impersonally.
- ◆ They value logic and objectivity.
- ◆ They naturally see flaws and can be critical.
- ◆ They value truth more than diplomacy.
- ◆ They are often businesslike and assertive.

Feelers (F) show these characteristics:

- They consider the effect of their actions on others.
- They value empathy and harmony.
- They like to please and help others.
- They are often very sensitive to criticism.
- They avoid arguments, conflict, and confrontations.

Are you more of a thinker or a feeler? _____

Agent to Agent _____

The authors of *Do What You Are* provide good instruction when they say, "Since the right job flows directly out of all the elements of your personality type, you need to spend some time figuring out what makes you tick. By making a conscious effort to discover the 'real you,' you can learn how to focus your natural strengths and inclinations into a career you can love for as long as you choose to work."

Judgers or Perceivers

Judgers and perceivers represent the ways people choose to organize their lives.

Judgers (J) show these characteristics:

- They are happiest once decisions are made.
- They have a strong work ethic: work now, play later.
- They set goals and work toward achieving them.
- They derive satisfaction from completing tasks.
- They are organized and take deadlines seriously.

Perceivers (P) show these characteristics:

- They value spontaneity and like to keep their options open.
- They have a play ethic: enjoy now, finish the job later.
- They change goals as information changes.

- They like starting projects better than finishing them.

- They consider deadlines to be "elastic."

Are you more of a judger or a perceiver? _____

Based on these brief descriptions of the different type preferences, record below the four letters that you think represent your Personality Type:

_____   _____   _____   _____

E or I   S or N   T or F   J or P

This exercise is not a validated test and is only designed to give you a *best-guess estimate* of your type. To get a more accurate read of your type, I recommend you take the more complete Personality Type assessment and read the accompanying profiles at www.personalitytype.com.

Next, I review each of the primary careers available to the real estate agent and discuss some of the ideal personality types for each. Although I use the term *ideal*, in reality all types can and do succeed in all aspects of real estate. But some types are much more naturally suited to, and therefore more likely to succeed in and enjoy, certain real estate careers.

Residential Sales

Ideal personality profile: Extrovert, Sensing, Feeling, Judging (ESFJ); Extrovert, Intuitive, Feeling, Judging (ENFJ); Extrovert, Sensing, Feeling, Perceiving (ESFP); Extrovert, Sensing, Thinking, Judging (ESTJ).

As a residential sales agent, you will help clients buy and sell residential properties, encompassing single family homes, condominiums, and multifamily compounds. You will develop expertise with local communities and their economics, neighborhood statistics, schools, parks, commuting, and shopping options. You will, in other words, become immersed in your local communities and make a living doing it. This is by far the most popular of the real estate professions—80 percent of agents choose it as their field.

Residential sales agents are attracted to home buying and selling due to the highly personal and social nature of the field. Helping clients define the living environment that suits their needs naturally entails a personal analysis. It calls upon many different aspects of your persona, from decorator to therapist to lawyer and all things between.

You will sometimes be called upon to handle emotional family issues, which can arise in a family home purchase. You will be in touch with the visual and decorative side of real estate, because personal creature comforts are at issue. In just a single day, you will wear many different hats and interact with many people.

These are some of the reasons that the vast majority of agents turn toward challenging and diversified residential sales. Because of the popularity of this field, this book looks most closely at the residential sales agent. Much of the next chapter is dedicated to examining a day in the life of the residential agent, along with her career experiences prior to becoming an agent.

FYI!
The median income for all agents is $62,300 with the highest to property managers and commercial agents and the lowest to residential agents and brokers.

Extroverts prefer this field because the residential agent tends to have a commanding presence in transactions. You are a salesperson and have an assertive, outgoing nature with a good measure of confidence and persistence. You should have good people skills that come most naturally to people who are both extroverts and feelers. All these traits are discussed in more depth in Chapter 8.

FYI!
In *Do What You Are,* the sales agent personality profile of Extrovert, Sensor, Feeler, Judger (ESFJ) is described as follows:
"ESFJs are motivated to help other people in real and practical ways through direct action and cooperation. They are responsible, friendly, and sympathetic. Because ESFJs place such importance on their relationships with other people, they tend to be popular, gracious, eager to please, and talkative. Practical and realistic, ESFJs tend to be matter-of-fact and organized. They attend to and remember important facts and details. They are aware of and involved with their physical environment and like to be active and productive."

Although all people have the ability to use both their sensing and intuition, both aspects come in handy in residential sales since common sense and attention to detail and imagination and creativity are all part of the successful agent's repertoire. Because of the personal and emotional aspects required of this career, feeler types usually enjoy residential sales more than thinkers. The residential agent needs to feel her client's considerations and understand them on an emotional level.

Real estate professionals who are judgers and those who are perceivers bring different gifts to the job. Judgers are usually well-organized, very productive, and closure-oriented. Perceivers are usually more spontaneous, flexible, and able to shift gears quickly—all characteristics that are required of agents on an almost daily basis. The next chapter will take an in-depth look at a typical day in the life of Julie, our residential sales agent.

Commercial Sales

Ideal personality profile: Extrovert, Sensing, Thinking, Judging (ESTJ); Introvert, Sensing, Thinking, Judging (ISTJ); Extrovert, Sensing, Thinking, Perceiving (ESTP); and Extrovert, Intuitive, Thinking, Judging (ENTJ).

Commercial, industrial, and farmland sales are included under the commercial category. Commercial agents specialize in income-producing properties, including office buildings, apartment buildings, stores and warehouses, and shopping centers. In order for clients to evaluate investment potentials, you need to understand growth factors, *capitalization rates* based on past income, and tax laws relating to real estate investments. Much of this career involves competency in objective analysis, number-crunching, and an emphasis on return on investment. It is not based nearly as much upon relationships as it is on hard, cold realities. This is why thinkers clearly enjoy commercial real estate much more than feelers do.

def•i•ni•tion

> **Capitalization rates** represent the relationship between the value of the property and the income it produces.
>
> **Zoning** is governmental regulation as to the use of a property. For instance, a property may be zoned for use by a single-family residence or it might be zoned for business.

Industrial and office real estate salespeople specialize in selling, developing, or leasing property used for industry or manufacturing. As this type of agent, you will understand the specific needs of different types of industries to determine variables such as transportation, proximity to raw materials, water and power, labor availability, and local building, *zoning*, and tax laws.

Land agents deal in land for farming and acquisition of rural land by cities for residential, commercial, and industrial expansion. Success as a land agent depends on accurately establishing the income potential of the property. As a successful land agent you will acquire a good working knowledge of agricultural and land-use factors in order to determine project feasibility.

Commercial real estate is far more analytical than residential sales. This field will appeal to you if you enjoy working with numbers and analyzing investment possibilities. Commercial agents often earn more than their residential counterparts, making income a consideration. They also enjoy schedules that conform more to regular working hours.

As a salesperson, the commercial agent has to be outgoing and assertive. Your advice should be based on hard facts and objective analysis (sensing and thinking characteristics), but also the ability to see and present alternatives, creatively solve problems (intuition), and be flexible when circumstances change (perceiving) can contribute to your success. Jim, our commercial agent featured in the next chapter, enjoys the diversity of his job and the many different people he comes in contact with each day.

Mortgage Brokers

Ideal personality profile: Extrovert, Sensing, Thinking, Judging (ESTJ); Introvert, Sensing, Thinking, Judging (ISTJ); and Extrovert, Sensing, Thinking, Perceiving (ESTP).

A mortgage broker is a real estate financing professional who puts together a lender and a borrower. This is done after thoroughly reviewing the needs and capabilities of the borrower, the characteristics of the property, and the various lending programs available from a wide range of lenders. This occupation will appeal to you if you like working with numbers and monitoring the lending marketplace, which is constantly changing.

This occupation is deadline-intensive since loan approval is the last *contingency* in the transaction to be removed. You will have lenders, appraisers, real estate agents, and clients continually meeting deadlines through your services. You should therefore work well under pressure, possess good people skills, and have the ability to run an efficient, organized communication center. (Three key characteristics of judgers are deadline-driven, organized, and efficient.)

You also will be discussing confidential information with clients and should be sensitive to your clients' predicaments. As Jeff,

def•i•ni•tion

A **contingency** is a condition that is built into a purchase offer to make it conditional. The offer is conditional until such time that the conditions are removed. Then, the offer becomes unconditional and binding. The most common contingencies in the real estate transaction are the loan, the physical inspection, and the review of the title.

the mortgage broker, describes in the next chapter, this job can be highly rewarding because clients are usually happy and appreciative after they get their loans. Jeff finds his job as a mortgage broker highly challenging and gratifying.

Property Managers

Ideal personality profile: Extrovert, Sensing, Thinking, Judging (ESTJ); Introvert, Sensing, Thinking, Judging (ISTJ); Extrovert, Sensing, Feeling, Judging (ESFJ); Extrovert, Sensing, Thinking, Perceiving (ESTP); and Extrovert, Sensing, Feeling, Perceiving (ESFP).

The property manager's principal role is to manage properties in order to produce the highest possible return on investment over the longest period of time. Managed commercial properties are likely to be office buildings and shopping centers; residential properties may be rental homes, apartments, and *condominium* developments. Property management generally brings higher financial rewards to its agents than other fields of real estate. Property management also invariably involves more time commitment than its sister fields, as tenants must be found, qualified, and maintained, while the property itself must also be kept in good repair.

def•i•ni•tion

A **condominium** is property developed for concurrent ownership where each owner has a separate interest in a unit combined with an undivided interest in the common areas of the property.

Since property management involves accounting and bookkeeping as well as dealing with owners and tenants, both the introvert and extrovert do well in this profession. Good people skills are mandatory since you will deal with owners and renters on a day-to-day basis. (While introverts may be very good with people, extroverts are naturally *drawn* to others and energized by being with them.) You will deal with raw data in the form of comparable rental values to establish lease rates for your owners (an excellent use of sensing).

You also will deal directly with tradespersons in maintaining your clients' properties. Considering the number of people you deal with and the diversity of their capacities, patience is a requirement, not just a virtue, for a career in property management. Melissa, a property manager, describes in the next chapter the position she has been in for 21 years as anything but routine.

Appraisers

Ideal personality profile: Introvert, Sensing, Thinking, Judging (ISTJ); Introvert, Sensing, Feeling, Judging (ISFJ); Extrovert, Sensing, Thinking, Judging (ESTJ); Extrovert, Sensing, Feeling, Judging (ESFJ); Extrovert, Sensing, Feeling, Perceiving (ESFP).

Real estate *appraisers* do one thing and one thing only: they determine the value of properties. Real estate is appraised to determine many types of values: assessed value to establish property taxes, investment value for investor analysis, fair market value for market analysis, book value for accounting purposes, discount value for tax purposes, rental value for income projections, and insurable value for insurance purposes.

def•i•ni•tion

An **appraiser** estimates the value of property as of a particular date.

The science of appraisal presents varying methods to determine many different values. Most people think a property has one value and one value only—until they venture into a career in real estate appraisal where real estate is valued in different ways depending upon the purpose of the valuation. Appraisers must know acceptable principles of appraisal and have a good knowledge of mathematics, accounting, and economics. Appraisal is the most scientific of the many types of real estate careers. You might call these financial pros the CPAs of real estate.

FYI!

You also can use personality typing to increase your sales effectiveness. The book *The Art of Speed-Reading People* (Tieger & Barron-Tieger) teaches you how to quickly size up people and to speak their language. This book is available at www. personalitytype.com.

This job requires tremendous focus and attention to detail. Appraisers must be observant and accurate with facts. (Hence, all *ideal* types are sensors.) While a lot of the job is done by oneself (the reason most appraisers are probably introverts), appraisers often interact with different types of people including homeowners, town officials, and real estate agents, so the job can certainly encompass extroverted activity and variety (which appeals to sensing, perceivers) as well. Appraisers must rely on established principles of appraisal and comparable sales.

I think of the appraiser as the laboratory technician. Once he gathers supporting information, he establishes value according to a scientific system. The appraiser should be practical and oriented toward the use of methods and systems (which are also activities that appeal more to sensors). In the next chapter, our appraiser, Paul, describes the required personality traits as practical and analytical, pointing out that you must be both, not just one, for this career to be a fit.

Take Your Time

As you can see, there are many careers under the umbrella of real estate agent. A career in real estate can be highly rewarding as long as you take the time to choose the right field and the right office. In other words, your initial decisions are imperative to finding the right fit. While this chapter and the next assist you in choosing the right field, Chapter 6 mentors you through your choice of office.

> **FYI!**
>
> By spending more time typing your personality and assessing its suitability to your career choice, you should be able to head off impulsive choice making. Taking the time for this important analysis before you jump into a career can mean the difference between a gratifying life-long career and a frustrating short-term one.

Take your time when deciding which field is right for you because where you start will probably be where you end. It's true. As creatures of habit, we generally enter a career and spend the next cycle of our lives trying to make it work for us. The time to be selective is now. Choose a field that matches your needs and your personality and allows you to work with energy, enthusiasm, and spirit.

Maureen, a real estate appraiser, is a good example of someone who didn't take the time to scout the field before selecting her career. Maureen had worked as a tax preparer for six years when she realized that tax preparation was not what she wanted to do for the rest of her life. She decided that a career in real estate would give her more versatility, income, and the people contact she missed. She took the required courses and passed the real estate licensing exam. Her neighbor was an appraiser and offered her a spot in his firm.

Maureen began there, stayed there, and never realized her dream. Again she found herself working with numbers, which she likes, but she still does not have the interaction with people she desires. Maureen wishes she had taken her time to research the field better before choosing appraisal. She feels that commercial sales would have better suited her personality and her passion for working with numbers, but once she became established in appraisal, she did not feel like making yet another career transition. Maureen's story is an example of what can happen if you settle into a field before you carefully scrutinize the available career options.

Although the majority of real estate professionals I interviewed for this book shared positive stories about their real estate career choices, Bill had a story similar to Maureen's. Bill obtained his real estate license after brokering securities for more than a decade. He fell into mortgage brokering when he answered an ad from a national bank. The interview went well, and he accepted the position. Early on, he had inklings that mortgage brokering wasn't for him. The money was good, but he felt that office leasing would feed his creative juices far better. Each year he vowed to make his transition, but never did. He stayed where he began and feels frustrated and disappointed that he doesn't have the gumption to make the change.

Research the Field

Do yourself a favor and take your time when evaluating your options. You want to perform your analysis long before you begin your prelicensing study for three important reasons. First, your investigation of the varied real estate career choices may tell you that the profession just is not right for you. Why take the required courses and the examination when real estate is not your answer? Second, some real estate prelicensing courses involve elections between varying courses. It would be wise for you to tailor your prelicensing education to the career you have determined is best for you. Third, when you study the required courses, you will naturally give greater attention to those involving the career you intend to make your own.

There is no rush when it comes to making a choice for the rest of your life, or at least for the foreseeable future. Talk to people, research, intern, join professional groups. Do anything it takes to introduce yourself to the inner workings of each facet of the real estate world. Ideally, you will undertake this level of examination while you are still involved in your current profession or schooling.

When you speak with others about your choices, take their advice with a grain of salt. Chapter 8 encourages you to be an independent thinker, which means not subjecting your ideas to public opinion, or if you do, not taking public opinion to heart. When you contemplate a change, conduct extensive research, but do not seek advice from others.

The independent thinker moves ahead despite public poll, oftentimes turning negative comments into reasons to be challenged. Each time I begin a new endeavor, while I often find a mentor to assist me with my transition, I do not seek validation from

Agent to Agent

Peak earning years for people used to be in their 40s. Now it's mid-50s to 60s.

others. There is a distinction between sharing your ideas with others and the discerning process of receiving mentorship through your transition, both of which will be discussed later in this book. Get your mentorship but do not take public opinion to heart.

Remember also that you will most likely be guided away from the real estate agent profession by existing agents. They have found a good thing, and they want to shelter their territory from interference by new wannabes. Through the processes described in this book, find your own passion and make your own decision.

What's Your Passion?

Since 93 percent of agents come to real estate in a career transition, the odds are good that you are in the midst of your own professional evolution. Realize that you're in a natural life cycle. You have changed as you have progressed down the path of your life. Take time up front to investigate and try on these career options. If you don't, you may end up in a career choice that will invite yet another transition.

Agent to Agent

What's your passion? Your passion may be bicycling. Specialize in a certain neighborhood and bike to client's homes. Your passion may be writing. Create the most laudatory, poetic brochures imaginable. (You will have a lot of competition in this department.) You can fit just about every passion you have into a career in real estate.

There is so much diversity available within the real estate field. It is very important to choose the field that is right for you. If you do, you will have the very best opportunity to stand out because you will enjoy what you do. The question then becomes one of exactly what it is that is right for you. What is your passion? Chapter 8 explores this important question more fully. Now that you have reviewed the career choices and are about to step through a day in the life of each, pause to make this important inquiry of yourself.

Take a deep breath. Take another. Now close your eyes. Ask yourself, "What would I do as a career if I were guaranteed success no matter what?" Ask yourself a number of times. You have an answer. We have all thought about this. We may call our thoughts dreams, but dreams can be attained if they are acknowledged. What did you say? Say it again. Write it down. Remember, you cannot fail. You can have it.

Write your answer here:_____

You have to know that you cannot fail in performing this exercise. You have to know you can be whatever you want to be. When I performed this exercise fifteen years ago, my passion was writing books. Within a year, I was writing my first book. It is powerful to acknowledge what you want within the safety of knowing you cannot fail. You can then look at the fear of failure that stands in your way in a more objective manner, and perhaps even dismiss it as a factor that is no longer relevant in your life. For me, I realized that it was more important to go after my dreams than to fear some failure that may never happen.

Looking at our work on a more philosophical level, our work in life is so much more than just making a living. It is, in fact, one of the most vital places for us to grow and express our creativity. When you consider that many of us spend 50 percent of our waking time working, finding the right avenue for our work is certainly a pursuit worthy of some considered analysis.

I recently read a survey of a hundred people on their deathbeds who revealed that their greatest regret is for the risks they never took. They wished that they had followed their dreams. Now's the time to make your dreams come true through choosing the right real estate career and adopting a positive state of mind.

Carving a Niche

A niche is a specialty. It may be a special area of sales or a special location or a unique demographic target. As you review the standard careers described in this chapter, know that there are niches to be woven throughout the real estate field. Think of what you might specialize in. Once you have your license and begin accumulating experience, there is no limit to the niches you can carve out for yourself. If you understand from the beginning of your real estate career that the field is ripe for the building of niches, you will approach your career with a niche-building state of mind.

For instance, my real estate business is both niche-based and *cyclical-oriented*. Over my career, I have taken a little bit of this and a little bit of that and contoured my own special arena. Residential real estate appealed to me because I enjoy decorating and working with families. I was also interested in investment property because my residential clients often round out their real estate portfolios with tax-motivated purchases. I have melded

def•i•ni•tion

Cyclical orientation allows your practice to thrive whether the real estate market is on an upward or flat trend. When the market changes, you orient your practice to help real estate purchasers and owners deal with the current trend.

these two aspects into a real estate brokerage practice which caters to the market as it goes through its cycles.

Early in my career, when the real estate market was flat, I began to specialize in *equity sharing*, partnering investors and home buyers in equity sharing transactions. In the early 2000s with the stock market downturn, my practice took a turn toward moving clients out of retirement accounts invested in the stock market and into the more reliable real estate market. More recently, as the real estate market has softened, equity sharing and more creative techniques have again gained popularity. My real estate practice keeps shifting with the opportunities created by changes in the economy.

def•i•ni•tion

Equity sharing is a real estate co-ownership strategy whereby one party, the occupier, lives in the property and pays its expenses, while the other party, the investor, puts up the down payment funds. They share tax deductions and profit. Many other structures are also possible, but this is the most common.

Carving out a niche is finding what you're good at and creating a professional position within the ever-changing real estate marketplace. It's about staying in tune with the market and learning and growing with it. The real estate market and its many faces are an enormously rich industry in terms of financial power and people power. It provides a changing stage on which to repackage yourself.

The Least You Need to Know

- There are many choices of careers within the real estate field.

- Knowing yourself and your personality will help you choose wisely among career choices.

- Each field has its advantages and tends to fit specific personality profiles.

- Take the time to research each of the real estate fields and determine your own passions before you leap into a specific field.

- Think about how you can develop a special niche for yourself that gives you opportunities to follow your passions.

Chapter 3

A Day in the Life

In This Chapter

- Julie, a residential sales agent—her story and her day
- Jim, a commercial sales agent—his story and his day
- Jeff, a mortgage broker—his story and his day
- Melissa, a property manager—her story and her day
- Paul, an appraiser—his story and his day

Did your personality profile spell property manager or sales agent? Are you more of an extrovert or an introvert? While the last chapter focused on personality profiling as a way of determining which career is right for you, this chapter looks at a typical day in the life of each real estate professional. This is the hands-on chapter, while the last chapter was a seat in the psychologist's chair. While this chapter focuses primarily on the residential sales agent, it also explores a day in the life for each career professional.

These agents also share their reasons for picking the fields they chose and how their careers have evolved over time. By the time you complete this chapter, you should have a very good idea of whether or not the real estate profession appeals to you and which field fits best with your own professional interests.

For those of you already in the business, step through this chapter to familiarize yourself more fully with what your real estate peers do. If you don't already have solid referral relationships with these professionals, now is the time to develop them. In Chapter 9, I talk extensively about building your important Power Team with these other professionals.

Residential Sales

Since 80 percent of agents choose home sales as a career, I'll start with residential sales. I think that the hokey pokey was created to depict the life of a residential real estate agent. You put your feet in, your hands out, your elbows in, you shake it all about, and then you do the old soft shoe. It's the life of the residential sales agent, a never-ending flutter of people and activity. In just one day this agent can step through more roles than any other agent, ranging from mentor to decorator to therapist to financial analyst.

Julie's Background

Julie is our residential sales agent. She's on her way to Top Dog status. Julie's schooling and licensing were in social work. Working with people is her lifeline, but after ten years as a social worker she found it emotionally depleting and difficult to continue working within the confines of public agencies. The red tape was frustrating and unproductive. Seven years ago she left the profession to have her children. After that, she wanted to return to a career, but one without the structure or aggravation of social work. Following is Julie's story in her own words.

> **Agent to Agent**
>
> The average Realtor nationwide entered the profession at age 39 and has been in the profession for 9 years; as noted in chapter 2, the average age is 52 years of age.

Why Julie Chose Her Career

After researching various professions, my career decision was a toss-up between real estate agent and financial planner. Because I have a knack for finances and a good business head, I felt financial planning would be a good choice, but I also felt that these talents would serve me in the real estate field. I had to complete a lot of classes to become licensed in financial planning, but I wasn't really interested in going back to school for a long time.

Since real estate investment has always been part of my plan for financial independence, I felt that a career in real estate made a lot of sense. I also felt drawn to real estate because it involves working with people and an adjustable work schedule. I picked residential real estate sales because I like dealing with people and it is in line with my enjoyment of home decorating.

I knew some successful agents through my children's school activities and my yoga classes. After researching local residential brokerage firms, I interviewed at the international real estate firm that one of these agents worked for. I went with this firm because it had excellent support for its agents, an extensive program in real estate fundamentals, and continuing education courses presented at the office.

Julie's Career

I liked the office manager and felt comfortable with the other agents and staff. Then I arranged for the agent I knew to be my mentor. My initial assigned work area was small and unappealing, but I decorated it and made that little space work for me. Initially, most of my work was done at the office where I could get support from others and get as much floor time as possible. Now I do most of the paperwork from home before I go to the office and when I return home from my day. The office is primarily where I meet with clients and other professionals, get support, and attend office meetings.

I've been licensed for six years now. I'm very happy with my decision to work in real estate sales. I have been able to handle a full client load and take care of my young children and their schedules. I have taken a number of computer courses so that I can use technology fully in my business. I now have all the latest in computer equipment, and I know that I use technology more than most of my peers. I've incorporated the computer into much of my activity, and I find that correspondence, property searches, and general tasks go very smoothly because of this.

After I had been an agent for three years, I completed some additional real estate planning and investment courses, which were helpful to my clients and to me personally. I'm known as the office tax whiz. I've purchased a duplex as my own real estate investment, and it already has a positive cash flow. I focus my continuing education courses on sharpening my real estate tax and investment skills.

Initially, I started with a 60-40 commission split where 40 percent of my commission went to the real estate company I work for, but now that I have a proven track record and my broker's license, I get a 70-30 split in my favor. I earn far more then I ever thought I would. If I worked more, I would make even more. I put in about 35 hours a week, and I cherish my time off. It took me about a year and a half to get going and build my own clientele. There were periods of uncertainty and scarcity, but I expected it to be rough as I started this new career.

After I had been a residential sales agent for four years, I started doing some business in the commercial residential market. That was a turning point for me. I began offering my clients multi-unit residential properties. I took my broker's examination and I am now licensed as a broker. I am still with the same firm, but if I decide I want to work harder I could go off on my own. I'm mentoring another agent who joined the firm a year ago.

I got a larger space in the office after I had been an agent for three years and I hired an assistant for 15 hours a week. My assistant now works 30 hours a week, mostly from her home. Last year I earned $140,000 from real estate sales and paid $22,000 to my assistant and paid about $20,000 in other expenses. The duplex I bought is bringing in another $550.00 a month above expenses. I love the diversity in my work, and I enjoy helping people find the right home and the right investment property.

The Appeal of Julie's Career

This career will appeal to you if you like working with people and have good people skills. For independent people who like having their own business and control over their time, it is the perfect profession. You have to be organized, though. The money and personal satisfaction are good, as well.

Many agents were formerly managers, salespersons, teachers, homemakers, or administrators. It's no surprise since agents are typically highly self-directed and independent.

A Day in the Life of Julie

Today is Saturday. It is June and business is very busy. Yesterday was a day off for me so today is also a catch-up day. My assistant is not working today so I send her e-mails to take care of when she works on Monday. Both my assistant and I receive our e-mail at home. I am set up to receive my e-mails at the office and at home. In the field, I also can send and receive e-mails from my cell phone or my laptop with the use of an air card.

Between my assistant and me, we produce beautiful sales flyers; staff open houses; write magazine ads; prospect for new clients; follow up with old clients; work with property inspectors, appraisers, and mortgage brokers; and handle the many steps of the sales transaction. Yesterday my assistant put my open house package together and dropped it off at my house. Everything is ready for today's open house.

Julie's Journal Entry for a Day

Julie's typical day begins at 9:00 A.M. and ends at 5:00 P.M. Here are her entries for one day.

9 A.M. Journal Entry: An Offer

My first voice mail message is from another agent who has an offer on one of my listings and wants to present the offer. I return his call and coordinate a presentation time of noon. One of my clients in contract to purchase a vacation home is set to remove her *inspection contingency* tomorrow. I call her and ask if she is satisfied with the condition of the property. I explain that this is the time to ask for a seller credit if she feels the price she has offered does not reflect the condition of the property. It is also the time to cancel the transaction if she is not satisfied with anything found in the inspection reports. My client feels she wants a credit of $7,000 for some work that will need to be done. I prepare a release of her inspection contingency subject to the seller crediting her with $7,000.

10 A.M. Journal Entry: Hand Holding

I receive a call from clients who are feeling nervous. They are concerned because their home is listed for sale, but they haven't found a suitable new home. In the past ten days I have shown them every home listed in their price range and the location they want to live in. None of these homes have appealed to them.

def•i•ni•tion

The **inspection contingency** is the period during which the buyer has the right to perform inspections he feels necessary to discover the condition of the property. This period may be as short as 15 days in a fast market.

Although the market is more of a seller's market than a buyer's market, it still is not typical for sellers to sell subject to finding a replacement home. They have reluctantly agreed not to make finding a replacement home a contingency of the sale. I just held the broker's open house on their home, and interest was high. I am expecting competitive offers in the next day or so.

My clients want to take their home off the market, concerned that they will be left without a place to live. I drive over and talk with them. We agree that the best way to proceed is to build in a customized clause that will give my clients a replacement home contingency, but one that will be more acceptable to a buyer than the typical open-ended contingency.

Noon Journal Entry: An Open House

I return to my office for the noon offer presentation with just enough time left to phone my clients and tell them the offer terms. At 2:00 P.M. I am holding an open house for another client. I like to do the open houses personally, because they are often excellent places to find new clients. My assistant has bought fresh flowers, some refreshments, the usual music to play, and printed marketing brochures. I drive by her house, pick up the supplies, arrive at the home early, and arrange the house with a few last items.

Last week I suggested to my client that professional *staging* of her home could make a big difference in marketability. A stager spent a day doing interior decorating, re-locating furniture, and placing rental plants and artwork throughout the home. The changes were the perfect touch to make this client's property one of the most appealing homes on the market in its price range. The broker's open house was earlier in the week and this is the day to present the home to the public.

def•i•ni•tion

Basic **staging** involves giving the property an objective eye-over and rearranging the furnishings and accessories in the most appealing manner. Advanced staging involves basic staging and possibly minor remodeling and landscape improvement.

The open house brings about 25 people; some may be potential clients. The people who come to an open house sometimes have a house they are thinking about selling. Two couples sound very interested in buying a house. One has an agent already; the other wants to look at a few more houses but sounds interested in making an offer through me. Two couples found that the home did not meet their needs, and we took a little time to review listings on my laptop. Next Wednesday I will show some other properties to one couple.

4:30 P.M. Journal Entry: The Day's End

At 4:30 P.M. I return to the office. I have frantic calls from a client whose *loan contingency* is due to be released in a few days. She reports problems obtaining loan approval. I have an e-mail from another agent inquiring about a property I have listed. But, before dealing with these issues, I call the clients whose home I received an offer on today to coordinate delivery of the offer to them and a meeting tomorrow to respond to the offer. I return a few more calls and leave messages that I will be available tomorrow between noon and 5 P.M.

def•i•ni•tion

The **loan contingency** is the period during which the buyer obtains loan approval. The buyer makes the offer contingent upon obtaining the loan described in the offer. The loan contingency often expires 30 days prior to closing.

Julie's Opinion of Residential Sales

Following are closing comments Julie made about a career in residential sales:

- ◆ **Personality type:** You need to be able to handle several deals at the same time, which requires a great deal of multitasking and multi-role-playing. Patience and persistence are part of every activity since a transaction can easily fall apart if you don't track it closely and stay in touch with everyone.

- ◆ **Character traits:** I think that honesty, a genuine liking of people, a calm demeanor and conversation, and an ability to track detail and understand options are all part of the successful agent. It may be that honesty is too high on my list, but the consequences of even a small white lie are not worth it. I like my clients to trust me, so my assistant and I do everything by the old golden rule.

- ◆ **Biggest rewards:** Satisfied customers; knowing that you got the buyer or seller what he wanted in the transaction and that you did it professionally; you are your only boss; being rewarded well for doing what you enjoy; being able to see your children off to school in the morning.

- ◆ **Biggest pitfalls:** This is not the profession for a disorganized person. There is no room for forgetting a detail or confusing the needs of clients. Real estate draws its fair share of lawsuits, which is always a concern to me and most in my profession.

FYI!

Lawyers are known as deal breakers in real estate. They have reputations for analyzing all the should haves, would haves, and could haves, and often scaring their clients out of transactions. Real estate transactions end up in litigation more often than most other types of transactions. Generally, it is the buyer who sues the seller. The agent or real estate office also often is named in the lawsuit. A typical lawsuit is for failure to disclose a known condition to the buyer. Many buyers think the seller warrants the property's condition similar to a new product warranty. Actually, the seller's duty is to advise the buyer of *known* conditions. If the roof leaks and the seller did not know of the leak, he cannot be held liable.

Commercial Sales

While the majority of agents choose residential sales, commercial sales agents are sometimes thought of as the financial wizards of the real estate field. Commercial agents analyze investment potential and tax criteria of properties whereas their residential counterparts are primarily focused on property features.

Jim's Background

Jim is our commercial sales agent. Seventeen years ago, after three careers, he got his real estate license. Jim had lived on both the East Coast and West Coast where he owned a boys camp, was a teacher, and then owned and operated a book publishing company. He has a *CCIM* (*certified commercial investment member*) designation and is in the top 10 percent of his profession. He has his broker's license, works for himself, and has a part-time assistant. He has a Bachelor's degree. (We will meet up with Jim again in Part 6 of this book, where Jim will share more details about his CCIM designation.)

def•i•ni•tion

The **CCIM (certified commercial investment member)** designation is granted by the National Association of Realtors upon successful completion of a prolonged course of study and experience. CCIMs are recognized experts in commercial real estate brokerage, leasing, asset management valuation, and investment analysis.

Why Jim Chose His Career

I backed into commercial real estate as a result of selling my book publishing company. During the transaction, I was impressed by the broker who was a specialist in *business opportunities* as well as commercial investment properties. He was smart and professional and had a good sense of humor. We got to be friends, and he suggested that I get a real estate license and join his small independent company of three brokers. I like people, action, and making a good living, and commercial sales seemed to fit the bill. I obtained my license and joined the firm. In my state, I was able to skip the agent's exam and sit for the broker's exam because I had a B.A. degree.

I usually work about forty hours a week, Monday through Friday. Sometimes I meet with a client on the weekend. I spend most of my work time in the office, although I

def•i•ni•tion

A **business opportunity** is a business for sale, generally with a proven track record.

PDA stands for personal digital assistant. This is a generic name for a handheld device that keeps address and phone information and schedules. Some of these devices have phones and some have Blackberry Internet capability as an all-in-one.

have a home office set up. I use a laptop computer and a *PDA*. I now own and operate three commercial properties, and about 30 percent of my time is spent on my own properties. I have made a very good living in part from commissions and in part from my own investments and taking an ownership interest in properties in lieu of commission.

The Appeal of Jim's Career

For a small investment of time and money, you can work for yourself and have control over your work time and play time. You also can make a good living from commissions, and you can make a lot of money by investing in real estate. I wish I would have started in real estate when I was fresh out of college.

A Day in the Life of Jim

I arrive at the office at 9 A.M. and return two calls about my office complex listing. I e-mail information to these people. I call the *Wall Street Journal* to run an ad for a new listing of a medical office building. At 11 A.M., I meet with the owner of the office building to receive the rent roll and other tenant information so I can work up a package to present to the monthly commercial-investment marketing meeting next week. Commercial sales are tied to the income received by the property.

At 1 P.M. I have lunch with a prospective seller of a building. He wants to sell and lease back his office space. He is interviewing several brokers and wants a competitive commission arrangement. Since I work for myself I can work out any arrangement that suits me and my client. He also wants a broker who is a CCIM, and I qualify.

At 3 P.M. I meet the appraiser at an apartment building, now in escrow. At 4 P.M. I go to the same apartment building for a contractor's inspection. We encounter a problem with two tenants who will not allow us into their apartments without 24-hour notice, which was given by phone yesterday but not acknowledged by the tenants. I reschedule the contractor to see these two apartments tomorrow at the same time. At 5 P.M. I return to my office to answer e-mails and phone calls. I begin to work up a medical office building package for a building a client will *exchange* out of, and then I submit the initial numbers to my client's accountant. As you can see, my days are often quite full.

def•i•ni•tion

An **exchange**, also known as 1031 Exchange or Starker Exchange, allows an owner to sell a property and reinvest in another property of equal or greater value without any tax consequences.

Jim's Opinion of Commercial Sales

Following are closing comments Jim made about a career in commercial sales:

◆ **Personality type:** Outgoing, friendly, patient, flexible, energetic, and detail-oriented. If you like and understand numbers well enough to do your own tax return, you may be good in this field.

◆ **Character traits:** I work with people and with their finances. I think a thorough understanding of investment returns is essential in order to represent income property. I also find that good listening helps in working with clients, especially the ones who are looking for space for their own businesses. It also helps to like being part of various community service groups, because networking is essential in the commercial sales business. I am active in two business networking groups and two civic organizations.

◆ **Biggest rewards:** Knowing both parties of a transaction are happy about the outcome. I also thoroughly enjoy finding investment opportunities for myself. Each day is completely different from the one before.

◆ **Biggest pitfalls:** Liability for things you say or don't say. There are a lot of lawsuits in this business, so I keep careful records and am scrupulous about my paperwork.

Agent to Agent

If you decide to become your own broker, make sure you get liability insurance, also known as errors and omissions insurance. Real estate transactions end up in litigation quite often. An agent should never practice without insurance with good limits of coverage. The agent who owns investment property also would be wise to own these properties in the name of a limited liability company to protect these assets from any personal judgment that may arise against him. Asset protection and good insurance coverage are a winning combination.

Mortgage Broker

Mortgage brokers are tied to the phone and the office more than any other agent. They have to be available during regular business hours and must continually stay in contact with changing interest rates and loan product criteria. These financial pros need to have nerves of steel to stay calm amidst ever-changing details and never-ending loan deadlines.

Jeff's Background

Jeff is our mortgage broker. He has been brokering for nine years. His wife is also a broker with the same company. Jeff graduated from college with a B.A. in Economics and became a commodities broker. He transitioned to mortgage brokering because he was looking for more client satisfaction. In commodities, he felt his clients were never happy.

Why Jeff Chose His Career

I always liked finance and real estate and felt mortgage brokering provided the ideal blend of my two interests. My choice also was based on the fact that I liked determining my own income instead of someone else deciding for me.

The Appeal of Jeff's Career

This career will appeal to someone who enjoys working with numbers and likes challenges. It is the ideal profession for someone who enjoys independence and being his or her own boss.

A Day in the Life of Jeff

I arrive at the office at 9 A.M. and immediately gather lender rate sheets for loans to be *locked* in. I retrieve voice mail and e-mail messages, and pass some on to my assistant. I review pending loans with my assistant. We lock in rates for clients whose loans are in a ready-to-lock status. I work on tough-to-qualify loans, repackaging them for lender submission.

def•i•ni•tion

A loan is **locked** in when the lender guarantees the loan's rate and terms.

I answer the phone, which rings about 75 times a day, and read and respond to e-mails from clients, Realtors, and title companies. I usually spend about one hour a day prospecting for new clients, although 95 percent of my business is referral-based. I spend about an hour a day speaking with loan representatives discussing the loans I have to place. Nearly all of my time is spent in the office except for about five hours of golf with my networking team each week.

Jeff's Opinion of Being a Mortgage Broker

Following are closing comments Jeff made about a career as a mortgage broker:

- **Personality type:** In this business you have to be personable and outgoing.

- **Character traits:** You need to be detail-oriented, able to listen and process what a client is saying they are looking for. You need to be adaptable and creative in your thinking to package your loans, especially the difficult ones, for the best lender presentation. You need to be a good problem solver because most loans have problems one way or the other.

- **Biggest rewards:** Everyone loves you at the end of the transaction. Your income is dependent upon how hard you work. If you are organized, you can play a lot of golf and still have a good income.

- **Pitfalls:** Don't promise your clients anything until you lock them in. The market fluctuates continually and the rate you promise could be gone tomorrow when the loan is ready to be locked. A commission structure can be challenging when you first start out or when interest rates climb and no one wants a loan. I also wish I could have found someone to train me better at the beginning of my career.

Property Management

The property manager is a facilitator and a juggler all in one. This professional works with property owners, tenants, and trades people simultaneously. The job can require the patience of a saint, the people skills of a couple's therapist, and the ability to multi-task to the extreme.

Melissa's Background

Twenty-one years ago, at 19, Melissa became a receptionist for the property management company she now owns. Prior to that she worked for a title company, which she found to be repetitive and uninteresting. Real estate has been her only real career. She now has seven employees, has her *Master Property Manager* (*MPM*) designation, and has served as President of the National Association of Residential Property Managers. (Melissa also will be featured later in Top Dogs.)

def•i•ni•tion

Master Property Manager (MPM) is a designation given by the National Association of Residential Property Managers (NARPM), a trade organization for the residential property management industry, to an agent with extensive experience.

Why Melissa Chose this Career and the Appeal of It

I loved the "never-a-dull-moment" day of the property manager. Why might others choose this career? Property management is an exciting career. It is a salaried position for some people and provides a lot of people interaction.

A Day in the Life of Melissa

There is never a routine day. I start my day going through paperwork in the office. Many days in the late morning and early afternoon I meet with prospective clients. I am on the phone a lot returning calls and speaking to owners regarding repairs, prospective tenants, or the rental market. I usually work a long day that generally flies by, leaving plenty to do the next day. Many people call wanting to set up an appointment to see a specific rental that same day. Since I manage seven employees and own the company, there is a good amount of management work to perform.

Melissa's Opinion of Being a Property Manager

Following are closing comments Melissa made about a career in property management:

- ◆ **Personality type:** Property managers should be friendly, social people. They need to be able to handle several things at once and pay attention to the details and follow-up.

- ◆ **Character traits:** You are handling someone else's investment property and their money, so I recommend being honest and competent in bookkeeping. You are dealing with people from all walks of life from owners to tenants to trades persons, so liking people and being fair with them is also important. I remind everyone that we treat each rental as a business. This means never skipping credit checks on potential tenants because we might feel sorry for them. Decisions should never be based on how we feel about the owner or tenant.

- ◆ **Biggest rewards:** The variety and the excitement keep me hopping. I love the many different things I do in my day. I get a feeling of satisfaction in the upkeep and appearance of the properties I manage, and the high rate of occupancy I achieve for my clients. I enjoy working with the service people who do good work for me, like painting, carpet cleaning, groundskeeping, and more.

- ◆ **Pitfalls:** Sometimes an owner may be unwilling to keep his property in good repair. I hear many complaints every day from tenants and from owners. I also hear some sad personal stories from tenants who are not able to pay their rent on time, and I have to make some difficult calls in those situations. Complaints are the nature of this business since you are managing properties. You cannot take them to heart.

The Appraiser

When appraisers number crunch they can estimate value to a decimal point. These mathematicians of real estate assign numbers to features such as view, design, functionality, and outdoor space, to name a few. Through comparing these features to other similar properties recently sold, they arrive at an appraised value.

Paul's Background

Paul was a policeman and then a loan manager, when he gravitated to appraisal about 20 years ago.

Why Paul Chose this Career and the Appeal of It

I considered appraisal to be the area of real estate lending that allowed a good deal of independence. Since I was already in real estate lending, I thought that my employer and others in the lending field would probably be a good source of business. I liked construction and am good in math, both of which are helpful in the appraisal field.

I also was drawn to the freedom of being my own boss and working out in the field. Anyone who cherishes independence should consider a career as an appraiser. A person with good math and computer skills who enjoys analysis would enjoy this field. I'm out and about a great deal, and I enjoy the process of valuing properties.

A Day in the Life of Paul

I usually set my appointments for early in the morning, so at 8:30 A.M. I might be taking front, rear, and street pictures and measuring a large home. I pull *comparables* before I go out to the property so when I finish the inspection, I drive by the comparables and take pictures of them. Back in the office I start populating the appraisal report software with floor plans, pictures, maps, and data. When the report is completely filled out, I convert it to a PDF file and e-mail it to my client.

It takes about a day to complete a simple appraisal. Appraisals for attorneys and tax professionals involving income property require more in-depth analysis and can take as long as several days. I sometimes feel like a scientist at work since I pinpoint the value of a property through all sorts of logical steps.

def·i·ni·tion

Comparables are similar properties recently sold located in the same proximity. Recent is about six months. Proximity is within a mile or so. Other factors considered are amenities and condition.

Paul's Opinion of Being an Appraiser

Following are closing comments Paul made about a career as an appraiser:

- ◆ **Personality Type:** Independent people who like working on their own and have a bent for math and technology are good appraisers.

◆ **Character Traits:** You must be practical and analytical. If you are just practical, you might be a contractor. If you are only analytical, you might be a loan officer. If you are both, you can be an appraiser. You need to be able to use a computer and to describe things simply.

FYI!

An average single-family home appraisal takes about an hour or so on-site, an hour to drive around the neighborhood and photograph comparable properties, and about four hours to gather some comparables and write the report.

◆ **Biggest rewards:** The biggest reward is freedom, lots of freedom. The money is also good. You also learn about good investment opportunities because you are often in on the first stages of someone wanting to sell a property. Another nice perk is that business is rather impersonal. An appraisal is ordered, it is worked up based on statistical information and methods, and it is produced. You have little dealing with clients and the problems that can crop up in representing them.

◆ **Pitfalls:** Most of the time the people that you deal with do not really want an appraisal. They call in an appraiser because they have to get one. They may be nervous if they want a low appraisal for tax purposes or a high appraisal for loan qualification purposes. You can't always plan your time in advance, because appraisals often must be done and submitted in a tight timeframe. Over the past few years licensing of appraisers has become far more complicated. There are all kinds of requirements and categories of designations that did not exist when I started in the profession.

The Least You Need to Know

◆ There are many career options under the umbrella of real estate. Each option has different characteristics and individual activities that make up a typical day.

◆ The residential agent has a flurry of activity and has the most personal involvement with clients.

◆ The commercial agent is similar to an investment analyst in some respects.

◆ The appraiser is like a scientific professional through his or her use of valuation methods and mathematical analysis.

Chapter 4

Your Prelicensing Education

In This Chapter

- ◆ A summary of prelicensing requirements
- ◆ An overview of the real estate principles course
- ◆ An introduction to property rights and the ways to hold title
- ◆ A look at the differences between condos and co-ops
- ◆ A survey of deeds used to transfer property

If you're reading this chapter, you have made the decision to become a real estate agent. Congratulations! You are about to enter an exciting and abundant profession. In all states and provinces, licensing is required to become a real estate agent. You have two steps in front of you to achieve your goal. One is to satisfy the prelicensing educational requirements. The second step is to take and pass the licensing exam.

This chapter covers step one, satisfying your state's prelicensing educational requirements for real estate agent licensing. Each state's requirements differ. A few states have no educational requirements. Most states require an average of 60 hours of education, while California and Quebec, Canada, tip the scales at 135 hours and 240 hours, respectively. Requirements should be obtained from the Real Estate Commission in the state where you want to practice.

FYI!

The following states and Canadian provinces require 90 hours or more of courses before you may take the agent exam:

Arizona, California, Delaware, Idaho, Kentucky, Louisiana, Nevada, Ohio, Utah, West Virginia, Alberta, and Quebec. Some of these hours can be filled within a year or two after licensing.

The Terminology

FYI!

Appraisal is covered separately by a certification procedure, and is beyond the scope of this chapter. The entry-level certification is "residential appraiser," while the advanced designation, "general appraiser," requires additional education and experience. California has four levels of appraiser certification.

Here's how the real estate profession works. There are two categories of agents. The *entry category* is a salesperson. Some states refer to this entry licensing as broker associate, agent, or sales associate. The *advanced category* is the broker. Broker licensing is conferred on the agent after experience and additional education levels are met.

In this book I refer to each licensed real estate professional as an agent unless he has become licensed as a broker, at which time he is referred to as a broker. Part 6 of this book, which focuses on becoming a Top Dog, addresses advanced licensing and the examination of brokers. This chapter deals with licensing of agents only.

Requirement Exceptions

In most states licensed lawyers or graduates of law schools are exempt from some, but often not all, course requirements. For others, an exemption may apply if you took the required courses at a recognized college or university and achieved a passing grade. Most states also accord reciprocity to licensees of other states, requiring that only their state's portion of the exam be taken.

Some states also provide exemptions from broker experience requirements, allowing qualified candidates to bypass the agent exam and go directly to the broker's exam, if you have …

- ◆ A four-year college degree or a higher level of education.

- ◆ A certain amount of recent experience as a real estate professional in certain job categories not requiring licensing.

Cave!

Not all states and provinces have education or experience exemptions. Be sure to check on your particular state's requirements.

If you are exempt from the agent exam, then you may read the last section of this book on becoming a Top Dog, which discusses the broker exam and its prelicensing requirements.

Prelicensing Course Procedures

The vast majority of states and Canadian provinces require license applicants to take prelicensing educational courses accredited by their state licensing agency before they qualify to sit for the exam. In other states, applicants can take these educational courses within a specified time after being licensed. Still other states require prelicensing courses to be completed before taking the exam as well as postlicensing courses targeted for one to two years after being licensed. There are significant differences between states. These additional courses are over and above annual continuing education courses that are required in all states to keep your license current.

FYI!
The following is a partial list of supplemental courses offered in California where other courses must be completed in addition to a course on real estate principles. If your state has supplemental course requirements, it is good to know which real estate career you intend to pursue so you can gear your courses toward that field. ◆ Real Estate Appraisal ◆ Property Management ◆ Real Estate Finance ◆ Real Estate Economics ◆ Legal Aspects of Real Estate ◆ Business Law ◆ Escrows ◆ Mortgage Loan Brokering and Lending ◆ Computer Applications in Real Estate

Prelicensing courses and the state exams cover the general real estate principles described later in this chapter as well as state-specific courses covering the laws specific to your state. Some states have additional course requirements. In those states, licensees often are given the option of selecting courses from a course list.

Determine Your State's Requirements

The best way to determine your state's licensing requirements is to search the Internet for "(name of your state) real estate commission." This search should bring you to the agency that regulates the licensing of real estate professionals. Mark the site as a favorite on your web browser so you can easily return to it.

Take note of the following requirements and exemptions:

- License requirements, such as age, citizenship, and other factual information
- Prelicensing course requirements
- Postlicensing course requirements
- Course requirement exemptions
- Agent licensing exemptions

With this information you will know what courses you need to take, how many hours these courses involve, whether you can skip the agent exam and just take the broker exam, and whether there are courses you will have to take after licensing to complete the process.

Prelicensing Courses

Companies providing prelicensing instruction have programs tailored to meet state prelicensing course requirements. Some states allow all course work to be done online or in correspondence courses. Some states require all or some classroom study. To find these companies, do another Internet search for "(name of your state) real estate prelicensing courses" or look in the Yellow Pages under Real Estate Schools. Some large real estate firms also offer prelicensing programs to qualify you for the exam and prepare you to take the licensing exam.

FYI!

You want to locate a company that provides the training that suits you best. If online methods suit you and comply with your state's requirements, find an online company. If you feel you do better with human interaction for your instruction or if your state requires it, find a company that fits these requirements. These companies are set up to conform with your state's requirements. The vast majority of prelicensing instructors offer state-specific courses.

When you search for course instruction, make sure that the company you sign up with also has courses that prepare you for the real estate exam itself. You may wonder why you need an examination preparation course after you've just completed all these real estate courses. In Chapter 5, you will understand why. There is an art to taking the real estate exam, and there are courses to make you a master at the exam-taking process.

Timing and Surviving

On average, it takes about three months from the time you enroll in the prelicensing courses to take your licensing exam. The average time for students to complete the prelicensing courses is six to eight weeks. You then receive your certificate of completion, apply for the exam, and take the exam, all of which takes four to five weeks. In other words, three months may elapse from the day you enroll in your prelicensing courses to the day you sit down and actually take your state exam.

It's a good idea to take your coursework and the exam while you're still employed elsewhere. Start saving money on the side. Build up approximately six months of seed money so that you can start your new career without money concerns. Don't forget that you will be paid on an irregular basis by commissions earned, and in the beginning you may not earn a commission for some time. It takes a good amount of wherewithal both financially and emotionally to jump-start a new real estate business. But anything worthwhile takes some good advance planning and a strong dose of persistence.

Cave!

Ideally, when you begin your practice you will want to have a nice car to tour clients in, a portable phone, a laptop computer, a PDA, and a digital camera. All of these cost money. Make sure you are financially set to acquire this equipment and live your life comfortably for about half a year before you start your new career.

Start telling everyone you know of your intentions to enter the real estate business and load up your database with names and contact information so you will have prospects to contact when you start your real estate business. Don't leave your employment until you have a good stash of cash and have passed the examination.

Real Estate Principles

The remainder of this chapter touches on the general real estate principles that are covered in your prelicensing courses and on your licensing exam. Of course, these principles do not include state-specific laws. For each course description, there is an average percentage of how much of the licensing exam you can expect each subject to cover.

Nature of Real Property and Ownership

The nature of real estate property and ownership should make up about 20 percent of the total exam.

Types of Real Property Rights

Real estate rights exist in many forms. The visible, or apparent, rights are the land and its improvements. Other rights also include the air, water, mineral and oil, and gas rights. There are also *real property* and *personal property* rights. Real property interests also come in varying types of estates, including *fee simple* (absolute and indefinite), life estates (measured by a lifespan), and leasehold estates (leases).

def•i•ni•tion

Real property is the land, its rights, and anything attached to it. The improvements (home, barn, or anything built on the property) are considered real property. Real property is transferred by deed.

Personal property is anything on the land that is not affixed and is moveable. For instance, furniture and farm equipment are personal property since they are not permanently affixed to the land. Personal property is transferred by bill of sale, not deed.

Fee simple is the most complete ownership one can have in a property. It establishes ownership of a property without limitation by time or any other factor. Most people own property in fee simple.

Here is an example of how property rights and ownership work: if I buy your property, you will most likely transfer fee simple title to me. With that title, I also receive the right to the air above the property, the resources below it (oil, for example), and the improvements on the property.

Holding Title

Title may be held by one or more persons and various different recognized entities. Methods of holding title, each of which have legal and tax significance, differ between the states. In some states, individuals can hold title in *joint tenancy*, meaning that the survivor of the owners becomes the sole owner without the necessity of probate. In other states, married couples desiring this type of *survivorship* hold title as *tenants by the entirety*. Community property states, representing a minority of states, permit holding title as *community property*. Your prelicensing course will instruct you on the ways for holding title in your state.

> **FYI!**
>
> If you live in an area where views are important, your neighbors may claim they have the right to a view over your property. They don't. Generally, you have the right to use the air above your property (the view) however you choose.

def•i•ni•tion

Joint tenancy is a way co-owners hold title in nearly all states if they want a surviving co-owner to receive the deceased co-owner's interest without probate. The co-owners do not have to be married.

Survivorship. The co-owner automatically receives full title without the need for probate when a co-owner dies.

Tenants by the entirety is the way a husband and wife hold title in 27 states if they want the surviving spouse to receive the deceased spouse's interest without probate. It is similar to joint tenancy used in other states.

Community property is a way of holding title without survivorship by married persons in states that have community property laws.

Community property with right of survivorship is a way of holding title by married persons in some states that have community property laws which allow the surviving spouse to receive a deceased spouse's interest without probate.

Tenants in common is a way for co-owners to own property together without survivorship rights. Their interests pass to their heirs, not to one another, when they die.

California and a few other community property states now permit married persons to hold title as *community property with right of survivorship*, a combination of joint tenancy and community property and similar to tenancy by the entirety. *Tenants in common* is usually the way co-owners hold title if they are not married. Each state's real estate laws provide detailed information on holding title.

FYI!
Community property states are Arizona, California, Idaho, Louisiana, Nevada, New Mexico, Texas, and Washington.
Tenancy by the entirety states are Alaska, Arkansas, Delaware, District of Columbia, Florida, Hawaii, Indiana, Kentucky, Maryland, Michigan, Mississippi, Missouri, New Jersey, New York, North Carolina, Ohio, Oklahoma, Oregon, Pennsylvania, Rhode Island, Tennessee, Utah, Vermont, Virginia, Washington, West Virginia, and Wyoming.

Here is an example of how holding title works: if a married couple (Papa Bear and Mama Bear, for example) wants to hold title so the survivor receives the property without probate, they will hold title as "Papa Bear and Mama Bear, husband and wife, as tenants by the entirety."

If this married couple lives in a community property state they would hold title as "Papa Bear and Mama Bear, husband and wife, as community property with rights of survivorship."

If Papa Bear and Mama Bear are not married but want the survivor to have full title, title would be held as "Papa Bear and Mama Bear, as joint tenants."

If Papa Bear and Mama Bear do not want the survivor to receive title but instead want their heirs to inherit it, title would be held as "Papa Bear and Mama Bear, as tenants in common."

Common Interest Developments

Common interest developments consist of *condominiums* and *cooperatives*. In condominium ownership each unit has its own deed and is separately taxed and mortgaged. Governing functions are most often carried out by an elected association which assesses association dues to the condominium owners. Documents called *conditions, covenants, and restrictions* (*CC&Rs*) define what owners can and cannot do with their properties. Cooperatives are different since owners do not go on title, instead receiving shares in the cooperative and a lease of a unit.

def•i•ni•tion

Condominiums are properties developed for concurrent ownership where each owner has a separate interest in a unit combined with an undivided interest in the common areas of the property.

Cooperatives are ownership of property by a corporation in which each resident owns a percentage share of the corporation, but does not hold title to the property.

Covenants, conditions, and restrictions, often referred to as **CC&Rs,** are rules that govern how a property looks and is used. These limitations are most commonly recorded on title on properties in a subdivision by the developer of the property. They are common with condominiums and multi-use properties, but may also pertain to single-family homes.

Here is an example of how common interest development works: if I purchase an interest in a condominium, my name goes on the title and the legal description to the property shows exclusive occupancy of my particular unit and a nonexclusive right to use the common area of the property as a whole. For a cooperative, I would receive shares in the corporation and the lease of a unit, but my name would not go on the title.

Property Restrictions

Property restrictions include factors that restrict the use or ownership of a property. *Easements* and CC&Rs restrict the full and free use of property while judgments, liens, and mortgages affect the *equity* of the property. All of these restrictions are recorded on the title to the property.

Here is an example of how property restrictions work: an example of an easement is a right my property gives to a neighbor to run drainage pipes across my property at a certain location. In that location, I cannot build in a way that interferes with the easement right. There is an easement recorded on my property in favor of my neighbor.

In addition, CC&Rs recorded on my property may require that I must obtain the consent of the design review committee if I want to add onto my outdoor patio.

def•i•ni•tion

Easements are rights to use the property of another person for a specific purpose. Easements are recorded on the title on both the property enjoying the right and on the property burdened by the right.

Equity is the difference between the value of the property and the loans against it.

An example of a lien is when my lender records a lien (a deed of trust or mortgage depending on the state) on my property in the amount of $200,000 since they loaned me this amount. When I sell the property, this amount must be paid off. Another example is a money judgment someone obtains against me and ends up as a lien against my property.

Governmental Limitations

The use of properties is subject to governmental restrictions in the form of zoning ordinances (regulation of the building of structures and use of the property for certain purposes) and building codes (standards of building and permit regulations). A process called *eminent domain* allows a governmental body to *condemn* a property for public use and pay the owner just compensation.

def•i•ni•tion _____

Eminent domain is the governmental right to take private property for necessary public use as long as it fairly compensates the owner. The process by which this occurs is called **condemnation.**

Here is an example of governmental limitations and how they affect property rights: my property is in an R-1 zone, which allows one, single-family home per one acre. (R stands for residential and 1 represents how many homes are permitted.) If the government decides it needs my property for the public good to extend the freeway, it exercises its eminent domain powers and must compensate me for the value of my property.

Land Description

The ways of legally describing a property consist of government survey systems (grids), *metes and bounds*, and subdivision lot and block numbers.

def•i•ni•tion _____

Metes and bounds is a method of identifying a parcel by reference to its boundaries and its shape.

Here is an example of a land description: a metes and bounds description begins with a point of beginning and uses the four quadrants of the compass by use of degrees and feet, in other words, "beginning at the intersection of Main and Minor Streets thence along the south side of Little Street for 150 feet, thence south 45 degrees east … (360 degrees covered) … to the point of beginning."

Valuation of Property

The valuation of property section of the exam makes up about 15 percent of the total exam length. The following sections discuss the various aspects of property valuation.

Appraisal

Appraisal is the process of creating an opinion about value by the use of accepted practices. It takes comparable recent sales, size, amenities, and condition of the property, *depreciation*, and several other accounting principles into consideration, depending on the type of property and the type of appraisal.

def•i•ni•tion

Depreciation is the allocation of the cost of an improvement over its life according to a set formula in the form of a tax deduction.

All lenders require an appraisal of a property to justify the real property loans they make. If I want to know the value of my property, the best method is to obtain an appraisal.

Taxes and Assessments

Income tax advantages relating to principal residences, vacation homes, and investment property are covered. The principal residence owner enjoys deductions for payment of loan interest and property taxes and exemptions from gain on sale. The investment property renders depreciation and other investment deductions and the ability to sell through a *tax-free exchange*.

def•i•ni•tion

Tax-free exchanges, also known as 1031 exchanges, allow taxes on profits to be deferred for real estate owners selling investment, rental, business, or vacation real estate and investing in other real estate.

The deductions an owner can take depend on whether the property is her principal residence, a vacation home, or investment property.

Financing of Real Estate

Financing real estate accounts for about 20 percent of the exam. The following sections discuss the aspects of financing you can expect on the exam.

Types of Loans

There are many types of loans, including *VA*, *FHA*, and conventional loans. For example, if I am a veteran or qualify for an FHA-insured loan, I may be able to obtain a more favorable loan through these branches of the government. This is more of a memorization exercise than anything else.

Mortgages and Foreclosures

Nearly all properties are purchased with a loan that takes the form of a mortgage or deed of trust recorded on the title. These loans allow the lender to *foreclose* in the event of *default*. Lender requirements are discussed as well as consequences of default.

For example, if I buy a property worth $300,000 and the loan is for $250,000, the lender will record its security interest on the title as a deed of trust or mortgage, depending on the state the property is in, and will foreclose on that interest if I default on the loan.

def•i•ni•tion

VA is the acronym for Veterans Administration. **FHA** stands for Federal Housing Administration. FHA loans allow qualified borrowers to obtain loans with as little as a 3 percent down payment.

To **foreclose** on a property means to liquidate the property for payment of a debt secured by it.

To **default** is to not meet a legal obligation.

Transfer of Ownership

Transfer of ownership accounts for about 15 percent of the exam.

Deeds

Types of deeds are *warranty deeds*, *grant deeds*, and *quitclaim deeds*. The type of deed used confers the type of guarantee given when a property is transferred. The wording of the deed is important to make the deed a valid contract. The process of *recording* deeds as well as the concept of *adverse possession* as a means to acquire title to a property are important to understand.

Here is an example of a deed: if I sign a quitclaim deed, I make no title warranty to you. If I sign a warranty or grant deed, I do make title warranties to you. To claim your property by adverse possession, I file an action in the court system to quiet title (obtain title) to your property.

def•i•ni•tion

A **warranty deed** guarantees that the title is free and clear. A **grant deed** has fewer guarantees than a warranty deed. A **quitclaim** has no guarantees.

Recording is the act of entering deeds and other similar documents affecting title to a property in the public record.

Adverse possession is the acquisition of property through prolonged and unauthorized use of someone else's property.

Closing Procedures

The acts of approving of *clear title* through a *title report*, ensuring a clear title through the purchase of *title insurance*, and completing the act of transferring title by recording the deed all serve to finalize the transfer of a property. *Settlement statements* allocate the amounts each party is charged for transferring title and itemizing its expenditures.

def•i•ni•tion

Clear title is ownership of property subject only to the claims described in a title report.

A **title report** is the report issued by a title company or closing attorney reporting the condition of the title to a property as disclosed by a search of the public record.

Title insurance is a policy guaranteeing that the title is clear and the property is legally owned by the seller. Basic coverage does not involve a site inspection by the title company whereas extended coverage may. A site inspection allows the title insurance to provide coverage for more conditions.

A **settlement statement** is a detailed accounting of buyer and seller debits and credits in the transaction.

The title report tells you whether there are easements, CC&Rs, or other restrictions affecting the property you intend to acquire. Title insurance ensures that you have clear title. Recordation of the deed in the public record makes the transaction part of the public record. The settlement statement describes how much you pay at closing for interest, insurance, purchase price, loan charges, agent commission, taxes, escrow fees, and so on.

Real Estate Brokerage

Real estate brokerage accounts for about 30 percent of the exam. The following sections describe the aspects of real estate brokerage.

Agency

Agency relationships describe the obligations between the agents in the transaction and the buyers and sellers. For example, if I represent you as your agent in a transaction, I have an agency relationship with you. I become your legal agent, and you become my principal.

There are many agency relationships, including seller's agent, buyer's agent, and *dual agent.*

Listings

A *listing* is the employment contract between a broker and a seller. These contracts provide for commission amount, term of the listing, agent's duties, and a description of the type of listing. Most listings are *exclusive right to sell* listings.

Here is an example of a listing agreement: when my client lists her property for sale with me, my exclusive right to sell listing agreement states that the listing is for four months, the listing price is $250,000, and the total commission to be paid is 6 percent of the sale price.

def•i•ni•tion

A real estate **agency relationship** is one where your client, or the principal, is represented by you, the agent, to act on their behalf. There are many legal obligations that arise because of this relationship.

A **dual agent** represents both a buyer and seller in a transaction.

A **listing** is a contract between the agent's broker and the owner that gives the broker the right to sell or lease the property.

An **exclusive right to sell** is a type of listing agreement between an owner and an agent's broker that pays the broker a commission even if the property is sold by someone else during the listing term.

Sales Contracts and Options

Purchase agreements include all the terms by which a buyer will buy and a seller will sell. It provides for the price, closing date, contingencies, and remedies on default. *Option agreements* are distinguished, as they establish a right to buy at a later time.

For example, the offer I make on a property becomes a purchase agreement after it is accepted by the seller. It regulates the entire transaction.

An example of an option agreement is if you agree to sell me your property in two years for a specified amount, I have an option agreement with you.

def•i•ni•tion

Option agreements give you the right to buy a property at a later specified time and price.

Federal Laws

You must be aware of fair housing laws relating to discrimination and disabilities, regulations that make loan procedures more understandable to consumers, and federally regulated environmental risks. Environmental issues include radon, asbestos, lead-based paint, and underground storage tanks.

In the practice of real estate, you need to be aware of protected rights afforded by discrimination and disability laws. These laws require specific steps to be taken by agents when dealing with certain classes of consumers. Fair housing laws must be memorized so you may be aware of when a particular law comes into play.

Consumer protection laws regulate the way loans are introduced to the public. These laws require finance charges and annual percentage rates to be expressed in simple, understandable ways. As agents, we must be aware of the requirements of these laws.

The government, too, protects buyers with respect to an ever-increasing list of environmental conditions. Sellers are required to disclose information relating to these conditions. As agents for buyers and sellers, we must be aware of the laws relating to environmental conditions and continually monitor this ever-changing body of law. For example, in the last many years, natural hazards such as earthquake propensity, the presence of mold, and the presence of lead-based paint have been added to the list of environmental conditions. The list seems to get longer with each passing year.

Property Management

The role and duties of the property manager, landlord-tenant relationships, leasing law, and laws relating to fair practices come under the heading of property management. There is a comprehensive body of law regulating leasing practice, which should be understood to some extent by all agents, even if they do not work as property managers. This body of law also involves fair housing practices, which protect renters from prohibited landlord acts.

Course Challenges

The previous discussion represents a highly summarized but rather complete overview of the real estate principles you will study in your prelicensing courses and what you will encounter on your licensing exam. Some of these subjects you will never encounter again in all of your real estate practice while others will be involved in your day-to-day activities. Your exam preparation course, described in the next chapter, will cover these subjects in detail.

The Least You Need to Know

- It can take three months to study and get your license, and longer to obtain your first commission.

- Each state has specific requirements for getting licensed, and there are entry-level licenses and advanced licenses, with requirements for each level.

- The course work can be very interesting, with valuable information on property rights, ways to hold title, and differences in types of deeds.

- Property restrictions, such as easements and CC&Rs, can affect an owner's property rights.

- The steps you take in a real estate transaction are fully detailed in the prelicensing course.

Preparing for and Taking the Exam

In This Chapter

- ◆ Applying for the exam and taking it
- ◆ Looking at a typical breakdown of the real estate exam
- ◆ Taking a real estate exam-preparation course
- ◆ Practicing for the exam
- ◆ Employing exam-taking strategies

You've completed your prelicensing courses. Now you want to apply for the exam, take an exam-preparation course, and take the exam. You're almost there. This chapter covers these steps and includes sample exam questions so that you know what to expect when you take the exam.

A Checklist of Exam-Preparation Tasks

Follow a systematic checklist approach when preparing to take the exam. In this manner, you cover all bases, allowing you to walk into the exam with confidence and assurance. These are the steps to take in the following order:

1. Apply to take the exam.

2. Determine exam procedures.

3. Gather information on exam content.

4. Take an exam-preparation course.

5. Simulate the exam conditions.

6. Master exam-taking strategies.

7. Adopt the right attitude.

8. Implement good exam-taking policies.

Apply to Take the Exam

Return to the website for your state's real estate commission and follow the instructions regarding applying for and taking the exam. Apply to take the exam before you undertake your exam preparatory work so that when you're done, you'll be ready to walk into your exam. You should find everything you need online.

After reviewing your state's requirements, you should be able to answer the following questions:

- Do you need a broker to sponsor you, attest to your good character, or put up a bond for you?

- What is the cost to apply to take the exam, to take the exam, and to have your license issued?

- What documents must you submit, such as proof of age, financial responsibility, high school or college completion, and residency?

- Are you required to submit photographs and/or fingerprints?

FYI!

A sample exam question: Which of the following is the best evidence that the title has been conveyed?

A. The deed has been recorded.

B. The deed has been delivered to the grantee.

C. The buyer is in possession.

D. The deed has been acknowledged.

Answer: B.

  ◆ Do you have proof of completion of your state's course requirements?

  ◆ Do you have proof of veteran or disabled veteran status, if it is applicable?

When you have your complete package assembled, send it by priority mail, or drop it off yourself if the office is close by. Keep a copy of everything in case your package is somehow misplaced.

Determine Exam Procedures

Obtain the dates and locations of examinations. Some states offer exams only twice a year and only in one location, typically the state's capital. Others offer the exam frequently and in many different locations. Depending on your state's policy, you should be able to schedule your exam date for when you are done with your examination-preparation course. This is the information you want to ascertain when determining exam procedures for your state:

  ◆ Examination dates and locations.

  ◆ What is the deadline to apply for your exam date of choice?

  ◆ Exam format, whether pencil and paper or examination machine.

  ◆ What you must bring to the exam: registration confirmation, pencils, scratch paper, application documents, calculator.

  ◆ Exam-grading procedure: is each section separately graded or are the sections added up basing your score on an overall score?

  ◆ Exam grading: how long will it be before you are notified of your results?

  ◆ Exam performance notification: are you directly notified or is someone else notified, such as your sponsoring broker, about how you did on the exam?

  ◆ Exam result advisory: are you advised about your score or just informed of whether you passed? Will you be able to review your exam to see where you excelled or where you made mistakes?

FYI!

A sample exam question: We call the instrument used to remove the lien of a trust deed or mortgage from record a ...

A. Satisfaction.

B. Release.

C. Deed of reconveyance.

D. Certificate of redemption.

Answer: C.

- License issuance: is your license automatically issued or does it just make you eligible to apply for licensing? How long do you have after passing to obtain your license?

- Retaking the exam: how soon after failing the exam may you retake it and how many times can you retake it?

- Pass score: what is your state's passing score? (In most states you have to get 70–75 percent of the questions correct to pass.)

- Time allowed to take the exam: most states allow between three and four hours to take the agent exam. A few states allow two to three hours. The broker exam is most often a full day.

- Pass statistics: what is the pass rate in your state? Most states average a 65 percent pass rate for the agent exam.

Gather Information on Exam Content

All exams are multiple choice consisting of 100 to 150 questions. Most state exams consist of two parts: a longer portion and a shorter portion. The longer portion with typically 80 to 100 questions is the general real estate exam covering the real estate principles you studied in your prelicensing course described in the last chapter. The shorter portion, typically 20 to 50 questions, covers licensing laws in your particular state.

Your state's Real Estate Commission or the company it hires to administer the exam will provide you with a wealth of information about the exam, including sample questions and exam content. Some states give you a breakdown of the percentage of questions relating to certain subjects.

As an example of the information you'll gather, I've noted here a summary of what is on California's website:

> **What the exam tests for:** Appropriate knowledge of the English language, including reading, writing, and spelling; arithmetical computations common to real estate and business opportunity practices.

> An understanding of the principles of real estate and business opportunity conveyancing; the general purposes and general legal effect of agency contracts, deposit receipts, deeds, deeds of trust, chattel mortgages, bills of sale, mortgages, land contracts of sale, and leases; principles of business, land economics, and appraisals.

A general and fair understanding of the obligations between principal and agent; the principles of real estate and business opportunity transactions, and the code of business ethics pertaining thereto; provisions of the law relating to real estate as administered by the Real Estate Commissioner.

Examination topics and percentage of exam coverage:

◆ Real property and laws relating to ownership (approximately 11 percent of exam), which includes ownership of property, encumbrances, and public power over property

◆ Tax implications of real estate ownership (approximately 8 percent of exam), which includes knowledge of current tax laws affecting real estate ownership

◆ Valuation/appraisal of real property (approximately 15 percent of exam), which includes methods of appraising and valuing property and factors which may influence value

◆ Financing real estate (approximately 17 percent of exam), which includes sources of financing, common clauses in mortgage instruments, types of loans, and terms and conditions

◆ Transfer of property (approximately 10 percent of exam), which includes title, escrow, and reports

◆ Real estate practice (approximately 22 percent of exam), which includes listing of real property, sales contracts, and marketing

> **FYI!**
>
> California's website lists 50 sample questions. You can get there directly by searching on the Internet for "California department of real estate salesperson exam sample questions." The first listing takes you directly to the sample questions under "the real estate license examinations." These exam allocations are similar to those described in Chapter 4.

◆ Broker's responsibility for agency management (approximately 17 percent of exam), which includes state real estate laws and regulations, laws relating to fair practices, knowledge of trends and developments, and knowledge of commonly used real estate forms and math calculations

Take an Exam-Preparation Course

After you apply to take the exam and gather information on it, take an examination-preparation course. You need it. The real estate exam is unique. You want to take a preparation course that will tutor you in the art of multiple-choice testing and in repetition of the concepts studied in your prelicensing courses. Your intent is to take the exam once and move on into your new career from there. The best way to do that is by taking a preparatory course. The pass rate for the exam is about 65 percent. The pass rate for preparatory-course attendees is 85 percent. Convinced?

The company you took your prelicensing course from also has exam-preparation courses geared toward your state's exam. Most courses cover about 2000 questions which are very similar to what you will encounter on the exam. These companies have reconstructed the exams so that their sample questions nearly simulate the licensing exam. They are also aware of the topics that cause the biggest problems for examinees and emphasize these problem areas throughout their practice exams.

Generally, real estate math and contracts are considered the most challenging areas. Math is what you took in the seventh grade. You're just a little out of practice. About 25 percent of the general examination covers math. Most states allow the use of a pocket calculator. Math principles that are covered include commission, interest calculations, depreciation, *prorations*, and *amortization*.

def•i•ni•tion

Prorations are the division of a property's expenses between the buyer and seller as of the property's transfer date.

Amortization is the gradual paying off of a debt by periodic payments.

Contracts intimidate people because they think that only lawyers can understand them. Don't buy into this. The principles are easy and pertain to agreements we make every day of our lives. What did you agree to do, and what did they agree to give you in return?

Find the course that is best for you. Courses are offered in person, by correspondence, and online. Find what best suits your needs and your level of discipline. If you feel you will need support from instructors or students, find a course that you can attend in person. Some people consider exam simulation to be highly valuable. The in-person courses put you in a room while an exam is administered under circumstances very similar to those used by your state examiners. If you do not require interaction and want to work at your own speed, go with an online or correspondence course.

Simulate the Exam Conditions

Some states require good old-fashioned pencil and paper while some states require computer usage for taking the exam. Know in advance what your state uses and simulate it many times before taking the exam.

Pencil and Paper or Computer Terminal

Some states use computer answer forms that you fill in with a pencil. The instructions ask you not to write in the exam booklet or on the answer sheet other than filling in your answer choice. You should then indicate to yourself which questions you want to come back to and which questions are math-related problems that require your math analysis hat. Note on a separate piece of paper "to come back to" (for questions you get stuck on) and "math questions" (for all math questions so you can tackle them at one time). Then come back to those groupings of questions after you complete the rest.

Most states are converting to computer entry instead of pencil and paper entry. You are placed in front of a keyboard and monitor similar to what you might have at home or at work. Questions with their answer choices are displayed and you enter your answer on your keypad in the blank provided. You can erase an answer and scroll back and forth to advance and return to questions.

FYI!
A sample exam question: When an obligation is paid on an installment basis, it is known as …   A. Acceleration   B. Conversion   C. Amortization   D. Depreciation   Answer: C

If this is the method used by your state, make sure you are familiar with computer use. The last thing you need is to spend valuable time fumbling with the computer. The exam administrators will provide detailed instructions on use of the equipment and give you a brief practice session. But this is not really enough time to become comfortable with computer test taking if you don't know the basics of using a computer.

The Simulation Process

If upon completion of your examination preparation course you do not feel comfortable with exam taking, buy one of the many books or online courses and practice more. In this case, practice does make perfect. Sit yourself down with a simulated examination according to the rules that will be followed in your exam. You have probably already done this in your preparation course. Use all the exam-taking strategies discussed in this chapter in your simulation sessions.

Master Exam-Taking Strategies

The national part of the exam is always multiple choice. Most states also use this format while very few states have a true/false or fill-in-the-blank format. If you gather information and take an exam-preparation course, you will know your state's format in advance. Here are some practical tips on answering questions:

1. For multiple-choice questions, realize that you are looking at the right answer. You do not have to pull it out of your head. It lies before you.

2. Identify keywords. Often these questions have keywords that guide you to the answer. The first step is to locate the keyword and relate it to the answers. Often, keywords come in the following forms: *always, never, not, but, if, incorrect, must, best, normally,* and *except.* Make sure you choose the answer that incorporates the keyword distinction. When you see these words, train your mental alarm clock to automatically go off.

3. Go with your first impression. It's usually correct.

4. Don't make it complicated. These exams test for minimal levels of competence. Don't look for the hidden meaning. There is no hidden meaning.

FYI!

A sample exam question: A, B, and C are joint tenants. A conveys his interest to D. This changes the ownership as follows:

A. B, C, and D are joint tenants.

B. B, C, and D are each one-third tenants in common.

C. D owns one third as a tenant in common with B and C, who now own two thirds as joint tenants.

D. None of the above.

Answer: B

Adopt the Right Attitude

Adopting the right attitude is an important step to achieving success on the exam. It consists of the following:

+ Shore up your confidence

+ Feel good and sleep well

+ Look at the worst-case scenario

+ Look at the best-case scenario

+ Walk into the exam with a positive attitude

Shore Up Your Confidence

If you have been out of school and out of practice taking exams, you can equip yourself to handle any jitters. After completing your prelicensing courses and an

examination-preparation course, you will have all the knowledge you need. In your preparation course, you will take several practice examinations. You will probably obtain sample questions from your state licensing body. You know exactly what the exam will consist of, and you will have mastered multiple-choice testing. The only unknown is the exact wording of the questions. In other words, you have taken all the right steps. There is no reason to lack confidence.

Cave!

The lowest pass rates are in Alaska, Arkansas, California, Colorado, Kentucky, Pennsylvania, South Carolina, Tennessee, and Utah.

The following states have the highest pass rates: Arizona, Georgia, and South Dakota.

Sleep Well and Feel Good

Rest and relax the day before the exam. The day before that, do a little studying, especially on subjects you feel weakest in. If you do opt to study the day before, don't spend more than a few hours studying and make sure you are finished at least two hours before your regular bedtime. Get some exercise the day before and do something to take your mind off the exam. A movie or something that takes your mind off the task of taking the exam is ideal.

Don't eat a heavy meal the night before or the day of the exam. Get good directions to the test location, including where to park and how to get into the building. Make sure you arrive at your testing location early. If you arrive late, you will not be allowed to take the exam.

Look at the Worst-Case Scenario

The pass rate in most states is 65 percent. The worst that can happen to you is you will be one of the 35 percent who do not pass. If you took the suggested preparation course, your odds of passing have increased to 85 percent. Do you really think you'll be one of the unsuccessful 15 percent? What is it that makes you feel that you will be among those who fail? The facts before you do not support this conclusion.

Look at the Best-Case Scenario

Chances are almost nine out of ten that you will pass. You've taken all the right steps to put yourself into the eighty-fifth percentile. Why wouldn't you pass? Why look at the glass as half-empty when it's nearly full?

Have a Positive Attitude

What's not to feel good about? You've looked at your career options and made a decision to have a career in the real estate field. You've taken and passed the courses you need to qualify for the licensing exam. You have most likely taken an exam-preparation course to prepare for the big exam. If you have taken your examination-preparation course in person, you have a group of other attendees to support you and positively influence you.

Your life is about to take a turn in a new direction entirely of your own making. Your decision has come out of a desire to make your life better. Keep these thoughts in mind as you take the exam. This is an exciting time for you and everything is looking up. Bring your positive attitude with you when you walk through the examination door.

> **FYI!**
>
> A sample exam question: Which is true of a *lis pendens*?
> A. Only a court order will remove it.
> B. It may be recorded no matter what the lawsuit is for.
> C. It may affect title to property based on the results of the lawsuit.
> D. None of the above.
> Answer: C

Implement Good Exam-Taking Policies

The following is a checklist you may want to adopt when you take the licensing exam:

◆ Don't pay attention to anyone else. If you do, you will think everyone else is calm and you are nervous. Everyone is nervous, but some people don't show it as much as others do. Do not look around during the exam when you are stuck. Just move on to the next question. Most states use several different test versions in each sitting. The person in your view will most likely not even have the same test you have.

> **FYI!**
>
> **A sample exam question:**
> An apartment building costs $450,000. It brings in a net income of $3,000 per month. The owner is making what percentage of return on investment?
>
> A. 7 percent
>
> B. 8 percent
>
> C. 11 percent
>
> D. None of the above
>
> Answer: B

◆ Read the instructions. Do this to make sure you understand the rules.

◆ First answer the easy questions. Some people get stuck on a question, run out of time, and are unable to answer the easy questions. Don't let your focus and attention become distracted by one question. Remember, you can get up to 30 percent wrong. If you answer the easy questions first, you will have a number of correct answers already in your bank account. Your primary objective in the exam is to answer as many questions as you can correctly. You will not get more credit for the ones that are more difficult. So, why belabor one when you can move on and potentially get five more correct?

◆ Answer the math questions at the same time. In this manner, you can put your "calculating hat" on instead of taking it off and on. You will have your calculator, if your state allows one, and your scratch paper and you'll save time by working one problem after another.

◆ Come back to the hard questions after you have answered the easy ones. On your second pass, do the same thing you did initially. Spend a little time with each question. If you're stuck, move on to the next one. Give yourself a little more time than you did with the first pass. However, don't struggle or stay on one question too long. You can come back to it, or just leave it as one of the 30 percent you are allowed to get wrong.

◆ Answer every question. Most exam proctors will provide warnings at certain time intervals before the exam ends. When you receive that warning, make an assessment of where you are in the exam. For instance, if you have ten questions you are stuck on, give yourself enough time to choose an answer. First, eliminate the answers you know are incorrect. Then choose one of the remaining answers.

Agent to Agent _____

Some of the professionals you met in Chapter 2 had the following comments about the licensing exam:

"The salesperson exam is definitely not easy. The subject matter is very technical. What helped me the most was the practice exams that were included in my preparation course. They were very similar to the real exam. The exam seemed very familiar to me when I tested, due to the many practice exams I had taken."

"The exam is difficult. The secret is to take lots of practice tests."

"The test items are often ambiguous. The best way to pass the test is to take a preparatory course and memorize answers to hundreds of test questions you get in the preparatory course."

"I rate the exam eight on a scale of one to ten, with ten being the hardest."

"I made sure that I was averaging 90 percent or better on the practice exams, which made the real thing seem easier. Practice; it makes a difference."

What's the lesson to learn here? Although the test might be difficult, the preparatory class and practice questions really do prepare you to pass.

- You should know in advance whether there will be a time warning. If there isn't one, keep track of time yourself, and make sure you know when there are only 15 minutes left before the exam ends to give yourself the time to make final decisions.

- Don't leave the exam early unless you feel sure of all of your answers. Spend the extra time to review any questions you have concerns about.

- Every once in a while take a few deep breaths and stretch your arms.

The Least You Need to Know

- The Real Estate Commission for your state can provide information about licensing requirements and the exam.

- The Real Estate Commission for each state often provides a complete breakdown of the exam, so you know what to study for.

- The real estate agent exam is usually half a day long, while the broker exam is usually one day long.

- The main secret to passing the exam is practice.

- A real estate exam preparation course is helpful and highly recommended before you take the exam.

Part 2

Getting Started

Although many career choices are available to the real estate agent, this book focuses on the residential sales agent. This part takes you through the business formation stage so you can successfully launch your business with a solid working foundation. The building blocks consist of …

- Choosing the right office.

- Formulating and instituting a good business plan.

- Incorporating personal and professional power into your business.

- Creating a power team of professionals to support you.

If you've already launched your business, this chapter could give you just the tools you need to take it to the next level.

Chapter 6

Choosing Your Office

In This Chapter

- The importance of real estate associations

- A checklist for interviewing the office you join

- Training and support from your office

- Fees and commissions you pay the company you choose

- A list of regrets from seasoned agents

Although many career options are available to the real estate agent, this book focuses on the residential sales agent. This chapter is about choosing the real estate office where you will begin your real estate sales career. This choice is one of the most important you will make since the office you select will mentor you into the practices and principles that will mark your career.

At the end of this chapter you will benefit from the hindsight of agents who wish they had started out their careers differently. A majority of them said they would have chosen their first office more carefully and begun their careers with more office involvement and better initial training.

Before you begin looking at which office might be right for you, you should develop an understanding of the real estate industry. I refer to it as the real estate country club because it consists of a closely-knit community of very social people. You don't have to be a social butterfly to be a member of the real estate community, but if you are, you have found your niche.

Socializing with the Real Estate Country Club

The real estate club is made up of agents and affiliates of agents. Its members consist of lenders, property inspectors, title and closing professionals, and the many categories of real estate agents. The agents are members of the local real estate association and its multiple listing service, while the rest are affiliates. The affiliates provide services to the agents and their clients and are always courting the agents.

The real estate professional is part of a large, active community. It's as if real estate has a flashing sign that says "Join me and you will never be lonely or broke again." It's true. Real estate takes care of its people. While you don't want to test your local real estate agent by asking to be personally invited into their well-protected domain, the real estate community itself is a large, highly cordial, supportive group of professionals.

Some people would contest this viewpoint, finding the real estate industry to be a cutthroat, fiercely protective community. However, this book is written from the perspective of *The New Ideal*, where old competitive attitudes give way to more compassionate, integrity-based ideals. Where generosity gives way to abundance both in terms of financial, emotional and spiritual prosperity. You become a valuable resource not only for your clients but for your fellow agents.

Agent to Agent _____

More than any other group of professionals, real estate agents will steer you away from their terrain. They will not admit to the merits of their profession, nor will they make you feel there is room for you. "It's a dog-eat-dog industry. You really do not want a part of it. We work 24 hours a day, seven days a week. There is no rest for the agent. We really don't make a lot of money; it's a myth."

Don't Believe All Agents

Real estate is bountiful. It provides unlimited financial opportunity to those who know how to tap into it. While the average income for agents is $62,000 a year nationwide, those who become Top Dogs earn extraordinary sums. Real estate is social. Real estate is flexible. It assures independence. Your typical agent works 46 hours a week, including driving time, with a schedule entirely of his or her own making.

The local real estate association you may join is a constant flurry of activity. They're always sponsoring educational programs and social events. The events can make you feel that life is one big party. The educational programs draw top motivational speakers, trainers, and educators providing the latest in information and methods. Between the firm you choose to affiliate with, the professional board you may join, and your mentors, you should be able to get all the support, both socially and professionally, you will need.

FYI!

To get an idea of what your local real estate association offers, search on the Internet for your locality and "Association of Realtors," for example, "Boston Massachusetts Association of Realtors." Some of these sites require membership and passwords to access some information, but you still may be able to get a good idea of the programs and services they provide. When you interview an office manager, ask him or her to step you through an online tour of what their office and the local association provide in terms of education, training, and community. Chapter 7 provides more information about the many benefits association membership offers.

Understanding the Relationship

If you are still researching the real estate sales field, undergo what I call job-security training. The would-be agent needs to understand that there is no job security whatsoever in real estate. Understand this before you even decide to study for the licensing exam.

This step consists of contacting a firm that you are considering joining and interviewing the office manager to gain preliminary information about the office and its services. Note that I said you will be interviewing them. I mean this. You will be paying them up to half of your earnings and additional fees. You will begin your real estate professional career under their tutelage. There is a lot you need to know about this office to determine whether you should associate with them.

They should be happy to discuss your potential career choice with you; they would prefer to dispel any doubts now instead of after you've joined their office. The purpose of this meeting is to get an idea of how the office operates, what they offer for training and support, and the financial arrangement you can expect. There's no need for a resumé or any other type of formality.

In fact, with some larger firms that provide license exam-preparation training, you can begin your association before you get your license. In this way you join the team before you're licensed and go through the prelicensing process with others of similar interest.

The job of the office manager is to recruit new agents as well as manage existing agents. They are always looking for new talent. The real estate sales office thrives on agents making money for them. Their policy is the more the merrier, although they do want you to produce if you are going to take up space in their office. When you contact an office asking to meet with the manager, recognize that this is a standard part of the manager's job.

Potential real estate licensees often have a misconception about the career they are considering. The number-one confusion in real estate sales is that you will be employed by one of these offices. This is not true. Although you will work under the name of the company, you are not employed by the company. You are an independent contractor.

The analogy is more of a franchise than one of self-employment. You purchase the right to come under the logo of the company you join and to use its tools. Let me repeat: you *purchase* the right. There are no benefits or pay provided by the company. In fact, it's the other way around. You pay for everything you get either through splitting your commission with your office or a monthly or transaction fee.

You will pay for errors and omissions insurance, board dues, multiple listing dues, desk fees, and administrative fees. You may pay for any training you receive. You will pay for the equipment you may need: typically a laptop, a fax machine at home, a cell phone, a digital camera, and a PDA for use in the

Cave!

Your skill as a real estate agent ultimately determines your income and success. There usually isn't a benefit package or retirement package to rely on. Always know that being a real estate agent means working for yourself but giving a part of your income to someone else. After working for another firm, you can become a broker and work for yourself if you choose.

Cave!

As an independent contractor, you work for yourself, pay your own taxes, and track your own deductions. One of those deductions will probably be a car lease. You need a good-size, four-door, high-quality car for driving your clients to view property.

field. You will pay for your car, auto insurance, and gas. You will pay for your health insurance and retirement benefits.

And on top of that you may share a significant portion of the commissions you earn with the office you join. You pay the company you hang your license at a high price for the privilege of using its name and placing your license with that company. When you have your broker's license, you will still pay these fees, but your commission split will probably be more in your favor. Over time, as you bring in more commissions, you will keep a bigger percentage of it.

As the real estate industry and its compensation hierarchy change, agent fee payment structures do too. Where the norm for the new agent once was splitting your commission 50-50 with your office, now there are many different arrangements to choose from. You can give up support and other optional features for more money in your pocket, or get more support and receive less commission. Some offices have set up a per transaction fee; others have monthly flat fees regardless of the number of transactions you do. Now you can choose the structure that best fits your budget and needs depending on which office you select.

Supporting the Fable

It is quite common for an office manager to watch the potential licensee's face turn white as she describes the financial aspect of the office-agent relationship. Both the agents and the real estate offices encourage the misconception that the agent works for the firm. According to a recent survey of real estate owners, their choice of agent is often due to the reputation of the firm they are associated with.

FYI!
Most people believe that the real estate firm has invested significant time and energy in their employee-agent relationships and continues to do so throughout the agent's career. This could not be farther from the truth. Once the agent concludes any required office training, which can be as brief as a few hours or as long as ten days, the agent is on his or her own. While the office broker is legally required to oversee your transactions, her presence is often more of a supervisor touching base than anything else.

So you see that your future is all of your own making. Take the steps described in this book and you will achieve a success that will make you proud to have chosen real estate as a career. It's not an easy career to begin, but once you define your market and implement good work habits and a productive business plan, it can be a very fulfilling one.

Choosing the Right Office

How do you know which office is right for you? You want to choose a company that will mentor you in customs and practices that will serve you throughout your real estate career. Many factors will go into your decision: your own personal needs, the firm's reputation, the office manager's style, and the agent package the firm offers. Selecting the right office is second only to choosing the right business partner.

The following categories will guide you in making this very important career decision:

Agent to Agent

Choosing your first office is like hiring a mentor. It is essential that you get the right training and support when you start out your real estate career. This training will set the tone for your business practices and ideals throughout the rest of your career.

- Company ideals
- Training and support
- Company reputation
- Financial considerations
- Office manager
- Company-generated business for you
- Office spirit
- Your working area
- Awards and clubs

You should analyze the benefits each office has to offer for each of these categories and then decide which best meets your needs.

Company Ideals

As with all industries, the real estate brokerage industry is experiencing massive change. Some companies encourage high integrity and focus on clients' needs as top priority, while others continue to rely on old-fashioned selling techniques and outdated business practices. The office you choose will mentor you into your new professional life, so choose carefully.

As with all times of change, innovative new companies are springing into existence. Some of these new companies have grown quickly and have gained both a national and international presence. They have a more democratic way of doing business with their agents, supporting teamwork. They also encourage and advocate higher integrity in interacting with and representing clients. Naturally, this type of company fits in with The New Ideal stressed in this book.

Make sure your research of the firm you are considering includes their philosophy on the following issues:

- ◆ Does the firm promote high-pressure selling techniques?

- ◆ Does the firm endorse the client's interest first and foremost, even if it means losing the deal?

- ◆ Is the firm technologically innovative? Does it support agents' use of computer-based, contact-management programs and agent web pages?

- ◆ How much does the firm charge agents, whether by commission split or other fees? Does the firm have any type of profit sharing or retirement programs for their agents?

When you sit down with the office manager, explore every one of these subjects.

Training and Support

One of the most important benefits you will receive from the company you choose is training and support. You want to establish good habits early on and set up tools to support you throughout your career. Some offices have full-blown training programs; others give you a cubicle, desk, and phone and say, "Go get 'em." Some Internet-based brokers don't even have offices, nor do they provide one for you. Typically, the larger the firm's national presence, the more training they offer. Remember, though, you pay for the training the same as you pay for everything else you receive from your office. Why? Because you are not an employee of the firm.

The training you may receive from the office will vary. Some offices offer highly sophisticated, in-depth new agent training by experienced trainers with a full curriculum covering agency relationships, *fiduciary duty*, the listing agreement, the purchase agreement, dealing with contingencies, seller disclosures, buyer due diligence, prospecting, and marketing. All of these subjects are discussed in Chapter 20, as they warrant a chapter of their own.

def•i•ni•tion

In a real estate transaction, the agent has a **fiduciary duty** to his client. A fiduciary duty is acting on behalf of your client with the utmost of care, integrity, honesty, confidentiality, and loyalty. Your mission is to take all steps with your client's best interest in mind. You are your client's trusted advocate.

Although you pay for everything you receive, at least it's there for the asking. It can be scary and lonely to be the new kid in the office and not have any support. With the tools and education provided by the larger firms, you have an abundant supply of resources for any type of situation. A highly detailed training manual can be an invaluable resource for the beginning agent. It's the built-in mentor that never leaves your side.

At the end of this chapter, you will find a list of steps agents would have done differently if they had to do it all over again. One of the most common regrets agents have is that they did not receive good training and support from their first office.

FYI!

Some cutting-edge firms provide ongoing empowerment programs for their agents. These are designed to increase personal productivity and provide career development. These online *universities* provide education, training, and tools. Some forward-looking companies provide peer partnering, matching agents with similar goals and production levels. These partners mentor each other and hold one another accountable for their goals. Some of these partners choose to share their work and profits and become true business partners, a subject that will be discussed later in this book. Others limit the relationship to acting as coaches for one another, which can be an extremely useful tool to the new agent.

A type of training offered by one national firm is called *mastermind training*, which stimulates its participants to expand their thinking in a setting that motivates and mentors them. *Shadowing* is another variety of training where the agent spends the day with a top producer, focusing on personal productivity, time management, and goal-setting techniques. This type of hands-on mentoring can jump-start the career of a new agent.

Some companies have online systems for their agents to download forms, promotional materials, and prospecting kits. Some firms offer ongoing online and in-person courses to increase the agent's technology base, marketing, time management, and legal and life skills. Some have online and conference-call coaching programs by top trainers to motivate you to higher production. Some have tools you can download to assist you in setting up your own website. Others ask you to download your listings directly to their website. Some provide in-house and online continuing education programs.

On the agent-support websites for many companies, you get a shopping cart, fill it with the support you need, and pay as you go. You could get this type of training and support just about anywhere in the classroom or on the Internet, but these firms offer everything in one handy spot. When you begin your real estate career, it's a good idea to avoid the urge to reinvent the wheel.

Cave!

As a new agent you can become insecure and alienated if you don't immerse yourself in your office and the real estate community. You need to get experience and these contacts are very helpful sources.

Multitudes have come before you. The process is all set up in a cookie-cutter fashion; you just need to decide which process you want to call your own.

Sizing Up the Company Reputation

Throughout your affiliation with the first company you sign on with, you will be thought of as an extension of that company. You therefore want to very carefully select the company that will hold your license, train you, and share its image with you. Research the company well to ensure that it has a solid history, credibility in the community, and a good share of the market.

Real estate relies on looks. What does the office look like? What do its agents look like? If you were a property owner about to sell a home, would you receive a good impression of this firm by walking through its doors? Does it have an image that shows responsibility and credibility?

The *multiple listing services* (*MLS*) provide statistics on how much of the market share each firm has. Have someone run those statistics for you before you join an office, or better yet, ask the office manager you're interviewing. Consider those numbers when you choose your firm. Drive around the community and observe the presence of this company on for-sale signs. Look at its presence in the local real estate section of the newspaper. Talk to other agents and property owners. Get the hard facts about this company; it will appear on all your cards, contracts, and flyers for years to come and will earn up to 50 percent of every cent you make.

def•i•ni•tion

A **multiple listing service** (MLS) is the database of properties listed for sale and rent within a certain locale. Only real estate agent members may use it. It also includes tax information, member information, and market statistics.

Sizing Up Financial Considerations

Since the real estate sales industry is undergoing enormous change, the industry standard for financial arrangements with agents also is undergoing changes. Not long ago, it was fairly standard for a new agent to share his commission 50-50 with the company, and most often the agent paid no expenses after that. Now, the split is all over the board.

With some companies, you earn the full commission and pay a per-transaction fee or a monthly fee. Some charge you fees in advance, which can be intimidating when you're paying for a new car, a new image, and your traveling high-tech office; and you are not yet bringing in an income. Some take some commission and charge some fees. Those that split commission have sliding scales depending on your sales volume. Get a copy of their scale. Some flat fee-based companies allow you to pay for only what you use.

> **FYI!**
>
> Some firms have instituted profit-sharing for their agents in an effort to address agent long-term financial planning objectives. These more-innovative companies encourage their agents to incorporate income-producing strategies into their business plans. Previously, this type of support of independent contractor agents was unheard of. Now it is just starting but will spread through the industry in the future.

Find out how much you pay the company and what they give you in return. Only you can evaluate whether what you pay justifies what you receive. Make a detailed list and scrutinize the options, the way you might compare loan options when buying a house. When analyzing your choice of office, there are important distinctions unrelated to company charges that can tip the scales in favor of one office over the other, such as company reputation or team spirit.

Sizing Up the Office Manager

The office manager will be your mentor on some level for years to come. This will be a very important person in your early career development. Spend some time with him or her discussing office philosophies and procedures. Describe situations that might develop and ask how they should be handled. For instance, you're handling the floor at the office and something comes up that you don't know the answer to. The manager is not in. What should you do? Is there a backup person in charge, or can you contact your manager when you're in a pinch for the first few months?

Get permission from the manager to interview the agents and receive their candid
input. If you do this, the agents will be far
more willing to talk about their experiences.
You need to be able to know that this manager will be there to support and guide you
through your first year of practice. Make
sure you know you can work well with this
person and will receive support when you
need it.

Agent to Agent _____

A recent survey of 1,500
agents showed that the top
three reasons agents joined
their current firm were company
image (54 percent), broker's
ethics (41 percent), and the
company's business philosophy
(34 percent).

Getting Leads from the Company

Your focus here is to determine what this office does to develop business for you.
Does it regularly promote the services of the company? How frequently? What is
the quality of its advertising? Does it have a good web presence? Will you be able to
upload all of your listings to its site in addition to your own site?

How much floor time will you have? In the beginning of your career, you may depend
on folks who walk in the office or phone the office as vital lead sources. You want to
make sure this office does not have too many agents who would limit your floor time.
With the increasing use of agent direct phone lines, floor time is quickly becoming
something of the past. If the company you interview has a floor time policy, examine
it carefully. For the new agent, floor time is invaluable in terms of acquiring leads and
clients.

Office Spirit and Agent Support

Does this office operate from a base of teamwork, or are the agents working strictly
on their own? Many offices give lip service to teamwork, but operate as a collection
of competitive individuals. Other offices are built on teamwork, providing in-house
mentorship to new agents. As a new agent, you want to operate within a team environment as much as you can. Talk to top agents in the office and find out whether you
can work as an assistant for them for a while until you can break away on your own.
In this manner, you will receive the best hands-on training available and receive pay
while you learn.

Agent to Agent _____

Teamwork and support are very important to agents starting out. If you can find a mentor and are comfortable with most of the other agents in an office, you can gain immeasurably from their experience. At the end of this chapter, you will see that teamwork and support were priorities for a majority of agents when choosing their first office.

Find out whether agents in the office are open to your sitting at open houses for them and even shadowing them for a day. See whether agents in the office are open to letting you "house sit" their listings while they take short vacations. Talk to agents about whether they will refer business to you that they don't want or can't get to in exchange for a referral fee from you. The best way to approach these issues is to have a generous attitude, not one of selfishness. In other words, your intention is to contribute to their well-being while they contribute to your learning and well-being.

Do some agents within the office partner with one another for mentoring purposes? Are some also partnering as full business partners? If you can find an office that has a long practice of team spirit, weigh this strongly. The office that provides very little in the way of formal training and high-tech strategies, but has good old-fashioned manager-agent relationships and team spirit, will guide you smoothly through your apprenticeship. At the end of this chapter you will see that agents regretted that they had not created more teamwork at the office they joined.

Sizing Up Your Work Space

This issue is based on personal preference. One person can be put in the bullpen cramped in a small cubicle in the loudest area of the office and be delighted. Another may find this a reason to have her head examined. Make sure you have a good idea of exactly what your work area will look like and whether you will be sharing it with others.

What will it feel like when the office is full of agents and their clients conducting business? In your first year, you will probably want to spend most of your time in the office where you can get support, rather than in your home office. How conducive is your space to your own personal productivity? Only you can answer that.

Getting Recognition

Many offices have special awards, clubs, and distinctions to honor achievements of their agents. Real estate is a social club and the offices are part of this. The larger offices have all kinds of awards and designations to celebrate staff. There are the million-dollar clubs, the best of the office, the best new agent. It's like being back in school again.

The agents receive their awards, and then publicize them to their sales communities. Yesterday they were just an agent. Today, they are a member of a multimillion-dollar club, tomorrow it may be the President's Club, and in the not-so-distant future it could be the Chairman's Circle of Excellence.

Some companies have their very own designations they give to experts in a given area of specialization, such as luxury home specialist, vacation home specialist, new home specialist, and farm and ranch specialist. It's another gold star on your business card that makes clients feel you are the top of your field.

Awards and designations are very important to agents. On their business cards, after you get past the gorgeous smiling mug, note the many designations and awards the agent has. These days it doesn't take much to join the million-dollar club. In areas of the country where the average-priced home is $700,000, you're in the door with one or two sales. Official designations are another story to be covered in later chapters.

Interviewing Firms

For this interview, you should bring a resumé that details your education, prior work experience, and affiliations. Make it one page, choose an impressive font, and use sturdy paper. There is a way of taking factual information and presenting it impressivly. It's not misrepresenting; it's making the most out of what you have. You need to learn this art for real estate sales, so you might as well begin with yourself.

The interview is the time to cover all the bases you discussed in this chapter. Bring this book and refer to it, or photocopy the pages you need. You'll be quite impressive when you present these topics for discussion. It will show that you are serious about your vision and intend to make the most of your career.

Agent to Agent

If you don't have prior resumé preparation experience, search the Internet on resumé preparation or pick up a book on the subject. You will soon prepare a bio for clients based on your resumé. Spend a little time cultivating your resumé-writing talents. You may want to pick up a copy of *The Resume Handbook: How to Write Outstanding Resumes and Cover Letters for Every Situation* (3rd Ed.) by Arthur D. Rosenberg and David V. Hizer.

You will probably already have many of your answers from the preliminary research you have done. There will be areas to be discussed and negotiated. Most importantly, you need to evaluate the level of rapport you have with the office manager. The interview should take an hour to an hour and a half.

You should interview at least three companies. If you were interviewing someone you wanted to hire, you would be sure to interview at least three people. Make sure you do the same with the company you will hire. Then, take time to compare your notes and deliberate over your important decision. You should know which office is right for you. If you don't, interview more companies until you have a strong feeling that you have found the office for you.

New agents are often unaware that *they* are in high demand, feeling intimidated by the interviewing process. When an office manager invites them on board, the agent gladly accepts, so pleased to have been accepted. If this is your inclination, put the shoe on your other foot. Nearly every office you interview with wants you in their money-making pool. Always remember, you are interviewing them; they are not interviewing you. Make your choice prudently.

Regrets of New Agents

You don't have to say, "I wish I had known then what I know now." Hindsight is always 20-20, and with this list of agent regrets you can learn from others who came before you. Here is a list of some of the major obstacles new agents face. Take each of these ideas to heart and consider them seriously when you begin your new career.

One agent points out that you have to be the one to seek out help from others:

> I wish I had involved myself more fully in my office. There is nothing that makes you feel more insecure than watching these gung ho producers handle five deals at a time and you don't even know the first step to take. Don't sit there. Find mentors, go to open houses, scout out a subdivision and find out everything about it, ask agents in your office to let you tag along.

From this agent's advice, you learn that discipline is important when starting and sustaining your real estate career:

> I should have disciplined myself more from the first moment, but most especially when I felt I wouldn't make it in the business. The last thing to do when feeling insecure is to cut back on good work habits. Always remember, the road to success is under construction. You can only pound one nail in at a time, but you've got to be disciplined to finish the job.

Other regrets not as high on the list include:

- ◆ I wish I had learned more about technology.
- ◆ I wish I had understood the agent smiling at you will stab you in the back.
- ◆ I wish I had understood that my choices have nothing to do with my client's choices.
- ◆ I wish I had understood the low regard agents are held in so I could build a model without those traits.
- ◆ I wish I had understood the official designations and received some early on.

This agent comments on the importance of building niches:

> Real estate sales is about creating markets everywhere you go. The best way to do that is to continually build niches. You live in a community. Be the agent who specializes in the 10-block radius around your home. Do this from day one. Also, make sure you use technology as much as you can, and have your own website.

Concerned about money when starting out? So was this agent. Here's some advice:

> Building a new career and a new business can be overwhelming if you don't have a stash to get you through the first year. Yes, I mean a year. You'll more than make up for it after that many times over again. In the beginning, though, you need to focus on the many challenges of your new business instead of worrying about making ends meet.

This agent comments on choice of office:

> I wish I had chosen my first office more carefully and found more mentors to guide me through my first year. I would have chosen my office based on its training program and its new agent support. I needed a training manual that was far more detailed than the skimpy notebook they handed me. I would have preferred an office that set me up with a mentor-agent to help me through my first few transactions.

Cave!

The National Association of Realtors reports that the typical agent has been in the business for nine years, having been with the same firm for five years and only one firm prior to that.

This agent comments on creativity in the business:

> I wish I had opened my mind to the many creative ways an agent can make real estate work for them as a source of creative income, excellent investment potential, and for creating a specialized career niche.

These "if-only-I-had" regrets are discussed throughout this book.

The Least You Need to Know

- Your local real estate association sponsors educational programs and social events for agents and affiliates.

- When you join an office, you become a franchisee of sorts, paying the office while, in turn, you receive support.

- Selecting the right office involves many factors: your own personal needs, the firm's reputation, the office manager's style, the agent package the firm offers, and more.

- Throughout your affiliation with the company you sign on with, you will be thought of as an extension of that company.

- Evaluate the philosophy and ideals of the company you intend to join to ensure that they are in line with your own philosophies.

Chapter 7

Building Your Business

In This Chapter

- ◆ Real estate associations and the multiple listing service
- ◆ Your small business as a productive, organized enterprise
- ◆ Lead generation as your top priority
- ◆ An intensive tutorial in understanding market indicators
- ◆ Technology as the foundation of your business

This chapter is a recipe for beginning your career with a solid foundation. After all, you've just become the CEO of your own company. It's time to implement a plan so you can capably steer your new company to success. When you start out in real estate sales, a good business plan is a must because you are beginning not only a new business, but an entirely new career. To ensure your success, you need many levels of business-building training.

FYI!
Many excellent books have been written about setting up your new business. Don't reinvent the business model. Follow the steps in this chapter, but also read some books on small business procedures. The Small Business Administration has all kinds of resources and information on its website at www.sba.gov.

This chapter only touches on the basic steps you will need to take to set up your new business. These are just the starter steps, whereas later chapters on marketing, computer technology, database management, and representation of your clients will round out the training you need. They didn't build Rome in a day, and you won't build your new business in one day either. If you begin it according to the steps in this chapter, it will be assured of a good foundation. The first step to take is to get some reality training.

A Dose of Reality Training

Realize that you are not prepared for the job ahead. Many people earn four- to eight-year degrees in institutions of higher learning to engage in professions that feel like kindergarten class compared to the transactions you will handle. Yet the real estate industry turns out agents to handle complex, multifaceted real estate sales transactions with just a few months of preparation. You therefore have a tremendous reality gap to bridge between what you know and how to make a living in real estate.

Unless you spend two years assisting a top producer before you handle your own deals, you must come to terms with the fact that you will not have enough time to gain the experience you need. You may make some serious and frustrating mistakes. For the first year or two anything that can go wrong will go wrong in varying stages of your transactions.

FYI!
Ask each of the experienced agents in your office whether they will let you track one transaction with them. This will be invaluable for you. If you limit your request to just a single transaction, you are more likely to receive a gracious response to your request. Although busy agents are hesitant to commit to mentoring you for any period of time, offering to help them on one transaction has an altogether different ring.

It often works like this: you master multiple listing entry, but then handling contingencies plagues you. You get contingencies down, and then dealing with price reductions becomes the new monster. You feel like you're back on track, and then a title issue comes in the side door. In real estate, where there are so many different roles and issues to deal with, the only way to ward off problems is to be a seasoned agent.

New agents are often taken advantage of by the public; often clients expect new agents to drive them all over the universe. You are likely to be abused by other agents who forget they were once in your position. You may also be led down a rosy path by those who see new agent naiveté written all over you. You may even make legal mistakes, and you might get involved in unethical situations without even knowing it.

When these things happen, as they shall, don't be surprised. If you're not surprised, your clients and peers won't be surprised. Stay calm, and sit down with your mentor or your manager and discuss situations as they arise. Don't take these issues to heart, but learn from each situation. With that said, let's plan your business so you can get through your experiences with as much ease and support possible.

Obtain Office Training and Support

Remember the number-one regret agents had about the beginning of their careers? Let me remind you in the words of one agent who mirrored what a large group of her peers had to say:

> I wish I had involved myself more fully in my office. There is nothing that makes you feel more insecure than watching these gung ho producers handle five deals at a time, and you don't even know the first step to take. Don't sit there. Find mentors, go to open houses, scout out a subdivision and find out everything about it, and ask agents in your office to let you tag along.

The very first step is to immerse yourself in your office. Hopefully, your office will have a well-developed training program and a good office manual. If the mentoring you need isn't available, find it. Your local association, discussed later in this chapter, will have a variety of programs and support aids available. If your office manager or the rest of the agents are not very forthcoming, you may have to reel them in. Everybody is busy doing what they were doing before you joined the office, so it is probable that you will have to build your own office support.

FYI!
Recall, seasoned agents have often looked back and wished they had chosen their first office based on the quality of its training program and new agent support.

If your office manual isn't detailed enough, supplement it. It is helpful to everyone in an office, and others are often willing to participate in sharing information with you because they will benefit from your product. A detailed office procedures manual is worth its weight in gold. It will get you through those inevitable, difficult times during your first year when you have no idea what to do. Statistics show that you will stay at your office for at least seven years. It is worth spending the time to set up a system that works for you.

You should also establish relationships with key players in your office. Don't come with a "what you can do for me" attitude. See what you can do to assist others and become a member of their support team. Determine who the top producers are and offer to assist with their transactions without pay, or offer to act as their administrative assistant. Seek to learn and contribute to the office. Top agents are the very best training tools you could ever pay for. Give thought now to choosing a person in your office to act as your mentor and possibly another person to partner with you.

Finally, and probably more important than anything else, always remember that you and only you are responsible for your success or failure. While you want to eke as much mentorship as you can from your office, you do not want to rely on them to either motivate you or make your business grow. Hopefully, you chose this office for its training and support, but the most important mindset you can have is, "No one is going to do it for me." Don't ever sit around the office waiting for something to happen. Follow the lead generation model in Chapter 13 and know that you will succeed; it is just a matter of time.

Agent to Agent

Did you know that the term *Realtor* is trademarked by the National Association of Realtors and can only be used by members? Go to www. Realtor.org to find out more.

Make Lead Generation Your First Priority Every Day

This chapter contains several steps you should take to make your business a success. By no means, though, should you make these steps more important than lead generation. Marketing for optimum lead generation is something you will do every single day for at least two hours a day. It is only after your lead generation activities are complete that the steps of this chapter come into play. You will encounter your marketing choices in Chapter 10 and your Master Marketing Model in Chapter 13. Just be aware that two hours of each day will be spent on marketing. Do not ever let yourself slip on this. Leads are your lifeline.

Participate with Your Realtor Associations

After you seek training in your office and after you make the best of your office situation, obtain training and support from your local real estate association. Each locale has its own real estate association that provides social and educational support to its members and affiliates. Along with your office, your local association will become the heartbeat of your real estate community. Get to know your local association and its staff. This association is like family to Realtors, and you can reap the benefits of its education, social events, and unbeatable community.

When you join an office, you become a member of your local association. You also may choose to join the statewide association and the National Association of Realtors. None of these memberships is mandatory. The only mandatory membership is with the real estate commission that issued your license and monitors your continuing education requirements. Your local Realtor association will have a continually growing list of educational programs and social events. The educational programs are usually very good as top educators and motivational speakers tour the real estate associations providing quality programs for continuing education credit.

The social events are usually loads of fun. There are bowling events, ski trips, golf trips, gambling excursions, and cruises. The local Realtor groups celebrate everything. And if there is nothing in particular to celebrate, there is a dance or an auction just for a reason to get together. They also sponsor events supporting local charities. Real estate has a unique sense of vitality and community that is not as common to other professions.

Your local real estate board, your state's board, and the national board also have websites with databases of statistics and other valuable information you should review regularly. These excellent websites are sources of legal, economic, and educational information as well as standard transaction forms.

Your local association also has a store where you can purchase signs, forms, and just about anything you'll need to practice real estate. You can lease your *lock boxes* and keys through the association. Your association also has boards and committees you can serve on. This type of service doesn't network you with clients, but it does present valuable opportunities to learn and to bond

def•i•ni•tion

A **lockbox** is an attachment to a door that holds the key to that door. Agents have access to the lockbox so that they can obtain the key to a property on-site. Many areas have adopted electronic lockboxes that track which agents visited the location, so that the listing agent has another tool for follow-up.

with your fellow agents. In the bigger picture, this type of service will gain you recognition from both clients and other agents as you will be thought of as one of the movers and shakers of the real estate community.

Know the Market

It's time for boot camp. Put on your boots, or at least your comfortable walking shoes, and walk the market, talk the market, and see the market. It will take time for you to talk market, but you will begin to if you saturate yourself in it. So how do you get prepared?

Check Out the Multiple Listing Service

Each locality has a multiple listing service (MLS) for its sales and rental listings. Most multiple listing services operate independently from real estate associations. Just about every licensed agent or broker belongs to the MLS, which provides a database of current and past listings of properties for sale and for rent. Through the MLS, the agent lists a client's property for sale or rent, and all agents belonging to that service can view the listings. Some services provide listings for an entire region; others handle one specific geographic area.

FYI!

The listing on the MLS will tell you specific information about the land, its building(s), and its listed price. It also will tell you commission amount and the property's showing information. There is a photo (or multiple photos), an embellished description, and contact information for the listing agent. There may be additional information, such as a date that all offers will be received, or any special terms, such as whether the owner will carry back financing or a special closing period.

Most services also provide a great deal of information beyond listings. For example, they provide tax assessor information and other agent and office data so you can track market share. We now have the capability for e-mails of new or changed listings to automatically be sent to designated clients and prospects. Marketing is at its best when it happens entirely without you. The more computer-savvy you become, the more benefits you will obtain from the MLS.

The MLS is your best course in real estate economics and statistics. Using the MLS is the course you did not receive in preparation for your license, but it *is* the one that really makes you a real estate agent. Once you understand the local real estate market and its statistics, you will begin to think like a real estate professional.

Here is a list of the primary statistics to study and compare to the same timeframe from the year before:

- Active listings in the area of your practice

- Average list price

- Average sales price

- Average time on market before sale

- List price versus sales price ratio

- Number of sales year-to-date

- Current interest rate for 30-year, fixed mortgage

Each MLS tracks these statistics. They are easy to retrieve, but you need to *understand* them. Sit down with your mentor or office manager and talk about these numbers. Only by comparing current statistics with one another and with statistics from the year before can you establish and track the economics of your market. You will see how prices compare to the year before, whether the market is slowing or quickening, and whether it is a seller's market or a buyer's market.

Now see how your area's statistics compare with surrounding areas and with the state and country as a whole. The website for your state association will provide data on where your area ranks within your state. How does its median home price compare to the immediate surrounding areas? Compare your local and statewide median home price to the national median by going to Realtor.org, the site of the National Association of Realtors. It gets very interesting when you start to put these statistics into perspective.

Agent to Agent

The National Association of Realtors has two websites, www.Realtor.com for the consumer and www.Realtor.org for agents. You should familiarize yourself with the consumer site so that you can direct your clients there. The agent site includes business management tips, breaking news, and the latest industry statistics and trends, sales and marketing tools, legal tips, and educational opportunities. In Canada, the national website is www.crea.ca.

Tour Houses

Study homes on the MLS, the inventory that makes the statistics. It would take you three hours to physically tour three properties. On the MLS website, you can tour at least a hundred in that time. It's not like opening the kitchen cabinets or walking through the garden, but you can see all of the properties' statistics along with a variety of pictures for each.

Through a careful study of the current active and recently sold listings, you will begin to understand value in a specific area. You will also start to understand per-square-foot figures when you divide the square footage of homes into their sale prices. You will see which areas appreciate more than other areas, and you will gain a sense of how long homes take to sell.

To complete your boot-camp training, move offline and into the field with some of the active listings you studied, physically touring these properties. This is where it gets fun. The numbers you've studied become homes and gardens. Hold the listing in your hand as you tour a property so the property's statistics are at your fingertips. Make sure you know the number of bedrooms and baths before you tour. Know what the siding is and how many fireplaces there are, and so on. Your primary reason for touring is to match up the physical product with its listing price and listing features.

Cave!

Go to properties on your own or with your mentor, hold the listing in hand, and make believe your clients are with you. Now's the time to perfect your touring style, not later when potential buyers are bombarding you with questions.

The market statistics you studied and the physical features of these properties will begin to relate to one another. An updated bathroom spells value, whereas a fully landscaped garden may spell work. Watch these listings as they travel through sale, and you will understand what makes one property more marketable than another. You may get a feel for why one property gets an offer in just a few days while another one goes through multiple price reductions and becomes stale.

Let seasoned agents in your office know you want to be included in listings they have obtained. Offer to sit for them when they hold open houses. Keep up your study of the market and tours of properties until you have a true understanding of value, property features, and your own local real estate market. Make sure you track the status of properties you tour. This type of monitoring will give you the very best sense of your local market.

Get to Know Your Local Neighborhoods

Tour a different neighborhood every few weeks. Pull the active and sold listings for that neighborhood. Get a feel for neighborhood value in relation to your entire area. Drive around and become acquainted with the amenities that make a certain sector a unique community. Know its proximity to transportation, major city centers, and other neighborhoods. Find out about the local schools and their reputations. Develop a neighborhood analysis based on your observations and the values you have established. You want to begin farming at least one neighborhood. Choose the neighborhood you want to make your own so when you get to the chapter on marketing you will have identified your farm.

It will take about three months of constant study and touring about ten homes a week to get a real feel for the market. If you religiously perform neighborhood analysis for the same period of time, you will develop a good understanding of your area as a whole and the difference in value among neighborhoods. You will tour a home and know which improvements increase value and which features make it more marketable. You will develop the ability to look at homes and come close to estimating the value without even reviewing computer statistics. One day you will drive by a house for sale, a price will come to mind, you will stop and pull the flyer—and you will be on the money. You will become a real estate pro without even realizing it.

FYI!
When you become a real estate licensee, bring out the teacher in yourself and develop a program accredited by your state real estate licensing organization. Through this, you will be more closely connected to the community and become recognized as an expert in the subject you teach. Why not teach a course on helping new agents set up their new business after you get yours running smoothly?

Upgrade Your Image

Real estate is both a highly visual industry and a fast track business. First impressions make or break you. This is probably a good time to hire an image consultant, but if this is not in your budget, step back and take a good objective look at how you

Cave!

Find an image consultant in the Yellow Pages under Coaches and Communications Consultants. If not under that category, look under Decorator or Interior Decorator and locate one who also handles personal décor. Also search the internet for someone local under any of these categories.

present yourself. In a people business like real estate, you have to capture your client quickly. This requires a full assessment of your business surroundings in order to capture your greatest market wherever you go.

The major components of your image are: how you look; what you say; and the appearance of your car, your office, and your marketing materials. Before you begin to build your business, you want to make sure its basic foundational components are the best they can be.

How You Look

Do you feel good about your appearance? If not, this is the time to do something about it. Buy those better looking glasses, get a new hairdo that fits the image you want to project, commit to a program to lose the weight you put on while studying for your real estate exam. Use this as a time to upgrade yourself. Not only will you feel more confident about yourself but people will naturally respond better to you.

Do you have the wardrobe required to present yourself as a competent real estate professional? If you are in doubt about attire, wear something more businesslike than not. If you don't have the clothes that make you feel successful, you will not have your best chance to succeed. If new clothes are not in your budget, go to a second-hand store. There is no reason to settle for less when it comes to appearance in a highly visual field like real estate.

Once you're looking just how you want, go to a professional photographer and have a few pictures taken. You'll need one for your business card, your marketing brochure, your web site, and your car sign. In real estate it's not the properties for sale that get all the fanfare, it's the agents.

Your Car is Your Calling Card

Since real estate is a field-intensive industry, you will be closely identified with your car. Does it project the image you desire? Look at the clientele you will target. What are they driving? You want your clients to feel an affinity with you, a similarity. Is your vehicle passenger and technology ready? You will be carting people around from home to home even if you primarily represent sellers because your sellers will also buy. Make sure your car is an inviting, comfortable place for them.

You also want to ensure that your vehicle is office ready. Are you able to set it up with all the materials you will need to efficiently operate out in the field? Is it easily adapted to charge your cell phone, PDA, printer, and laptop? Is there room to write offers and review documents? Does it have a global positioning system to direct you to listings? Some of these features can be deferred until you make your first few commissions but the basics should be on board from the get-go.

Now that you have your car ready for business, make it your mobile advertisement. Get a nice looking sign that magnetically attaches to your car and leave it on at all times. This sign will literally be your calling card. You are ready to broadcast your new profession to everyone you come across. You may as well take advantage of advertising as you drive the byways of your life. You will be surprised by how many people start real estate conversations with you just because of your sign. You won't have to prospect for clients. They will drive up right next to you.

Since you will probably choose to farm your own neighborhood, the neighbors might as well know exactly where you live. What better way than to have your car in the driveway with your marquee visible to everyone who drives by. You might even want to invite them to drop in and see you and even leave real estate requests in your mailbox. We call this reverse prospecting—letting people know where you are so they can come to you.

Make Your Office an Inviting Space

Size up your office. Is it organized? Does it present a picture of competence? Will a buyer or seller feel comfortable in it? Is your computer monitor capable of touring buyers through listings as if they are on site? The more virtual touring you can do in your office, the less time you will spend carting clients around to properties.

Create a 30 Second Spiel

Don't reinvent the wheel each time you encounter a prospect. It takes too much time and energy. Once you have assessed

Cave!

Don't take your energy away from the real estate business by becoming a computer nerd. Get some basic training in how to connect your equipment and how to share information. Find a person who knows computers to help you. Otherwise, you'll add a level of frustration to your business that will decrease, not increase, your productivity.

the markets you feel most comfortable in, you will know where your specialty lies. Are you good with decorating and can guide clients in preparing their properties for sale, will you provide a rebate to clients, will you provide a stager at your cost, will you specialize in certain communities?

You will discover your particular unique calling when you put your professional marketing package together. At that time, sit down and create a short, pinpointed commercial about yourself and what you can do for your client. Then memorize it. When you network and encounter prospects, look them in the eyes, connect, and give them your spiel as if you just created it in their presence.

Create Professional Marketing Materials

Use the professional photo you had taken on all your marketing materials. To begin with, your print products will be business cards and a mailer. Make sure all your marketing materials, including your car marquee and open house signs, match. You want to convey one direct message in a visually consistent way.

Manage Your Own Business

When you decided on a career in real estate, you made a decision to become a small business owner. If that scares you, a career in residential real estate sales is not for you. Although you come under the umbrella of a real estate office, you are actually the owner and operator of your own real estate sales practice. There are some important administrative steps you must take as a small business owner. The following sections explore these.

Incorporate Technology Fully

Because the MLS is Internet-driven and the business model in this book is computer-driven, it is imperative that technology become the foundation of your business. Thus, Chapter 12 is devoted entirely to it, covering the computer programs you will require to manage contacts, e-mail, calendaring functions, word processing, Internet access, and accounting. Most agents have two offices and field locations from which they need the ability to access information and to communicate by voice, fax, and e-mail. The challenge of the highly portable nature of your business is solved with a laptop, a cell phone, and a PDA, all of which must work together.

FYI!
The vast majority of Realtors now have their own website in addition to the one provided by their office.

Include Web Technology

Web-based technology is a subject you need to understand and incorporate into your business fully. The way we communicate with others and receive our information has changed, as has the way we market ourselves. Just as every business has a physical address, they now have an Internet address too. The office you work for will have a web presence. But you also want to have your own.

The Master Marketing Model in Chapter 13 will guide you to the best website options. These days you can get a feature-rich website with database management and campaign-generating tools all built in. All you do is push a button and your Internet-based contacts receive your current newsletter. You don't even have to prepare the newsletter—it comes packaged with your website, all for less than $500 a year.

Open Your Bank Accounts

You will need a business operating account for the commissions you earn and a client trust account for costs your client may deposit with you for payment of expenses. Your business operating account will be the main account for your small business where you will keep track of the income you receive and the deductions you take. You'll pay all your expenses out of this account, so you must therefore track them to count as deductions on your tax return.

The trust account is required by law if you hold funds for others. It will hold any funds your client has entrusted to you which are to be used on their behalf. Until these funds are spent according to their instructions, they belong to the client and must be kept in a separate trust account. You are not required to have a separate trust account for each client, but you must separately account for their funds within your trust account.

Agent to Agent

Your trust account may have money from your clients for various expenses. Perhaps these are fees to a stager, a painter, or a carpet-cleaning service. Sometimes the client is not local to the property and asks you to coordinate with many people to prepare a property for sale.

Prepare for Tax Time

Now that you work for yourself, you are responsible for calculating and paying your own taxes. The days of receiving paychecks with taxes already deducted are gone. You have state and federal income, Social Security, and Medicare taxes to pay. You will pay a rather steep *self-employment tax* for the privilege of being self-employed. I realize it should be the other way around, but it is not. These taxes can easily eat up 40 percent of your net income.

You will need to make tax payments as you go along by paying quarterly estimates. You don't want to get to tax filing day without budgeting for taxes. There are penalties if you do not make tax deposits as you go along. With most accounting software programs, your tax payments can be calculated as you deposit commissions.

If you have employees who are not *independent contractors*, you will also have to calculate and pay their taxes. An assistant will most likely meet the criteria of independent contractor, which means the assistant pays his own taxes. Workers are considered independent contractors if they have the right to direct and control the way they work, including the details of when, where, and how they do their jobs. If your assistant works out of her home at her own pace and works for others in addition to you, the independent contractor test has most likely been met. Virtual assistants are always independent contractors.

def•i•ni•tion

Self-employment tax is Social Security and Medicare tax paid by self-employed taxpayers on the net income from their trade or business.

An **Independent contractor** is a worker with the right to direct and control the way he works, including the details of when, where, and how he does his job. The independent contractor receives a 1099-Misc form by the end of January if he has earned over $600.00 from you.

When and if you hire an assistant, make sure you have him or her sign an independent contractor agreement that says what is described above. There is a fine line between employee and independent contractor status, so always watch that you do not cross it. If you do, the taxing authorities can assess you for any taxes that have not been paid both by you and by your employee. The very best way to stay on the right side of the independent contractor fence is to define only the work you want done, leaving your assistant to control how, when, and where the tasks are accomplished.

Deduct Most of Your Expenses

Now that you are self-employed, all business-related expenses are deductible. You pay self-employment taxes, so you want to meticulously claim all the deductions that you can as a small business owner. Pay all tax-deductible expenses out of your business operating account and itemize these expenses under the appropriate deduction category.

Know what deductions you can and cannot take. Your car is now a business expense, as is the business use of your home. All expenses you pay for education, including books you read, are deductible. Dues for clubs you join are also eligible as a deduction. Office equipment you use for your business is deductible. If the expense is related to business, take it as a deduction. This also applies to gas, auto repair, and auto insurance expense.

Save all your receipts for business travel, entertainment, and restaurants. You are required to itemize the specific people you met with, the dates you met, and the business purpose. This is the reason those big, ugly manila envelopes exist—to hold all your receipts in case you are audited. The reason is not to pull the receipts out at tax time and tally them up. You should implement a far better accounting program that tracks these expenses on computer as you go along.

FYI!

Here is a list of common deductions available to the real estate agent who works as an independent contractor:

- Advertising
- Assistants and virtual assistants
- Automobile expenses and lease
- Books and publications
- Business travel
- Dues to business-related organizations
- Education
- Entertainment necessary for business
- Equipment (including computers, phones, PDAs)
- Gifts to clients (all those gifts described in the referral stream system in Chapter 15)
- Home office use
- Insurance
- License renewal
- Supplies (including software)
- Postage
- Professional services
- Rent for office space
- Stationery and printing
- Telephone
- Website hosting and bundled services

There is a whole world of deductions available to you now that you are self-employed. From now on, whenever you pay an expense, go through the mental process of determining whether it is an expense related to your business. If it is, be sure you deduct it. The best way to track expenses is to pay them all through your business operating account or a business credit card. Make sure you have separate business and personal bank accounts and credit card accounts. The accounting becomes simple when everything associated with your business accounts is segregated.

When you pay your business credit card each month, allocate each item to its deduction category with your accounting software. You "split" the total bill into your deduction categories. For instance, your bill is $1,500, $230 of which was for advertising. Itemize this expense as "advertising." The categories you use should be the same categories you will use on your tax return.

It is especially important to scrupulously document your deductions because they determine the net income your taxes will be based upon. You therefore want to have as many deductions as possible. If you earn $75,000 and deduct $15,000 for expenses, your taxes are based on $60,000 net. Your expenses are your way to receive tax-free income as long as you choose them carefully and document them well.

Set Up Your Retirement Accounts

Many agents miss out on retirement planning because it dawns on them late in the game that nobody else is going to do it for them. We CEOs of our small businesses don't get the huge stock option packages others do, nor do we automatically have retirement accounts building for years as we toil away. We get nothing, a big zip, unless we begin saving for retirement early. When you set up your office, set up your retirement accounts. Build retirement into your overall business plan. If you set up these accounts with automatic payments from your operating account each month, you won't even feel the bite.

FYI!

Take the time to consider available retirement options and build them into your business and accounting plan. Go to www.irs.gov and click on *business*, then *small business*, to review the simple information the government provides on traditional IRAs, Roth IRAs, Simple IRAs, and SEP-IRAs. A SEP-IRA is a simplified employee pension plan tailored to ideally suit self-employed people and small business owners. It is voluntary, and its contribution level is geared to increase as your income increases.

When you start out knowing you are the only one who will take care of your retirement, you will build in the steps required to fund your retirement. Don't just automatically open a basic IRA. Review the options, talk to your accountant, and determine whether a Roth IRA or SEP-IRA, or other retirement option, is the best plan for you. Why pay taxes on income when you can legally divert income into tax-deferred or even tax-free retirement accounts? Setting up the maximum leveraged retirement accounts and creating future income streams (addressed later in this book in Part 6) will assure you financial abundance throughout your later years.

Package Your Business

Set yourself up as an entrepreneur with an entrepreneurial state of mind. Every successful entrepreneur sets up his business according to business opportunity resale standards to be sold later when it's a profitable venture. Any business that has a long-standing client list and a good history of income can be sold as a business opportunity. The longer the business has operated and the more net income it receives, the higher its value.

This is the frame of mind you want to have when setting up your business. The last section of this book describes business opportunity resale packaging of your business in more detail. It is important to set up your potentially sellable business now in its beginning stages for resale later. Here are a few tips to consider:

- ◆ Keep good, clear, verifiable records.
- ◆ Have a good accounting program that tracks all income and expenses.
- ◆ Have your tax return mirror your accounting income and expense categories.
- ◆ Set up systems for doing business that will allow your buyer to operate your business as successfully as you did.

Each step you take with your business plan takes into account the marketability of your business. Will this feature make this business more marketable when later sold as a business opportunity? If you revise your business procedures, do it in a simple, straightforward way. If you have a choice between technology and archaic methods, choose technology.

Agent to Agent

Surf the Net for business opportunities to get an idea of resale standards. Just having the intention to build an enterprise that will have resale value gives you an entrepreneurial state of mind. See if there are any real estate practices for sale in your area. Why start from scratch when you can step into someone else's successful shoes?

Make sure your records, both on the computer and hard copy, are clear. Keep your client base well organized in your contact management program. Your intention is to sell your flourishing enterprise when the time is right, even if it remains a one-person business.

Check Your Insurance Coverage

You also will need to contact your vehicle insurer to report that you are using your vehicle for business and chauffeuring clients. Otherwise, your insurance may not cover you for a business-related loss. Your office will also likely require you to list it as an additional insured on your policy. Your vehicle insurance will increase, so be prepared for that.

def•i•ni•tion

Errors and omissions insurance is known as E & O insurance. This insurance provides legal defense and coverage for claims made against you in your capacity as an agent. Most real estate offices provide this insurance for their agents as part of the fees they charge or in exchange for the commission split.

You also want to check on your new professional liability insurance. Lawsuits are a part of real estate. They go with any territory that involves high stakes. Real estate is about as high as you can get. Your liability insurance is called *errors and omissions insurance*, and covers you for any claim made against you for your real estate services. You pay your insurance through the office you hang your license with. Make sure the coverage is high and your deductible is low.

Take Construction and Architecture Courses

Real estate lingo is a vocabulary of its own. You need to know the industry-accepted terminology for all parts of a building, its components, its décor, and its land. The appraisal industry has its way of speaking. The construction industry has another. Architecture has a third. Decorating has its share, and landscaping has yet another. You need to know them all so you can intelligently communicate the names of features of a property. Some you met up with on your real estate exam. Much of this terminology may be new to you.

FYI!

Here are a few sample terms you will come across:

- ◆ **Construction terms:** dormer, wainscoting, rafters, trusses, load-bearing wall, joists
- ◆ **Decorating terms:** foyer instead of hallway, swags, cornices, valances
- ◆ **Furniture styles:** Chesterfield sofa versus the camelback sofa, Chippendale leg versus French provincial leg
- ◆ **Architectural terms:** crown molding and cove molding; peninsulas and islands; granite, marble, slate
- ◆ **Landscaping:** hardscape and softscape
- ◆ **Engineering:** septic systems, wells

When you get your license and become involved in the real estate industry, you are immediately catapulted into a whole different language. Read books on these subjects. Watch Home & Garden television and acquire an education in a week that will serve you well in your new career. Surf the Net. A dictionary of real estate terms will do once you know the words, but until then you need to learn what each feature is by touch, feel, and sight.

Take Continuing Education and Specialty Training

As with most other professional licenses, you must fulfill continuing education requirements to retain your license. These courses advance your expertise in your chosen field of real estate or help you to transition into another real estate field. If you plan ahead and choose your continuing education courses wisely, you will continually enhance your practice by broadening your marketplace and establishing your competence in chosen fields of expertise.

Although your job is not to give tax advice or legal advice, by honing your understanding of tax laws and contractual issues you will become indispensable to your clients and

Agent to Agent

Continually monitor the continuing education courses offered by your local real estate association, your state association, and the national association. Why not take the best courses to help you specialize and become a Top Dog? You may want to begin working toward a special designation like Certified Residential Specialist (CRS) or Graduate of the Realtor Institute (GRI) offered by the National Association of Realtors.

yourself. You will stand out as a career specialist who understands and takes advantage of the full benefits and ramifications of real estate ownership.

Build in continuing education, not just because it is required by your license, but because you want to be a Top Dog in your business. Don't wait until your continuing education hours are due to be turned in to take the week-long Real Estate Agent's Grand Riviera Gambling Cruise. You may get a good tan and have a lot of fun, but it won't boost your career in the least. Instead, continually monitor courses and pick and choose the ones that will enhance your marketability, your personal knowledge, and your own entrepreneurial skills.

The Least You Need to Know

- ◆ Your local, state, and national associations provide educational tools, statistics, and other valuable resources.

- ◆ The information and statistics on your local multiple listing service will become your education for the rest of your career.

- ◆ Consistently use lead-generating tools to build your business—and never stop.

- ◆ Now that you are a small business owner, payment of taxes, claiming deductions, retirement allocations, and resale value should all be built into your business plan.

- ◆ Training in computer technology allows you to market and organize your business and bring it everywhere you go.

Chapter 8

Building Personal and Professional Power

In This Chapter

- Understanding the seven principles of personal and professional power
- Viewing work as an extension of your passion
- Having an independent way of thinking
- Being powerful means having self-discipline
- Practicing good people skills is essential

This chapter describes the character traits and ideals that lead to personal and professional power. Cultivate these principles as the core of your real estate practice. While a good business plan and computer technology can make the difference between financial success and mediocre achievement, personal and professional power assure you of wealth of a different kind. It brings your heart and soul into your work and makes something more than profit your bottom line.

I refer to your real estate business as a real estate *practice* because personal and professional power is based upon the premise that you render a quality professional *service* to your clientele. Your business is far more than a high-pressure real estate sales office. It is a real estate practice based upon customs that dispense client-first loyalty and high-ethics service.

The Seven Principles of Power

Powerful people believe in themselves and their ability to make things happen. They have confidence that their ideas will manifest. They subscribe to the centuries-old concept of "you are what you think." They have mastered the skill of empowered thinking, a talent essential to achieving success.

FYI!
The philosophy of "you are what you think" began centuries ago when Buddha expressed it as, "All we are is the result of what we have thought."
In articulating a religion called Christian Science, Mary Baker Eddy affirmed that if you hold a thought of perfection, you will be perfect.
"Think who you want to become and you will become it" is the foundation of Napoleon Hill's formula to personal achievement and enrichment in his empowering book, *Think and Grow Rich*.

Dale Carnegie, Thomas Edison, Henry Ford, and Franklin D. Roosevelt all based their success on the ability to hold a vision and work toward it. The "you are what you think" concept is expressed in more modern times in many ways. Affirm what you want and it will be yours. Be positive even if you don't feel it, and you will begin to feel positive. Do not fear failure; it is just a stepping stone to success. Believe you will achieve, and you will. Seek your passion, and you will find abundance. An open mind leads to true abundance.

The following seven principles represent the ideals found to be most essential to achieving personal and professional power within the real estate sales field:

- **Principle 1:** See your work as your passion.
- **Principle 2:** Develop a burning desire to succeed.
- **Principle 3:** Be an independent thinker.
- **Principle 4:** Have a positive attitude.

- **Principle 5:** Be self-disciplined.

- **Principle 6:** Be ethical.

- **Principle 7:** Have good people skills.

Personal power is premised on the belief that you can affect an outcome through the power of your thinking. Self-defeating attitudes are replaced with empowering ones. You think it, affirm it, and expect the result. Whether you prescribe to personal empowerment philosophies doesn't matter. These principles have worked for centuries to create personal and professional success. What does matter is whether you are willing to use these tools to have the best chance to achieve personal and professional prosperity in your real estate career. If you are, the steps follow.

Agent to Agent

If these concepts appeal to you, read Napoleon Hill's book, *Think and Grow Rich*, published by Fawcett Columbine, New York. It was one of the important books that assisted me with my path to personal achievement. Many other books and tapes on personal empowerment will coach you with this concept. Tony Robbins, Joe Girard, Dr. Norman Vincent Peale, Zig Zigler, and Og Mandino, to mention a few, are available as your mentors.

Principle 1: See Your Work as Your Passion

Proverb: A little of what you fancy does you good.

The first step to personal and professional power is to see your work as the source of good things, as the outlet for your passion. This takes a transformation of the way we as a society feel about work. For as long as history tells the story, we have suffered in our work, equating pain with work and pleasure with home. We must shake loose of these archaic attitudes that announce that the source of our livelihood has to be hard in order to be worthwhile.

In many other professions, it is difficult to adopt a change of heart regarding work. Finding passion and meaning in a career is in conflict with the typical corporate hierarchy and its rigid chain of command. Most of us have taken that path. When we couldn't reframe our views about work from within that culture, we went in search of fulfillment outside of it. In real estate we recognize that our work can be an outlet for our personal passion.

Cave!

You cannot find your passion unless you believe that you can make a difference to more than yourself. This is presented in Chapter 15. It is about treating our clients in a more integrity-driven manner, and bringing our deeper morals and creative spirits into our work as a whole.

In Marsha Sinetar's book *Do What you Love, the Money Will Follow*, she pronounces that when we do what we are passionate about, abundance follows—not just financial abundance but personal abundance as well. The soul-searching question then is, "What do you love doing? What feeds your spirit?" In real estate it's not hard to find the answer because the job encompasses such a diverse range of qualities. Architect, analyst, attorney, therapist, decorator, negotiator, marketer, and advocate are just a few. My passions are property staging, negotiating, and problem solving. The real estate practice I have developed feeds each of these passions and gives me a wealth of personal and professional power and satisfaction.

Go on your own personal hunt to determine what it is that speaks to your soul. What gets your juices flowing? Just looking at your day and pinpointing specific roles you play that make you feel good will result in a new appreciation for what you do. Instead of experiencing a day that just passes like any other, doing too many things with not enough time, your day involves several roles—a little bit of decorator, a lot of an advocate. Sometimes you'll play the role of marketer or of a therapist.

If your passion does not exist in your day, bring it into your day. If you love to drive and should have been a race car driver, take the long route, get off the beaten track, and drive. If gardening is one of your passions, spend more time in clients' gardens. Help them spruce up their gardens when they buy or sell. If marketing brings out the best in you, as you'll find out in Chapter 10, Marketing is your middle name. You'll have no trouble putting this talent to use and frolicking in the results as well.

The answer to enjoying our work is really in knowing that work can be a source of pleasure and in taking the time to incorporate the activities you feel passionate about into your daily work life. The proverb goes, "A little of what you fancy does you good." Let's change it to "A lot of what you fancy does you really good."

Principle 2: Develop a Burning Desire to Succeed

Proverb: Where there's a will, there's a way.

In his work, *Think and Grow Rich*, Napoleon Hill used the term "burning desire." His philosophy is that in order to acquire deep-seeded abundance, you must have a burning desire. You must desire your objective so fiercely that you are willing to persist time and time again in the face of defeat. You must taste it, feel it, see it. You must use your five senses to visualize it. Then you must dream it until it bursts inside of you. Once you have reached this stage, you will find that the dream has manifested into reality. Hill even went so far as to call the fully developed burning desire an obsession.

This is how I became the national expert on equity sharing. It began with a good concept in its embryonic stages. I obsessed on it for about five years, and before I knew it I was writing a book, doing radio shows, touring the country, giving seminars, serving as an expert witness, and facilitating equity-sharing transactions across the country. My obsession with equity sharing has brought me satisfaction, enjoyment, a well-known reputation, and a good income stream.

FYI!

For some of us strongly motivated by a desire to serve, you may want to change the name of this principle to "a burning desire to serve." Since service is at the core of the real estate profession, it's really just a philosophical difference between a desire to succeed and a desire to serve. For you to succeed in real estate, service has to be a goal. The reason equity sharing appealed to me so strongly is I was born with a deep desire to bring equality to others. Is it any wonder that something called equity sharing became my obsession?

This willingness to be fully engaged in our work is one of the essential elements of powerful people. When you begin to pinpoint your passion and cultivate it in your work, you will automatically want to commit yourself more fully to your work. You will feel more interested in and satisfied by it. Each day that you practice these principles, you will engage yourself more fully in your work and you will naturally reap the rewards of your commitment. It takes a strong commitment to be the very best. The result will be that you will operate with confidence, diligence, ethics, and passion.

The real estate field is like no other. It is enormously wealthy with unlimited possibility. It is easy to find something that interests you, like equity sharing did for me, and tap into it. If it has not already been created, Principle 2 coaches you in how to build it. Let "where there's a will, there's a way" be your motto. Combine it with Principle 3, independent thinking, and these principles will carry you a long, long way.

Principle 3: Be an Independent Thinker

Proverb: Life is what you make it.

Another essential ingredient to personal and professional power is independent thinking. You have to believe that "Life is what you make it," and have the vision to make your dreams happen. Most people tap their creative visions but are soon derailed by the opinions of others. They fail to commemorate their dreams, instead subjecting them to the negative thoughts of others.

Real estate abounds with independent thinkers. Many people are drawn to real estate because of its unstructured environment and flexibility. Far too often, the attraction stops there. Most agents say, "I'm so glad to be out of the rat race of the workaday structured world. I have independence and financial reward in my work," and independent thought ends.

> **FYI!**
>
> As Napolean Hill so aptly put it, "Opinions are the cheapest commodities on earth. Everyone has a flock of opinions ready to be wished upon anyone who will accept them." Successful independent thinkers don't share their visions. We think out of the box, create out of the box, and do not subject our ideas to the scrutiny of others.

In the real estate field, you are in the middle of a goldmine as long as you retain your independent thinking. We are exposed to deals every day of our lives. Just think of how many times in a day or week you are asked if you know a source of ready cash or a good real estate deal. The independent thinker jumps on these opportunities, continually expanding her vision, and is always on the lookout for deals.

The independent thinker sees a need and fills it. She thinks of real estate as an investment first and the source of a commission second. She keeps track of good real estate deals and puts people together, herself included, to provide funding for these deals. She acquires an investor state of mind and builds future income streams that sustain her throughout her career.

Real estate's possibilities are infinite. As you increase your professional expertise, you serve your clients and manage your own investments better. In real estate, if you follow your passions and let your dreams evolve, you can build a business that will sustain you for years to come. I know this from personal experience. I started out in real estate law, then ran the gamut to real estate litigation, mediation, sales, equity-sharing facilitation, exchange facilitation, real estate seminars, consulting on real estate issues, and writing real estate books. The entrepreneurial-minded independent thinker can find a place in real estate's expansive universe and create a niche that will attract clients, wealth, and opportunities. "If you build it, they will come."

Principle 4: Have a Positive Attitude

Proverb: Count your blessings.

A positive attitude is essential to the achievement of personal power. When you enter the real estate profession, you see cheery people everywhere. Not only is the agent's smile plastered across business cards, it is who the agent is—at least who the successful agent is. Real estate draws people who are able to look on the positive side of things. After all, they've chosen a profession that is marked by freedom and flexibility. What's not to smile about? Let it be a touchstone for you. It can be contagious if you let it. Remember, "you are what you think."

Take real estate legend, Danielle Kennedy, for example. When she became an agent she was six months pregnant with her fifth child, yet through persistence and a positive attitude she achieved success few have seen. Within four years she closed on over one hundred homes and has since become a well-respected motivational speaker and author of several sales books. This lady was empowered and determined to make the grade. Read her fine work, *How To List & Sell Real Estate*.

FYI!

If you have a positive attitude, you see the glass as half-full. Back in the early twentieth century, when men of unparalleled fortune and power like Franklin D. Roosevelt and Thomas Edison needed to create a state of mind that was essential to getting what they wanted, they used the power of affirmation. They affirmed what they wanted on a continual basis and watched it materialize. Just start acting like a positive person, associate with positive people, and pretty soon you will find that you have a positive state of mind.

Once you cultivate a positive attitude, it's time to create a positive work environment. The first step is to identify and limit your susceptibility to negative influences. Watch your everyday life, both work-related situations and the rest of your life. What causes you to feel negativity? Write these conditions down.

Next, spend time noting the things that make you feel good. Create a "count-my-blessings" list. These may include beautiful

 Cave!

Negative influences come in various shapes and sizes. They may be conditions with family members and friends, the media constantly sensationalizing negative events, the agent in the next cubicle relentlessly complaining about her husband, and so on.

scenery, pleasant company, your family, and satisfaction with your achievements. Stop, watch, and identify exactly what makes you feel good. Then set boundaries to protect against the negative influences and to bring in the positive ones.

The final step of the positive life plan is to deliberately seek out people and circumstances that influence you positively. Positive people are magnetic. Everyone wants to be near them. People are drawn by their genuine smile and their contagious feeling of good will. Take steps to attract and surround yourself with these people. When you choose real estate as a career, select an upbeat group of people to surround yourself with. Let it work for you. Pick Power Team members (discussed in the next chapter) who have a positive spirit.

FYI!
I often take my dog to the office with me. I drive over the Golden Gate Bridge just for the joy of it. It does help that my office is only ten miles from San Francisco. I take my morning walk each day before I work. I have my afternoon tea. I sit with clients and help them resolve their real estate woes day in and day out. If I find a client is impossible, I gently pass them on to some other less discerning professional.

Creating positive spirit can be a real challenge for the new agent who often sets up shop in the least desirable spot in what is probably already a crowded office. In addition, everything he's doing is brand new. Setting up your workspace after you have conducted the previous analysis makes the difference between a haphazard work environment and one that supports a positive state of mind. Bring in a picture of the dog if you can't fit your dog under your desk. Wear headphones if you can't concentrate because your cubicle is in the middle of a busy walkway. Build in those creature comforts that make you feel like a worthwhile creature.

Principle 5: Be Self-Disciplined

Proverb: If at first you don't succeed, try, try, and try again.

Henry Ford and Dale Carnegie knew it. You can have a burning desire to the extent of it becoming an obsession, but if you don't have the self-discipline to go after the object of your desire, you will never get it. Self-discipline, therefore, is a necessary quality for true personal power. In real estate you've got to have self-discipline for about a hundred reasons.

The number-one reason you need self-discipline is that you work for yourself and you are the source of your income. Number two is that you work for yourself, but the show goes on without you. Most self-employed people have to show up to get the show rolling. That in itself is an incentive for self-discipline. In real estate, the office opens, the phones are answered, and life marches on without you. There is no office rule that says you have to be there. Number three is that when the show goes on without you, you earn no income. Your business makes no money without you. And, in offices where you pay fees on top of commission, you lose money when you don't show up.

The best way to start out on the right foot is to act as if you have a regular job. Of course you don't, and that's why you're smiling. But if you adopt the work ethic an employer would require of you, you will develop a discipline that will serve you for the rest of your career. Keep regular work hours. Get there early. Be part of the team. Allow the office environment to work for you. Let your office and your other support team members be a central part of your business. Without self-discipline on the part of all team members, you and your team will not have power.

> **FYI!**
>
> Remember, one of the major regrets of seasoned agents is lack of self-discipline. From day one agents felt they should have adopted better work habits, such as starting work at a certain time and building in repetitive tasks at the same time each day.

The number-one obstacle of self-discipline is that nasty human foible called procrastination. When you join the real estate club and its share of amenities, determination and persistence are the name of the game. There is no room for procrastination. If you stop working in real estate, very simply, real estate stops working for you. The business moves too fast to allow procrastinators aboard its fast track for more than a short ride.

I would like to share a story about the life of one man we all know and respect. His story may be a bit historical but it so perfectly depicts the self-discipline a person develops when he manifests a burning desire and perseveres until he achieves his goal. Here is this famous gentleman's resumé:

> **Agent to Agent**
>
> M. Scott Peck's *The Road Less Traveled*, published by Simon & Schuster, discusses self-discipline when he begins his international bestseller with "Life is difficult." He describes self-discipline as one of the tools required to solve life's problems. I highly recommend this book.

- ◆ 1831 Failed in business
- ◆ 1832 Lost election for the legislature

- 1834 Failed in business again

- 1835 Sweetheart died

- 1836 Nervous breakdown

- 1838 Defeated in second political race

- 1843, 1846, 1848 Defeated for Congress

- 1855 Defeated for the U.S. Senate

- 1856 Defeated for the vice presidency

- 1858 Defeated for the U.S. Senate

- 1860 Elected president of the United States

Agent to Agent

Here are some inspiring quotes from Abraham Lincoln:

"Leave nothing for tomorrow which can be done today."

"I have been driven many times upon my knees by the overwhelming conviction that I had nowhere else to go. My own wisdom and that of all about me seemed insufficient for that day."

This man is Abraham Lincoln. He is a deeply inspiring model of what happens when you burn with your desire to the point of obsession and persist until you achieve your goal. For the thirty years before he was elected President of the United States, he was continually defeated in all his major undertakings. Hopefully, we don't have to lose a loved one or have a nervous breakdown to achieve our goals in the real estate field. But it has been my experience that the most successful of us come through a fair share of life challenges before we discover our own personal and professional power.

Principle 6: Be Ethical

Proverb: As you sow, so shall you reap.

Good ethics are at the heart of personal power. The New Ideal (see Chapter 16 for more information) mandates that you represent your client first and foremost. Don't focus on the close and don't rush clients through the process. Focus instead on assisting your client by applying your highest integrity to each and every step of the transaction. Your mission is to make your client's welfare your top priority. After all, you are his or her legal agent.

Take each step slowly and carefully, explaining the many options available to your buyers and sellers. Allow yourself to be guided by your integrity as you skillfully discharge your legal duty. To the personally powerful agent, client advocacy and quality personal service is far more important than the close. The commission we make at closing is just a by-product of serving our clients according to this ethical code and our legal obligation. It's no longer a job of salesmanship. It is now a job of ethics.

Chapter 16 carries this principle farther. Let it now be a seed that begins to germinate within you. Erase the artificial line between business and personal ethics that was drawn so long ago. Because our work becomes the source of our passion, personal ethics come into play. They go hand in hand with true passion. Allow yourself to cross the bridge into a more conscious livelihood of ethics-based action. If you do, you will exude a professional power that draws others to you because "as you sow, so shall you reap."

Principle 7: Have Good People Skills

Proverb: Do unto others as you would have them do unto you.

Real estate is a people place. For the real estate professional, good people skills are mandatory. Everything you do involves relationships with clients, other agents, and various other professionals. Your work on behalf of your client is that of a counselor, a friend, a strong negotiator, a shrewd analyst, and a facilitator. In order to have personal power in real estate you have to develop strong people skills. You must develop the principle of "Do unto others as you would have them do unto you."

In the real estate field, good people skills mean the application of skillful listening. We need to hear what our clients have to say from both their words and emotions. As a society, our ears have failed as instruments of understanding others. We must learn to listen in new ways. Begin to give your clients 100 percent of your attention as they describe what they want. This is the only way to truly understand their needs. Remember, you are their fiduciary agent. Your job is to be loyal to them and take care of their interests above all else. How can you do this when you haven't heard what their interests are?

Problem solving is another people skill the powerful agent should possess. The residential real estate transaction is particularly susceptible to high levels of stress because of its fast track, high stakes, and personal nature. Clients can become unglued in any phase of the deal. Your role as the caretaker of these transactions makes you an essential member of your client's problem-solving team. Legally you become their fiduciary, but emotionally you become part of their problem-solving team. By continually cultivating sensitivity and compassion, you will have the patience and understanding to problem solve in a professional manner on these occasions.

Agent to Agent _____

For the next week, pay attention to the way others listen to you. You know the difference when someone is doing ten things at one time, and you are one of those ten things. In these days of quick action, particularly within real estate's fast pace, everyone seems to be continually multitasking. Be fully present when you are listening to your clients. Don't multitask. They know the difference, and so do you.

You will also be called upon to display your negotiating skills. At the drop of a hat, an emotional buyer or seller can come up with the most confounded demands. Your job is to take this transaction and carefully maneuver it through another phase that no one really planned upon. Armed with good people skills and effective negotiating expertise, you will work through this obstacle and turn it into a mere bump in the road.

Always draw upon the proverb of "do unto others as you would have them do unto you" when dealing with all parties in your transactions and your people skills will be a quality others will admire in you.

The Sum of the Parts

I have my seven principles on a card in my wallet, in my car, and on my wall at the office and at home. They are with me wherever I go. They have become a part of me, and I can truly say I have personal and professional power. It's been a long, soul-searching road, but one that I would not trade for all the money in the world. The richness you will receive if you incorporate these seven principles into your real estate career will be equally rewarding to you.

The Least You Need to Know

- Personal and professional power can come through a belief that you can affect your outcome through positive thinking.

- One way to become a powerful person is to enjoy what you do and express your passion through your work.

- Persistence and the application of independent thinking can lead to personal and professional power.

- Personal and professional power come to those who operate with high integrity.

- Because real estate is a field that deals with people, having good people skills and being a good listener are important traits to acquire.

Chapter 9

Building Your Power Team

In This Chapter

- ◆ Your Power Team members
- ◆ Partnering with another agent
- ◆ Where to find Power Team candidates
- ◆ Qualifying your Power Team members
- ◆ Team meetings and motivation

The foundation of every agent's business is his Power Team. Thus, one of the first steps you will take is to build your own essential team. Your Power Team members are real estate professionals who will make your transactions seamlessly travel through the many stages to closing. It is these professionals who become a pipeline for client referrals for a lifetime. You will refer to them; they will refer to you. And they will help provide professional service at its very best to your clients.

Be picky about who you choose for your team. Make sure your candidates provide quality service and have good professional ethics. Each member is vital to your reputation and your success. Talk to your mentor or office manager about candidates for your team. If you feel you don't have enough experience in the field to make these important choices, don't make them.

It is better to defer building your team until you are able to put together a team that is personally and professionally powerful.

When you interview members, have a mental checklist in place for the important qualities you seek in each. While reading this chapter, compose your own list of traits that are important to you. The checklist approach works best since you will apply the same criteria to a number of different candidates, some of whom will not meet your standards and some of whom will become qualified Power Team members.

Choosing Your Power Team Members

The Power Team members will consist of the following:

- ◆ Your mentor(s)
- ◆ Your agent partner if you have one
- ◆ Mortgage broker
- ◆ Closing professional
- ◆ Professional stager
- ◆ Pest control inspector
- ◆ General property inspector

FYI!

You can easily put together a Power Team at just one Chamber of Commerce mixer or civic organization meeting. When you are new to the business and don't really have many contacts yet, this may be an ideal way to assemble your first Power Team. In the beginning, the job is more about creating an energetic and supportive team. Over time the team will refine itself into an efficient, productive, and powerful group.

During the first year of your career, your mentor is your most important tool for motivation and guidance. If you cannot find mentor qualities in one person, select several mentors each with a different expertise. It would be ideal to get everything you need in one person, but if you can't, don't stop looking.

The person you choose should be a fellow agent and must be able to give you the time and expertise you need. Although your mentor will not officially be a member of your Power Team (at least the team that works together servicing clients and meets regularly), this guide should have many of the traits described in the prior chapter on personal and professional power. You want to learn from a pro—not just any old pro, but a personally powerful one.

Now on to your official Power Team members. If you have partnered with another agent, this agent will naturally become your most important Power Team member. If not, the mortgage broker is the most important member. There are two reasons why. First, a good mortgage broker can make the difference between a deal plagued with stress and a smooth, calm transaction. Second, this is the team member you are likely to get the most referrals from. Make sure your qualification of these team members is thorough. Act like you're getting married when you qualify both your agent partner and your mortgage broker members. These people can make the difference between a good life as an agent and an average one.

Other optional members are a real estate attorney, a certified public accountant, and an exchange intermediary. You should have affiliations with each of these professionals since their services are often required in transactions. Including them in your Power Team family depends on whether their presence has a benefit. If they enhance the team spirit, pass the team qualification test, and are willing to reciprocate with referrals, sign them up.

Partnering with Another Agent

It can be a real challenge to beat the time crunch of the swiftly moving real estate transaction. Given the importance of each step in a transaction and the brief period assigned to each, emergencies threaten even the most well-planned time off. Agent partnering is a welcome relief for the agent who feels pulled in many directions. Through job sharing, one partner is on call while the other is off, confident that her clients are being taken care of. The well-chosen partnership can be the ideal answer for weary agents who have felt captive by work and responsibility.

If you decide to partner with another agent, your agent partner will naturally be one of the most valuable members of your Power Team. Believe it or not, sharing your listings with the right agent-partner can be the way to increase your market appreciably. It may sound strange to describe sharing listings

Agent to Agent

When you are a new agent, consider partnering. When you're a pro, consider teaming up with a novice. As in anything else, selective partnering can make the difference between a solitary career experience and one filled with the sharing of rewards and woes.

as a way to increase a market. You might think that this would break a market or at least cut it in half. Actually, it can double your market and create a synergy that occurs when two people work well together.

New agents teaming up in partnership with one another can be the perfect solution to even the odds when pickings are slim initially. One commission between the two is better than no commission at all. In the beginning, it's also helpful to have a colleague in your corner when you're fumbling through new experiences, even when your partner fumbles with you. It can get lonely at the new agent's desk, facing a silent phone while you're trying to master a highly detail-oriented profession.

If you are a new agent and you find a seasoned professional to team up with, you are two steps ahead. The commission split between you and your partner will not be equal in this relationship, but the advantages are easy to understand. You have found a built-in mentor, someone who has learned the ropes and can guide you through the obstacle course. The skilled agent, on the other hand, will reap the rewards of sharing time and responsibilities and have fresh enthusiasm from you as his partner.

> **Cave!**
>
> Prepare a *written* partnership agreement signed by you and your agent partner that reflects what you have agreed to, especially how you have agreed to share your commissions. In this manner, you can eliminate areas for potential misunderstandings and future problems. Include a clause on how you will dissolve the partnership should either of you seek a change.

Arranging the Partnership

You and your partner can have any arrangement that suits your fancy. It can be a 50-50 split, a 10-90 split, or anything in between. You can have an on-call arrangement that does not involve commission splitting but is purely a time trade. For example, Tom and Anne have an on-call arrangement. Tom is on call for Anne's clients when she is off and vice versa. They do not share commissions.

Or you may choose a time trade coupled with a fee for time spent. In that situation, Tom and Ann would time-trade but keep track of the time they spend on the other's matters. At the end of the month, whoever has spent more time gets paid an agreed-on hourly rate for the excess time.

There are as many variables as you can dream up for agent partnerships. As long as everyone works in the same office, there should be no problem since everyone is on the same insurance policy, has a commission split with the same company, and has the same manager. Agents have found that job sharing and on-call partnering enhance their use of time.

Using a Professional Stager

Most agents who deal with high-end properties have a stager on their Power Team. The stager accompanies you to listing presentations. He provides design and decorating recommendations, hopefully in a very sensitive manner, on how to best stage the home for sale. Sellers usually find staging quite helpful and often engage the stager's services. I think every agent, not just high-end agents, seriously interested in listing a home for sale should recommend the services of a professional stager. This is why the stager is included on your Power Team.

Your stager is a designer or decorator versed in staging properties for sale. For high-end properties, a stager is hired with expertise in interior decorating, contracting, and landscape architecture. The value and condition of the property indicate which type of stager is used and the budget for this professional. Chapter 23 describes the role of the stager in more detail.

FYI!

You can find stagers in the yellow pages of your phone book. Look under Interior Designers, and note which ones have added home staging to their specialties. Pay attention to their suggestions so you can make similar suggestions for clients who do not want to pay for this professional service. I found my stager in the very next town through an Internet search that brought me to www.bhammil.com.

Stagers may use the furnishings already present or might rent furnishings, artwork, and plants for a home. They usually reduce the clutter so that the space shows to its fullest advantage. They also recommend painting and other spruce-up steps. These talented people can work wonders with very little expense. A staged home may greatly hasten the sale of that home.

Finding Power Team Members

Each real estate community has a number of professional marketing groups. If you can't find one, check out your local real estate board or the local chamber of commerce. These groups generally meet once or twice a month. Your local board consists of agent members and affiliates. Affiliates are your potential team members. You may want to monitor new affiliates as they join since they are probably new to real estate or to your territory and obviously want a larger market. They will be motivated. Of course, motivation isn't everything, but it is a start.

- ◆ Your local real estate board
- ◆ Your mentor
- ◆ Your office manager
- ◆ Yellow Pages and Internet searches
- ◆ Community groups
- ◆ Your agent partner

If you are partnering with an agent who has been practicing for any time, he will have his own Power Team in place. If you use his team, you won't have to build your own. Sometimes that is an advantage; sometimes it is not. Talk to your agent partner about his team with the thought of ensuring that this team is the very best for both of you.

Your partner may have wanted to replace some members, but has not had the time or has been embarrassed to do so. His partnership with you is just the excuse to reassess and revise the team as needed. If you perform your own interview of an existing team, do it with a good deal of deference. You're the new kid on the block, and they are veterans. Don't rock the boat, just watch and inquire with manners and humility.

If you're not partnering, ask your mentor or office manager for referrals. The people they refer you to may not be available to the extent your Power Team members need to be, but they can refer you to other potential candidates in their field. Go to the Yellow Pages under the category of professional you are looking for. Tell them you are interested in building a Power Team and would like to speak with them about their participation or a referral to someone in their field who may be a benefit to your group. If you have a group affiliation, look for your team members there. In this way, you'll be starting out with someone who has a similar outside interest. Sharing something in common, aside from career objectives, makes for a solid Power Team partnership.

Qualifying Power Team Members

As you qualify candidates, ask them for their lists of existing Power Team members. You may want to tap resources they have already found success with. You want to pick your Power Team members according to the criteria discussed in the following list:

- ◆ Commitment to a Power Team plan
- ◆ Availability

- Quality of services

- Personal and professional power

- Good people skills

- High integrity

Commitment to a Power Team Plan

One of the most important criteria of your team members is their ability to commit to you. Your candidate may already have one or more teams in place and may not be able to give you the service and referrals your Power Team needs. You want this relationship to be as important to them as it is to you. With that comes a commitment to continually upgrade services as the market changes and spend time with team members motivating and assisting one another.

As a real estate sales agent, your transactions always need the services of your team members, whereas their transactions rarely need you because they do not have agent choice in the majority of their transactions. This makes their ability to commit to you and give you quality service all the more important.

It may take some effort to find team members who can give you this commitment because often the quality candidates already have teams in place. You will probably end up with someone relatively new to their field, as you are new to yours. A new person may be able to give your clients more attention. If they have good practices in place, they may be as capable as someone who has been in the profession for a long time.

Availability

You want to make sure your Power Team members are available. Because of the flexibility afforded by the industry, many real estate professionals suffer from poor self-discipline when it comes to keeping a regular schedule. You want to be able to contact your team members during regular working hours to be able to keep your transactions on course and full speed ahead. Find out what their regular hours are and make

Agent to Agent

If e-mail will be your primary source of communication with Power Team members, make sure they have built e-mail services fully into their business model. Some people only use e-mail as a secondary source of communication. If you are e-mail-based, your Power Team members need to be as well.

sure their hours conform to your schedule and the schedule of the rest of your Power Team.

My team members primarily keep in touch through e-mail. When we are working on the same transaction, we include the rest of the team on communications with one another so everyone stays on top of the transaction's status. E-mail provides a highly efficient way of keeping everyone in the loop in the most time-efficient manner possible, as long as your Power Team members are technologically versatile.

Quality of Services

Your members should provide diligent, competent services. They should be professionals who will go the extra mile for you and your clients. When you put together a new team, you will not yet know how team members measure up to this standard. As you encounter someone who falls short, talk to him or her immediately. Make sure the situation is corrected. If, after thorough communication and a good opportunity to correct, your team member continues to fall short, replace him or her. Do it with permission of your team members, and do it compassionately, but do it.

You are building an important enterprise with your Power Team. Do not underestimate the value of each member, especially your agent partner, mortgage broker, and closing professional. You want to do business with and have your clients served by the finest in the field. Do not feel that you cannot have the best because you're new. You have made a commitment to the quality of service you will provide, and you will bring this distinction to any Power Team you build. Be proud of who you are and expect others to treat you with respect just as you treat them with respect.

Personal and Professional Power

Repeating the last chapter on personal and professional power here would be worthwhile. You want your Power Team members to share the qualities of personally powerful people. Develop a mental checklist of the qualities described in the last chapter. Your team members may not possess all criteria required of the person with personal and professional power, but if each team member possesses a few of these skills, you will be well on the path to creating a top-notch Power Team.

If your entire Power Team has developed its own version of personal power, your team will be exceptional. Each team member will attract his own market because he will be motivated to provide outstanding service, and clients will naturally gravitate his way. With this special synergy, your Power Team will be a magnet that will draw clients and their referrals.

Good People Skills

Your Power Team members should be likeable, since you will be working closely with them. You will pull them into every transaction you have. If you enjoy working with them, your clients will, too. In the beginning, check in with the clients you refer to team members at each stage and make sure they are well taken care of. If they aren't feeling taken care of, look at the reason why. Transactions can become stressful, and how we deal with one another during times of stress is extremely important. It is the difference between good people skills and bad people skills. You want each member on your team to demonstrate good people skills.

High Integrity

You want your team members to share your values relating to integrity and ethics. Your team should not only be capable and enjoyable to work with, they should be a team deserving of your respect and that of your clients. You want to stand out in what you do because of your sense of service and integrity, and you want your Power Team to do the same.

Your Power Team can produce phenomenal teaming power if each member is aligned with a similar mission statement about excellent service and caring for people. An ideal way to make sure your team shares the same vision is to develop a mission statement together. At your first Power Team meeting, put the creation of a mission statement on the agenda.

Team Motivation

If you aspire to have a truly empowered Power Team, a motivation plan is important. Your team might start out upbeat and positive, but it is susceptible to negative professional influences. Weekly or bimonthly meetings can provide just the right amount of motivation and support to keep your team upbeat and on track.

You may want to appoint one team member on a rotation basis to serve as the motivational coach each month. This person can perform the roles of the troubleshooter, problem solver, and facilitator for a period of service. Scheduled meetings provide an extra, all-important bond among members and a forum for open discussion of challenging situations.

Agent to Agent _____

My first Power Team gave monthly seminars to the community, sharing valuable information about the real estate purchase and sale process. By holding these seminars and becoming a quality team, we built a referral stream that lasted for many years. We also provided invaluable support to one another on both a personal and business level.

Title and closing companies often have conference rooms they will let you use to put on community service seminars. Use a flyer to announce your seminars to the community. You can also post notices in the community calendar of your local newspaper.

Transaction and Quality Control

Set up a method of communicating on each transaction so that all involved members can track the progress of a transaction. I set up individual transaction pages on my website so Power Team members and our clients can track the progress of our transactions. These pages are confidential and can only be accessed directly by knowing the URL of that page.

You also want to conduct your own diligent quality control to ensure that each member provides the level of service and integrity that your clients deserve. On your Power Team, quality control occurs as each member holds the rest accountable for timely, quality services promised.

The Least You Need to Know

- Your Power Team provides stability to your transactions and credibility to your business.

- Partnering with another agent provides you the ability to share benefits and burdens with someone else.

- Qualifying your Power Team members is essential to building a team that has a solid foundation and shares your values.

- Keeping your team motivated and in line with high ideals is as important as finding the right team members.

- Have regular meetings and monitor the performance of Power Team members.

Part 3

Building an Unbeatable System

Get out your tool belt. It's time to build your unbeatable system. It's a three-level structure constructed of the following:

Top level: Marketing and lead generating systems

Middle level: Time management and transaction coordination techniques

Bottom level: Technology to automate and synchronize it all

This part makes your business a market making machine. With the implementation of cutting edge technology and multimedia marketing, your business draws leads and services them virtually without you. Even sale facilitation becomes automated with form contracts that synchronize with transaction management programs.

10

Building A Lead Generating Machine

In This Chapter

◆ The importance of lead generation

◆ Your sphere of influence as your first market

◆ Broaden your community involvement

◆ Put up your own website

◆ Get ready to adopt our lead generating Master Market Model

Somewhere along the way a wise real estate agent once said, "Real estate is the highest paying hard work and the lowest paying easy work in the world." It's true. In real estate sales, the financial disparity between the producers and the loafers is extreme. There is a huge difference between big bucks and no bucks.

Two agents can spend eight hours a day, one just filling a slot and waiting for success to happen and the other conscientiously following a tried-and-true lead generating system. The passive agent will net the lowest pay for his easy work. Not only will the result be low pay, there will be out-of-pocket expenses for insurance, dues, and technology that will make this agent one of the many people who pivot in and out of real estate each year.

The diligent proactive agent will gradually but steadily increase her income until she reaches her goal of high paying producer. Consistent hard work pays off particularly well in real estate sales. It is important for you to realize now that it is at the lead generating level that the tough get going and the lazy drop out.

def•i•ni•tion

A **lead generating** system is one that captures prospects, usually at an Internet intersection, and drives them your way.

This chapter mainly deals with the importance of consistent lead generation and what you do to make your markets, while Chapter 13 sets your high-tech lead generating programs in place. First, let's take a look at the different types of focused marketing available to real estate agents. It will make you sensitive to markets and able to draw them to you.

Are You a Social Butterfly?

We've already established that the field of real estate is easy to enter and those who work hard with a consistent lead generating system succeed. But it takes something else, too. You must enjoy associating with a vast variety of people in order to achieve the greatest success. This, ladies and gentlemen, is the secret. You must enjoy people and take pleasure in helping them.

The simple truth is to become a real producer in the real estate field you must make Market your middle name and social butterfly your new job. Your job 8 hours a day is real estate agent; your job 24 hours a day is generating leads. You can have all the best credentials and a mile of intentions but in real estate, you must first have clients. Real estate is a people business more than any other. Always think of yourself as "on the job" because all those people you interact with every day are your bread and butter—and your lifeline.

Potential Markets Swirl Around You

Nearly everyone you bump into will buy or sell real estate, so you are continually surrounded by potential markets. Why not let everyone you meet know what you do? What you do is a large part of who you are, especially if you have come to your profession after having been down many other roads. This chapter will assist you in identifying and creating markets. It will start you out with your personal *sphere of influence* and take you through many different markets that swirl around you. It literally will transform you from a fledgling caterpillar into a magnetic social butterfly—and a million dollar real estate agent.

Your personality profile most likely targets you as butterfly material anyway. The transformation contemplated by this chapter shouldn't really involve changing your personality traits. Instead, we want to implement a makeover of sorts; an optimal reorganization of your social orientation in a way that scoops up markets as you go through your everyday life. You don't have to be an extrovert to be honest with people. Just quietly look them in the eye and let them know you want to assist them.

def•i•ni•tion

Your **sphere of influence** is everyone you have known or associated with throughout your life. Pull out those dusty yearbooks, tap into your memory banks, and remember all those folks whom you have had contact with. Track down your childhood friends and the parents of your children's friends. It is time to remember them all.

Generating Leads for Survival

Make sure you always remember the importance of generating leads, not just in the beginning, but always. If you lag, you will lose. Before you entered real estate sales, leads were about dancing or fishing. Now they're about survival.

One of the main problems agents have is once they get a good system going, they stop working it. When I finally implemented a system that began producing the leads I needed, I patted myself on the back and turned my attention to the listings I was getting. This was a bad move. Marketing to produce leads is your job before any other. If you don't consistently grease the wheels of the marketing machine, the machine will run slower, and slower, and you will end up having to rebuild it—after it chugs to a halt.

There is nothing that will suffocate your business more than a slow down in lead generation. Don't let this important system go into neutral, ever. Each morning you awaken know that you are first a marketer and second a real estate agent. Your secret to long-term success, even when you are a millionaire, is to understand that lead generation is not optional. It is the foundation of your business and no matter how successful you become, you must always make it your first priority and personally administer it.

For this reason you must always and forever block off time to administer your lead generation program. Make it be as important as shopping for groceries in your everyday life. If you

FYI!

The third most common thing seasoned agents wished they had realized in their early years is that real estate sales is about creating markets everywhere you go.

don't consistently do it, your business will not thrive. Even when its volume becomes overwhelming, the system stays in place. This just means it is time to hire more help. It does not mean you should cut back on generating leads.

It took me a while to find out that my sources for leads were subject to the ups and downs of the real estate market. If I did not carefully service my lead program, it would go into idle when the real estate market experienced its regular cycles of supply and demand and interest rate fluctuation.

Because lead generation is so vital to a thriving real estate business, I created a multi-media lead generation model for the new edition of this book, presented in Chapter 13. The Master Marketing Model hands you a powerful lead generating machine that you can adopt verbatim while the Lead Generating Projector tells you exactly how many leads you need each day to reach your targeted income. Armed with this type of definition, you can count your leads daily and spend the rest of your day with the assurance of knowing you have met your most important goal.

Where Do You Get Leads?

Which form of marketing is best for you? This is the million dollar question. Over time, you will identify the formula that consistently brings the largest amount of leads for the least amount of time and money. The answer is different for each person depending upon your locality, the market, and your temperament.

Any form of marketing works, just not for every person everywhere. It takes a quantity of time in the business to identify and master the best method for you. Don't just buy a lead generating program that someone else put together. It's too individual and too important to entirely delegate to someone else. Leads are the foundation of your business. Without them you will have no business. This is why it is important that you customize your lead generation model.

So, as a new agent, how do you put a marketing program together when you don't even understand the market yet? The answer is you don't. The number one reason agents fail in the first years of practice is because they can't figure out which lead generating practices are best for them. You spend valuable energy trying to replicate other agents' plans, buying expensive leads, and taking all kinds of steps that only lead to insecurity and confusion. Very simply, a new agent does not have the tools yet to develop the marketing plan their new business requires.

Instead, as a new agent you should capitalize on the key resource you do have—enthusiasm. You're excited about the new possibilities ahead of you. You have energy, drive, and motivation. Use it. Adopt our Master Marketing Model until you have three years under your belt and can customize a model to fit your evolving business. Don't sit around in confusion trying to find answers you cannot get. Be proactive. Follow the model in Chapter 13 to a T, work eight hours at least five days a week, and you will earn a good living and do it with ease.

The Master Marketing Model

To begin with, your lead generating model will consist of a variety of options that, when blended together, will give you a comprehensive, streamlined plan. The Master Marketing Model detailed in Chapter 13 will consist of the following:

- ◆ You will obtain your own lead generating website.

- ◆ You will procure a database management system and run targeted campaigns.

- ◆ You will have an 800 voicemail number.

- ◆ You will advertise in magazines.

- ◆ You will engage in networking and market to the leads you gain.

- ◆ You will market to your current sphere of influence.

- ◆ You will farm one selected neighborhood and market to them.

This is the plan I recommend for new agents and seasoned agents alike. It is high tech, state-of-the-art, and powerfully incorporates several different types of media to give you a global presence. I've devoted all of Chapter 13 to articulating this plan so you can adopt it as-is and begin initiating its multimedia lead generating magnets.

The rest of this chapter details marketing techniques both included and not included in the Master Plan. I want you to consider all marketing options so that over time you will begin to customize your Master Plan by adding on other marketing formats that blend well with your business. The Master Plan is a powerful beginning but it is only a beginning. Over time as your business begins to define its best markets you will tailor your Master Plan into a truly customized format that fits your business like a glove.

Tap Your Sphere of Influence

Let the bells toll and the story be told that you are now an agent. Announce your new profession to all your friends, relatives, acquaintances, shopkeepers, and everyone you meet. Don't forget schoolmates, past coworkers, neighbors, parents of your kid's friends, and anyone affiliated with activities you regularly engage in. Tell folks in your wider communities, such as religious organizations, parent-teacher associations, volunteer groups, exercise groups, country clubs, or golf clubs. Don't forget trades people and professionals you've done business with, such as doctors, lawyers, teachers, veterinarians, and gardeners. Did I forget to include everyone you have ever come in contact with from your first memory on?

These important people make up your initial sphere of influence, which will become your very first market to tap and a source of some of your very best referrals. Do not ever discount the importance of this select group of contacts. Sphere of influence contacts bring in clients far more frequently than networking contacts. Cherish this group, and when you input them in your contacts database, make sure you input as much information as you can to ensure a birthday and/or holiday card to each person.

Start assembling your contact list even before you are licensed. It is never too early to begin building the foundation of your business—the *contacts database* that will assure you a prosperous lead generation program. Don't let your mental critic send messages such as, "This is stupid. I haven't even passed the exam. What if I don't?" You will pass the exam. Everyone does eventually. So if you have the time before you are licensed and the flurry of activity begins, take steps right away to create your first contacts database. Chapter 12 describes your database management software options while Chapter 15 shows you how to input your contact group so your prospects receive the correct marketing output.

def•i•ni•tion

A **contacts database** is the computer-based program you use, such as Microsoft Outlook, for your address book, e-mail, and calendar. These programs allow you to easily manage a high volume of information in an organized, efficient manner.

When you have determined the spheres of your life, gather names and contact information (including e-mail addresses) for people falling within that category. For example, you meet with a book club once a month. List book club as a sphere and obtain names and contact information for that sphere. You don't even have to mention your purpose to these people. Input them directly into your contacts database according to the instructions in Chapter 15 and follow the instructions in that chapter regarding the marketing materials they will receive.

If you have decided to partner with another agent, tap their sphere of influence. Many agents from the old school focusing on salesmanship instead of what this book advocates as The New Ideal (a new, more-ethical way of representing clients described in Chapter 16) may never have marketed to their own sphere. Even if they have, this is the opportunity to notify them again. Why? You have something to announce. The two of you have teamed up to provide unparalleled service to clients.

Making Markets Through Networking

If we all walked around with our professions taped across our foreheads, especially personal service providers, we'd probably have a better world. After all, who we choose to give our business to is often an emotional decision. It usually comes down to, "Do I like this person and feel comfortable in his or her presence?" Putting your profession on your forehead isn't really practical, nor is painting your career on the side of your car, although these are good steps!

All-important personal contact is numero uno. In-person networking is by far the best use of your informal lead generating time. So when you meet up with potential clients, let them know what you do at your first possible opportunity. If you mention your profession right at the start, your contact can begin his mental and emotional assessment of you early on in the conversation. As you converse, place your card in his hand, reinforcing what you said both by touch and by a card he can carry with him. This is one very good reason why your photo on your card is important. Your contact will remember his conversation with you, and when he comes across your card, he is more likely to remember his contact with you by looking at your picture.

Go to at least two networking activities a week. Real estate is a social club and remember, you have now become a social butterfly. Joining organizations is something we do because we are always busy creating new markets. You will find an abundance of agents buzzing around at any social or fraternal organization. Why? Because agents are community-minded. Our job is to service the real estate needs of the community. Community service is therefore essential to a flourishing real estate career, and it feeds your constant need for leads.

There are so many types of organizations to choose from. Watch the community calendar in your local newspapers. Your town will have a chamber of commerce. There are benevolent societies. Find activities that align with your philosophies and make that group a part of your community. These groups are all about engaging with and serving one another; in other words, carrying out the job of your middle name.

Agent to Agent

Search the Internet for real estate investor groups in your area, look in your local paper under Real Estate Investor or in the Yellow Pages. Ask other agents at your local real estate association meetings.

In Chapter 13 you also will encounter less formal groups to market your services to. These groups are just those activities you normally engage in that you should now see as ideal networking opportunities.

I will travel quite a distance to meet with a real estate investor networking group. These people are exactly who you want as clients, and they bring repeat business. These groups meet in most of the larger cities around the United States. They can be a goldmine for developing new reliable contacts.

Adopt a Positive Networking Style

Make sure that when you do flutter into your varying markets, you look the part. Chapter 7 suggests the right dress and decorum for a well-respected real estate agent, not only in your attire but in your marketing materials. You don't want to just show up; you want to show up in the best way you can with the most credibility. In this way, when you enter each market you will make an immediate positive first impression and it will be easy for you. You will have a cookie-cutter presentation that follows you everywhere you go.

Let your contacts all know you are ready to assist them with their real estate needs. Don't limit it to the sector of real estate sales you have entered. Tell them to come to you with any real estate matter, and you will handle it if it is your specialty or refer them to someone who will do a first-rate job for them.

The first reason you want them to come to you for everything is that you will be the best person to research the field and find the best person for them if you are not suited for their situation. The second reason, and I do mean second, is that you will receive a *referral fee* from the lucky agent you refer them to.

def•i•ni•tion

A **referral fee** is a fee paid for referral of a client.

I have always invited people to come to me for any real estate or legal matter. They think of me as law and real estate. Most of the time, I refer them to someone else since I am quite specialized in what I do. But they enter my marketplace first. And, when they come, they are served well. They are either served by my office, referred to my Power Team members, or referred to others who will provide good service. The true marketer knows that what goes around comes around. My Power Team members refer people to me. Those who come to me and are referred out, refer to me. Other professionals who receive referrals from me reciprocate.

Do More of What You Like

The very best place to market yourself is where you are most happy. In line with the principle of "do what you love and the money will follow," build your business around your passion. If you enjoy golf, play more and let everyone know what you do. Make golf and real estate go hand in hand. In fact, they do. The golf course is one place where business is done and is done well. If you're an avid hiker, hike more and do it with hiking groups whose real estate needs you will fill. If cooking is your thing, create delicacies to serve at open houses. Sailing is what you enjoy? Join the local sailing club and jibe less and talk real estate more. If you enjoy reading, join a book club.

Bring your passions to your work and you will be a magnet for others. You will dazzle. Even if it doesn't bring business, and I cannot imagine that it wouldn't, at least you will be enjoying yourself. Instead of forcing yourself to make cold calls, do something you love where you gather with others. Entertain the many ways in which you can join your passion with your work. Got a dog? Walk the dog and talk to other dog lovers. I meet more people and do more business when I walk my dog than when I engage in some planned marketing activities. When you orient your business around your likes rather than your dislikes, it's surprising how much fun you can have and how much business will show up in your path.

Market to Your Neighborhood

The next step of your lead generation program is to market to your selected neighborhood. This is referred to as farming in the real estate business. A specific farm for each residential agent consists of neighbors—neighbors at home and neighbors where your office is located. You will be surprised to find that even the 15 other agents in your office haven't tapped this valuable group of prospects. For the commercial agent, your market is your commercial neighbors. Let them know you are down the street and well aware of the market for their properties. People like doing business with people in their locality. They feel they are doing business with someone they already know, a neighbor.

A farm is no more than 200 to 300 residences. Assemble a marketing list using one of the cross-indexing services available through an Internet search for mailing list vendors. Even easier, get one from your local title company or perhaps the tax database in your MLS includes this feature. Four times per year, your newsletter will go to these people. Your newsletter should include an area to personalize with your biographical information. If you have a family and feel comfortable sharing about them, include their names as well. The goal is to be perceived as the person to turn to when they want to buy or sell. You want them to feel as if they know you. You will have a sign on your car that identifies you so as to further personalize your presence.

Your quarterly newsletter is discussed in more detail in Chapter 15. You may choose to include a sheet of recent *comparables* folded inside your newsletter. The comparables listed are not even properties you have sold, but these recipients are interested in this type of information because they own properties with comparable values. When I get mailers, I throw everything away except the ones that give me comparables for the real estate I own.

def•i•ni•tion

Comparables are similar properties recently sold located in the same proximity. Recent is defined as within about the last six months. Proximity is defined as within a mile or so of each other. Other factors considered are amenities and condition.

You don't even need an affiliation with a neighborhood to make it your market. All it takes is carving a niche by letting people know you specialize in a particular area. The job then is to find out everything you can about that area and let your name be known in that area in as many ways as you can. A blimp would be ideal, a banner across city hall would be better, and then there are more traditional ways, like magazine advertising which we recommend in Chapter 13's Master Marketing Model.

Have Your Own Website

You want to have your own website and be able to customize it yourself. Having your own website is no longer optional. In today's real estate world, a web presence is mandatory. Your clients and prospects expect you to have a highly visual web presence to advertise their listings and to display properties for them to search. They have become accustomed to the wide array of tools real estate sites now make available to them. They want to search the MLS on your site, obtain a market analysis, and determine their mortgage requirements. If they are going to pledge their business to you, they want you to have all the consumer tools at their fingertips.

Capturing internet traffic is as equally important as providing a resource to service your clients. You cannot afford to miss out on the Internet consumers you will capture if you have a lead generating website. The number of Americans who search the Internet as part of their home buying or selling process is close to a whopping 80 percent.

Your office will have its own websites, but you also want to have your own. You will miss out on all this internet traffic if you do not have your own website. More and more people are looking to the Internet when researching products and professional services. It is just around the corner when more people will find agents by searching the web rather than browsing the yellow pages. The agent who does not have web presence will be unable to compete.

Remember, you are now a small business owner and lead generation is your new business. You want to start out your new business with a high-profile visual presence and with lead generation built into your business model. Your website, 800 number, magazine advertising, and referral stream system are your greatest self-promoting tools. They promote you 24/7 and generate all-important leads without your efforts. I believe having your own website is so important that the Master Marketing Model in Chapter 13 is built around it.

In summary, if you want Internet searches to bring you a market, you should have a lead generating website. If you want clients and their referrals to include your site in their resource center, make sure you choose a format that gives them all the tools they'll need to make their real estate decisions. If you're new to the business or tired of your old site, go to a vendor who will give you a site with all the bells and whistles for less than $500 a year. Chapter 13 goes into more detail about website choices and the consumer-rich, lead generating tools available. In the current marketplace you can have a website that begins generating leads in a snap of your fingers and a shake of your piggy bank.

Agent to Agent

Go to the Internet and search under keywords that describe the services you provide. Now, narrow that search by more specifically describing your service and the location in which you provide it. Through this process you should be able to identify a service you perform or will perform that is unique enough to come up in the top 30, as long as your site is indexed correctly. The truly creative agent searches for a specialty few others share and begins to specialize in it! Your next step after you come up with the right keywords is to make sure your website is properly coded so the search engines index your pages under these keywords. Go to www.websitetrafficbuilders.com for more.

Promote Your Listings on the Internet

A website that displays your listed properties gives you and your listings additional exposure. Some agents do a grand exposé on unique properties complete with historical and legal data, comparables, and a picture gallery that vies with most virtual reality tours. Clients love it. It also makes buyer and agent calls very easy. Just refer them to your website.

Web listing has become so popular now that you will sometimes see a website address dedicated to just one listing. For instance, your new listing is at 287 Hometown Drive. Your sign includes a rider that says see www.287hometown.com. The website process has become so easy that vendors such as www.iHOUSEweb.com give you a domain name using the home's address and unlimited photos for less than $100. iHOUSE features this product as a listing Spotlight, and they provide tools for buyers to calculate loans and find community information. But what's even more valuable is the button that provides password-protected access to your transaction details and documents. Your client and the many professionals who will later be involved in the sale can access the transaction details without having to go to a different website for online transaction management. iHOUSE will give readers a discount off their normal fees if you use promotion code IG906 (this is capital I as in Indian, G as in Guru) when you sign up with them. You can also create a free preview website for your listing to show during seller presentations prior to making a purchase.

Planning Your Website

Many real estate associations have vendors they recommend for website production, or you can do a search on the Internet for these professionals. Real estate agent website developers have the website production process down to a science. When I put my site up over a decade ago, the process was expensive, complicated, and unsophisticated. Now, it is affordable, simple, and streamlined.

Cave!

Do a search on the Internet, this time searching for "real estate website developers." This search will give you companies that develop agents' sites for a living. Just be careful with the extra fees they charge. Make sure you ask all the questions and get all the answers when it comes to ongoing extra charges and making changes to your site. Or just go to Chapter 13 and adopt our recommendations for an excellent website provider.

If you want to make changes to your site to add new listings and other information on your own, make sure the company that creates the site for you is able to give you that capability. Some will not give you this flexibility, wanting to obtain payment for each change and requiring you to take extra steps that make the updating process frustrating. Before you begin your research, however, read Chapter 13. You may very well want to go with the vendor we recommend.

Remind Past Clients

Never lose track of your past clients, or better said, never let your past clients lose track of you. Include them on your list to receive their closing gift, your newsletter, and birthday and holiday cards each year according to the guide in Chapter 15. If your list is still a reasonable size, follow up the mailing with a quick call to check in. You'll probably get an answering machine, but your voice will remind them of you and your services. Your past clients are your very best market as they will return to you and refer their people to you as long as you stay in touch and continue to provide excellent service. Never lose contact, even if it is just by way of your smiling face on your newsletter.

Give Free Seminars

People love getting something free. It's just a part of human nature. Why not begin your own free seminar series alone or with your Power Team members? It is where I can be found every Tuesday evening. Weekly may be too often for you, but it works for me. Talk about some part of what you know that will be of interest to your market.

I have become an institution in my area through providing weekly public service seminars for over a decade. My seminars are information-packed and on cutting-edge real estate subjects. They provide a community base for people to come and bring with them their real estate and legal issues. They are also a magnet for people who need my services.

Don't feel that you are not experienced enough to give a seminar. People like to come together just for a place to share their ideas. Sometimes it's not you they come to hear; it's the subject

FYI!
An interesting seminar will bring you a market year round as long as your primary motivation is to give information, not to sell your services.

Seminar title: How to Make Maximum Profit on the Sale of Your Home

Place: XYZ Title Company

Price: Free

that interests them, and they have their own thoughts to impart. Successful seminars can consist of a room full of people sharing their ideas with others. Real estate is always a subject of interest to people because it is a part of everyone's life.

Remember that the purpose of the seminar is to provide community service, not to market your services. You will nevertheless want to add the names, addresses, phone numbers, and e-mail addresses of the attendees to your ever-growing contact list, include them on your mailers and keep in touch as warranted.

Advertise Wisely

There are many ways to advertise, and savvy agents know that this is the key to successful marketing. Agents advertise more than any other profession because the game is market, market, market. You see these agents' faces peeking out at you everywhere: in the newspaper, on supermarket carts, and even bus benches. They believe in getting their name out even if they have to pay dearly for it. Since many of these forms of advertising are expensive, the cost must be measured against the results obtained.

There is a lot to be said for repetition. An agent can become well known through seeing her name continually in the same media. The Top Dogs have so many "for sale" signs broadcasting their names that they do not have to worry about using paid-for advertising. Some do, though, and that's one of the reasons their signs are everywhere.

> **Agent to Agent**
>
> Here's an example of an advertisement slogan a local agent runs in the real estate section under the town where she specializes: "Audrey Agent, specializing in Middleburg luxury homes." Audrey identifies herself with the Middleburg luxury home market because of her constant advertising. If she provides excellent services as well, she may have a corner on that market.

A face photo is one of the trademarks of agents. Not any old mug shot, but one that's personal, friendly, and close up. Agents are famous for plastering their smiling faces everywhere. We are now beginning to see agents smiling from their "for sale" signs. Forget the name of the company. Give us an agent smiling, and that's all that matters. It's a reminder about the social nature of real estate.

Your decision as to which type of advertising is best for your business will depend upon the market you want to capture and the amount of your advertising budget. As part of our Master Marketing Model we recommend that you regularly advertise in the most current national real estate publication. Right now that is Real Estate House. We also suggest that you subscribe to a 800 call capture service which will allow your calls to be serviced 24/7 without you through voice mail information blurbs, fax back, and on-the-spot paging. This combination is the hottest new way to get leads and service listings without any work on your part. See Chapter 13 for more information regarding this powerful advertising combo.

Prospect for Gold

The word *prospecting* always reminds me of mining. I see the miner's light on a sooty forehead searching for gold. Although the new agent is looking for clients, not gold, his clients are his gold. Prospecting in the real estate world means contacting potential clients with one purpose in mind: to see if you can be of help. Two of the most valuable ways of prospecting in the real estate world include working the expired listings and For Sale by Owners (FSBOs).

People with expired listings or FSBO properties need help since they obviously have a property to sell and no one to help them. While prospecting to these two groups was an important part of an agent's marketing plan, it has become more difficult because of the Do Not Call Registry. You can no longer call these people unless they initiate contact with you.

Thus, I still include them as an important market, but remember you cannot cold call them. This limits your direct contact with them to in-person meeting, probably by showing up at an open house for the FSBO or knocking on the door of both the FSBO and expired seller. Indirect contact will come by mailing an attention getter to them, such as a concise plan about how you will team with them to get their property sold.

def•i•ni•tion

Prospecting in the real estate business is a way of targeting potential clients and appealing to their real estate needs. The choice of term is good since in real estate our clients bring us financial reward similar to the miner's reward when he strikes gold.

The Philosophy That Works

If you are able to speak with them, ask these prospects why their listing expired or why they are selling on their own. Ask them to share their war stories. Be generous. Share useful information with them. Don't push them. Leave them your name and number and tell them to call if they want more help. Then continue to check in with them on a weekly basis.

Many FSBOs have had bad experiences with agents in the past. They do not want to repeat their mistakes. Those with expired listings probably feel let down by the agents who were unable to sell their properties. They will be reluctant to deal with you because of this, and nothing will change that except for genuine sincerity.

The sales trainers give you scripts with which to prospect. You just need to pick the right one out of your bag of tricks to fit the right situation. As you will see in Chapter 16, prospecting within The New Ideal has nothing to do with trying to pull a fast one on someone. It is not about instilling fear in others as a way to get their listing. Your purpose is to genuinely offer your help, and if they don't want it, that is their prerogative.

Former President Clinton demonstrated the importance of making one's desire known to others. His slogan in his presidential campaign was "I desperately want to be your president." I'm not saying that this is the exact terminology to use with this less-than-friendly group of prospects, but do let them know you have the answer for them and make no bones about the fact that you want their listing. Authenticity and good service make an unbeatable combination.

> **Agent to Agent**
>
> The National Association of Realtors reports that agent sales of comparable properties resulted in sales prices 27 percent higher than those sold by FSBOs. This means that if the FSBO is selling without an agent to save money, they are not accomplishing their objective.

Dealing with FSBOs

The FSBOs are found through buying FSBO lists for your area and reviewing the classifieds. They are the advertisements that say FSBO, or do not say agent. Many FSBOs can be downright hostile to agents. They have issued a directive to the world that says, "I am selling on my own, and I do not want to use a real estate agent."

If they are in the initial stages of marketing, they are gung ho and ready to take on the world. All the new agents and some of the old ones approach FSBOs, each trying out their best script from their sales technique bag of tricks. This type of prospecting is not what The New Ideal encourages its professional real estate agents to do.

Instead, be real. The biggest mistake agents make with FSBOs is to come on strong when the FSBO has just begun his job. FSBOs resent agent intrusion more than you could ever know. They have made a decision to do it their way without your help, and they do not want you taking their job away from them. Go ahead and contact them early on in their marketing, but be gentle.

Tell them you understand their reasons for wanting to sell on their own, and that you're an agent who has signed on to The New Ideal; then invite them to tap you for help as they go along. If you have a web page for FSBOs on your site, direct them there. In other words, you're agreeing to no listing and offering free help.

If you are still at the stage of your career where handling an open house would be advantageous, offer to handle your FSBO's open house free of charge. Explain that it's an opportunity for you to meet prospects and help him all in one sitting. You will earn your FSBO's appreciation, possibly his listing, and probably a few more prospects, too.

FYI!

Offer FSBOs the following proposition: "Fred, I'll prepare you an in-depth comparable market analysis supported by current market data. My package also includes a market analysis sheet that is useful in understanding current market statistics. I'll prepare a property profile that shows where your property lies in conjunction with your neighbors. If you still don't want my help, take these documents and use them to sell on your own. They will help. If you want my help, it's there for the taking." It is hard to say no to this kind of proposition, especially when the agent really means it.

Dealing with Expired Listings

You find the expired listings through a simple database search on the MLS. Then you match up the property with the owner name through tax records. Most multiple listing services also include tax records. Title companies also will provide you with a *property profile* containing the information you need. In the real estate world, information is plentiful. In this industry, where there is a will, there is a way.

Many listings expire because they are priced unrealistically. The owner undoubtedly insisted that her price be used rather than the market price. This is a conversation you will want to have and perhaps you will be able to explain this in a manner that will be more palatable to your prospect. Price is always a touchy subject with the seller who knows it all. All you can do is be honest and sincere, watch the listing, and check in from time to time.

def•i•ni•tion

A **property profile** is a report a title company provides as a customer service that includes a property's title vesting, loan, tax information, its legal description, and information on surrounding properties.

Specialize

One of the best ways to create a self-fueling market is to specialize. There are as many categories to specialize in as you can dream up. Once you define the spheres in which your life has traveled, you will have a good basis for identifying markets. For instance, if you previously worked with retirees, or you are a member of a country club with many retirees, you may want to specialize in marketing to people retiring or downsizing after the kids have left home. This group often trades in a large home for a smaller one or a multilevel home for a single-story home. They also have a high degree of interest in purchasing in a retirement community.

Agent to Agent

Here is a list of general categories you can specialize in that might interest you:

- Relocation
- Buyers agent only
- First-time home buyers
- Military housing
- Retirement housing
- Luxury homes only
- A specific town, residential only
- A specific neighborhood

The list of specialties is never-ending. If you live in an area with many golf courses, specialize in golf course homes. If you're in a beach area, focus on beachfront properties. In Sedona, Arizona, you might specialize in spiritual centers. If you live in an area with an influx of baby boomers, specialize in relocation. Retiring baby boomers make the best clients of all since they are moving to new, less expensive areas and buying lots of real estate.

If you practice in an area where baby boomers are exiting or arriving in droves, consider making relocation your specialty. Look into your office's alliance programs. More than 40 percent of all real estate firms participate in some type of referral program, and one-fifth of all firms have their own affinity programs to generate leads.

You can earn an excellent living by the revolving relocation real estate door. Your clients sell and you earn a commission on their home you sell. You then refer them to an agent in the location where they will relocate and receive a referral fee through an alliance program. If you are on the other end of relocation, you get the referral in and pay a portion of your commission out.

The Least You Need to Know

- Anyone you meet is a potential client and should be added to your contact list.

- Consider targeted e-mail campaigns, a 800 voice mail number, and magazine advertising as a lead generation package.

- Keep your name in front of your potential clients with mailers and other forms of advertising.

- Have your own lead-generating website.

- Scrutinize existing markets that surround you and consider specializing in one or two of those markets.

Chapter 11

Managing the Time Demon

In This Chapter

- Setting boundaries with your clients
- Qualifying prospective clients early on
- Hiring an administrative assistant
- Dealing effectively with contingencies
- Working with the closing professional

Controlling time is a constant challenge in the real estate business. The real estate train moves along at a high-speed clip. Not long ago, the sales transaction took sixty to ninety days to travel its many steps to closing. Now that technology has expedited the loan process, closings are taking place in half that time. This situation has caused many real estate agents to lose control of their time. They have let time become their enemy, robbing them of the very freedom and versatility that brought them to the real estate profession.

Don't give in to the time demon. You can't create more time, but you can learn to manage it more efficiently. One way is to master organization and computer technology, the subject of later chapters. In this chapter, we look at identifying the cause of time pressures and how to set up systems so those time pirates do not rock your organized and orderly boat.

Use Your Time Well

The new sales agent is easy prey for poverty consciousness, which incessantly whispers, "You're on commission—the more time you spend, the more money you'll make." Don't give in to it. It is not spending time that will get you there, it is the effective use of time that will. There is so much to learn, a new business to operate, and clientele to cultivate. After about two or three years, your business will have matured some, and you will be on your way to a successful real estate career.

The time to begin building boundaries against the time bandit is when you are first starting out and implementing your work ethic. Set regular hours for yourself and do not work beyond those hours. So many agents become prisoners of their work, schlepping it around everywhere they go. You see them everywhere. They are the ones talking on a cell phone in the middle of the restaurant. This is not good for your self-esteem or for gaining your clients' respect. It's also debilitating to your family and friends if they continually have to play second fiddle to your work.

Act like you have a regular job. Go to the office regularly, and if you want to be successful at maintaining personal time, do not work much more than forty hours a week. Unless you have an unusual time-intensive matter, don't check in again until your regular hours start. Be proactive so that you control your time. Your clients and your peers will respect that you are not a puppet to their whim and call. And your personal life will thrive because it will be first in your book, as it should be.

Cave!

Start out your real estate practice with balance. Your personal life has to be sheltered from your work. Otherwise, it will be gobbled up into your practice. Little by little, day by day, your personal time will disappear if you don't pay attention to time-management issues.

Don't Be a 24/7 Person

There is no time that is not a good time for real estate. It lives and breathes at all times. It seems to have a life of its own. However, you do not need to be perpetually on call. It is not good business. Some agents try to claim market share by being the most available. Unfortunately, your availability also carries a sign that says, "I am so unproductive or unsuccessful that I have to work all the time." You can be sufficiently available with regular hours. You do not have to be the all-day, all-night real estate store.

Agent to Agent

The National Association of Realtors reports that the typical agent works 46 hours a week.

Being On-Call for Your Clients

Whether you're in residential or commercial sales, your clients tend to do business with you on their off-hours. They want to get their own work done during regular business hours. You can work out a compromise so that your schedule and your clients' schedules work together.

You will want to work one weekend day, and probably both Saturday and Sunday in the beginning. There's no getting around the fact that residential real estate happens on the weekends in a big way. Also, dedicate a couple of days when you can start later to work later. If you do, you can accommodate clients who want to meet with you after normal business hours. The rest of the week, maintain regular business hours. Put your business hours on your card so clients will know when to contact you.

The time demons will also tell you that you've got to work sixty hours a week to make a living in the dog-eat-dog real estate world. Don't believe them. The disorganized real estate agent who has failed to adopt healthy work boundaries may need to work sixty hours a week to keep up. You don't have to be that kind of agent. You can be one of the Top Dogs who achieve abundance both financially and personally and have regular work schedules. In fact, you'll only become a Top Dog if you adopt good, healthy work strategies and manage your time effectively.

> **FYI!**
>
> Your clients will continually try to get your schedule to coincide with their *off* schedule. It takes strong determination to reinforce your boundaries repeatedly, but you must. You are a professional and deserve to have your boundaries respected. If you don't respect your time, clients won't respect it either.

Beware of High-Maintenance People

You also need to have defined boundaries with clients, especially with potential clients. Always be on the lookout for high-maintenance people (HMPs). I have special antennae trained to detect these time demons. HMPs will suck you dry if you let them. The more you give, the more they want and the less they appreciate you. It's a skirmish that never ends. The new agent, especially, is easy prey for HMPs.

Real estate is often a place where you act as a therapist to soothe and support a client. Budget only a short amount of time for these people, or you will find yourself unable to deal with the rest of your schedule and your other clients. In the real estate business, your time is a precious commodity.

Agent to Agent

There is a huge difference between professional courtesy and being taken advantage of. Know the difference. You are not here to please the world; you are here to deliver quality professional services to your clients in a way that supports and serves them.

I have met and supported high-maintenance clients—you know those people who demand your attention ten hours a day? When they call for my services again, I thank them for considering me, but I tell them I have too many clients right now and will not be able to give them the attention they deserve. I then refer them to my referral source for high-maintenance people. I receive the best of both worlds when I receive a referral fee and I do not have to deal with people who keep me on the run.

Once people pass the high-maintenance test, they must be qualified. Are they ready to act or are they just in the information-gathering stage? As part of your public service orientation, you should be willing to give a certain amount of time to people who are researching and shopping. After that, it's time to set your boundary and qualify them by using the checklists set forth in later chapters.

Peer Pressure

Sales has a built-in rush factor. The sales demons realize that excess time encourages indecision, especially when it comes to high-priced real estate. Thus, the real estate sales transaction races on a fast track. The whole real estate industry can be one big pressure cooker. This is one of the major reasons for agent burnout. The unsophisticated agent gives in to this mentality. They interact with peers who perpetuate the rush syndrome and find themselves being pushed along as part of the mad dash to closing.

Anything done from a hurried place is susceptible to error and confusion. There is enough time in this transaction, especially if the steps are taken in an organized, well-thought-out manner. As long as you monitor steps when they need to be performed on both sides of your transactions, not just your side, there will be no reason to rush or to be unreasonably surprised.

In fact, by not rushing through sales transactions, you will stand out among the rest because you will be confident and calm while other agents nervously fidget. While others are trying to keep up in an atmosphere of chaos, your time and energy can be directed to more productive activities.

Hire a Helper

More and more, agents are defeating the time demon by hiring assistants. While transaction coordinators can provide relief, they generally cannot provide the support a busy agent needs. For the high producer, there is nothing like having a good assistant. In fact, the choice to employ an assistant is not only good business sense, it proves to be first-class financial sense. The National Association of Realtors conducted a recent survey, which found that agents who have assistants earn twice as much as those who don't. Those same statistics also show that only one in five agents have an assistant on their team. These agents are the Top Dogs.

Assistants are versed in the real estate transaction and can ease the load considerably. They have become so valuable in the real estate field that there are now courses certifying these professionals. Just as lawyers have certified paralegals to assist them, the agent may have a certified real estate assistant.

Agent to Agent _____

The National Association of Realtors provides Real Estate Professional Assistant Certification (REPA), as do many state associations. The two-day course provides an intensive introduction to the real estate business and to the specific ways to support the agent's busy practice. Some highlights of the course are …

- ◆ Understanding the business of real estate.
- ◆ Knowing what MLS is and being familiar with input forms and reports.
- ◆ Knowing how to manage the transaction.
- ◆ Understanding the difference between licensed and unlicensed activities.
- ◆ Understanding the types of agency representation and disclosures.
- ◆ Comprehending key marketing concepts.

Go to www.Realtor.org for more information on this course.

You don't have to employ these assistants full time. You can share an assistant with one or more other agents. Your tools to freedom in the real estate sales world are technology and a good assistant. If your assistant is a career real estate assistant, he or she can train you in real estate procedures. These support professionals are one of the most important assets to running a chock-full streamlined practice.

As is described in more detail in Chapter 22, unlicensed assistants cannot do anything that requires a real estate license, such as showing property, explaining a contract or other document to a client, discussing property attributes with a prospect, and conducting an open house. But other than that, they can make your life much easier. An enormous amount of detail goes into the daily practice of real estate sales. Your assistant can handle most of the administrative functions and coordinate the contacts that need to be made. While your assistant is handling the routine transaction steps and tracking calendar and marketing tasks, you are able to focus on developing new business and listing and selling real estate.

The National Association of Realtors (www.Realtor.org) has a checklist of functions that can be performed by an assistant and those that require a real estate license. Simply stated, if an activity is directly related to listing and selling properties, a license is required. When you train your assistant (or he or she trains you) make sure that her duties do not fall into the category of those requiring a license. The distinction can be blurry at times. It makes it a lot easier if you have a handy description of what the assistant can and cannot do for easy reference.

def•i•ni•tion

A **virtual assistant** is a support professional who provides administrative, creative, or technical services on a contractual basis. Virtual assistants use advanced technological modes of communication and data delivery, which allow them to work remotely.

In your first years, the relief you need might be to hire *virtual assistance* on a per-transaction basis, or just to take care of some tasks to ease up your load. Throughout this book we reference virtual assistance and virtual transaction coordination as a means to get help without actually hiring an in-person assistant. There are a number of excellent online services that can provide you with as little or as much help as you need, and at a budget-conscious price. One such service can be found at www.teamdoubleclick.com.

Partnering with Another Agent

This subject was discussed in relation to building your Power Team in Chapter 9, but it is worth mentioning again here since agent partnering can be the ideal solution to the time crunch. For some busy agents, the only way they can feel relaxed enough to enjoy meaningful time off is to know another agent with similar standards is taking a turn at the helm of their ship. Although your assistant can be extremely valuable when it comes to organization, she cannot handle major transaction issues that require the expertise of a licensed agent.

The Loan and Inspection Contingencies

The physical inspection and loan contingencies can complicate transactions more than any other issues. If you begin each transaction by continually shepherding these contingencies, you will significantly increase the chances that your transaction will close without a visit from the contingency scoundrel.

Agent to Agent _____

Often it is the physical inspection contingency that causes a transaction to fall apart. It sometimes happens that the buyer obtains inspection reports that say a certain amount of repairs need to be made and the seller refuses to credit the buyer the amount needed to make the repairs. The seller sometimes says the price the client agreed to pay reflects the need for these repairs, refusing to compromise.

Keep careful track of these contingencies even if you are on the seller side. Stay in touch with the buyer's agent and repeatedly ask for status reports. By keeping the other agent and your clients on track, you will decrease the likelihood of problems and last-minute issues. When you represent the buyer, take steps toward removing contingencies on the first day of the contingency period. These all-important, sometimes hair-raising contingencies are addressed in depth in Chapter 19.

The Title Contingency

Review of the title report is another buyer contingency that can lead to surprises, cancelled escrows, and their accompanying time pressures. The buyer has a short period of time to review and approve the preliminary title report, or prelim. Make sure this report goes to the buyers as early as possible so they have sufficient opportunity to analyze the property's legal criteria.

Title reports contain easements and covenants, conditions and restrictions, and other legal conditions that can drastically affect both the use and value of a property. The buyers need to examine the nature and scope of any such restrictions, which may mean consultation with a professional to obtain advice. The time to do this is before the contingency is removed. The title contingency is addressed in more depth in Chapter 19.

Work with the Closing Professional

The *closing professional* serves as a neutral intermediary facilitating the transaction. In some states, the title company acts in this capacity; in others, attorneys do. They take buyer funds in the form of buyer deposits and lender deposits and distribute them to sellers, lenders, and real estate agents. They give lenders recorded security instruments and give buyers deeds. They handle the paper and money exchange required in the real estate purchase and sale process.

def•i•ni•tion

The manner in which closings are handled varies depending on your location. In some areas, the **closing professional** is an attorney who also conducts title search. In others, escrow and title companies perform these functions. The choice of a closing professional is at the discretion of the buyer in purchase and sale transactions.

Sometimes the closing professional may wait until the last minute to get everything ready for signing and recording. You can reduce this potential stress builder by staying in close contact with the closing professional, who should be part of your Power Team. Typically the buyer's agent opens *escrow*. But, as with everything else, you want to facilitate all steps of the transaction because the buyer-seller steps are all contingent upon one another. A buyer surprise is a seller surprise.

Early on make sure the closing professional has all the information required to close out the transaction. Call a week ahead of closing and ask for an *estimated closing statement*. This will cause the closer to finalize the details of the transaction and complete anything not yet finished. Of course, the easiest way to keep your professionals on track is to use an online transaction coordination system, described in Chapter 12, so all team members have online access to the transaction information.

def•i•ni•tion

Escrow is the independent third party that holds the funds and distributes them according to buyer and seller instructions and processes and prepares the transaction documents. Depending upon your location, escrow is either an escrow company or a closing attorney.

An **estimated closing statement** is one of the last steps the closing professional performs in a transaction. It is a detailed accounting of buyer and seller debits and credits in the transaction. Once the parties approve of the estimated statement, the final closing statement is prepared prior to closing on the transaction.

The Least You Need to Know

◆ If you do not set boundaries with your clients and associates, your personal life will be swallowed up by your business.

◆ If you do not qualify potential clients early on, you will be run ragged by shoppers and high-maintenance people.

◆ Hiring an administrative assistant or partnering with another agent could be your answer for beating the time crunch.

◆ Physical inspection and loan and title review contingencies should be carefully monitored throughout the transaction, even if you are representing the seller.

◆ Work closely with the closing professional from the very beginning of the transaction to ensure an organized and orderly closing.

Chapter 12

Technology

In This Chapter

- ◆ Using technology to the max to streamline your business
- ◆ Reviewing the hardware and software you will need
- ◆ Having wireless technology everywhere you go
- ◆ Using online transaction management and contact management programs
- ◆ Utilizing the multiple listing service

Technology is so important to success in real estate sales that it warrants an entire chapter. You can get along without becoming a technology wiz, but you will not be able to tap your peak performance unless you make technology the cornerstone of your business. I have three recommendations for you to achieve real estate business goals: first, research all tools available, second, buy the best tools that you can afford, and third, use them!

In the real estate sales business, technology is required not just because it has become a business standard, but because technology is your pipeline. Agents must have real-time access to the multiple listing service and their all-important leads. The challenge for the active agent is that we are highly portable. We need to conduct business from various locations—a regular office, a home office, a client's home, and anywhere in the field. The only answer is for you to become technologically savvy.

This chapter covers some of the tools you will need to get your high-tech real estate practice in gear. Chapter 14 shows you how to organize your technology and duplicate it at home, in your vehicle, and elsewhere.

No More Excuses

After you get your real estate license, your new mantra becomes "Be organized and be high-tech." There are so many details in real estate sales that you cannot afford the luxury of being disorganized for a moment. To be a Top Dog, you must embrace technology and recognize it not only as an essential ingredient of your business, but as its foundation. Technology efficiently tracks an enormous amount of contacts, details, communications, and scheduling in addition to the multiple listing service's thousands of listings. It also keeps you in real-time contact with your clients and leads.

It's true that many old-timers were incredibly successful without the use of technology. When they built their business model, technology was not what it is today. Now they are dinosaurs. In this age of advanced technology, especially in the fast-paced real estate world, you must make technology an extension of yourself to be a peak performer. There is just no getting around it. The excuse that you are not high-tech will not work any longer. Today's real estate business requires real time, which is only met through up-to-date technology.

Agent to Agent

An acronym for technology that works for anti-technology people is Terrific Extra Chance to Heighten Natural Organization and Leverage Optimum Gains for You. When technology is seen in this light, it opens the mind.

As a sophisticated agent you require technology to perform a multitude of functions. Today, you prepare your contract documents on computer, not by hand, and many are now using transaction management programs. Managing your leads and prospects through a comprehensive contact-management program is essential for you to fully canvas your market and conduct Internet-based marketing campaigns. You also require a calendar program to record important contract dates and to follow up with leads. E-mail and interaction with the MLS is mandatory.

Your High-Tech System

In the high-tech model this book advocates, your laptop will travel with you to all locations except where laptop access is inconvenient, where you will use your PDA. Computer technology has become so advanced that some lock-box keys now operate through PDAs or cell phones. With a computer at your fingertips in your many locations, business will travel with you everywhere you go. This, you will find, affords the ultimate freedom and flexibility—one reason you chose this job.

Now you can sit at the coffee shop and review the multiple listing database you uploaded to your PDA that morning. Or better yet, go online and search new listings in real time. Make business calls with your cell phone and schedule appointments on your PDA, which you will upload to your calendar and contacts database on your laptop or online when you *synchronize*. You can send and receive e-mail with your wireless technology and surf the net for new client closing gifts.

def•i•ni•tion

When you **synchronize** your databases, you usually use a docking station or interface cable connected to your computer in conjunction with a software program that comes packaged with your portable device. Information such as contacts or calendar entries are compared on the two devices and any new entries or modified entries are added or updated. The result is that both the device and the computer have the same information. If your database is now Internet-based, you will synchronize with the Internet website that houses your information.

You will find that a sizeable portion of the real estate industry is not yet as high-tech as I suggest, but if you want to be on the cutting edge and a peak performer, heed these steps. Don't let your peers get to you when they tease you about your technology entourage. They're just jealous!

The Hardware You Will Need

Before you purchase any computer hardware, do the research. Don't rely solely on the salespeople in the computer store. Make sure the literature for everything you buy confirms what the salesperson says. I have a cabinet full of interesting technological devices that were not compatible with my other technology, or didn't do what the salesperson said they would do. The following list is the suggested basic technology you will need in your life as a mobile real estate professional:

- Laptop computer
- Cell phone
- PDA
- Digital camera
- Printer, copier, scanner, and fax machine, or an all-in-one unit with all those functions.

If you are going to be high-tech, ask all the questions and confirm all the answers before you buy. It is easier to do this in advance than to worry about connectivity, synchronization, or a host of other issues after you have made the investment. It would be prudent to also investigate the post-sale services of the vendor such as customer service, technology support, and repairs.

Laptop

The office you join will probably provide a desktop computer for your use. Use your personal laptop instead so your information will follow you wherever you go. In this manner, you will be far more flexible, which is one of the reasons you came to real estate to begin with. The first consideration when buying a laptop (or any computer) is what operating system you want. To determine this, consider what software packages you will use. Note that any Internet application such as the MLS can be accessed by any operating system. Whichever machine you buy, make sure you get the best you can afford. Make sure your laptop has built-in wireless capability, a PCI slot, and enough USB ports to plug in flash cards and other pieces of equipment like a printer, scanner, and so on.

You want a good size screen and quality display so when you show clients properties they can see a clear visual picture. You will be able to cut down on driving and showing time if you introduce your clients to prospective properties by computer and if they display almost as well as being on site. Many agents just print out listings for client preview. These properties look far more visually appealing on the computer screen.

Some of us also still use desktops at home or at the office to benefit from the larger monitors and keyboards. If you do, make sure your laptop has a networking card so you can easily network the two computers to synchronize their information and back them up. You will also want to be able to synchronize with your PDA. If you choose to have your database online as many people are doing these days, you will synchronize your computers with your online database.

Agent to Agent

You will have your laptop in the field with you, so you want to make sure its casing is well protected and will withstand being carted around. Most computer companies provide two lines of computers, consumer quality (home systems) and business-class quality. By spending the extra cash up-front for a business-class quality laptop you will ensure built-in protection for instances where your laptop is dropped or otherwise inadvertently maligned. In addition, buy a well-padded briefcase for your machine. I cannot stress this enough, having learned from experience. You pay a price for the freedom of portability if you don't build in the appropriate safeguards.

Real estate specialty developers are finally putting together hardware products customized to real estate transactions. While these products do not have the track record of traditional technology, you may very well want to consider them instead of building your own real estate-based computer. VREO, Inc. (www.vreo.com) has developed a Tablet PC just for real estate agents. Although I have not personally checked it out, it seems to have all the built-in gadgets the portable agent needs, including digital signature capability. Just make sure that it will run the other software you will need for your business, discussed later in this chapter.

Laptop Field Requirements

Since my laptop is my lifeline, I have Internet connectivity bases covered. My first choice is Wi-Fi because you get the speed of DSL. You either have Wi-Fi capability built into your computer or you get a Wi-Fi card. Wi-Fi is based on radio signals and is faster than other wireless options. Your computer searches for a Wi-Fi hotspot and connects if it finds one. Many consumer-oriented facilities have what they call Wi-Fi cafés. While many aren't actual cafés, some of them are, like Starbucks. They are more often shopping center lots, hospitals, hotels, truck stops, or campgrounds. They are popping up anywhere people gather in large numbers.

If I can't get Wi-Fi, I use my WWAN (wireless wide-area network), which is a card I put in my PCI slot, and I'm online in seconds. All cell providers have these wireless cards. They use cell signals instead of the radio signals Wi-Fis use. I use Verizon's air card. If you don't have wireless capability built into your computer or a wireless adapter, you can use your cell phone as a modem by connecting your cell phone's data port to your computer's USB port. Either way works. The connection is clear and constant and while it is not as fast as DSL, it isn't as slow as dial-up.

I use my laptop extensively in the field, which sometimes brings me outdoors. If you plan to use your computer outdoors, make sure you have a screen protector to reduce the glare. I wrote most of this book outdoors at an RV resort. Weight may also be a consideration if you travel a great deal with your computer slung over your shoulder. You can find several suitable laptop models that weigh in at just a few pounds.

Cave!

If you think laptop crashes are a remote risk, think again. I have been a victim more than once. Your best protection is to pad your case well and back up to another device or to an online database. I now also obtain crash insurance when I purchase my portable devices.

If you plan to use your laptop where electricity is not available, make sure you have extensive battery power capacity. I have both replacement batteries and an adapter that plugs into my cigarette lighter. If you also plan on printing make sure your portable printer uses the same connector as your computer.

Cell Phone

You will need a cell phone. Because you often use your cell phone when driving, consider one with voice recognition so you can program it to dial for you when you speak a certain name. Install some form of hands-free capability so you can drive with both hands and talk with the use of a headset or microphone. Purchasing a cell phone with Bluetooth capabilities allows you to use a wireless headset. These are relatively inexpensive headsets (under $100) that obviate the need for the wire between your cell and your headset and are very convenient.

The features on cell phones might make you wonder if it is a cell phone, a PDA, or a very small computer. Cell phones not only take phone calls, they can store your contacts and calendar as well as allow you to receive and send e-mail and access the Internet. At the very least, you need a cell phone that includes a contacts list.

When choosing your cell phone if you want the capability of using it as a modem for your laptop to access the Internet, make sure it has a data port. The data port can also be used for synchronization of information with your other computers. Also, ensure that you charge your phone every night and have a car charger in your vehicle. You will be astounded at how much battery life is used up over the course of the day. Better to have it charging in the car and always ready than to be out and about and incommunicado because your cell phone battery went dead.

Agent to Agent

Many products now exist that are pretty good all-in-one devices. The Palm Treo 650, for example, is a great cell phone with all the extras such as Bluetooth and voice recognition, a good contact database, an Outlook-compatible calendaring system, and fairly good e-mail capability. Add a touch screen with great resolution and the capacity to smoothly synch with Outlook or other organizers and you are set to go.

Personal Data Assistant (a.k.a. PDA)

A PDA allows you to bring your address book, calendar, contacts, e-mail, and multiple listing data everywhere you go. In addition, some PDAs double as a cell phone and can provide dial-up Internet access. If you decide to use your device to access e-mail directly from the Internet, you may find Blackberry is the best. However, other brands such as the Palm Treo Smartphone have made inroads into Blackberry's superiority in this regard and incorporate a better cell phone capability than Blackberry. Personally, I have not mastered the tiny keyboards on phones. Others are annoyed by the alternative method of multiple keystrokes to record a character when composing e-mails.

Your PDA is synchronized with your laptop or desktop as well as the MLS with the use of a docking station. This synchronization process is discussed in Chapter 14. Then again, you may choose to have a web-based contact management system, also discussed in Chapter 14. There are so many products on the market today it's almost like being a kid in a candy store. Prices have come way down on many models and there has been a proliferation of products that multitask, giving you even more options.

If I have any choice at all about which computer device to use, I choose my laptop. I bring it nearly everywhere I go—to the beach if I have business to do and to the relatives on family occasions. I work much better with the size of its screen and keyboard and its processing power. Although PDAs have large-size keyboards you can attach as an add-on and expansion cards for additional memory, there is only so much you can do with a hand-size device. So yes, I am the person you've seen at the hairdresser's sitting under the dryer with my laptop perched in front of me.

Digital Camera

You will need a digital camera to take pictures of the properties you list. There is a variety to choose from. Some are built into your cell phone, though these usually have very low resolution. Others can be purchased as accessories to your PDA. To open the picture on your computer, you need the software application that relates to the digital image. Most cameras come with their own photo software. This software allows you to tweak the picture until it achieves the look you are after. You will use your photos for your marketing materials and to include with your listings on the multiple listing service and on your website. You can also e-mail your digital photos to interested buyers. Multiple listing services now have the capability to show a large portfolio of pictures of a property. You also can take your own slide show, or hire one of the many companies that prepare virtual slide shows for you.

> **Agent to Agent** _____
>
> Sit down with a basic computer book like *The Complete Idiot's Guide to Computer Basics* so you can understand the basic terminology and concepts of computer networking.

Printer, Copier, and Fax

Your office usually provides this equipment for use at the office. You will need to provide for home and in the field. If you do not already have this equipment, you might choose to get your own fax, printer, scanner, copier, or an all-in-one. Your research may indicate that the more features, the more susceptible the device is to problems. Take a look at consumer reports and make your own evaluation. In particular, pay attention to the quality of the printer in all-in-one devices. If you plan on any printing of higher quality generally these devices do not suffice.

I recommend that you have your own fax machine with a dedicated line at the office and at home to ensure that your faxes come directly to you and that the line is available to you at all times. Even more important, with your own fax line, when you leave the office, you can forward your faxes to your home fax machine. If you want to be truly high-tech, you don't even need a fax machine to send and receive faxes anymore. You just sign up with a company (www.efax.com, for example) that gives you a special e-fax number. Faxes are then forwarded to your e-fax number where they are converted to e-mail format and sent to your e-mail address. Faxing out is handled in a similar manner.

E-fax is undoubtedly the better solution so your faxes reach you wherever you go. With e-fax, you end up with faxed documents right on your computer so you can save them directly in your client's computer file. You also can send faxes by e-mail in the same way. In this manner you can be truly portable as you send and receive e-mail, voice mail, and faxes at any location. Additionally, you can secure the privacy of your transactions.

Having a color printer is an asset in the highly visual real estate business where color is the norm. If you plan on building a vehicle office, you will want a portable printer that will connect to either your laptop or PDA. This is especially handy for obtaining client signatures in the field.

Becoming Paperless

I couldn't live without a scanner. I conduct business primarily by computer technology and strive to be paperless. The scanner turns my paper products into an image that I then store on my computer to complete my transaction database and e-mail to others involved in my transactions. Portable scanners are available, too, for scanning while out in the field.

As you go along, you can evaluate how important a scanner is for your particular needs. I find e-mailing documents to be a handy alternative to faxing, especially since clients often have e-mail but don't have a fax machine. I will do just about anything to not have to transmit documents by snail mail or by a fax machine.

Now that I am using a transaction management online database, I just upload documents into our online transaction and give team members passwords for viewing. In this manner, I am paperless in my transactions, with the exception of the documents that need signatures. We are still stuck with hard copies for obtaining signatures on documents until such time as digital signatures are authenticated in real estate transactions.

There is, however, new technology that incorporates digital signatures into transactions. The software must be run on a Tablet PC, not a regular laptop, but the innovative company that provides this software also provides the Tablet (www.Vreo.com). Federal law now authorizes the use of digital signatures, and no doubt states will soon follow this mandate. The real estate industry is clearly headed in this direction, and you may choose to be on the cutting edge by using paperless technology now.

The Software You Will Need

You want your operation to become a high-level multitasking operation through the efficient use of computer programs. While this chapter describes the programs, Chapter 14 shows you how to integrate and organize them so they work together. The software functions you will need are …

- ◆ An office suite for contact management, calendaring, e-mail, word processing, working with numbers and spreadsheets, and for visual presentations

- Accounting and check writing
- Transaction management
- Scanning and possibly character recognition for editing
- Photo management
- Internet access
- Multiple listing entries and searches
- Security (for backups and virus protection)

You are probably familiar with many of these applications and will only need training in a few areas. Your goal is to use and manage your applications in such a way that these tasks are easy and compatible. Open one program and you're ready to write a letter. Open another and send an e-mail or fax. There is no need to duplicate information between programs since this information is in your contact database, which can be accessed for the rest of your programs.

An Office Suite

You will need an office suite for basic functions such as contact management, calendaring, e-mail, word processing, working with numbers and spreadsheets, and for visual presentations. The most universally used suite is Microsoft Office featuring Word, Excel, and Outlook. If you do not get these programs packaged together, such as through the Microsoft Office Suite, you will need to obtain them individually.

Microsoft Word is a word processor used for the production (including composition, editing, and formatting) of documents. Excel is a spreadsheet program for mathematical and financial analysis. Outlook is a personal information manager and e-mail communication software. Although often used mainly as an e-mail application, it also provides calendar, task and contact management, note taking, and journal ability. PowerPoint is a popular presentation program. It is used to create slideshows, composed of text, graphics, movies, and other objects, which can be displayed on-screen and navigated through by the presenter or printed out on transparencies or slides.

It is wise to use applications that are widely accepted within the business community. Microsoft Office fits that criterion. While the program you use is clearly a matter of personal preference, when you send documents by computer you have to ensure that the other party can easily read them. Therefore using a popular program such as

Microsoft Office would be wise. Also, make sure your software is up to date. While updating your software can be expensive and sometimes frustrating, not doing so can also present problems.

Another reason to utilize a universally used model like the Microsoft Office Suite is to ensure that the program you use on your laptop or desktop can be used on your other hardware and with any Internet-based server you may choose to store and manage your information. You want to make sure that you can synchronize and export between devices and servers. Following the high-tech Master Marketing Model discussed in Chapter 13, the new contact information and client meeting you entered into your PDA while at lunch is exported to your online database and updates it so that you can pull the information up on your laptop at home later that evening.

FYI!

Make sure you specify your return address and signature line in your e-mail setup. This should include your full name, company name, address, telephone, fax, e-mail, and web address. Some states may require that you also provide your real estate license number. Check with your Association of Realtors or state licensing division to be sure you are compliant in your area.

Don't forget to provide a link to your website. Also include a brief mission statement or specialty motto if you have developed one. I colorize my name and use a font that looks like handwriting for my signature. It almost looks like I have personally signed the message.

Learn how to use all the features of these programs. They will make your life much easier and transform the agent-juggling act into one efficient and highly organized system. Once you input a person's or company's contact information, you never have to do it again as long as you know how to access it from different programs. If you want to send someone an e-mail, just click on his or her e-mail address. A fax calls for a click on their fax number. If you want to send a letter by snail mail, your contact program address book provides their address for the letter in your word processing program.

Contact Management Options

There are several issues you should look at in choosing a contact management program, such as Outlook. One is the template used to index contacts. Another is whether you will use your program in conjunction with an online database management provider.

Cave!

Some brokerages offer a contact management system exclusively designed for their company. It will probably have numerous features—most of which you'll probably never use. The broker may have purchased or leased this program because it does many administrative functions necessary for the broker to run his business, but not necessarily expedient for the sales associate. Understand, there is a cost associated with your participation on the broker's system. Sometimes the agency will include the cost as part of a larger group of fees, sometimes called desk fees or monthly administrative fee. Be cautious; it can be expensive. More often than not with a little research you can find the same or similar product available on the open market for much less than you would pay your broker.

Some agents feel that Outlook does not fit the real estate sales business model well enough, and they instead choose ACT!, Top Producer, Realty Empowerment Systems, or FileMaker Pro, to name a few. These programs allow you to index each contact under any number of categories, either preset or customized. All you do is check the category you want to apply to a contact.

But you also can use Outlook in conjunction with a product available from Sonoma Enterprises (www.SonomaEnterprises.com) called Active Agent. This program, when downloaded onto your computer, will change the contact template used in Outlook, Top Producer, and a few other programs. Instead of the standard contact form, it modifies the template with a real estate theme so you can enter the information and designate real estate categories for that contact.

Consider Web-Based Contact Management

You should consider contact management systems that are web-based products. These are accessed from any computer that is connected to the Internet. Our high-tech Master Marketing Model featured in Chapter 13 adopts a web-based product with lead generating capabilities and 24/7 marketing of your services. While the merits of this type of product are discussed in later chapters, here are some basic advantages of a web-based product:

◆ Flexibility of accessing your information from any computer connected to the Internet wherever you happen to be. No more synchronizing your phone, PDA, laptop, and desktop so they all have the same information.

◆ Earlier concerns about the security of the information on the web have been quelled. Your stored information is extremely protected from corruption, hackers, viruses, and so on. Plus, it is backed up several times a day to ensure its integrity. You will be freed of these time-consuming security tasks.

◆ Some people are uncomfortable not having all their information on their laptop. Over time, these feelings are eliminated in the face of the benefits of having the information on the web. But, you can download files onto your laptop whenever you desire.

Cave!

If you are contemplating using a web-based product ensure that the company and its ISP provider are financially solvent. I would investigate how long they have been in business, their reputation within the real estate community, and so on. Talk to some of their customers. Most of the vendors will gladly provide you with a list of clients or testimonials for you to review.

When choosing a web-based product make sure that you can download your information easily and quickly. You must consider the big picture. What happens if you decide to switch to another product later on down the road? Will you be able to easily retrieve your information and upload it to your web-based contact manager? These are all important factors to consider.

Accounting and Check Writing

Many agents still write checks by hand and then spend at least a week organizing, categorizing, and totaling receipts for tax purposes. There is no reason to live in the dark ages any longer. Technology provides tools to make these activities simple.

Use an accounting and check-writing software program. These programs automatically itemize your deductions as you write checks. They will also keep track of your trust account and separately itemize client deposits. With these accounting programs, preparation for filing your taxes becomes simple. All expenses are tracked under the correct deduction category as you pay them; then, at tax time a report shows each category, all expenses in that category, and a total for those expenses. Always think as a small business owner should: Does this payment qualify as an expense? Which category does it fall under?

Agent to Agent

A good accountant is a handy asset and an absolute necessity when setting up your business! He or she will guide you to understanding how to fit your expenses into the most advantageous categories and will steer you away from deductions that are on the IRS "red flag" list.

Pay for everything by check or business credit card. When you pay your credit card bill, take a moment to itemize each expense into the correct category. When you write your checks each billing interval, you just pull up the contact information for that vendor. There is no need to input vendor information again as it is already there. All you do is change the amount of the payment if it differs from the time before. Handy window envelopes allow the vendor name and address printed on the check to be seen through the window for mailing purposes.

Transaction Management

There are now transaction management programs available to guide you through the myriad steps your transactions require. What was once a highly complex process with a multitude of contract terms has now become a streamlined, organized practice. This important transformation has come through the advent of standard contract forms that integrate with transaction management programs.

Not long ago we had hundreds of contract forms. Now, across the United States contracts have become more standardized. For the most part, we use ZipForm in most states and WINForms in California, both available online and as product downloads. These standard forms now integrate with transaction management software, such as Relay Online Transaction Management (www.rebt.com) to simplify transaction documentation and management so that even a new agent can make sense of what is without a doubt a highly sophisticated and detailed process.

These transaction management programs offer customizable checklist templates that identify each transaction step, offering forms to complete each step and calendar dates for accomplishing them on a timely basis. As you will see in Chapter 14, diary dates end up on your calendar and you are e-mailed a reminder in advance of each event.

Furthermore, since the entire transaction is online, the many parties involved in your transaction can review the status of activities and integrate their activity with yours, making the transaction far more collaborative than when each person works solo. The database becomes more unified for the many transaction participants to join together as a unified team. Of course, no one will view the private details of your transaction unless you give them password permission.

I suggest you take two steps with transaction management. One is to use either ZipForm (www.zipform.com) or WINForms (www.winforms.com), depending upon where you practice, and use transaction management software (www.rebt.com), preferably online, that integrates these standard forms. The second is to obtain the assistance of professional transaction coordinators to help you carry out the massive number of transaction steps.

FYI!
When you use an online transaction management system you can set levels of access for guests. You can give your client permission to view documents but not your notes. You can give the title company access to view just the documents they will need to process escrow. You can give an assistant or transaction coordinator permission to edit documents. You can control the transaction any way you like and give as much or as little permission to as many people as you desire.

You can obtain transaction coordination virtually (online) or in person. Virtual assistance is available through companies like Team Double-Click (www.teamdoubleclick.com). The charge is $300 per buyer or seller side per transaction. Or perhaps your office provides transaction coordination assistance. If you use a transaction coordination system like Relay or SettlementRoom, you want your coordinator to have experience with the same program. The two of you will complete the steps online so each of you can be aware of the transaction's progress.

Agent to Agent

For those unique question-intensive listings, you can refer agents and interested purchasers to your website or your 800 fax on demand number. Make sure everything they need is provided by technology. Your time can then be spent in more productive areas instead of responding to a never-ending barrage of questions about the property.

Mastering Computer Attachments

Learn how to attach files of all types to e-mails and e-faxes. For instance, your contracts and other forms are most likely stored on the computer. If not, go to www.Zipform.com or www.WINForms.com (California agents) and begin using the right form for you. Instead of being limited by the paper shuffle (printing out documents and transmitting them by fax, by mail, or by hand, and receiving them back in the same manner), you are able to attach these documents to an e-mail or e-fax and send them from your computer. If a file is not online or stored in your computer, you can scan the document into a computer file and attach it.

Attachments aren't only for forms, you can attach pictures, other e-mails, and address book pages. By using an attachment to e-mail instead of inputting directly into the e-mail, formatting is better retained and transmission may be faster. There are all kinds of tricks of the trade that will make your computer experience much easier and more productive. Take the time to get some training and spend some time with each of the features of your contact management program.

Scanning and Editing Software

You will need to scan documents in order to get them into a computer format so you can store them on your computer or send them to others as e-mail attachments. This is done with scanning hardware and the software that comes bundled with it. If you also want to edit the documents you scan, you will need character recognition software.

Photo Management Software

Most cameras come with their own photo software. This software allows you to tweak the picture until it achieves the look you are after by adding more light or color, centering the picture, or resizing it, to name a few of a multitude of options. You will want to use these features to their fullest so you can make your listings look more appealing.

Internet Access

Everyone needs access to the Internet these days. If you have e-mail connectivity, you also have Internet access. The Internet is an amazing source of information and tools. Of course, you have to consider the reliability of the source depending on the type of information you find. The Internet can be a multi-purpose tool, useful for gathering information and for marketing your services and advertising your client's listings.

To connect to the Internet, you need the service of an *Internet service provider* (*ISP*). You will have to connect to the Internet to get your e-mail, access the MLS listings, or gather information from other websites. A dial-up connection is the most economical, but can be very slow and inconvenient when viewing graphic-intensive pages or accessing applications like the MLS. No truly high-tech person can do without a high-speed connection such as DSL or cable. The additional cost will be worth the time you will save not having to wait to view pages.

Make sure you understand your Internet browser and its capabilities so you can make the most of the world of information available through Internet access. The Internet is quickly becoming the place where a lot of marketing takes place. Keep abreast of what the Internet offers. It changes daily. Its potential is unlimited.

def•i•ni•tion

An **Internet service provider** (ISP) is a company that sells you connectivity to the Internet. This service often also comes with one or more e-mail addresses.

Multiple Listing Service

The multiple listing service (MLS) is a membership-only website, although there is now a public version called IDX featured in the next chapter. The MLS site includes many sophisticated features that allow you to perform complex searches for properties for sale or rent and to locate comparables. There are also prospect-matching functions that allow you to automate e-mails of new listings to prospects without even touching your computer. Your prospect receives a full-color display of new listings without any continuing effort on your part.

There are also tax records to search and important statistics to access. Most MLS programs also include desktop art features for professional creation of flyers, brochures, and other marketing materials. Make sure you receive thorough training in the use of this service. You will receive some training through your office, but you should also sign up for some courses through either your local board or the multiple listing service itself. Agents often underutilize computer technology. As you can see, this would be a big mistake for you.

Security (Backups and Virus Protection)

This section should have a big warning sign that says: "If you rely on computer technology, you must have a backup and an antivirus system in place." Because your computer contains your real estate world, you must safeguard its information.

Virus protection is easy. Make sure you have virus protection software, such as Norton AntiVirus, installed on each computer, and that each is updated at least weekly. Backing up takes a little more work.

 Cave!

Because everyone is worried about viruses, you want to let your e-mail recipient know the attachment is virus free. Be sure you set up your virus checking program to scan all incoming and outgoing messages.

Some ISPs are now offering excellent antivirus and firewall software to their subscribers. This can be a big plus to you and your computer. You can download the software at no additional cost to you and have complete protection from virus infection. Not having virus protection on your machine is tantamount to driving with your eyes shut. You will eventually run into something and it could be fatal to your computer and its database.

The convenience of having a portable computer has its own downside: as it is transported from place to place, it becomes susceptible to crashes and loss. Always back up your information to another location that does not travel with you or utilize an online database management system.

In my office, we have multiple computers that are networked together. One computer acts as a server that all information is backed up to. If you have just one computer or have no network capability, you will have to use writable CDs/DVDs, USB drives, Zip disks, or tapes as your backup medium. Consult a professional or a technology-savvy friend if these processes and terms are unfamiliar to you.

Whatever you do, don't ignore backups! Backup utilities come bundled with the latest Microsoft operating system as part of its highly accessible system tools or can be purchased separately from other vendors. Some backup utilities are included with writable hardware like CD/DVD writers and Zip drives. It just takes a few clicks to initiate a backup. You can set the backup to occur automatically with just a few more clicks. One week is the maximum time to elapse between backups. I back up only my documents, since my software is available and filed away.

Now that we have affordable Internet-based servers available to house our information, backing up and virus protection are reinforced. Currently, my office is transitioning all our server information to an Internet-based server. The result will be ease of information synchronization and improved virus protection and security.

Connectivity

Because you will have multiple locations where you access information, it is necessary to understand computer connectivity for e-mail, fax, and Internet access. This means knowing how to track your Internet service provider's access numbers and change your access to conform to that number if you use dial-up access. You will want to know how to make these changes on the devices that will travel with you: your laptop and your PDA. Although I am on land line at the office and home, I use wireless while in the field whenever possible. It's easy because it finds its own cells to interact with.

FYI!
You may have occasion to use a program like PC Anywhere to dial in to another computer to obtain its files. I have a desktop at home and another at my office, and a laptop and PDA that travel with me. I use PC Anywhere between the computers to access and update files. I also synchronize via a network, my laptop computer, my assistant's desktop computer, and my desktop computers whenever I am in the office. Now that we are moving to an online database, we will have only one place to synchronize all computers with.

Synchronization

You will want to synchronize data throughout all of your devices, which involves having the right hardware and software. Some PDAs have software applications that will not "sync" with the applications used on your laptop. Do not purchase these devices. Get those that are compatible with the applications you use on your computer. If you use an Internet database, make sure all of your files will be exportable to the online system.

The answer to full integration is twofold. First, make sure that each computer device you purchase is fully compatible with your contact and calendar applications. Second, make sure your computers have the right ports so they can physically network with your other computers or your online database so you can exchange information between computers. Again, if you don't understand the issues involved in making these devices compatible with each other, consult a friend or technically savvy person who can help you.

Obtaining Computer Training

For some programs you will require hands-on training, for others online instruction will do, and for others self-instruction will suffice. It all depends on your level of interest and discipline. You will probably use a combination of these sources. Most software programs have handy tutorials that step you through the basic processes. Some classroom training is advisable for the programs you will use most often.

There are many places to acquire the skills necessary to become fluid with your computer programs. Local community colleges have night and day courses on the most common programs. The private sector has many good courses to offer, too. Some are quite economical while others can be pricey. You can take many courses online in the convenience of your own home or office. Ask at your local Association of Realtors.

Often they provide technical assistance. Check with the title companies, too. They have a multitude of programs that you may take to sharpen your computer skills.

FYI!

I encourage you to become a certified E-Pro agent. This is an Internet mastery certification offered through the National Association of Realtors. This course, called E-Pro, is offered online and confers the E-Pro certification which can be used after your name. This program was designed to help you thrive and compete in the world of online real estate. This is a partial course description as described on the NAR's website, www.realtor.org:

- **Getting Connected**—Getting connected is more than going online, it is about creating an Internet presence.
- **E-mail, a new way to communicate and a new way to market**—Master your e-mail software, using it as a tool to communicate before, during, and after the transaction. Learn great risk reduction and marketing techniques.
- **World Wide Web**—Learn the obvious and the subtle advantages a web-marketing plan can have. Create your own Internet Listing Presentation content. Use the WWW to publish information valuable to your prospects as well as your clients. Do your homework before you "buy" a website or pay for an "exclusive territory."
- **Tying it all together**—Bring the aspects of ancillary technology such as PDAs, digital cameras, virtual tours, and MLS systems to the attention of the e-PRO.

Stay in Touch with NAR

The National Association of Realtors is up to date on technology. Join them and make sure you get on their weekly e-mail update. They provide weekly information advisories that include the newest, latest, and greatest of everything to keep your business cutting edge. Don't just get these advisories. Read them.

The Least You Need to Know

- Technology is the key to an organized, highly efficient real estate practice.
- A laptop computer, cell phone, color printer, copier, fax machine, and digital camera are essential equipment, while a PDA is optional but highly recommended.

◆ Software functions must cover an abundance of activities, including contact, e-mail and calendar handling, accounting, transaction management, word processing, MLS, and Internet.

◆ The MLS has many services that can make your work easier, such as the ability to perform a detailed search of listings and other critical information.

◆ With Internet technology comes the constant need to virus protect and back up.

A Multimedia Lead Generation System

In This Chapter

- ◆ Meeting the Master Marketing Model
- ◆ Incorporating multimedia marketing in real estate
- ◆ Generating leads through your website
- ◆ Automating campaign functions with your contact database
- ◆ Using the Lead Projector to calculate daily leads

A thriving lead generation system spells the difference between success and failure for the real estate professional. New agents have no idea how to define their market nor how to build a reliable system to consistently drive leads their way. Even the veteran agent can be lost these days in a high-tech world that is challenging to embrace but must be incorporated to capture market share.

While this chapter utilizes a new licensee as an example, the system presented is for all agents who want to benefit from a state-of-the-art lead generating system that utilizes technology to the max. What's so good about it is it is prepackaged for you. You don't even need to understand technology to have a marketing model that includes the most technologically advanced lead procurement systems.

The aim of this marketing model was to answer the questions agents asked as this book gained popularity, "How many leads do we need to generate each day to reach our financial goals? How do we drive these leads our way using high-tech self-generating systems?" They asked for the tools to project the number of leads they will require to meet their financial goals and for a cookie-cutter system to get those leads on a consistent ongoing basis.

For the new edition of this book, I have built the Master Marketing Model and the Lead Projector, a two-tiered cutting edge system that answers these questions. The Master Marketing Model gives you a multimedia system that incorporates the most cutting-edge forms of advertising into one streamlined package while the Lead Projector tells you exactly how many leads you need to meet your financial goals.

The New Agent's Quandary

The new agent is particularly vulnerable when it comes to creating a lead generating plan. You're new to the business. You don't really understand what your market is, not to mention how to generate those all-important leads. Can you afford a website? Would a toll-free 800 number be the answer? Should you buy a lead generating program? You know you need leads; you realize they are your lifeline but you do not know how to customize a plan for yourself.

FYI!
Almost one-third of real estate firms have an agreement with a lead generation company that provides the firm with customer contact information.

All too often as a new agent you sit at your desk roaring to break into the real estate field just to find questions like this plaguing you—with no answers and few resources from which to get them. You may feel lost in a sea of uncertainty without the experience to identify how much of a market share you need to make it or even how to draw any market at all.

Even Top Dogs Need Technology Upgrades

This chapter is not just for the new agent. Maybe you are an agent who has been licensed for some time, but you have not been able to pull in self-generating systems or Internet market share. You know you are missing out on an important market and believe you are being squeezed out by your technology-based competition. Whether you are new to the business or a Top Dog, the tools presented in this chapter will provide the lead generating components your business needs.

The Master Marketing Model is one of the most cutting-edge real estate sales lead generating system ever presented. It incorporates the very latest in technology-based products to give you the most comprehensive plan that for the most part works without you. Even you Top Dogs may want to replace the website you've had for years with a more innovative one that feeds leads directly into a built-in, campaign-driven contacts database. Four hundred dollars a year certainly makes this choice affordable. Why not have a website that does the work you hire assistants to do for 1 percent of the price?

How the System Works

The Master Marketing Model gives you a lead generating plan that cannot fail—as long as you follow it to the T. This model identifies each and every step you need to take to implement a powerful lead generating machine—one that is affordable to even the newly licensed agent. The Lead Projector, a simplified economic analysis, on the other hand, will quantify the number of leads you will need to generate the income you target. It will give you a quantifiable bottom-line goal to market toward. These tools work together by implementing a defined marketing model to fit your income needs.

Any model is best illustrated with an example. Cynthia, a new agent wanting to earn $80,000 her first year, is the example we have built this chapter around. Again, this system is not just for the new agent. It is for anyone who wants to take advantage of a lead generation system that does the work for you. Cynthia has enough money for start up costs and to pay living expenses for six months and has just started in the business. She has all her technology tools—both hardware and software. She has taken the right steps thus far, but now she needs a solid marketing plan.

The Master Marketing Model Defined

Your *lead generating* model consists of a variety of options which, when blended together, will give you a comprehensive, streamlined master marking plan. Your model will be composed of the following:

- Obtaining your own lead generating website

- Procuring a database management system and running targeted campaigns

- Having an 800 toll-free 24/7 listing info-line

- Advertising in magazines

- Marketing to your current sphere of influence

- Engaging in networking and marketing to the leads you gain

- Farming one selected neighborhood and marketing to it

The Secret to the Master Marketing Model

The secret to the Master Marketing Model is that it has a global reach through its multimedia features and its 24/7 built-in constant market pull. By incorporating various methods of interaction, it is virtually multidimensional. In essence, it reaches the many senses of your consumer base by utilizing Internet interface, voice interaction, in-person connection, and written media. The system is set up to cycle your consumer through each format, thereby exposing them to multiple dimensions of your marketing information.

Marketing research indicates that when marketing is repeated in different media formats, your market reach escalates. The handshake and eye contact have a certain personal connection that is stored in one compartment of the brain. Written media presents another facet, which in turn gets stored in a different compartment of the brain. The more visual graphics of website interaction hits another sensory aspect of the brain and is stored there. When you factor in each of the Master Marketing Model formats, the brain's recollection points are activated at various sensory points causing prospects to receive a far more indelible memory of you.

The object of this marketing plan is to hit them on many fronts and many levels. While your lead will come in one sensory door, they will be exposed to your marketing on various levels. For instance, George sees your ad in a magazine and calls your 800 number. He then receives your voice mail message and interactively requests a fax back of information relating to a property he is interested in. He also is directed to your website. He now has received a brain memory of you on three distinct levels—audio, visual, and in print. If he were to stop by your office to talk with you, he would then receive an in-person impression of you which would be more distinct and lasting than the rest. By this time the memory of your message is activated in four sectors of his brain, and by all indicators, you should be in a position to make a client of this lead.

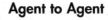

Agent to Agent

The purpose of multimedia marketing is to appeal to many different senses through many types of media such as video, audio, print, and graphics.

The Master Marketing Model in the Flesh

Our Master Marketing Model is more comprehensive yet more streamlined than any other system heretofore presented in the real estate field. The high-tech portion of our model consists of a personal website with an MLS search function, an all-in-one Internet-based contact management program with campaign capability, an 800 number call capture system, and *web-based paging*. To our technology-based model we add select print advertising, networking, and mailings to your sphere of influence and to your farm to round out our Master Marketing Model.

Each of these features and their prices are discussed separately below. The Lead Projector, presented later in this chapter, explores all yearly expenses an agent can expect to pay including the cost of this marketing model. This plan will only work if it is affordable to the new agent, and the market has made sure that it is.

def•i•ni•tion

Web-based paging notifies you via alphanumeric pager or text messaging cell phone when you receive e-mail.

Adopt a Master Marketing Mindset

Before I reveal the Master Marketing Model, I want to stress the importance of your mental attitude. You can have the best marketing model, but if you don't believe in it, it cannot flourish. There is a mindset you want to adopt to assure the very best results for yourself. You want to begin thinking in terms of success and see yourself as successful. Know without a single doubt that if you follow this marketing plan you will succeed. Don't second guess yourself. When results do not appear in one month, two months, three months, even six months, continue to know that your efforts will pay off.

Most people, especially in sales, insist upon seeing quantifiable results before they will believe in themselves. This thinking is backwards. As I pointed out in Chapter 8, success is achieved through holding a positive image and working towards it, not the other way around. Know you will succeed, take the steps to succeed, and you are guaranteed success.

> **FYI!**
>
> The median size of single family homes is 1,727 square feet. For first-time buyers it is 1,451 square feet and 1,920 square feet for repeat buyers. Custom-built homes are larger, with a median size of 2,186 square feet.

You don't point your car towards San Diego and wonder whether you will arrive. Although you must drive 2,000 miles to get there, you know you will get there as long as you keep driving in the right direction. You don't get to Texas and say, "Nope, not there yet. Let's turn around and go back." You know you will get there. The same philosophy applies to following this marketing plan. It is just a matter of time. Hang on, work this excellent program, and you will get there. I guarantee it.

The High-Tech Component

The Master Marketing Model begins with the high-tech lead generating plan, then gets supplemented with low-tech features like magazine advertising, networking, and newsletter mailing. These are the elements that comprise the high-tech portion of this dynamic plan and their prices:

Marketing Tool	Description	Provider	Yearly Fee
Agent Pro website	Enhanced website	iHOUSE	$398
IDX-Pro search capability	Incorporates MLS database	iHOUSE	$298
MarketReach	Contacts database campaign functions, calendars, etc.	iHOUSE	$149
Web Pager	Alerts you when e-mail comes in from your website	iHOUSE	$49

Marketing Tool	Description	Provider	Yearly Fee
ConnecTel	800 toll-free number listing info line (with 240 pre-loaded minutes per month)	iHOUSE	$298
High-Tech Annual Total			$1,192

You can now push buttons from one central command post, your computer, instead of engaging in time-consuming multitasking, all at an affordable price.

A 24/7 Self-Generating Model

The driving force behind our Master Marketing Model is that it is *self generating*. It delivers a 24/7 presence that works without you. While you orchestrate and monitor the control panel of your lead generating program, it does the majority of its work without you.

While there will undoubtedly be many providers of our high-tech marketing model over time, currently the provider we recommend is iHOUSE Web Solutions. Go to their website at www.iHOUSEweb.com and start test driving your very own website. Make sure you also test drive MarketReach, their lead generating contact management program too, to get a good understanding of exactly how each of their marketing features work. Their setup fees for the products we recommend is a little over $300. But iHOUSE will waive their setup fees if you use promotion code IG906 (this is capital I as in Indian, G as in Guru) when you sign up with them. [Note: offer good for annual purchase plan only, limit of one redemption per account, and code must be entered at time of purchase, promotion code valid for new orders only, offer subject to change at any time.]

def•i•ni•tion

A **self generating** system is one that generates leads from action it takes or responses it draws.

Below we explore each one of the features considered necessary to the high-tech component of your Master Marketing Model and why the elements are important.

Having Your Own Website

I can hear you saying, "I'm a new agent. Why do I need my own website? It's a luxury I cannot afford right now." My answer is, "It is not a luxury; it is mandatory." In the visually oriented real estate world, you must have a strong web presence to be taken seriously and to capture the technology-based consumer. A website has replaced the business card—and every agent needs a business card.

iHOUSE's personal customization options are endless, with hundreds of design templates to choose from, or you can just go with certain defaults. These turnkey sites offer your visitors in-depth listing searches and hundreds of pages of professional content. They are built to not only give you visibility 24/7 but to draw leads to your site and give them a productive, resourceful experience while they are there.

We suggest choosing Agent Pro, iHOUSE's intermediate website format rich in preloaded content and interactive tools. This format gives you a personal profile page, a do-it-yourself newsletter; mortgage information; daily interest rate updates; current real estate news; mortgage calculators; a dream home finder; a market analysis request form; tips for buyers and sellers in the form of informative articles and links to other websites; homeowner, title, and escrow information; and community information.

Agent to Agent

I first put up my website a decade ago. It was an amazingly expensive and complex ordeal. Now, ten years later, for $400 a year you can get a website rich with interactive market-making features to assure you of focused real estate lead generation.

The tools and tutorials are rich with all the information you need to reach the largest market you can with the most features available. Their search engine resources are comprehensive, allowing you to understand the significance of the proper keywords listed for your site and the importance of making your site "search engine friendly." They offer many options for both directory inclusion and priority placement with the major search engines. As you begin earning more in your business, you may choose to join pay-per-click advertising on Google or Yahoo or one of the other search engines. When someone clicks into your site as a result of your ad, you pay a nominal fee.

These turnkey websites also have unlimited e-mail forwarding, auto response capabilities, and a web traffic reporter to let you know how much traffic you're receiving. By comparing your traffic to the leads you get, you can understand if you need to add more lead generating options to your site to reach the goal defined by the Lead Projector.

Don't Reinvent the Website Wheel

As I was writing this chapter I received an e-mail from Ben, an agent who has been in the business for 16 years. He is with a major international brokerage company and just put up his own website. He paid $2,400 and spent about five weeks creating the content for his pages. The site lacks interest, navigation is not easy, and it has few resources. I suggested he take a look at iHOUSE. He got back to me with this message, "Why didn't you tell me sooner?" A few days later he dumped his site and signed on with iHOUSE, realizing that in just a few months with a self-marketing website he would make this money back. He just did not realize that the website wheel for real estate professionals had already been invented. He did not have to start the process all over again.

Adding a Comprehensive Search Feature to Your Website

The IDX-Pro feature of the marketing model we suggest allows your web visitors to search your local MLS listings in addition to the national database on www.realtor.com. In the beginning, if you feel your budget cannot encompass this option, leave it out but add it as soon as you can because MLS searches are the number one reason home buyers visit real estate sites on the web. Not only will you provide an exhaustive, up-to-date, heretofore secret inventory of properties for sale to your guests, you will automatically receive their confidential contact information in return.

This is how it works. iHOUSE's IDX-Pro online MLS search indexes your guest's search criteria and automatically sends them daily e-mail alerts from you describing new listings that match their requirements. Through lead tracker, an integrated contact management system, your new client's contact information is automatically added to your database of buyers who you can set up to receive automated buyer campaign products such as "How to Find the Right House at the Right Price" with a tool such as MarketReach, which we will discuss in the next section. With MarketReach, all this work is done automatically. All you have to do is decide which already prepared newsletter goes to buyers this month and click a button. You can even schedule campaigns in advance.

FYI!
Investment property home buyers have a median age of 47 years with a typical household income of $85,700.

Contacts Database with Campaign Capability

Lead generation and optimum servicing of those leads used to require multitasking at its best. You would get a lead, feed it into your database, and then decide how to service it. Your marketing program pretty much ran independent of your website. I had a snail mail monthly newsletter and a contacts database that needed constant attention aside from my website. It took a lot of time and talent and careful attention to the referral stream system discussed in Chapter 15. While I continually tried to get my website to fulfill all my marketing needs, I never made it.

The answer is to have a contact management database that is Internet-based and dovetails with your website. In this manner, web-generated contacts pour over into your database, pick up your marketing material, and go back out to your visitor page. The result is instant stop and shop while you tend to your existing clients. iHOUSE again fills this need with their product called MarketReach. Those of you with iHOUSE should use MarketReach for marketing, calendaring, and database management following the database entry steps in the referral stream system in Chapter 15.

This is how MarketReach and most other Internet-based contacts management programs work. They basically replace Outlook, Top Producer, Act!, or any other contact program you use. They also eliminate the need to synchronize databases. For instance, before an Internet based e-mail, contacts, and calendaring system, you had to synchronize all computers to update information between them. You would enter a contact or calendar event on one computer or receive an e-mail. You would then be out in the field with your PDA entering more information and receiving and sending more e-mails. You would return to the office or home and you would synchronize all computers to unify their information.

There is no longer a need to do that when you have an Internet-based program such as MarketReach where all your information resides in one unified place. If you're out in the field and don't have Internet access, input the information into your PDA and upload it to MarketReach when you're connected. Furthermore, the leads captured from your website or an IDX-Pro search end up automatically sent to MarketReach.

MarketReach contains a catalog of hundreds of eCards that are basically informative newsletters prepared by iHOUSE staff but customized as if they were personally prepared by you. You can select an informative mailer and choose a group of contacts (for instance, buyers) to receive it, and presto, all buyers in that grouping receive your informative newsletter. This is called an e-marketing campaign. Or select a group of newsletters (one about the importance of property inspections, another about home staging, and so on) and schedule them to send sequentially every week to your grouping (sellers here).

This is called a *drip campaign*. It drips into your market a little at a time. It only takes three minutes to select the informative newsletters and decide which grouping to send them to and how frequently they should be sent. Or, be lazy, don't take three minutes. Just hit the button that automatically sends drip campaigns out for you and choose the best newsletters to match them. And, last but not least, you can automate your marketing tools to auto respond to people with your products and services without even pushing a button.

def•i•ni•tion

Database management programs have campaign ability built in. The campaigns are targeted to certain prospect groups and consist of marketing materials determined to be of interest to that prospect group. **Drip campaigns** are scheduled to transmit these materials at certain frequencies over a set period of time; thus, the term "drip." These campaigns are transmitted by e-mail.

Web Based Pager

Before web-based paging, one obstacle I was never able to hurdle was being in two places at one time. My time invariably needed to be divided between receiving and responding to e-mail in front of the computer and in the field making new markets and servicing client needs. I'm a Gemini so I have the best chance of doing this, yet it never worked.

I tried every conceivable gadget to successfully connect to the Internet while out and about. Although air cards and Blackberry were great tools, web-based paging is better. Now with a web-based paging service, you add your alphanumeric pager or text messaging cell phone to your website. Online visitors contact you by filling in a form which is sent directly to your pager or cell phone as a text message. It's simple and effective!

800 Line Call Capture System

The hottest new way to get leads and service listings is through an 800 call-capture system. This is how it works. You list your 800 number on your advertising, all of which make it clear that the 800 number has free recorded information 24/7, not a live person. Market surveys show that people are 75 percent more likely to call a number that has recorded information as opposed to a live person. Because of this you receive nearly two times more inquiries than you would if your regular contact number were listed. Your targeted market comes to you instead of your spending countless hours and days prospecting and cold calling for them.

Your 800 number has various extensions which are matched with listings and other advertising. For instance, if a caller is interested in listing 2862, they call your 800 number, input 2862, and receive a series of options related to that listing. One option is to receive a fax back of listing information and photos. Another is to hear a verbal description of the property's criteria and price. Another is to leave you a voicemail. Another interesting feature ConnecTel has is the Find Me, Follow Me function. When this function is turned on, the system will attempt to reach you at multiple phone numbers where you may be located. Leads will always be able to find you—if you want them to!

But the best part of this model is this: within 20 seconds of anyone calling, you receive an e-mail, call, and/or text message with the caller's phone number (even if they have caller ID blocked) along with the listing or advertisement they responded to, and their name and address (if available). Real estate is an in-the-moment industry. Connecting with a buyer or seller when they are in hot pursuit is the best marketing you can ever do. When you receive their phone number, you auto dial them and connect with them in the moment that opportunity strikes. You overcome do-not-call registry obstacles and at the same time you are able to provide them with information they are seeking. It's the best of all worlds.

With this recorded info-line capability, instead of spending endless hours answering questions about your listings, your toll-free 24/7 info line does it for you. There's no more sending out property information, your 800 number faxes callers directly back with a property flyer. Your time is freed up to generate more leads and obtain more listings. By assigning a unique extension to each of your marketing sources (magazine, yard sign, website, etc.), you also can track the effectiveness of your advertising modes.

Most agents also include catchy advertising along with their listings, such as offers for a free market evaluation directing readers to your website or offers of rebates to buyers and sellers. If you are a new agent and do not have listings yet, there are many advertising options. Invite buyers and sellers to connect with you because you have something no one else has to offer. The possibilities are endless.

The Low-Tech Component of the Model

Our marketing model has a full sweeping effect because it gives you a presence both online and offline. It captures both Internet real estate consumers and your average low-tech Joe who picks up real estate magazines and drives around looking at houses. The rest of your Master Marketing Model is low-tech, but each element captures an important aspect of the market for you.

Magazine Advertising

Marketing tool	Description	Provider	Yearly cost
Print advertising	Advertising	Real estate book	*Varies

Begin a half page ad at $200 - $300 a month. When you have two or more listings, begin your full page ad at $350-$500 a month.

The Master Marketing Model's biggest expense is magazine advertising. A major benefit of magazine advertising is that you get a much longer shelf life than with other forms of print advertising. It is not uncommon for clients to still have copies of real estate magazines that are several months old. Agents can generate leads long after the issue date of the magazine. Expensive, yes; but I feel the cost is necessary to capture non-high-tech leads through the use of an 800 line call-capture system listed in print media. This has proven itself to be an unbeatable combination. The 800 number component was described above.

For print media, Real Estate Book (www.realestatebook.com) will give you the greatest and most reliable amount of leads. Their rates vary depending upon the area you are in but generally plan on spending $350 to $500 a month for a page and half that much for a half page. I recommend that you commit to a yearly contract to get these rates.

The Master Marketing Model staggers your participation with Real Estate Book. Start with a half page ad until you have the business to warrant a full page. If you have no listings and really feel uncomfortable with a half page commitment, wait until you have a listing. You probably will get the listing through your ad, but the choice is up to you. You have come this far, work the program and it will work. By the time you have your second listing, you should commit to a full page. If you do not have listings to feature, feature something unique about your services. There are many ways to get a real estate consumer to interact with you, especially when you have rich tools and features to offer them on your website. It will be just a matter of time when you have your own listings to feature.

Networking

Marketing tool	Description	Provider	Yearly cost
Networking	At least twice a week	Various	$1,200

There's no way around it. Real estate is a personal services industry. It's a touchy-feely business. Handshakes and eye contact are a big part of what makes it work. Referrals are its foundation and in-person contact creates referrals. "I like your smile; I give you my business." Although getting leads is a big part of networking, there is something even bigger: community. Real estate involves so many facets of life and so many different professionals to put a transaction together. You've got to have a community always swirling around you. And, with these community members, you need to socialize, handshake, and have plain old fun.

Our Master Marketing Model includes *networking* twice a week. We estimate that you will pay approximately $100 a month on dues, food, and beverages. The forum is your choice. There are numerous civic organizations to choose from. It could be a bowling league, a golf tournament, anything that involves an opportunity to stand on a chair or a golf cart and exclaim to the world, "I'm the best real estate agent there ever was." Not really, but really.

def•i•ni•tion

Networking is defined in many ways. I define it as the process of meeting people who can be of help to your career.

A networking event is any gathering where buyers and sellers or people who can refer business to you congregate and where you have an opportunity to socialize. Church qualifies if there is a social gathering before or after services. The intent is twofold: first, to put your business card in at least five hands per event; and second, to collect the business cards of the business leaders in that particular group. You will want to add them to your database and contact them on a regular basis, fostering your relationship with them. Remember, too, to bring your PDA to these gatherings and database manage while you socialize. See Chapter 15 for the best way to input into your database and socialize at the same time.

Newsletters

Marketing tool	Description	Provider	Yearly cost
Newsletter mailing	To your sphere of influence and your form	Newsletter on your iHouse website	$500

Your high-tech marketing model works for you 24/7 through your contacts database management program. You will have constant campaigns automatically e-mailed to all your leads in your database. Some will be drip campaigns; some will be individual, more focused campaigns. Many will automatically receive the monthly newsletter your web host provides for you. Or your list of sellers will automatically receive your informative article on the benefits of home staging.

But there are two groups of important prospects that require snail mail. Why? Because you don't have their e-mail addresses. The first group includes some of your all-important sphere of influence. The second group is your farm, the 200 or 300 people in a certain neighborhood you have targeted. Both of these markets are described in Chapter 10.

It may feel archaic to spend time printing newsletters out from your website, stuffing them into envelopes, and dropping them in snail mail. It is, but this is an important step in the Master Marketing Model. Your sphere of influence will transition to e-mail recipients over time as they provide you with e-mail addresses. But in the beginning when you only have their low-tech information, snail mail is it. These people are numero uno. They are extremely important to you because they know you better than anyone and have more allegiance to you than anyone.

There are companies that have the ability to handle the mailing function for you. For a nominal charge they will prepare it for either first-class or bulk mailing, and send it off for you. The cost of having them do all the prep work versus you taking time away from prospecting and servicing clients may make this a very cost-effective option.

Agent to Agent

Bulk mailing is the sending of a large number of identical pieces of third class mail at a further reduced rate. It requires special sorting and labeling and is less expensive than other types of mailing.

While your farm does not start out as a market with any apparent loyalty to you, you will find that over time they will become your clients. If you farm the neighborhood where you live or work, they will come to know you by sight, and sight breeds familiarity which soon turns into listings.

Your sphere of influence and your farm make up an important personal marketplace you always want to keep track of and service with at least a quarterly mailing by snail mail when you do not have e-mail addresses and more frequently by e-mail when you do. Estimate $500 annually for snail mail postage to this important lead group.

The Lead Projector

Now that you have your Master Marketing Plan down, it is time to work the Lead Projector. New agents reported that they need a gauge to know if they are on track to meet their yearly income needs. Many of them have never made a living earning commissions. They need a way to think in terms of leads, listings, and commissions. In the beginning when you're insecure about just about everything you are doing, the one thing you want to measure is your financial bottom line.

They asked for a quantifiable measuring stick to determine how many leads they need to generate on a daily basis to net their targeted income. Our team came up with a mathematical formula we call the Lead Projector. Not only does it answer the question, "How many new leads do I need each day to reach my targeted income?" it also projects the out-of-pocket expense you are likely to pay to receive that income.

For an illustration in this chapter, Cynthia, a first year agent in Arizona, wants to target a net income of $80,000 this year. I will apply the Lead Projector to Cynthia's scenario so you can see how it works and so you can then apply it to your own situation. It allows you to incorporate your unique criteria such as median home price in your area, your office commission split, and average work days per week. It evaluates and approximates the business expenses you will incur and adds them in to determine the gross income required to net the income you desire. It then calculates the number of leads you will require to meet that number.

How Many Leads Will Do It?

The Lead Projector uses industry norms to predict its bottom line—the number of leads you will need to bring in the door. These are the norms it incorporates:

- Every 30 leads turns into a client appointment
- 70 percent of leads that result in buyer or seller appointments end up as listings
- 70 percent of listings close

Please understand that these percentages are norms for both new and experienced sales agents. Your numbers may need to be adjusted according to how long you have been in the business and how well you work your program.

Commission Splits and Median Home Price

Commission split and median home price are two important factors that will affect the Lead Projector's bottom line. While agent-broker commission splits range across the board, many new agents split their commissions 50/50 with their office. Our model agent, Cynthia, does too. If your situation differs, just adjust the commission percentage to fit your situation.

Since commission is based on the sale prices of a house, median home prices will also affect your commission, and will therefore affect the number of leads you will require. Therefore, if you are working in a market where median home prices are $500,000, your lead and listing requirements will be half as much as the agent in a more typical market where home prices are $250,000. Cynthia lives and works in an area where the average home price is $250,000. (If yours differs, use your median home price in your calculations.)

The Results of the Lead Projector

Based on these assumptions, Cynthia needs to generate one lead a day (rounded up), five days a week to earn $80,000 a year. If you practice in an area where the median home price is twice as high as Cynthia's, you will need only one lead every few days. If your median home price is half of Cynthia's you will need closer to two leads a day. Of course, this is only if your office commission split is 50-50.

Let's take a look at the Lead Projector as it applies to Cynthia. Later in this chapter is a blank one for you to complete to determine exactly how many leads you will need to earn the income level you project.

Lead Projector

Criteria	Quantity
Net Income Desired (Pretax dollars)	$80,000
Gross Income Required to earn Net Income Desired (rounded)	$98,000
Formula: Net Income Desired divided by .82 (100% - 18% expenses)	
Operating expenses	$18,000
Formula: 18% of Gross Income	
Gross Commissions Required to net Gross Income Required	$196,000
Formula: For 50% office commission split, Gross Income divided by .5	
Gross Sales Required to meet Gross Income Required	$6,533,333
Formula: Assuming Commission is 3% of Sales Price, Gross Commissions divided by .03 (rounded)	
Closed Escrows Required to meet Gross Sales Required	26
Formula: Gross Sales divided by Median Home Price in your area ($250,000 here)	
Listings Required for Closed Escrows Required (using a 70% success rate)	38
Formula: Closed Escrows Required divided by .7	
Listing Appointments Required to produce Listings Required (using a 70% success rate)	54
Formula: Listings Required divided by .7	
Listing Leads Required to produce Listing Appointments Required (30% success rate)	180
Formula: Listing Appointments Required divided by .3	

Criteria	Quantity
Daily Listing Leads required (working 22 days a month, 264 days a year) (rounded up)	.68 = 1
Formula: Listing Leads Required divided by number of working days a year (here 264 days)	

Setting Net Income Desired

Very simply, this is pretax income you want to bring home yearly after expenses are paid. Cynthia feels $80,000 is within her reach with a *median home price* of $250,000. Remember, the net income we are talking about is gross income minus deductible expenses. This figure is pretax.

Agent to Agent

When determining the median home price, only one home price matters, that of the home in the middle. Of all the homes sold during a particular period, precisely half sold for more than the median price and half sold for less.

Finding Gross Income Required

In the first five years of your business, your operating expense should approximate about 18 percent to 20 percent of your gross income. (Later, as your income increases they may go up to as much as 30 percent.) Our formula uses 18 percent. To determine gross income required with 18 percent allocated to expenses, divide net income desired by .82 (100 percent minus 18 percent expenses) for a total of $98,000 rounded up. Cynthia therefore needs to earn $98,000 before expenses to net her $80,000. Our analysis must use gross income, not net, because the number of leads required must produce enough income to pay your expenses before you take home your desired income.

Identifying Expenses

The expenses we project are $18,000 (rounded up) representing 18 percent of gross yearly income (GYI) of $98,000. The following chart describes the expenses you can project for your first years in real estate sales and the percentage each expense is of gross yearly income. Everyone differs, but these expenses are based upon the Marketing Model recommended in this chapter. They should be close to what a new agent will encounter.

Expense	Yearly	% of GYI
High-tech marketing plan component	$1,200	1.2
Liability insurance/office fees*	$1,000	1
Wireless services ($150/mo.)	$1,800	1.8
Association & MLS dues/education*	$1,200	1.2
Supplies (gas, cards, mailer, gifts)	$3,500	3.5
Technology equipment	$500	.5
Networking	$1,200	1.2
Advertising	$6,000	6.1
Transaction coordination	$1,600	1.5
Total	**$17,870**	**18**

*Check out these figures to correctly reflect charges in your local market.

High-Tech Marketing Plan

The high-tech marketing plan, advertising, networking, and newsletters were described earlier in this chapter under the Master Marketing Model while the rest are discussed below. For seasoned agents, use your actual expenses, not these projections. While the seasoned agent's expenses may be as high as 30 percent of gross income, they could also be as low as 5 percent. It all depends on how much support staff you have.

Liability Insurance and Office Fees

One thousand dollars is an average for any number of expenses for which your broker may charge you. Some provide liability insurance free of charge while some charge a fee. Some charge desk fees or transaction fees while others don't. Others charge a flat fee as a business fee. Some charge for training courses they give. One thousand dollars is a good average to use. But check out the figures in your respective area as they do vary and will impact your expense allocation.

Wireless Services

I have lumped cell phone, text messaging fees, and wireless charges together for a monthly expenditure of about $150 and a yearly figure of $1,800.

Association and MLS Dues/Education

Average yearly association and MLS fees are about $950, and I have allocated $250 to yearly education. Although these expenses are expressed as a percentage of gross yearly income, they should remain fairly consistent throughout your career and will not adjust when your income increases. Check out the figures in your respective area as they do vary and will impact your expense allocation.

Cave! _____

Wireless charges can easily get out of hand if you do not have the right package for your use frequency. Take a moment to review your bill and the packages your provider has available. It could save you a bundle.

Supplies

I have included gas, postage, business cards, and client closing gifts in this category for a yearly total of $3,500 or 3.5 percent of your gross income required, itemized as follows:

Gas	$1800
Postage	$500
Business cards	$200
Closing gifts, gift certificates	$900

Gas I have estimated at $150 a month. Postage is for newsletters mailed initially to your sphere of influence, for quarterly mailings to your farm, and for birthday and holiday snail mail cards. Business cards are self-explanatory as are gifts (described in Chapter 15). These are just projections but they should come close to what you actually pay each year.

Technology Equipment

I assume you have already purchased all the technology you will need to be an optimum producer. This category should include only nominal yearly upgrades to your existing technology.

Transaction Coordination

The budget allows for transaction coordination. I feel it is important to get help in carrying out your transactions, especially in the beginning. Chapter 12 includes information about this important subject and refers you to providers of all the tools you will need to manage your transactions efficiently. With a net income of $80,000, only $1,470 is permitted for transaction coordination. But, as your income increases, so does your budget for transaction coordination.

Make sure you get the contract forms and transaction management software you need before you even write your first contract. In the beginning, your budget will only allow a coordination assistant for your first few transactions. Carefully watch how these coordinators carry out your steps and you will be well on your way to coordinating your own transactions.

Later on, you will be able to afford to hire a transaction coordinator for all of your transactions. You will find it to be a service you are not willing to live without.

Finding Gross Commissions Required

Cynthia, like many new agents, earns only 50 percent of commissions that come to her office from her work. Her required gross income must be divided by 50 percent to determine how much gross commission she needs to earn to net her half. If you have a different commission split, divide your gross income by the percentage of commission you receive.

Finding Gross Sales Required

To determine gross sales required to net the income you desire, the gross commission you require is divided by the percentage of sales price your office receives. We use 3 percent of sales price since most transactions are based on a 6 percent commission with half to each side—in most transactions you only represent one side of the sale. If you live in an area that has a different commission norm, such as a 5 percent gross commission with half to the listing agent and half to the selling agent, you will adjust 3 percent to 2.5 percent.

Find Closed Escrows Required

You will be able to pinpoint how many escrows you need to close each year in order to receive the net income you desire by dividing gross sales required by the median home price in your area. Cynthia needs to close 26 escrows to net $80,000 in her area with a median home price of $250,000. She has to work twice as hard as an agent in

California with double her median home price, but the California agent needs considerably more income to match the same lifestyle.

When you get to this point in your economic analysis, you have finally arrived at a more tangible number from which to determine the bottom line—how many leads you need to bring in to net the income you desire. It becomes far more quantifiable when you know how many escrows you need to close. But we're far from there since only a percentage of leads end up as appointments, only a percentage of appointments end up as listings, and only a percentage of listings end up as closed escrows. These percentages have to be factored in to determine how many listings you will need to close the required number of escrows.

Finding Listings Required

Industry norm is that about 70 percent of listings close escrow. Cynthia needs 26 closed escrows each year to produce the income she requires. But, since only 70 percent of listings close, she needs 38 listings per year to close on 26. To determine this number I took her 26 closed escrows and divided by 70 percent. Cynthia will need to sign up 38 clients to close 26 escrows. You will use 70 percent in performing your own calculations.

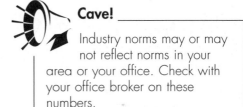

Cave!

Industry norms may or may not reflect norms in your area or your office. Check with your office broker on these numbers.

Finding Listing Appointments Required

Industry norm is that 70 percent of listing appointments result in listings on behalf of the buyer or the seller. Using the same formula, 38 listings divided by 70 percent, Cynthia needs 54 listing appointments per year to obtain 38 listings, 26 of which will actually close. Again, you will use 70 percent in performing your analysis.

Finding Leads Required

Industry norm is that 30 percent of *good* leads turn into appointments. The job here is to make sure your leads are good leads, meaning reliable leads that you have personally gathered or have come through reliable sources. The important thing here is to have leads that are qualified, people who can perform and are ready to become clients soon.

To find leads required, the number of listing appointments required is divided by .3. For Cynthia, she needs 180 leads per year to produce her required 54 listing appointments. If she works 22 days a month she will need to receive .68 good leads each day, which I have rounded up to be one bona fide lead per day.

The Lead Projector has given Cynthia a definitive number she can use each and every work day to gauge her performance. Each morning she will track her leads and will perform her marketing checklist until she has those leads. She will not deviate from her most important job, getting leads, until she has the number she needs for that day. Here, she only needs one lead a day.

Working Your Lead Projector

Now apply the Lead Projector to your practice and see how many leads you will require each day to meet your projected income.

Lead Projector

Criteria	Quantity
Net Income Desired (Pretax dollars)	_____
Gross Income Required to earn Net Income Desired (rounded)	
Formula: Net Income Desired divided by .82 (100% - 18% expenses)	
Operating expenses	_____
Formula: 18% of Gross Income	
Gross Commissions Required to net Gross Income Required	_____
Formula: For 50% office commission split, Gross Income divided by .5	
Gross Sales Required to meet Gross Income Required	_____
Formula: Assuming Commission is 3% of Sales Price, Gross Commissions divided by .03 (rounded)	
Closed Escrows Required to meet Gross Sales Required	_____

Criteria	Quantity
Formula: Gross Sales divided by Median Home Price in your area ($250,000 here)	
Listings Required for Closed Escrows Required (using a 70% success rate)	_____
Formula: Closed Escrows Required divided by .7	
Listing Appointments Required to produce Listings Required (using a 70% success rate)	_____
Formula: Listings Required divided by .7	
Listing Leads Required to produce Listing Appointments Required (30% success rate)	_____
Formula: Listing Appointments Required divided by .3	
Daily Listing Leads required (working 22 days a month, 264 days a year) (rounded up)	_____
Formula: Listing Leads Required divided by number of working days a year (here 264 days)	

Listings or Buyer Sales?

To generate leads you need to know what you are looking for. Do you want buyers, sellers, or both? Listing and selling a property both bring the same income. The dif-ference lies in the amount of time you dedicate to each and the amount of exposure you gain. It takes about three times longer to find and close on a home for a buyer than listing a property for a seller. This is because your listing work is basically done once you get the listed property's marketing package in place. It sells itself.

Agent to Agent

The typical vacation home buyer is 55 years old with a household income of $71,000. Eighty six percent of vacation home buyers do not rent out their vacation home.

Representing the buyer is far more time intensive. The average buyer looks at nine homes over eight weeks before they buy, and you are the one taking them through each. And, because buyer scrutiny is essential, you spend a good deal of time guiding your client through the buying process.

Perhaps more important is the visibility you receive when you list a property. Your signage, direct mail, ads, and open houses give you the type of visibility that earns you neighbor listings and drives potential buyers your way. With enough listings you get to a point where you do not need to market yourself anymore because your name is consistently before the public. Listings, then, are the leads you want to focus on if you have the choice. You want to list everyone's home for sale.

You will find that over time you will exclusively handle seller listings and either refer out buyer transactions or hire another agent to specialize in the more time-intensive job of assisting buyers.

Converting Your Leads

The cornerstone of your business will be your marketing-based lead generating program supplemented by active networking and utilizing the referral stream system described in Chapter 15. But the job doesn't end with capturing leads. These leads must be converted to appointments. I know countless agents with good marketing programs and leads pouring in, but they fail because they are disorganized. They have scraps of paper with names and important sales information sitting in disorganized stacks. They did the job of lead generating but failed to set up a system to service the leads once they arrived.

Think of these leads as hard green cash but only if they reach your database and receive an output action. You must have a system in place that ensures productive follow-up. If they sit in your database without an output designation, they will do you no good. This is where the referral stream system in Chapter 15 comes into play. Each lead receives an output designation which automatically triggers action either by you, by staff, or by your automated campaign system.

After you initiate an output you also want to follow up to seal the deal. Generosity begets generosity. Their listing or their friend's listing should follow in due course. With the computer technology we have these days, it is simple to schedule your next follow-up activity. The secret is to follow your calendar meticulously. If you don't, you have taken all these steps for nothing. Walk your talk and work your plan. Your success as a real estate professional is entirely in your hands!

The Least You Need to Know

- ◆ Lead generating is achieved with the Master Marketing Model—adopt it!

- ◆ Assume a master marketing mindset.

- ◆ Follow your lead projection numbers and meet your financial goal.

- ◆ Real estate magazine advertising listing your 800 call capture line will generate leads and process them for you.

- ◆ Low-tech networking and newsletter mailing services an important lead-generating market.

Part 4

Putting It All Together

Now that you have automated your business, it's time to institute the finishing touches. As they say in the interior design business, it's time to furnish and accessorize. This is the section that shows you how to take your technology based business and make it a truly professional real estate practice. The key elements consist of the following:

- ◆ Becoming a master of organization
- ◆ Building a referral stream system
- ◆ Following The New Ideal
- ◆ Making a winning listing presentation

Chapter 14

A Master of Organization

In This Chapter

- ◆ You can administer your business from anywhere, if you bring technology with you
- ◆ Coordinate information on your computer and PDA
- ◆ Use your calendar program efficiently
- ◆ Know how your various computer programs work together
- ◆ Set up your home office

This chapter covers organization and efficiency. Once you have your computer technology, your business plan, and your marketing plan in place, the next step is to efficiently integrate them all. Again, it begins with a capital *C* for *computer*. Whereas the previous chapters have addressed computer technology from a product selection and training standpoint, this chapter looks at technology from an organizational perspective.

E-mail, cell phones, and fax machines are the technologies that should serve as your communication core. This chapter shows you how to most efficiently use and integrate your computer technology and bring it with you everywhere you go—office, home office, vehicle, and anywhere in the field.

Make Your Computer Your Business Partner

Times have changed, especially where technology is concerned. If you want to move into Top Dog status in the real estate field, you *must* make your computer a top priority, and you *must* become computer savvy. There's just no two ways about this. We have too many technologically competent people entering the field for anyone who wants to claim market share to ignore the benefits of technology any longer.

Agents fight this state of reality, claiming that real estate is a people business that cannot be replaced by impersonal technology. The fact is that technology is not here to *replace* the personal touch; it is here to allow you to be more productive and efficient in order to give you more time to interact with clients and build relationships.

Not everyone has the desire to become a Top Dog, but if you do, organization is essential, and technology provides the key. There are three steps to achieving this goal:

1. Get the right computer programs.

2. Use these computer programs for *all* your business.

3. Bring your computer, either laptop or PDA, everywhere you go during business hours.

Wean Yourself off Paper

As described in previous chapters, a good contact management program which organizes your contacts, e-mail, and calendar is a must. The trick is not just knowing how to use it, but using it faithfully. Wean yourself off of paper. Make yourself use a computer for everything. I accomplished this by removing pens from my surroundings. I felt as if I was giving up smoking again. But it worked.

After about three weeks, computer entry becomes automatic for calendaring, lists of tasks, and contact information. Since we spend so much time in the field, your PDA is indispensable, but you've got to use it. The transition from pen to computer entry shouldn't require drastic measures; just don't let a pen get in the way.

Of course, the computer efficiency plan will not work for you unless you establish e-mail as a method of supplementing contact with clients, other agents, and peers. Nearly everyone has e-mail these days. Just train them to use it. Once they see the immediate benefits of instant communication and delivery of information, they will be converts. I have no trouble whatsoever mentoring my groups into using e-mail for transactions, and most people who are not as e-mail based as I am are flabbergasted at the resulting increase in productivity and interaction.

This fact is borne out by a survey the National Association of Realtors conducted recently that indicates that buyers and sellers who receive status reports by e-mail are the most satisfied with their agents because communication is more frequent. You will be met with opposition from many people, but hang in there. It is worth it.

Become a Computer Multitasker

To achieve high performance, you must also become a computer multitasker. It is only through complete familiarity with your computer programs that you will achieve your highest efficiency. Obtain the training that pulls all of your applications together in a unified manner. You should be able to sit at your computer and seamlessly click away as you write letters from scratch, modify real estate forms and documents, e-mail, fax, scan, search the Internet, update your contacts, keep up with your accounting, and calendar your reminders and appointments.

FYI!
I feel like Ms. Spock on my computer as I run several programs, simultaneously multi-tasking between them all. To do this, you need to know which program performs the functions you require and have the ability to use that function well. This ability only comes through experience, but when it comes, you know you have discovered the most efficient way of doing business. It's as if one day the light bulb comes on and after that, you are a lean, mean, computerized machine.

For instance, you're preparing a listing agreement. You receive an e-mail confirming an appointment. With one little click you reply to the e-mail. You open your calendar and diary the meeting within a matter of seconds. You open the multiple listing service to search for properties for that client. You e-mail your clients the listings you feel may interest them. You open your calculator program to determine the mortgage payment they will make. You get some information on loan rates from the Internet, and then copy that and paste it into an e-mail. Now, you return to the listing agreement you were preparing. You and your laptop become an efficient central office no matter where you are.

Bring Your Database Everywhere You Go

To become a Top Dog in the portable real estate business, you must train yourself to bring your database everywhere you go. While many agents have not partnered with technology to the extent this book suggests, you must if you want to be a Top Dog. Top Dogs use technology to claim market share and to service market share. With that said, let me illustrate the advantage of making technology portable.

Most busy agents spend at least two hours a day performing administrative tasks, even if they have an assistant. With the right technology at your fingertips, you can easily handle these chores as you step through your day. Can you imagine having two hours a day more than your competitors have? The answer is to have your laptop or PDA with you at all times.

Agent to Agent

In my car or in the field where inputting information is inconvenient or dangerous, I use the voice recorder built into my PDA to record information requiring notation. For instance, if I need to make an entry while driving and talking on my cell phone, I activate the voice recorder on my PDA and repeat the message. The recorder easily plays back for retrieval of information. When I arrive at my destination, I enter important information into my database.

Inefficiency and disorganization so often result from having information on your computer in one place while you are at another location. For instance, you've just returned to the office from a day (without your computer) in the field, delivering a listing presentation and meeting with various vendors and potential clients. You have a listing to input, dates to calendar from contacts you made in the field, new client information to enter, and so on. There are faxes that have been received and e-mails and voice messages to pore through. You're stuck in office administration mode for a few hours.

Multitasking in the Field

This is not the case for the high-tech agent who goes home from the listing presentation to spend quality time with his family. He has minimal voice mail to return since he had his cell phone with him and received most calls. At the listing presentation, he used his laptop as a visual aid (see Chapter 17), so when he signed his clients up, he entered their contact information into his database. He also completed and submitted the listing to the multiple listing service while with his clients, enabling them to respond to property-specific questions. He had his digital camera and took pictures and uploaded them when entering the listing on the MLS. He also installed a lock box and explained its security features in order to alleviate his new client's concerns over allowing agents access to their home. Instead of requiring several return visits to take pictures, install a lock box, and obtain information for the listing, the high-tech agent accomplished these tasks on the spot when the listing was received.

During the rest of his time in the field, calendar dates and contact information were entered on his PDA instead of on scraps of paper to be entered later. His faxes were automatically forwarded to his home. When he arrives home, instead of several hours of administration, he has a few faxes and some e-mail to review. Who would you rather be? The high-tech agent home with his family having administrated his day throughout the day, or the low-tech agent stuck at the office still administrating the details?

Even if you have an assistant administrating the office for you, it increases office productivity if you organize and administrate your time in the field. In this manner, there is little time spent transmitting information to your assistant later; just initiate the synchronization program on your computer and your information is transferred to your assistant's computer. Or better yet, use an online data storage service which allows you to synchronize directly to your database from anywhere as long as you are connected to the Internet.

Becoming a Calendar Wizard

Full use of your computer calendar is essential to maximum productivity in the real estate field. The business just moves too fast and there are too many details and people to rely on memory or scraps of paper. Even more important is the fact that transactions are deadline driven, and if deadlines are not met, the consequences are extreme.

Some real estate offices still train agents and support staff to use hand-written calendaring systems. I urge you to do it all on computer. If your office insists on using hand-written forms, check with your manager to see whether a computer-entered profile for each transaction will suffice. If not, still use computer entry as your primary tracking method while you conform to office policy using the written method.

Better yet, use the transaction management software we recommended in the previous chapter. These programs will automatically transfer transaction diary dates directly to your calendaring program and will e-mail you an advance notification.

def•i•ni•tion

A **contingency release** occurs when a contingency is released, either by satisfaction or waiver. There is a specified time period for this to happen. The agent prepares a release of contingency, which is signed by the buyer. If the contingency is not released within this time frame, the transaction most often terminates without penalty.

For matters that need advanced planning, such as a *contingency release*, I program my transaction management system to make a calendar entry for both the date of the release and a few days before the release. Everything that needs to be accomplished at a specific date or time goes on my calendar, not just transaction management dates. Allocate specific hours for prospecting and marketing and put them on your appointment calendar; then adhere to them as if they are actual appointments. You can set your calendar to provide a reminder for each item's entry. The reminder pops up on your computer screen at the lead time you specify.

FYI!

In most calendar programs, you can ask to be reminded of appointments and tasks. These reminders have a pop-up window and can produce a sound to notify you. You can specify how much time you want the reminder to occur before the appointment or task start time. For example, you can receive a warning 30 minutes before the scheduled time that you are to meet with a client. PDAs also notify you, so if you're in the field you will be alerted if your PDA is on. These notifications have saved me from many embarrassing moments.

Keep Track of Your Tasks

It is also important to calendar items on your daily task list in your calendar. On my task list I include every single thing I need to do, and I mean *everything*. Your calendar program should have an area for tasks, which is separate from time-specific items on each calendar date. As you complete your tasks, cross them off; as more appear, immediately put them on the list.

Print Out Your Calendar the Day Before

Especially in the fast-paced real estate business, the only way you can have an organized, self-directed day is to begin with a clear desk and an organized agenda. Before you leave either your home office or away-from-home office for the day, clear off your desk entirely and print out your schedule for the next day. It should be the only thing sitting on your desk when you begin the day. I have one calendar at home, one at the office, and one in my car. It should be full if you follow the steps recommended in this book.

So many agents are running through their days instead of running their days. The real estate business is a flurry of activity. It is possible to just show up and be madly busy for an entire day. This is what many real estate agents do. They are frantic because they do not follow an agenda.

By printing out your schedule for the next day at the end of your workday, you have time to think about what your next day will be. Planning ahead like this allows you to subconsciously formulate plans for the next day's activities, and when the calendar dishes them out you are ready to respond with well-thought-out actions. By managing your time in this manner, you can run a highly efficient, seamless business that will not run you.

FYI!

Your transaction management program tracks your transactions and reminds you when a task is to be performed. When you need to know the calendar dates for a transaction, just enter the name of the client in the transaction search field and it automatically assembles all calendar and task entries in one convenient transaction profile. You also can search your regular calendar by client name and receive a list of all calendar dates related to that client. With my online transaction management program my clients and Power Team members can track the progress of transactions with me.

Organizing Your Computer Files

When you enter the high-tech world, you need a filing cabinet. Of course, it's on your computer. Although the other steps in this chapter are mandatory for the high achieving agent, this step is optional. Personally, I couldn't live without my computer filing cabinet, but I utilize computer technology more than most of my peers. For those of you who want to achieve a good measure of computerized file management, this section and the next are meant for you.

I open a new computer folder for each client and file everything relating to that client in this folder. This includes e-mail I send and receive, contracts, letters, and spreadsheets that relate to the client. The multiple listings I enter or retrieve for my clients go in their folder. Because I also scan hard copies of documents if they are not already on my computer, my client computer file includes the entire transaction.

Instead of dealing with paper throughout the transaction, which can be inconvenient and time-consuming, I make computer data my primary source of information and my traveling data center. I still have a paper file containing signed copies and originals of documents for each transaction, which is retained by my transaction coordinator. But the day-in and day-out activities of my business are conducted according to my handy easy-to-retrieve computer database. Once you make the transition away from paper, you will find that having everything literally at your fingertips makes organization something that just falls into place—all on your computer.

More recently, with the advent of online transaction management programs, my file storage has begun to take place online. I just upload documents created offline into my transaction management program and synchronize data between them.

Maintaining Your Paper Files

You still want to retain paper files for transactions for the following reasons:

◆ Your office will probably require it.

◆ Although backing up is reliable, there is still concern that both the storage files and the primary files may be susceptible to crash.

◆ Some transactions still require the use of originals when the parties do not stipulate the use of copies in lieu of originals.

◆ Many people still do not use computer technology to the extent recommended in this book. You will therefore continue to receive many documents in hard copy.

Agent to Agent

I include the following term in the offers I prepare: "The parties agree that signed documents transmitted by facsimile or PDF file constitute originals for all purposes in this transaction."

In most of my transactions, I have the parties stipulate that signed copies of documents transmitted by fax or PDF file have the same effect as originals, thereby avoiding the need for transmittal of originals, which can really slow things down. If you decide to use this stipulation in your transaction, make sure you clear procedure with your office manager in advance.

In both law and real estate, the use of originals is deeply ingrained. Some people of the old school refuse to adopt new ways of conducting business. In those transactions we still use originals and labor under the inconvenience of transmitting originals back and forth between the contracting parties. For these transactions, hard copy files rule.

Synchronizing and Backing Up Data

Daily, either at the office or home, you will need to synchronize your equipment and back up your data. With synchronization, entries made on one computer should appear on the other. The synchronization process is more sophisticated than uploading and downloading information because of its ability to determine what has been added most recently on either device and duplicate that information on the other, all in one easy step. If you have an assistant, you need to synchronize with him or her as well. You will also need to synchronize your PDA with the MLS to update any listings that have changed or been added since you last synchronized.

Utilize a docking station and software that synchronizes your laptop with your PDA and vice versa so both devices contain up-to-date information. For laptop to desktop, if you use both, a network cable achieves the same result. And backup of one fully synchronized computer is essential.

FYI!

Your PDA will not have the capacity to download all MLS listings, although it should easily hold thousands of them. Download only those that define a specific market. Storage of recently downloaded listings on your PDA is not as good as obtaining real-time information, but it is far better than having nothing at all when you are in the field and unable to obtain direct access to the MLS database.

Build these steps into your schedule on a daily basis. I perform these tasks at home at the end of each day. All I do is integrate my computers with their docking stations or networking cables and hit a few buttons to synchronize, download, and back up. As I wind down from the day, these functions occur on their own. As long as you've set these features up correctly, the process is simple and fully automated. If your system isn't seamless, hire a computer consultant to work out the quirks.

You also can have your main database online and synchronize your computers with it, instead of synchronizing with your offline server. More and more agents are moving to online database management, not just for contact management and transaction management, but for everything. If you're online out in the field, you can access your files directly instead of having to later synchronize. Virus protection and backing up also become easier when these duties are performed by your online storage provider. Simplifying technology is what it's all about, and online data management does just that.

Establishing Your Home Office

In all likelihood you will set up an office in your home. It all depends on your habits and the benefits your away-from-home office provides, but you may find that you spend more time working from your home than from your office. One of the main reasons for choosing real estate is the flexibility, and having a home office provides flexibility in spades. You have to be careful, though, as the homey home office can be a big threat to a solid work ethic and self-discipline. Distractions are everywhere.

> ### Cave!
> If you choose to work at home any quantity of time, treat it like an outside office. If you don't, your personal life will become your work life and everyone, including you, will resent it. The real estate business by its very nature is personal and social. As such, it is almost impossible to separate it from your family life unless you build in boundaries from day one. Begin with your home office. Make it as separate as possible from the rest of your home.

Build in specific times when you work. Treat your home office just as you would your away-from-home office. Set it up like an office and build in all the high-tech creature comforts to make it a true business operation. Have a station for your laptop. Get a color printer, scanner, copier, and fax, or an all-in-one device. Make it an efficient, professional place to work.

Be disciplined. When you walk from your home space to your business space, act as if you have driven to the office. Get dressed for the office and bring your office mind-set with you. Don't lollygag in your slippers and robe. If you do, you will make your home office a part of your family life, and you will not be able to separate the two. Your efficiency in both business and personal matters will become impaired because you will not be totally focused on either one.

Transforming Your Home Office

The home office challenge is high on the list of agent obstacles to productivity. It comes second to controlling your time. For this, you must master self-discipline. It is always the case in life that our biggest pleasures can become our biggest pains.

Early on in my split-office routine (some time was spent at home; some was spent at the office), I observed that I was a completely different worker at home. I was not as thorough, efficient, or intelligent as I was at the office. When I examined the cause, I realized that I had failed to bring the essential qualities to my home office that made my regular office so productive.

I allowed too much of a relaxed, comfy environment to permeate my home office. My home office was kind of an office and kind of a retreat. When I was in it, I was therefore kind of a worker and kind of not a worker. I came to name it limbo land before it received its transformation because it was in limbo. A lot of agents and other professionals who sometimes work at home suffer from limbo land syndrome.

In no time at all, limbo land was transformed into a comfortable, aesthetically pleasing, highly productive space through careful evaluation and implementation of a plan I call commercial transformation. Commercial transformation is a process that duplicates your away-from-home office in your home office with one little twist—it's in your home.

Commercial Transformation

The commercial transformation process is comprehensive. You want to duplicate both the physical and emotional characteristics that make you succeed at the office. At the same time, you want to retain the characteristics about being home that drew you to a profession that allowed you to work from home. It's a fine line, but the process of commercial transformation will help.

For my commercial transformation, the following sections show how my report card ended up.

FYI!

This is how it's done. Spend one day at your office doing all the things you do. Make a list of what is in your office that includes the following:

- The equipment you use.
- The furnishings and utilities you use.
- Placement and accessibility that make you productive.
- The successful mindsets you hold.

Home Office Equipment

Both my home printer and fax machine needed an upgrade. My phone did not have headset or speakerphone capacity, so I upgraded it. My computer monitor needed to be upgraded to a larger size with a more pleasing display. With these upgrades, my home office duplicated my away-from-home office equipment.

Agent to Agent

You can connect your laptop to a full-size monitor for easy viewing. I use a full-size monitor both at home and at the office. It saves me neck and eye strain. You can also use a mouse and full-size keyboard with your laptop to make it more ergonomically friendly.

Furnishings and Accessibility

As for furnishings, several changes were required. My desk required ergonomic fitting so the keyboard sat in my top drawer. I needed better accessibility to my files, so I had the built-ins rearranged. I made some accessibility changes by reorganizing my desk for easier access to everyday supplies. I actually duplicated the organization I use at the office.

Although I have always been organized at the office, I never really carried commercial organization to my home office. It made a huge difference in work efficiency. Then I relegated my personal home files to a separate area, making my office primarily my efficient home real estate office.

def•i•ni•tion

Feng shui means "wind and water" and is the ancient Chinese science of balancing the elements within the environment. I recommend reading *The Complete Idiot's Guide to Feng Shui* by Elizabeth Moran to learn more about this subject, which has become relevant to the real estate field.

Finally, I changed the whole *feng shui* arrangement of my office furniture. While I still have a clear view of the yard below, my office is more *inner* directed than *outer* directed. It points more toward productivity than gardening. I moved the dog bed farther away from my immediate desk area so access to equipment is easier and my desire to commune with my pup is more subdued. It is important to access your immediate space and reduce its distractions. I also placed the seating in my office in such a way that it does not invite family members to sit down and gab. Now it says, "This is an efficient real estate office. Stay out unless you are an animal or have real estate to sell."

A Successful Mindset

With these physical changes in place, it was much easier to adopt the mental mindset that takes place when I walk over the threshold to my regular office. I now produce as well at home as I do at my traditional office. I still allow my home office to give me great pleasure because I get to be with the dog and have a beautiful view of my yard, but these steps have transformed my home office into a productive environment. I have no more excuses for doing less than the highly competent job I do at the office.

The self-discipline required to make the home office as successful as your other office takes a commitment to exercise rigorous willpower, but the rewards of flexibility and freedom that mark your career will be well worth the work.

Setting Up a Vehicle Office

There are an increasing number of agents with handy offices set up in their vehicles prepared to print out offers, more property flyers, or anything they may need in the field. With SUVs leading the way as a vehicle of choice and portability built into technology, it is now possible to bring your office everywhere you go. Why not have the technology on board when your client decides she must make an offer? Take her up on it, prepare the paperwork, and print it out right on the spot. The high-tech solution is a marked improvement to preparing a written offer on the hood of your car as we did not so long ago.

I know agents whose luxurious leather interior SUVs make comfortable offices in the back seat. A handy tray folds down where they set their laptop, a portable printer prints out their contracts, and wireless Internet and e-mail allows them to send and receive e-mail and multiple listing information. They sit their clients in their luxurious portable offices and fold down the other handy tray for client signing. One I've seen even had a minirefrigerator, which you might think is going too far.

> **Agent to Agent**
>
> SUVs come with a full array of options for use and convenience. Some also have space and adjacency plans to suit high-tech motorists. If you plan to use your SUV as an office, look into manufacturer options before you have the outfitting performed.

For those of us who relish convenience and like to work, the vehicle office is the perfect solution to utter portability. In my case, I often work from my RV. I can sit in the middle of the woods or on the beach in my RV and conduct business or write books, as I am doing right now.

Working Anywhere in the Field

You can now do everything in the field that you can do in the office. Receipt of faxes used to be a problem but now that we have e-fax services (www.efax.com, for example), you can send and receive faxes through your computer.

For postal mail, we have priority service so even originals can find you as long as you know where you will be. We will know that we've made it to a whole new level of flexibility when the priority mail carriers contact us by e-mail to let us know they are close to shipping so we can redirect packages to the location we have arrived at. I wouldn't be surprised if this convenience isn't available in the very near future.

You may not choose to be as computer capable and portable as I am, but it's comforting to know that technology is there to assist you if you do choose to be a high-tech, portable, lean mean real estate machine.

The Least You Need to Know

- ◆ You can store documents in a computer folder devoted to a specific client, and you can retain a paper file for that client with your transaction coordinator.

- ◆ If you utilize the technology at your disposal, you can eliminate catch-up administrative tasks that need to be done daily.

- ◆ A good calendaring program helps you organize your day and track transaction deadlines, tasks, appointments, and time for prospecting.

- ◆ Various computer devices need to be synchronized with your online or offline server so they each contain the most current information.

- ◆ Your home office, your field locations, and your vehicle all can be set up for efficient office use.

Building a Referral Stream System

In This Chapter

- ◆ Building your referral stream database

- ◆ Learning the basics of database management

- ◆ Planning for use of a PDA

- ◆ Choosing your client gifts wisely

- ◆ Utilizing a newsletter

A pioneer in the field of real estate training, John Lumbleu, moved the Rolodex system to the next level by implementing a color-coded 3×5 index card system for setting up your farm area and keeping track of your buyers and sellers. His program, while antiquated by today's technology, for many agents, established a foundational contact information base with a viable, serviceable contact management system. This program has been used by thousands of agents in a time before computers, the Internet, and high tech as we know it today.

While the system worked well it was incumbent upon the sales associate to keep meticulous records and log by hand on each index card various bits and pieces of information. Unfortunately, on occasion the agent accidentally dumped the box of cards on the floor, effectively destroying the entire system. Other perils such as the spilled cup of coffee, a gust of wind, or misplacing/misfiling one of the contact cards would be catastrophic.

In those days we had an excuse for clutter. Now we don't. With the simplified database management systems we have at our fingertips, anyone can be organized. In fact, in the real estate business where the never-ending parade of names and details are the backbone of your business, a foolproof system is a must. The best way I know of is to utilize computer-based contact management and make it Internet-based. Regardless, many agents are still fighting computer technology.

This chapter shows you how to build your contacts database into a referral stream system that will turn your business into a circle of abundance. It's all based on three easy steps—setup, input, and processing. For every input, there is an output and from that output there is a return in the form of an ongoing stream of referrals.

Meeting People and Keeping Their Information

Real estate is a people business. It's just plain and simple. You need to know everyone's name and a little bit of information about them. The people (contacts) you will keep track of in your database consist of service providers (peers and Power Team members), new and old clients (as distinguished from prospects), and prospects (people you'd like to have as clients). In the referral stream system you are about to build, each contact receives one or more marketing products. Here's an example: my next-door neighbors are entered in my contacts database and categorized to receive a newsletter and a holiday greeting.

Agent to Agent

As a people business, real estate is also a gift-based and thanks-based business. Appreciation and celebration are as much a part of the business as commissions and properties. If you set up your business in an organized, computer-based fashion as described in this chapter, you will grow into a referral-based business in no time. Although people think it's who you know, the secret is really how organized you are about the people you get to know.

If you work forty hours a week in the manner described in this book, keep an organized, up-to-date contacts database, and follow the referral stream system to a T, you will never have to prospect after the first few years of your business. This is known as the referral stream system because that's exactly how it works. Contacts are entered in your system, they receive gifts and mailers from you, and they give you a steady stream of business. When you couple this with your automated online lead generating 24/7 campaigns (described in the Master Marketing Model in Chapter 13), you will have a system that feeds you all the business you need.

Keeping Organized and Caretaking

If you step into the mindset of good organization, described in the previous chapter, vigilant caretaking of your database becomes one of the primary steps to creating professional and financial abundance. It is important to remember, though, that your contacts database has to go everywhere with you. That's why a smaller, more portable device, like a PDA, is essential. Get used to having this device with you and use it.

The referral stream model is based on the premise that every qualified person you come in contact with becomes a relationship you will have for the next 20 years. As such, they end up in your database under easily searchable criteria and on a list to receive one thing or another from you for the rest of your career.

Sounds like a big commitment, doesn't it, treating everyone as if you will know them for the next two decades? Actually, it's the only way to build a business that *will* last for twenty years. With this enduring point of view, your business becomes a flourishing hub of activity because what you give out comes back to you many times over. And you will be giving out a lot, both in terms of service and appreciation. This model is a highly organized, efficient system that makes you unforgettable because you go out of your way for people and you appreciate them. The system is simple and doesn't take much time, and the reward is abundance for the rest of your career.

The plan is built in three easy steps:

1. Setup

2. Input

3. Processing

FYI!

I use Microsoft Outlook for contact management because it is packaged with my other office programs and it provides the basic level of contact database management I need.

FYI!

Although multilevel marketing has a bad reputation, it is an excellent business model. In a sense, this type of contact management is multilevel marketing, which occurs within your contacts database based on the categories you set up. Every input receives an automated mailer. You meet a qualified person. You input them and assign them a category. Each category receives an output. The more people you meet and input, the bigger your network becomes.

Step 1—Setup

The categories you will need to set up in your contacts program follow. Feel free to substitute categories:

- Snail mail newsletter

- E-mail newsletter

- Gift certificates for referrals

- Buyer gifts

- Seller gifts

- "Nice to have met you" cards for prospects (NTHMYs)

- Holiday cards

- Birthday greetings

You set these categories up in your contacts database. In Outlook, you click the Category button on the bottom of the general contact page. Other programs have a similar feature. Then, when you enter a contact, you select the output you want them to receive. It all happens on the contact entry page described in Step 2, the "Input" step.

Snail and E-Mail Newsletters

Why a newsletter? Always keep in mind that Market is your middle name. You become your best mover and shaker when you consistently let people know you are moving and shaking. Because you cannot be in front of your entire contacts database on a continual basis, your personalized newsletter is the next best choice.

My system has two categories for newsletters: those snail mailed and those e-mailed. Your newsletter will go to your current sphere of influence by e-mail when you have addresses and snail mail when you don't. Later, you also will include your farm and any other important contacts you do not have e-mail addresses for.

Your sphere of influence contacts will all eventually transition to the e-mail newsletter category as you ascertain e-mail addresses for them. This choice is up to you. I continue to retain sphere of influence contacts as snail mail recipients because I believe in the power of print media. Furthermore, surveys indicate that while snail mail has a tendency to go in the garbage, it is more likely than e-mail to meet your contact's eyes. If you can carve out the time to snail mail to your sphere and your farm, keep them on the snail mail list.

Newsletter Choices

Those of you who follow the Master Marketing Model will have newsletter capability bundled with your website and with your database management program. It's all done for you, all you have to do is choose the newsletter you like the most. If you don't want to adopt the entire Master Marketing Model, sign on for MarketReach (www.ihouseweb.com) or any other real estate database marketing service that includes monthly newsletters.

Agent to Agent

To find companies that prepare personalized real estate newsletters, do an Internet search for "real estate marketing newsletter vendors," or a variation of that. Better yet, send your clients a beautiful customized magazine (without advertising) with your compliments. Recently, I was able to break into a hard-to-get market with this type of high-end product. Go to www.hbdmagazine.com for a sample.

You also can check with your state's Association of Realtors to see if they have newsletters for member use. For instance, as a service to its members, the California Association of Realtors provides a newsletter which updates each month free of charge. You just download it from their web site, personalize it, and mail it out. Go to www.car.org and click on Home Owner's Guide, Free Marketing Tool. More and more, Realtor organizations and brokerage firms are providing either free or more affordable resources to agents. Before you scout newsletter vendors, check with your office and your local associations to see what they have available.

You can customize all of these prefabricated newsletters to a certain extent. In the olden days we used to spend quite a bit of time customizing our newsletters. We discovered our time was better spent servicing listings or networking.

Don't spend significant time customizing your newsletter. The intent here is not to become a publisher. It is to repeatedly place your name before your contacts in a way that associates your name with real estate.

Frequency of Newsletter Transmittal

Your e-mailed newsletter will be transmitted to recipients automatically on a *monthly* basis. All you do is preselect the newsletter you want to send, schedule your database management program to send this newsletter to your group of e-mail newsletter recipients, and on the date you have selected, presto, e-mailing is initiated by your program. All this while you sit on the beach in Hawaii.

Because snail mailing is time and cost intensive, your snail mail newsletters are only sent out *quarterly* instead of monthly.

Evaluate Snail Mail Newsletter Costs

When you add postage and a long mailing list, a snail mailed newsletter can get a bit pricey, especially when your mailers go out four times a year. Yet snail mailed newsletters are mandatory, not optional. The place to cut the budget is not with the newsletter itself; it is with your decision as to who to send the newsletter to.

When you add a contact to your snail mail newsletter category, evaluate whether the expense of mailing to them is warranted. In other words, qualify them as much as you can before you add them to your snail mail newsletter list. Before adding a contact to receive my snail mailed newsletter, I go through a mental checklist to qualify them. Is this person relatively close to hiring me as their agent or are they someone who is recreationally shopping around? If the contact passes my test, I input them to receive a snail mail newsletter; if not, I will place them on my e-mail newsletter list if I have their e-mail address.

For a nominal charge, mailing services have the ability to process your quarterly mailing for you. The cost of having them do all the prep work versus you taking time away from networking and servicing clients may make this a very cost-effective option.

Personalize Your Newsletters

A personalized cover letter or header on your newsletter should accompany your first snail mail newsletter to both your sphere of influence and your farm. This message should be something that associates you with them and makes them want to read your mailer to discover more about you. This way they will be on the lookout for future newsletters and begin associating you with real estate.

In this message you don't really want to emphasize that you are new to the business because people do not really want to hire someone inexperienced to help them buy or sell their most valuable asset. It is probably best just to let them know you want to include them on your newsletter list and ask them to contact you if they need real estate help or refer anyone who does. I use a handwriting type font for these letters and try to personally sign them. Here are sample messages for your consideration:

To Your Sphere of Influence

I hope all is well for you. I wanted to share my newsletter with you so you can be informed about your real estate decisions. Feel free to call or e-mail me if I can assist you or any of your friends or family with a real estate purchase or sale.

To Your Farm

I am your neighbor at 123 Main Street. I wanted to share my newsletter with you so you can be informed about your real estate decisions. Feel free to call or e-mail me if I can assist you or any of your friends or family with a real estate purchase or sale.

Gift Certificates for Referrals

Anyone who refers someone who becomes a client goes on the gift certificate list, which you print out and process monthly. A referral source is typically already in the contacts database, but if not, you should enter the contact.

I have an account with an Internet merchandiser and my gift certificates are all sent by my vendor. Just pick a product you like, set up an account with the vendor, and when it comes time to order a gift certificate, all you do is give the vendor your client's delivery information. I do it all by e-mail.

Buyer Gifts

My buyer gifts change as I hear of new improved choices. Currently, I use www. charpics.com to prepare a rendering of the house my clients purchased. I just e-mail a picture to this vendor; they create a rendering and send it to the buyer with thanks from me. This is one of my most popular buyer and seller gifts. The sellers like to have a classy memento of their old home, and the buyers enjoy having something more than a picture of their new home to show friends and family. A long time favorite buyer gift is still an engraved brass or chrome door plate which greets them every time they walk through the door of their new home. These gifts are a nice gesture as well as a constant reminder of you.

Seller Gifts

My current seller gift is the rendering of the house they just sold described above. It seems to receive more applause than my prior gift, which was a brass alarm clock engraved with their old address and the years of their ownership of the home we sold. I offer gift choices such as freshly made truffles, chocolate chip cookies, and a bottle of wine to some clients who buy and sell frequently. I send them a few website addresses, and they select their own gift.

FYI!

While using local vendors is important to support your community, so is convenience. If you cannot easily locate a local vendor, just go to the Internet and locate a vendor with a product you like. My company orders everything from the Internet and we have never, and I mean never, had a vendor not send a product.

Nice to Have Met You Cards (NTHMYs)

A NTHMY follow-up card or e-mail should be sent to all potential clients, whether you gave them a formal seller or buyer presentation (discussed in later chapters) or just discussed their real estate needs. People appreciate good manners. You want each prospect to receive your message right after you meet with them.

In my business, NTHMYs are not handled by category selection in the contacts database. You can handle them that way if you choose and for this reason they are included as a category. I like to process them immediately so I handle them on a priority basis. When I schedule an appointment with prospects, I immediately enter them on my calendar for the day after the appointment to send a card. I never leave it to memory. I have e-mail and regular mail NTHMYs. I grab the one that applies when my calendar sends my reminder, include a brief personal greeting, and it's done.

When I enter my NTHMY contact, sometimes I include them in the newsletter category and sometimes I don't. It all depends on how much I want a relationship with that prospect for the next twenty years. Always think in terms of longevity. That's what makes this model so successful. When a prospect turns into a buyer or seller, they are added to the appropriate buyer or seller gift category. If they were not already targeted for a newsletter, they are added to the list.

Holiday Cards

I only do one mailing of holiday cards each year, at Christmas time. Just about every buyer, seller, prospect, and regular business contact is on the list. A simple card to wish these people well will do. I generally go with a generic message like "Season's Greetings" or "Happy Holidays," as some people do not observe this occasion as Christmas.

Another way to address the holiday season and remain politically correct is to send a New Year's card! A New Year's card is not as emotionally charged as a religious themed holiday card. Plus, it gives you greater flexibility in terms of time. You can send it before the new year starts or even a few days after the start of the new year.

One agent I know personally forgot to send his holiday cards in a timely fashion. Although they were all addressed, sealed, and stamped he had forgotten to take them to the post office. Now he had 350 holiday cards sitting on his desk just as they had been for the past two weeks. He sheepishly put them into a bag and stuffed them into the closet hoping to remember to send the next year. In the middle of the summer, as he was cleaning out his closet he discovered the bag of holiday cards. His business was a bit slow so he considered the ramifications of sending out his cards right then and there in the middle of July. And he did.

He received numerous phone calls from his friends, clients, and past customers all of whom were delighted to have received his card, albeit a bit late. In fact, each and every one of the calls blamed the post office for the delay. The result was an instant boom to his business and renewed relationships with the people he so desperately needed to stay in touch with.

Birthday Greetings

Anyone whose birthday was filled out in the contacts detail page under "birthday" should receive an e-mailed birthday card on their birthday when they come up on the calendar. If there is no e-mail address, cards should be sent by mail. You don't even have to perform a category search to send your birthday cards because the contact management program automatically displays each birthday entered on your calendar for that date. My office has one standard birthday card that is used for a year, and then we switch to a new one for the next year.

Agent to Agent

Do a search on the Internet for birthday e-cards. Most can be sent free of charge. You may need a real card as well, for those people who do not have an e-mail address or those special people you want to greet more personally with postal delivery. In these high-tech times, people often feel more appreciated when you take the extra time to send a greeting through the mail.

Step 2—Input

Here's an example of how this works. At the Chamber of Commerce meeting, I met Bill, a mortgage broker. I had my PDA with me. I find that just the process of entering contact information can bring about lively conversation. I was impressed with Bill and how he conducted himself. We exchanged cards and I said, "Bill, I want to make sure I have your information in my database. Do you mind if I enter you right now and ask you a few more questions?" People love the opportunity to speak about themselves. They are also quite impressed with your level of organization and computer competence. It took me two minutes of fun conversation to enter the information I need for Bill into my PDA.

Real estate is a people business, and you don't want to detract from its social quality. In the beginning, entering data can be clumsy and impersonal. Hang in there; it's worth it. Because you are already a multitasking real estate professional, you'll soon be a pro at inputting information and making lively conversation at the same time.

The information I enter includes the following:

- Name
- Address
- Telephone

- ◆ Fax

- ◆ E-mail

- ◆ Profession

- ◆ Birthday

- ◆ Notes, such as "Chamber of Commerce, in business for 20 years"

- ◆ Categories, such as "newsletter" or "holiday card"

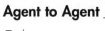

Agent to Agent

To locate a contact in a certain profession, in Microsoft Outlook, go to Tools, Advanced Find, Advanced, Field, Personal Fields, Profession. Other contact programs have similar search capabilities.

Simple. I made nine brief entries in the fields described in this list. In Outlook, these entries appear on the general and detail pages for a contact. Because I spent two minutes entering Bill's information, he will automatically come up on my newsletter mailing list and my holiday card list. He also will appear on my calendar on his birthday so we can send him a birthday card. Additionally, I will be able to send him an e-mail or fax by just clicking a button.

I will be able to access him for mortgage information and to send him clients without even recalling his name. Because I entered his profession as mortgage broker, he comes up under an advanced search for "mortgage broker" under the field "profession" along with all the mortgage brokers in my database.

When Bill called me a few months later, I didn't remember him. I could, however, search for his name (which took just a few seconds), and I could instantly see how I came into contact with him and all the important information about him. Quick and easy retrieval of information is invaluable, especially when your contacts database is brimming. On this call from Bill, he mentioned his wife by name, and so I added his wife's name to his contact information.

People love to be remembered and appreciated, especially in a service-oriented industry like real estate. Bill will be part of my business for all the years to come because I took a few minutes to record his information in my database and knew how to easily access it when he later called. My contact entry and recall system made him feel important and in turn he has made me important. Since our initial meeting not two years ago, Bill has referred six people who became clients.

If you cannot bring yourself to engage in database entry at these events, don't give up. You can follow these same steps writing on your contact's business card, but you must religiously input the contact when you next reach your computer. To save entry time, there is scanning software (www.cardscan.com) that will transfer business cards into easily manageable computer data.

Step 3—Processing

Step 3, processing, is the final step before the referral stream begins to take hold. The gift department processes gifts monthly while the snail mail department performs its processing at varying intervals. The processing department at my office is my assistant who looks a lot like Mrs. Santa on processing day.

The Gift Department

The gift department in my office processes the following gifts monthly:

◆ Gift certificates for referrals

◆ Buyer gifts

◆ Seller gifts

Agent to Agent

The Internet vendor will send either an e-mail gift certificate or a paper gift certificate. They handle the mailing. All I need to do is select from e-mail delivery or regular mail delivery, and supply the recipient address. Oh yes, I forgot: I also have to pay for this certificate. I, of course, use the business credit card because this is a deductible expense.

The gift department does everything by e-mail. Because gifting in these categories occurs monthly, I just use the fourth Friday of every month for gift certificates, buyer gifts, and seller gifts categories. On that day, I click a button and receive contact information for anyone coming under those categories, with each category run separately.

For gift certificates, I go directly to the Internet vendor I have selected for gift certificates and enter the recipient name and address. It takes a minute per person.

For buyer and seller gifts, I e-mail a list of those contacts to our respective vendors who include a nice thank-you card from us with their deliveries.

The Snail Mail Department

Now to the snail mail department. This department handles the following categories at the intervals specified:

◆ Snail mail newsletters

◆ NTHMY cards

- ◆ Holiday cards

- ◆ Birthday cards if recipients are not regular e-mail users

Your snail mail list is produced by calling up all contacts that come under the specified category. Your snail mail newsletters are mailed quarterly. If you follow the Master Marketing Model you just have color prints made of the newsletter you choose from your website or contacts database program. If you are signed up with a real estate newsletter publisher, every quarter you receive your shipment. These arrive automatically after you're on their quarterly list. Most of these companies will also mail the newsletters for you.

> **FYI!**
>
> If you send a personalized newsletter, consider having the publisher do your mailing. All you need to do is e-mail your contact list to the publisher. If you do the mailing in house, it is fairly easy to print out labels for all contacts within a specific category. The labels get slapped on, postage or bulk mail is applied, and that's it. You can easily and quickly head up the mailing department in your early days and sit around for a few hours with your family enjoying a little time together growing your business.

In my company, for holiday cards we use a service or my assistant does them. We calendar a month and a half ahead of time for ordering the cards. NTHMYs and birthday cards are sent by snail mail or e-mail on the day they come up on the calendar.

Reviewing the Referral Stream

The example above of Bill, the mortgage broker, illustrates how you should enter a contact into your database. So far you haven't seen the stream of referrals resulting from the referral stream system. Here is an example of a seller. Carol and James sold their vacation home with my help. After they received their seller gift from us, they continued to appear on the holiday card and newsletter list.

Carol and James referred eleven people over the next seven years, three of whom ended up as buyers and two as sellers. Three of the other referrals did not become clients, but they referred clients which resulted in two more purchases. The remaining three have not culminated in any business or prospects. One of these three is still on our quarterly mailer list.

Agent to Agent _____

We also added Carol and James to the gift certificate category when a client was referred by them. By showing our appreciation, they will continue to remember us whenever any-one mentions real estate.

Cave! _____

If you share your commis-sion with an office, your commissions will naturally be reduced accordingly.

The three buyers Carol and James referred have resulted in fourteen referrals, which have resulted in five sales. One was a repeat sale. The two sellers they referred resulted in two purchases, because they both purchased when they sold, and seven referrals which have resulted in two sales. You can see the result of doing a good job for Carol and James and keeping in touch with them via the referral stream system. Just considering these three levels of connections brought in thirteen purchases or sales, which at an average 3 percent commission for properties worth $250,000, resulted in commissions of $97,500.

Was it worth spending the time to run the referral stream system to send gifts, holiday cards, gift certifi-cates, and quarterly newsletters to Carol and James and the same to the other twelve clients to earn $97,500? I would estimate that to earn this referral income stream of $97,500, the time spent inputting contacts or automating my system was three hours and the cost of gifts and mailers was about $2,200. Of course, that doesn't include the time it took to service listings and find buyer homes, but it shows that the referral stream system is well worth the time and money.

Examining the Philosophy

When you do a good job for people, they remember you, but only for a little while. When you do a good job for people and give them a gift, they remember you a little longer. When you do a good job for them, give them a gift, and continually stay in touch, they remember you forever. That's the philosophy of the referral stream sys-tem. And it works.

The system is based on principles of psychology and sociology. You show people your competence, and they remember you in the competence sector of their brains. You give them a gift and let them know you appreciate them, and you are also remembered in the nice person sector. When you continually remind them of you, you reactivate the places in which your memory is stored. With Carol and James, I was in two areas, which were activated five times a year with my quarterly mailer and our Christmas cards, not including gift certificates they received. I was therefore on their minds whenever they thought about real estate.

Tips on Making the System Work

Don't be cheap with your gifts. Remember, you will know these people for at least twenty more years. You are an important part of their lives when you assist them with their transactions, and they contribute to your financial abundance through the commissions they pay you.

Choosing recipients wisely is another important step. Make sure the people you add to your referral stream system are qualified. Establish a definition of your own as to who is qualified. Buyer, seller, and prospect checklists for qualification are presented in later chapters. Good common sense and the ability to recognize the difference between qualified people and nonqualified ones is essential to making your model work well. If you aren't discerning, you could end up spending too much time inputting contacts or too much money on gifts or mailings. If you follow the suggested criteria, your database contacts will all be qualified and your time and money will be justified because the result will be an enviable referral stream.

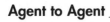

Agent to Agent

This efficient plan won't work if the gift department spends too much time shopping, shipping, or shuttling. That means choosing your products well and setting them up for automatic delivery. You need to work with reliable and efficient vendors who can receive your orders by e-mail and deliver those orders to your clients. In this way, your vendors become your shipping department. Otherwise, your new job will be managing the processing department. With a full client base, processing at my office takes no more than two hours a month. We have more important things to do than process gifts and mailers.

A final note is, why spend your time cold-calling people you've never had contact with, which no one enjoys? Why not spend it setting up a good marketing system and working the system? You still need to get out there, greet your market, and put contacts into your system. But after you've got them in the system, you can keep them if you stay on top of your system. I guarantee it.

The Least You Need to Know

◆ The referral stream system is built on the premise that for every input there is an automated output.

◆ If you choose your gifts and mailers carefully, your recipients will appreciate your taste and generosity and will remember you.

◆ The referral stream system must be vigilantly followed both in terms of input of contacts and processing of gifts and mailers.

◆ The success of the referral stream system lies in its ability to get your name and your goodwill to recipients on a regular basis over the long term.

◆ Consider use of a mailing service for your newsletters and holiday cards.

The New Ideal

In This Chapter

- The New Ideal in representing your clients
- Sales pitches are a thing of the past
- Understanding your fiduciary duty to your client
- Your client's endless decisions
- Extending The New Ideal to your peers

In other real estate sales books, this would be the chapter on sales. In this book, it's on dealing with your client and peers in a more authentic, professional manner. It presents *The New Ideal* for the services agents render their clients and the way agents treat their clients and one another.

During the last two decades, the hard sell was the standard for real estate and how real estate agents represented their clients. As a result, the real estate sales profession entered this new century with a reputation that requires serious bolstering.

The New Ideal presented in this book is about bringing the real estate profession up a level so that we are treated as the professionals we deserve to be and our clients receive the quality service they always deserved.

The Times They Are A-Changin'

Times have changed, but some agents often use the same old high-pressure sales techniques advocated by sales trainers. The style of agents who fancy-talk their clients with sales scripts and other trickster routines is outdated and certainly not in pace with our sophisticated and savvy modern-day real estate clients. Nor does it fulfill the agency obligations agents have to clients.

Real estate buyers and sellers no longer want to be assaulted by sales gimmicks of yesteryear. They ask their real estate legal representatives to pressure them less and treat them more like respected clients in need of reliable guidance. They want to be treated intelligently and honestly, not as though they can be tricked. Sincere and willing agents want to be thought of as more professional. However, we have not yet bridged the gap between pushy salesperson and professional representative.

Agent to Agent

The National Association of Realtors reports that only 40 percent of sellers used the agent who assisted them with the sale of their previous home for their most recent purchase. This statistic alone shows that real estate consumers are dissatisfied with the representation they currently receive.

The problem isn't only client dissatisfaction. Legal issues exist. The use of sales techniques practiced on clients does not legally satisfy your fiduciary duty to a client. The law gives one important legal directive to agents while outdated sales training techniques give another. They are in conflict.

If you follow The New Ideal set in this book and put the interests of your clients ahead of your financial success, you will find legal, moral, and financial satisfaction in abundance. You will be rewarded with commissions, referrals, and your clients' high regard. In addition, your clients will receive the fiduciary representation the law always said they should have.

Performing Your Fiduciary Duty

A fiduciary duty is the legal duty an agent owes his or her client in a real estate transaction. Exactly what is this important relationship that all real estate agents should aspire to maintain with clients? A fiduciary acts on behalf of his client with the utmost of care, integrity, honesty, confidentiality, and loyalty. Your mission is to take all steps with your client's best interest in mind. You are your client's trusted advocate.

This is the highest duty the law imposes. The fiduciary relationship is therefore the most important legal relationship any two people can have. It is a relationship built on the highest trust where the agent is designated the legal caretaker of his client. It is actually more consequential than marriage because the fiduciary relationship legally requires one to act in the other's best interest; in marriage, the obligation is mostly moral. Even the lawyer-client relationship does not meet the very high standards legally imposed on real estate agents.

Recognizing the Sales Scripts

Some sales trainers compare the real estate agent-client relationship to hunting. The correlation goes like this:

> When you go hunting, when would you load your gun—when you see the rabbit or before you start walking? If you wait until the rabbit appears, by the time you get your gun loaded, it's certain to have scampered off.

You are instructed to treat your client as the rabbit you are stalking, to hold your unsuspecting rabbit in your focus, and continually berate him or her with sales scripts. The purpose isn't really to kill the client; it's to push him or her to your only objective: closing on a deal.

Motivational sales trainers describe clients as "sitting on the fence" when they are faced with concern and indecision. They tell you this is the time to hit 'em with a script. Pressure does it. Get 'em while they're down.

FYI!
If your client isn't ready to sign a listing, sales trainers instruct you to hit her with the following:
Are you sure you can afford to wait? You never know when the market is going to begin its downward spiral. I have seen too many clients wait just long enough to miss a good market and have to sell at a much lower price.
If the client isn't sure whether to make an offer, trainers use fear again:
This property has attracted a lot of interest since it hit the market. I hate to see you lose it. Nice properties like this don't come along very often. In fact, when I spoke with the listing agent this morning, I think she mentioned something about expecting an offer later today.
This canned script has nothing to do with the property. It is quite effective, though, in getting client buyers to sign on the dotted line.

There are hundreds of sales scripts for every occasion. Some are tailored to be delivered in particular rooms of a house. Some work in any room. One is the very sad story of your last client who waited and lost the home they loved. They never bought another. There wasn't another one like the one they lost. The well-trained agent is able to deliver these lies with sincerity and emotion, thereby instigating the emotion of concern in the wavering buyer.

Agents are often instructed to hide blank offers in a notepad they carry around so they can pull one out just as they are ready to strike their unsuspecting buyer client with the closing script. There isn't time to open your briefcase and take an offer out. You've got to strike quickly.

Some trainers teach you that you must drive your buyer clients to properties. One reason is to maintain control. The other is to condition them by the careful delivery of sales scripts while you have them in your car. There are scripts about getting them in your car so you can feed them these scripts. For the challenging situation when there are too many buyers to get in your car, the answer is to scoop up the children and take them in your car. This ploy is called "kidnapping the kids." The parents are guaranteed to show up when you have their children, and you can work on the impressionable kids in your car.

> **Cave!**
> Stay away from sales gimmicks. If you were trained with them, think before you speak. If it's a sales script, replace it with a genuine desire to facilitate what your client needs and wants.

The sales script is aimed at one thing and one thing only: inducing pressure and fear in clients. These scripts are professionally designed to work these two human emotions to motivate the unsuspecting client. And they do work. They cause buyers to buy when they should pause and evaluate. They cause sellers to sell when another course of action might serve them better. The result is the demoralization of a profession that should be revered as one that discharges the highest legal and ethical obligation to its clientele.

Participating in the Transformation

The rabbit-hunting analogy and the kidnap-the-kids routine blatantly depict the grave need for a transformation of the real estate sales profession. The sales script may have had its place years ago when the modern real estate agent industry was still in its infancy. Now that real estate has matured into a multibillion dollar industry and a most popular investment choice, the time has come to overhaul the foundation of the agent-client relationship.

You've come to a profession that is held in low esteem. On the ladder of disrespect, real estate agents come just above used-car salesmen. You therefore have an image problem to overcome, and The New Ideal is your tool. The first step is to look more closely at the fiduciary relationship you establish with your client and the legal obligation it imposes.

When does the fiduciary relationship begin and end? It begins the first moment you have contact with the person who becomes your client and continues all the way through the last step you take on behalf of your client. The person to whom you are pitching sales gimmicks in your listing presentation is the person with whom you are forming a fiduciary relationship. How can you, in good and legal conscience, serve this potential client with anything less than bona fide goodwill and good real estate practice? We look at how in the following sections.

Dropping the Hard Sell

Real estate does not require the hard sell. Nor do your services. However, you are often told that you must master your sales skills and apply them expertly for anyone to hire your services. I disagree. I believe that you have a professional service to render but no product to hard-sell.

Real estate trainers often analogize real estate sales with sales of other products, such as computers, cars, and cellular phones. They talk apples and oranges. In product sales you need to talk up your product in comparison to another product. Product sales are competition driven, for instance, comparing an IBM to a Dell computer. You answer the question of why your product is better than theirs. In product sales you must be one up on your competition and a salesperson in every sense of the word.

> **FYI!**
>
> You don't hear doctors or other professionals walking around saying they want to sell their services. "Hey, fella, how about a nice kidney transplant?" Doctors, accountants, and other professionals are facilitators of services. Real estate agents, too, are facilitators of purchases and sales of real estate. Why, then, are real estate agents pushed to become master salespeople?

But real estate sales are different. You are not direct-selling a product. You work with listings on a centralized database through which real estate sells itself with your skilled representation. You offer your professional representation to a client who has real estate to buy or sell. The way to do this isn't with sales pitches; it is through the delivery of quality professional services.

Demand for Agent Services

The statistics on real estate appreciation are compelling, and become even more so when tax benefits are considered. Over the past two decades real estate has become the top investment choice for a growing segment of society. Everybody needs a home, many people need real estate investments, and others need real estate for their businesses. Real estate is in high demand, especially because the stock market has proven unpredictable. There is more need for an agent's services than ever before due to the increased demand for real estate.

The ever-increasing complexity of the real estate transaction also means increased need for agent services. The routine purchase and sales transaction has transformed into a complex, multistage operation. Property disclosures become more complicated every year, as do the number of details and players involved in a real estate transaction.

In a single transaction, an agent may deal with as many as 35 people. Agents work with people and computers; they complete contract documents, coordinate professionals, and review complex disclosures and reports; and they use psychology, analysis, and other people skills. Agents deal with valuable and coveted assets, sometimes in the million dollar range. In addition, agents must navigate their clients through all these transactions during high times of stress and in very brief timeframes.

Given the breadth and depth of what agents handle, it doesn't make sense to perceive them as salespeople. The real job is for agents to adopt a new mindset. We must provide quality, professional services to our clients, not to get their listings or sign on their purchases, but because we are their fiduciary representatives. If you make your client's interest more important than your own, you will attract and keep far more clients than the master salesperson. You also will be meeting your legal obligation.

Appreciating the Client's Decisions

Clients are making the biggest decisions of their lives and may be making the largest financial investment they have ever handled. That alone makes clients vulnerable to the most nerve-racking reasons for indecision. Equally as mind-boggling is the fact that the home purchaser is trying to satisfy the personal and emotional needs of his entire family. Home buyers must evaluate their most basic human needs affecting how they live and where they live. The investment property buyer is investing money into what she hopes is a valuable investment for her and her family.

These days there is also another layer of analysis a buyer must make. How will they hold title? Should they have a living trust, and what about a *family limited partnership*? With an investment property, should they utilize *asset protection* and form a *limited-liability company* to hold title?

def•i•ni•tion

A **family-limited partnership** is a specially designed limited partnership consisting of one or more general partners and one or more limited partners, which can provide asset protection from personal liability and discount valuation for estate tax purposes.

Asset protection refers to the sheltering of assets from excessive taxation and lawsuit-taking by the use of irrevocable living trusts, family limited partnerships, house trusts, and limited liability companies, to name a few.

A **limited-liability company** affords its members limited liability similar to shareholders of a corporation and pass-through taxation similar to a sole-proprietorship or partnership. It can provide asset protection and discount valuation for estate tax purposes.

The following is a partial list of decisions clients face when purchasing a home or an investment property:

Decisions About a Home Purchase

- Is this the right home for our family?

- Can we afford this home? What are our financing options?

- Will this home be easy to sell when we are ready to sell?

- Is this the best home for the price?

- Will the commute to and from work be difficult?

- Are there good schools and other children in the neighborhood?

- Is the structure of this home sound? Are there any repairs we will need to make?

- Is there room for a garden? What is the weather like?

- Is it in an earthquake or flood zone? Will I be able to get enough insurance?

- What will the expenses be for utilities and repairs?

- Have we been careful enough with the inspections? Are there any hidden problems?

- Are DSL, cable, and satellite available here?

- Where are the property boundaries? Are there easements affecting this home?

- Is there development nearby that will threaten our privacy and property values?

- Is this a safe neighborhood?

- How should the title be stated?

Decisions About an Investment Property Purchase

- Will its income justify its expense?

- What are its tax deductions?

- Will *depreciation* represent a good deduction for my portfolio?

- Can I take any *passive losses*?

- Can I *exchange* tax free into this property? Can I exchange out of this property?

- What is my tax basis if I exchange into this property?

- Would I be better off just putting my hard-earned money in the stock market?

- What is the rental market for this property?

- What are the terms of the existing leases on this property?

- Can I increase the rent for the existing tenants?

- Can I occupy any of the property?

- Would I be better off creating a limited liability company and taking title in its name?

- Will insurance cover me in the event of a lawsuit?

def•i•ni•tion

Depreciation is the allocation of the cost of an improvement over the life of the asset in the form of a tax deduction.

Passive loss is a loss in excess of income on a rental property.

Exchange is trading a business or investment property or properties for others to avoid taxation of profits.

As the purchaser's agent, you will often be involved in your client's deliberations when considering these vital issues. As their advocate, always be aware of the consequences of the decisions that face them. It is only through this awareness that you can best discharge your obligation to support their best interest in the transaction.

Supporting Clients

You will find yourself involved in client deliberations or decision-making. In the course of transactions, some clients attempt to second-guess themselves and try to undo what they have done. I am never surprised when clients turn around and head in the other direction. As their advocate, you want to take away the stress and give your clients the space and support they need to make well-informed decisions. The very last thing they need is their trusted agent feeding them scripts intended to move them to buy or sell irrespective of their needs.

FYI!
If your clients lean in favor of terminating a transaction, suggest they see an attorney. Do not try to strong-arm clients with threats of a potential lawsuit from the other party or that they are breaking the contract. Some agents even go so far as to tell their clients that they have earned their commission and they intend to enforce their commission rights against them. Don't turn your back on your clients, especially in a time of high stress when your clients need your support the most. There are legal rights, and then there is personal integrity and fiduciary responsibility.

Replacing the Scripts

When you're having an interaction with a client or potential client and you don't know what to say, just be honest and put their interest first. Your client interactions are just that—conversations between two people, one of whom has a fiduciary relationship with another. If you don't know an answer, say you don't know. If you do know an answer and your interest conflicts with theirs, choose your client's interest.

Here are some typical client questions followed by a typical sales-trainer script and what the agent following The New Ideal might say. It is quite telling to compare the difference in flavor between the scripted response and The New Ideal response:

Question 1: "Won't you reduce your commission?"

Script: "Which services do you want me to cut, marketing or listing?"

The New Ideal response: "This is what we charge to give you the very best service. If we charged less, we would have to give you less. We don't do that."

Question 2: "Another agent said he would list my property at a higher price."

Script: "The truth is that many agents will tell you anything, especially a listing price not justified by the market, to get you to sign on with them."

The New Ideal response: "The listing price I suggest is based on a detailed and careful analysis of the market based on the comparables I shared with you. A higher price is not supported. I feel it would be a disservice to you to list the property at a higher price."

Question 3: "We would like a shorter listing term."

Script: "It takes a good six months to sell a home. If we don't give this six months, I can't do a good job for you."

> **Agent to Agent**
>
> When you are responding to a client question, try to keep in mind the principle of "Do unto others as you would have them do unto you."

The New Ideal response: "Whatever term makes you most comfortable is fine with me as long as we start with an initial term that gives me a good chance to fully market your property. We can always extend after that if it doesn't sell and you are happy with my services."

Question 4: "We want to think it over."

Script: "Are you sure you can afford to wait? You never know when the market will go south. The market is good now. That's all we know."

The New Ideal response: "Sure. Take your time. Your choice of agent to sell your valuable asset is very important. I don't plan to be away so contact me when you're ready, and I will stay in touch. In the interim, review my package and give me a call if I can answer any questions for you."

Question 5: "We are thinking about renting our property out instead of selling it."

Script: "Recently I spent time with an agent who rented his home in this area. … [long story] … so instead of receiving rent, he had to hire an attorney, file a lawsuit, and refurbish the property. It all cost him $12,000 in addition to the rent he lost." (This is not a true story, but it is the script you are urged to give.)

The New Ideal response: "Our database also includes rental prices. I can provide you with some rental figures for the area if you like so you can further analyze this option. It's all up to you. Whatever you want is right for me."

Relating to the Competition

The problem hasn't just been the relationships between agents and clients. We need to transform the way we treat our fellow agents as well. As we change our client relationship from salesperson to facilitator, we also must change the competitive way we treat our peers. Competitiveness is part of sales mentality. It is not a part of *professionalism* and high integrity.

Competition consciousness goes hand in hand with high-pressure sales. It takes fear of others pulling ahead of you to fuel your motivation. The result is the real estate field becomes a back-biting, dog-eat-dog industry full of agents willing to do just about anything to get business. This attitude does not speak highly of the profession, and it takes its toll on the relationship between agents. The New Ideal, therefore, also extends to upgrading the way we treat our fellow agents.

def•i•ni•tion

There are two definitions of a **professional**: (a) one who is worthy of high standards; (b) one who practices a profession for his or her livelihood. The real estate agent with The New Ideal fits both definitions.

Here are some examples of how the New Ideal agent and the competition-driven old ideal agent relate to their peers:

Agent 1: "I just can't seem to get this listing I'm after."

New Ideal Agent: "Why not show them how staging can increase their home's market appeal and offer them free staging services. I have a video to show them I can lend you."

Old Ideal Agent: "What was that person's name and number?" (So I can get their listing myself.)

Agent 2: "I've got an emergency and need someone to baby-sit one of my listings".

New Ideal Agent: : "Let me do it for you."

Old Ideal Agent: "What portion of the commission will you give me if I do?"

Agent 3: "I have a prospect who wants to list with me but requires a lower commission than my office will allow."

New Ideal Agent: "Do you want me to take the listing and give you a referral fee?"

Old Ideal Agent: "What was your prospect's name and number? (So I can get their listing myself.)

Predicting the Result

If you follow the steps in this book, you have chosen real estate sales as your profession because you are willing to discharge your legal obligation to clients in a professional way. You are genuinely interested in helping people find their next home, office, or investment property that will serve them through the upcoming years. There's really no good reason why you should strong arm someone into hiring you. You're good at what you do. You enjoy doing what you're doing. People need your service.

Find your clients through successful marketing described in the chapters on marketing. Genuinely and intelligently offer them your professional services to represent them in their purchase or sale. Let them know you are not part of the old soft shuffle. Define the fiduciary obligation you have to them and commit to your willingness to fulfill it.

Realize that real estate is in high demand, as are your services. Discard salesmanship and competitive attitudes as you embrace The New Ideal. The natural result of practicing this type of high-integrity professionalism is that you will gain market share and you will feel a pride that will permeate your professional life. Hopefully, someday soon sales mentality will be a thing of the past in real estate sales. You will be on the cutting edge and clients will naturally gravitate your way because you are part of The New Ideal. High integrity and competence draw people like a magnet. They are an unbeatable combination.

The Least You Need to Know

- The hard-sell tactic puts you in the same category as the slick, used-car salesman.

- The law has decreed that you have a powerful fiduciary relationship with your clients.

- Buying and selling properties are complex transactions and require that the client make many difficult, important decisions.

- Acting with high integrity and putting the client's interest first results in a good conscience, an excellent reputation, and a stream of referrals.

- Treating your fellow peers with respect instead of competitive disregard will improve your relationship with peers and clients alike.

Chapter 17

A Winning Listing Presentation

In This Chapter

- ◆ Qualifying potential sellers
- ◆ Putting your listing package together
- ◆ Making the listing presentation
- ◆ Conducting the comparative market analysis
- ◆ Using the listing agreement and sample net sheet

This chapter is about qualifying your seller prospect and making your listing presentation. Qualifying the seller is essential to cutting down on the time you spend with a seller prospect. After you qualify your seller, prepare your listing package, make your presentation, and have the seller sign a listing agreement.

The components of your listing package are of vital importance because they set the stage for your listing presentation. This chapter describes each document that should be included in your listing package and exactly how you should present the listing package. The next chapter is on representing the seller after you receive the listing. Chapter 19 covers representing the buyer, and Chapter 20 addresses what to do when you are asked to represent both the buyer and the seller.

Qualifying Sellers

Time is a most precious commodity. If you don't have a clear plan in mind in the real estate field, you can easily end up spending too much of your time with potential clients who are not ready to buy or sell. You want to help them, and you understand that it takes time to prepare to buy or sell. However, your income depends on commissions.

Client inquisition is my terminology for the process of a potential client taking up far too much of my time just learning about real estate. The only way you can control your time is by setting boundaries. To do this, you must qualify your potential clients early on. If they don't qualify, you can certainly assist them, but at least you will know where they stand so you can gauge your time accordingly.

Let's walk through the steps of the important qualification process. Assume that through successful application of your marketing skills and your referral stream system, you are in communication with a seller prospect. Now what do you do? If your prospects are not in a seller state of mind, it will not behoove you to dedicate large quantities of time and energy to them. There is no such thing as a perfect client, but you can come close to finding one by qualifying your potential sellers. If they qualify, you give them the full-blown listing presentation. If not, put them on your list of prospects to receive newsletters.

Here is a list of questions to ask of your seller prospect. These questions will serve both to qualify a seller and to get helpful information for preparation of your listing package:

1. When do you plan to move?

2. How soon do you want to list your property for sale?

3. After you list it for sale, how long do you anticipate it will take to close on a sale?

4. How much do you think your property is worth?

5. How did you arrive at this value?

6. If this is a home you intend to replace, have you begun to look at other homes? Have you found any you are interested in? What is the price range of your replacement home?

7. If the property in question is not your primary home, do you intend to buy another property?

8. How far are you in the agent-interviewing process?

9. What is the most important factor you will consider in choosing to list your property with one agent over another?

10. (Include this question if you feel the prospect is qualified.) Can you give me the amount you owe on the property so I may prepare some figures for you as part of my listing presentation?

11. (If warranted) When can I come by to see your property and give you a brief listing presentation?

12. (If warranted) May I bring my professional stager with me? She is a wiz at deciding what steps, if any, should be taken to get the top price for your property. (Professional staging is covered in Chapter 23.)

> **Agent to Agent**
>
> Qualifying your clients is probably one of the most important time-saving steps you can take. After you have done this about 15 times, the process will come naturally to you. In the beginning, a checklist approach helps.

> **FYI!**
>
> The National Association of Realtors reports that sellers of homes typically interviewed just one agent before selecting the agent who ultimately sold their home.

If your potential seller is ready to list the property within the next 60 days or so, you will know it from the answers you obtain through this qualification process. If the seller is ready, you can take the next step, which is preparing your listing package.

Listing Presentations

The sales trainers make a listing presentation sound like you're auditioning for a part in a Hollywood movie. They suggest you spend two hours selling your potential client on yourself. The big to-do is all very contrived, dramatic, and unprofessional. They give you yet another inventory of fancy scripts to spew forth in order to bring the big one in for a close.

Let's put away the script and begin anew in an entirely different way. Remember, it is a fiduciary relationship of the utmost trust and confidence we are building here, not selling a horse. The listing package you prepare will form the basis of your presentation, so let's take a look at what that package should consist of.

But first, let me suggest that you bring your professional stager along to your listing presentation when warranted. Your stager should be prepared to conduct an onsite analysis of the property and recommend prelisting steps that will enhance the marketability of the property. I find that clients are quite impressed when a stager is brought to the listing presentation. You will have to make the judgment call for the area in which you practice and the property to be listed.

Your Listing Package

In real estate, looks are important. When preparing your listing package, make it look good. Use nice paper and a good color printer. The seller will assess your marketing abilities by the presentation of the documents in your listing package. Make the very most of this opportunity.

Every listing presentation is worth giving your all with intelligent, well-delivered information and an earnest desire to help. The listing package you prepare will serve as your calling card. The seller will review it many times over. It will be compared with other listing packages. If it is good, you may be assured it will receive the review of many eyes.

We also provide a listing DVD to our clients. It is not tailored to their particular property, but it gives them something visual to sit back and watch and once again emphasizes what you will do for them. Some offices have these on hand for agent use. If yours does, you may still want to consider having one personalized with you as the presenter.

I suggest your presentation package consist of the following, either bound or neatly organized in a professional preprinted folder and in the following order:

> **FYI!**
>
> In my area of the country where prices are off the charts, high-end offices put together 35-page, full-color, glossy, bound listing packages. They are no less than works of fine art and literature. Very impressive.

- Current market trends page and marketing plan

- Your office and personal bio and mission statement

- Your most recent newsletter

- Comparative market analysis in full color

- Sample net sheet

- A sample transaction if you use a transaction management program

- Your agency disclosure form and a sample listing agreement

Your listing package will make your listing presentation simple because it will be your guide to exactly what you cover during the presentation. Have a copy for yourself and one for your client so you can review these documents together. If your stager has analyzed the property in advance of your presentation, include your stager's recommendations and cost estimate. Your listing presentation should be no longer than one half to three quarters of an hour. Bring your laptop computer so you can show your prospect exactly how a new listing appears on the MLS.

Provide a Current Market Trends Page and Marketing Plan

Include a page on current market trends. This should be colorful and include graphs showing statistics that will be important to this seller. Don't just pull these figures. Explain them to your prospective sellers.

In your marketing plan, tell the seller exactly how you intend to undertake the job at hand. Describe the *broker's open house*, the frequency at which you will hold *open houses*, newspaper advertising and frequency, lock box use, and other marketing methods you will use. Detail the features of the property that you will highlight in your marketing. If you plan to feature the property on your website, or give it a website of its own, describe your plan. Let them know you have really thought about this, because you have thought about it.

Have your laptop set up with your website on the screen. Show them exactly how their property will be featured. Also step them through the other tools on your site which may help them with finding their next property. If you have IDX, the public MLS search feature, on your site, the sellers

def•i•ni•tion

The **broker's open house** is the property showing for the agent community as opposed to the **open house** which is for the public.

will be able to search for replacement homes on their own. And, as the coup de grâce, as recommended in Chapter 10, set up your prospect's property with its own home address website through www.iHOUSEweb.com. Pull up the site and watch your prospect's faces. As they see their home on the internet with a website address of its own they will transform from prospects to clients before your very eyes. They will be impressed beyond words with your motivation and your competence.

FYI!
Important statistics your market trends page should include are: ♦ Number of properties listed in the same category as the seller ♦ Average list price for the properties listed in the same category ♦ Average days on the market until closing ♦ Average list price compared to sale price ♦ Your or your company's statistics in comparison

Prepare Your Bio and Mission Statement

Clients want to know who you are almost as much as what you will do for them. They are interviewing you for the important job of selling their valued asset. Include a mission statement that distinguishes your services from the rest of the pack.

Include information about the company you work for, but keep it to a minimum if you personally have an impressive listing history to show. If not, include the company's listing and sales statistics, but also include information about yourself.

If you do have an impressive history, list current and past listings. Include client contact information (if those clients have given you permission). Attach letters your clients have written thanking you for your help.

Agent to Agent

Agents often shy away from talking about themselves, especially boasting about their past successes. If this is the case for you, your inclination will be to leave the reading of your bio to the seller. Don't. Make sure you cover your bio in your oral listing presentation. Although sellers often review listing packages after presentation, you can't rely on that. Why blow this important opportunity by leaving out what may be the most important factor to the seller? If you have multiple transactions under your belt, you may want to have a separate bio aimed for the seller, and one directed at the buyers.

I keep clients' complimentary letters in a file called Testimonials. These letters are added to my website and my resumé. Keep your bio to one page if possible, excluding attachments. Make it look professional by using standard resumé format and impressive by using classic fonts. Include some color. Depending on your bio, it can be the most important component of your listing package.

Include Your Newsletter in the Listing Presentation Package

Include your most recent newsletter with your listing package. Some agents have a mailer covering a variety of topics. If you have one tailored to the steps in a transaction or the services you will provide to the seller, include that as well. If you give free seminars, include your schedule.

Comparative Market Analysis

Multiple listing programs allow you to prepare a professional looking *comparative market analysis* (*CMA*) of a property with the click of a few buttons. You can personalize these reports to include your potential client's name, address, and other identifying data. Better yet, use Top Producer or some other real estate marketing program and you will impress your clients all the more.

The CMA states your recommended list price for the property. Print out a full copy of the comparable properties your package lists. The comparable listings serve as backup for your recommendation. These reports are incredibly useful for discussing the property value in a scientific, objective manner. Sellers can be highly charged over price, feeling their property, especially their home, is worth far more than the market will bear.

def•i•ni•tion

A **CMA**, or **comparative market analysis**, is a summary of comparable properties in the area that have sold recently, generally in the last six months. Comparable properties are those with similar numbers of bedrooms and bathrooms, square footage, and lot size. This report, which is akin to a mini-appraisal, includes color photos of the comparable properties and recommends a listing price.

One of the many useful functions of the CMA is to flush out seller price issues early on. Always be prepared for a seller to have a dream price far greater than the current market price. There is a fine line between alienating a seller in love with his property and presenting an objective view of the market. Make sure you never belittle the seller's point of view or his property. People's homes come high up on their list of emotional importance. You don't want to step on any emotional toes.

Prepare the Sample Net Sheet

This document helps the seller understand how much the closing costs will run and how much they will net from the sale. It deducts loan payoff, commission, and other estimated closing costs from the recommended sales price. This simple document should be completed at your listing presentation unless the seller has provided you with loan payoff figures in advance.

It is at this point that your knowledge of tax law comes in handy, not to render tax advice, but because you want to show the seller that you are competent and aware of sale ramifications. Depending on the tax law at the time, your client may have taxable gain requiring some analysis as to how to reduce or defer it. Of course, you don't actually want to render tax advice; however, because you are savvy enough to raise such issues, the seller will be impressed by both your integrity and your knowledge.

Include a Transaction Management Sample

If you use a transaction management program, include a sample transaction so your sellers can see how professionally their transaction will be handled. If your transaction management program is online, show them how they also can track the progress of their sale online. Tell them that statistics show that transactions handled with a transaction management program have a higher incidence of closing than those not so coordinated. Explain to them how all of the professionals who will be involved in their sale will be able to follow the status of the transaction online. They will be impressed by your professionalism and competence.

Listen to Your Clients

Before you discuss the listing agreement, give your prospects a chance to voice their concerns, issues, and thoughts. Ask them whether they would like to change anything about your plan. Inquire as to whether there is anything you left out. They know their property better than anyone else, and their thoughts and comments are valuable.

 Agent to Agent

Most multiple listing software allows you to enter a listing in the form without uploading it into the database until later. This allows you to assemble the required information without the necessity of uploading until you're ready to present your new listing.

Ask them whether anything about the sale process you have suggested makes them feel uncomfortable, because the plan can be tailored to meet their needs. They are the bosses. Are there any family issues you should consider? It is only through enlisting them into your plan that the sale of their property will evolve into a team endeavor, the most satisfying feeling for you and your client alike.

Include Your Agency Disclosure and a Listing Agreement

Include your agency disclosure form and a *listing agreement* as the last documents in your package. You will have made a thorough, impressive presentation, followed up with the agency disclosure and listing agreement that will cement your relationship with this seller.

def•i•ni•tion

The **listing agreement** is the contract between the seller and broker. It outlines what the agent will do for the seller and how much the broker will be paid. It also includes the price the property will be listed at and how long the listing will last. Listing agreements are usually exclusive rights to sell, meaning that the broker gets paid regardless of who brings in the buyer.

When you get to the listing agreement in your package, ask the sellers whether they are ready to sign the agreement now, or should you just step through it and they can think about it. (The listing agreement is discussed more fully in Chapter 20.) If your prospect is ready to sign, follow the high-tech agent's example in Chapter 14. Enter the property on the MLS while you have your client there to provide you with all the detailed information required. If the light is right, take your digital photos. You don't have to upload them to the MLS yet, but you'll have all your input work done. I have my stager take the photographs. She does her magic, and then she stages each photo she takes. She has a better eye for just the right shot.

If your prospects are not ready to sign up with you, tell them to take their time. There is no urgency. Real estate transactions are rushed along far too quickly. Clients' number-one complaint is that the process becomes a mad dash to the finish. Let your potential clients know that you feel this way, if you do, and that you believe that planning and good coordination can take the crisis mode out of the real estate transaction.

Utilizing Technology to Instill Trust

A laptop is indispensable at listing presentations. The MLS database can be used to justify the listing price you recommend and to gain seller trust. Potential clients appreciate seeing how the MLS is set up and how their property will be featured on it. They trust your CMA statistics more if they are able to see them on the computer. They also tend to trust you more because you have chosen to share the coveted database that most agents jealously guard. (There is no rule against showing listings to your clients. You just can't let them access the database without your supervision or let them view confidential remarks.)

Agent to Agent

Seventy-three percent of sellers contacted only one agent before listing their home for sale.

Do not skip this step. It may not seem like an important step to you, but it provides a real advantage in gaining client trust. Remember, you're dealing with what is possibly their most valuable asset. They want to see exactly how you come up with the value you assign. Emotionally, they want to be included and informed about the list price you recommend, and you accomplish this by sharing your database with them.

Allow for Rejection

Although your affirmation will be that this client will list with you, don't be discouraged if this doesn't happen. The seller needs to go through the very important process of agent interview and selection. We make a lot of money from selling properties. Listing presentations that don't pan out are just one of the costs of doing business.

Think of them as a public service. They are a part of what agents do, not just to get the listing, but as a service to owners in the community. If your presentation was thorough and it was if you followed this format, you gave the seller valuable time and information and it will come back to you. Good service always brings a priceless return.

The Least You Need to Know

- ◆ Time is precious, so qualify your potential seller clients before you invest too much time with them.

- ◆ In your listing presentation, provide information about yourself, an analysis of comparable properties and the market, and a recommended listing price.

◆ Evaluating and presenting current market trends lets you and your prospect gauge the market together.

◆ Let your prospect know exactly how you intend to market their property, including Internet exposure.

◆ Sharing information from the MLS with your client gives you an advantage over your competition.

Part 5

The Parts of a Transaction

This chapter looks at the residential real estate transaction from the following multiple perspectives:

- ◆ Representing the seller

- ◆ Representing the buyer

- ◆ Understanding the transaction documents, using them online and off, and managing the transaction with a professional transaction management program. As you'll learn in this section, representing the seller and buyer involve very different approaches to the real estate sales transaction. Each representation has its unique steps and issues. This part of the book takes a close look at the steps involved in client representation and concludes with a quasilegal analysis of the transaction documents so you may more professionally guide your clients through transactions.

Chapter 18

Representing the Seller

In This Chapter

- ◆ Staging the property for sale
- ◆ Listing on the MLS
- ◆ Conducting the broker's open house
- ◆ Conducting the open house for the public
- ◆ Handling multiple offers

Congratulations! Your listing presentation was successful. This chapter covers all the steps you will take on behalf of your seller client from signing the listing agreement to closing on the sale. Before showcasing your new listing, you want to perform a marketability assessment of the home. Should a professional stager be hired? Are there seller disclosure issues? Should inspection reports be obtained? Are there title issues that may arise?

After you have performed your assessment and readied the property for the market, you can feature it on the multiple listing service (MLS), show it to your fellow agents at the broker's open house, and then show it at the public open house. When an offer is received, you will undertake the all-important process of reviewing the offer with your client and responding. Once you're in contract, careful facilitation through closing becomes your most important job. This chapter assumes you have a signed listing agreement and you are now officially representing the seller as the *listing agent*.

def•i•ni•tion

The **listing agent** acts for the seller according to the terms of the listing agreement. The selling agent brings in the successful buyer. If the listing agent also acts as the selling agent, he is acting as a dual agent.

Professional Staging

Where prices warrant presale expense, properties are often professionally staged before they go on the market. We make a major production out of getting a home ready for its coming-out party. Staging the property to achieve optimum visual appeal is often the very first step you will take.

> **FYI!**
>
> My stager offers a basic staging flat-fee package. The flat-fee structure is more acceptable to the seller wary of hidden selling expenses. You, too, can sit down with your stager and come up with flat-fee basic plans that meet the needs of standard homes.

Evaluating Property Problems

The second step of your marketability assessment is to determine potential property issues and address them. Are there property conditions that may cause concern to a buyer? The days of buyer beware are over. Sellers have to disclose any problems they are aware of relating to the property. Some offices have a policy of staying away from seller disclosure issues. My policy is it's better to encourage full and complete disclosure and find out about any potential problems early on. Believe me, if the buyer decides to sue the seller later for failure to disclose, you will be named in the lawsuit as well. Head it off early. Handle it now.

Although a seller's written disclosures are often not due until after an offer is accepted, a good practice is to have the seller complete these disclosure forms now. The questions in these forms are targeted at flushing out property defects, and these are the very conditions you want to pinpoint early on.

One way to handle property defects is to hire a professional inspection company to identify the problems and have them repaired before listing the property on the MLS. In most states, the seller has to disclose this inspection and its report to a buyer in contract, so consider that issue as well. Depending on what the report says and the extent of the repairs recommended, the seller can either make the repairs or not.

Cave!

One question on a typical disclosure statement is, "Are there any conditions you have not described that materially affect the value and desirability of the property to a buyer?" In other words, if there isn't a question that specifically addresses a condition, there's a catch-all place to include it.

At least the seller will be informed of conditions when the buyers have their inspection done. The seller will be prepared to deal with these issues. It is wise to have one company perform the inspection and another company perform the repairs. In this manner, your inspection will be an unbiased opinion unmotivated by a tendency to recommend unnecessary and costly repairs.

One more condition to assess before the conclusion of your marketability analysis is title. Is the seller aware of any unusual conditions of title that may cause a prudent buyer concern? If you feel title issues may exist, order a preliminary title report or abstract of title as soon as you receive the listing.

Are there easements in favor of neighboring property? Are nonconforming uses being made of the property? Are there any boundary problems—for example, is half of their backyard actually the neighbor's property? Are there *set-back* problems with the side deck? Are there any improvements made without permits?

The time to tackle these problems is now for two reasons. First, the seller has to disclose these issues. Second, you can set a plan in place to either address these issues when they come up or head them off entirely.

def•i•ni•tion

A **set-back** requirement is established by zoning law or agreement between neighbors as to how far an improvement might be situated from a certain marker.

These are your problems as well as your client's problems. These are the types of issues that cause an otherwise highly marketable property to become stale and undervalued. If the property doesn't sell, you will not have done your best for your client and you will have spent what will ultimately be a great deal of time getting nowhere. The listing will expire with unsatisfied clients and no income in your pocket. Be proactive. Address these issues in the beginning and encourage your clients to take the steps their consultants suggest to make the property as marketable as possible.

Listing on the MLS

Now that premarketing steps are complete, you're ready to service your new listing. When the property is ready to be previewed, advise your office of the listing and place it on the multiple listing service. Upload as many digital pictures of the property as your listing service will allow or set up a *virtual tour* shoot.

def•i•ni•tion

A **virtual tour** is a depiction of a property as if it were photographed with a video camera. It takes you through the property as if you are viewing it in person. You can do this yourself with your digital camera or hire a firm to do it. Check with your local association for referrals.

When your listing is entered in the MLS, it will show up as a new listing on what is referred to as the Hot Sheet. This is your listing's most important day on the market as agents feast their eyes on the hit parade of new properties.

The listing is then automatically matched up with agent profiling in a process called prospect matching. For example, Agent B has a client who is interested in a three-bedroom, two-bath home in a certain town with a view of the water. He enters these criteria into the multiple listing service and asks for notification when a new property matching it comes on the market. This new listing matches, and the multiple listing program automatically notifies him of this new listing.

Hosting the Broker's Open House

When you enter your listing in the MLS, you choose a date—generally a few days to a week later—for the broker's open house. On that date, the agents working in the area of your listing tour the property. It's always a good idea to *host* your broker's open house by serving refreshments to your peers. The broker's open house is an important step in your listing's marketing program.

If your listing was well-received when it was entered on the MLS, agents have already brought their clients to see the property by the time you hold the broker's open house. Agents can be very quick when they believe a new listing is hot and they have client interest. They don't want to dilly-dally until the broker's open house, where the world of agents will converge upon this unsuspecting property and bring in lots of competition.

Agents sometimes ask those who show up for the broker's open house to fill out a suggested listing price form. If the client has pressured you into listing the property at above market value, these forms completed by fellow agents can go a long way in helping convince the seller that the price should come down. If agents feel the price is too high, so will their clients. They may not even show the property to a potential buyer because of its price.

The agents touring your listing are your gateway to buyers. The vast majority of listings are sold by other agents. Each of these agents leaves the broker's open house and broadcasts news of this new listing to their offices and their network of qualified buyers. It is only after the broker's open house that your listing has been fully marketed to the local real estate community.

Holding the Open House for the Public

When you entered your listing with the MLS you also selected an *open house* date. The open house is the agent's way of inviting the public to preview a home listed for sale. This event you advertise in the local newspaper. Although it has been advertised to the agents on the MLS, the agents are not really your market for this event. The public is. You also advertise the open house in the local paper and attach an open Sunday rider to your sign. Another good idea is to send postcards to the surrounding neighbors, inviting them to drop by an hour earlier than the general public for a personalized tour of the house.

def•i•ni•tion

The **open house** is just what it sounds like. The house is opened to interested buyers to tour. Buyers are notified by newspaper advertising, well-posted signs, and sometimes by agent mailers.

The open house brings people who are looking to buy or who may be about to sell. Buyers and sellers often frequent open houses before they are ready for their own purchase or sale. They want to see how it's done and what it's all about. The old adage is a property doesn't sell at an open house. This is true. But your *services* do sell at an open house. Especially because your middle name is Market.

At the open house you are showcasing yourself just as much as your client's property. People will ask your opinion about the market and inquire about your experience. It's your time to shine and to generously assist visitors with their real estate issues. It becomes your time to stand out, although first and foremost the feature of the day is selling your client's home.

Many agents say open houses are a waste of time. Their experience is that the crowds aren't interested in buying; for the most part, they are just getting an education. And if someone becomes interested, they make an offer through their own agent, not through the listing agent. I thoroughly disagree with this philosophy. I think an open house is everything but a waste of time. I refer to it as a goldmine.

Everyone who comes to the open house is a potential client. They are not just there for the refreshments, unless you're serving shrimp and champagne. They have come out of genuine interest in this home or they are interested in the sale process because they will soon become involved in real estate as a buyer or seller. What more can an agent ask for?

When you think of the amount of cold calling and prospecting agents do to turn up one live potential client, why would the open house that brings them to your very door be considered a waste of time? It's a jackpot. I know agents with similar thoughts who will handle open houses for other agents gratis just to have potential clients appear before their very eyes.

Your Open House Checklist

Here is the step-by-step process to follow when conducting your open house for the public:

1. Mail a notice to the neighbors. The customer service department at your favorite title company will be happy to compile a list for you and even provide you with mailing labels. You want to mail to the 50 neighbors that are closest to your client's home. Send them a notice telling them that you have listed the home at your client's address and invite them to come to the open house. Remember to invite them to a special "for neighbors only" preview of the home, one hour before the general public is to show up. Some agents will even follow this up with a Saturday face-to-face visit with the neighbors, reminding them about tomorrow's open house. This system is prospecting at its very best.

   Neighbors also make valuable sources of future potential sellers. Even if the neighbors have no interest of their own, you will have introduced yourself by your mailer. If they come to the open house, you will have a chance to meet them in person. Meeting potential clients when you are in the course of doing an impressive job for another client is the best possible introduction of all.

FYI!

Neighbors are an excellent source of buyers. They might have watched the house for years, hoping it would come up for sale. They might have relatives or friends who would like to live close by. They may want to purchase the property as a good invest-ment that they can keep their eye on. Familiarity is a property owner's best friend. Some people will do anything to stay in their neighborhood, even move across the street. They know the neighborhood and its services and conveniences. So when it is time to upgrade, they already know where they want to be.

---

2. Invite your buyer and seller prospects to your open house. This is a good way to allow people you've been prospecting to see you at work. It will give your seller prospects a good idea of what they can expect for an open house of their home. Your buyer prospects might even be interested in this home. Your prospects will be impressed, and their rating of you can't help but go up.

3. Place appropriate signage. If the home is in a high-traffic area, make sure your open house is posted in as many areas as possible. Do this days in advance for post-driven signage. On the day of the open house make sure your directional signs direct them to the home from all busy thoroughfares. Don't just depend on an address to get them there. Guide them in with nice-looking signs well posted from point one to point ten and all the points in between.

4. Complete your office preparation. Your open-house supplies should include the following:

   ◆ An ample supply of marketing flyers for the property, along with its plot map

   ◆ A review copy of advance inspec-tion reports that give the property a good report

   ◆ A guest book for people in attendance to sign

   ◆ Your bio and mission statement

   ◆ Your business cards

   ◆ Comparables supporting the listing price

Agent to Agent

Every handout should have your name and contact infor-mation on it. Provide pens for guests who want to make notes. If it is a hot property, hire another person to assist with the greetings and train that person to set up intros to you when appropriate.

5. Set up your traveling office in the property. Set up your laptop so you can access the MLS. You want access if the opportunity arises to search listings for potential clients, to review new listings if there is a lull in the day, or to send and receive e-mail. Make sure your property flyers and marketing materials are placed in an accessible location. Have your guest book in the same vicinity.

6. Ready the property for visitors. Make sure the property is ready for the open house by following these pointers:

   ◆ The sellers, their children, and their animals should be gone for the day; and their valuables and prescription medications should be locked up.

   ◆ Display fresh flowers, install some air fresheners, light a nice-smelling candle, and put on soothing music.

   ◆ Make sure the temperature is right. If not, put on more heat or air conditioning. If the weather permits, light a fire.

   ◆ Keep the front and back doors open for easy access if the weather permits. Open all the drapes. Turn every light in the house on. Everything should be bright and cheery.

Agent to Agent

The smell of fresh-baked cookies can add to a feeling of warmth and home. Some agents bake cookies in the kitchen oven and offer them to guests. Others use a frozen apple pie generously sprinkled with sugar and cinnamon and set on a low temperature to flavor the air with aromas that remind the prospective buyers of home and family. There are many ways to make a property appealing to each of the senses.

Greeting Buyers

When people arrive, introduce yourself, ask them their names, and find out whether they are neighbors. Ask them to sign your guest book. Give them a property flyer and graciously invite them to show themselves around and take as much time as they want. Invite them to ask you any questions they may have about the property or about the real estate market. Then leave them alone.

Before they leave, if they have not spoken with you again, connect with them and engage in simple, friendly conversation. Ask them questions you would ask anyone coming to an open house, such as, "Where do you live? How long have you been looking? Are you selling a home of your own?" If they are neighbors, the questions will be different. Just be friendly and interested. You won't have the look of dollar signs in your eyes; you will have the look of genuine interest instead.

Tell them you would be happy to assist them with any real estate matter they may have now or in the future. You're not being pushy. You're just being honest and sincere. Give them your card and your bio. On the back of your bio you may want to include a personal mission statement. For instance, if you have followed the steps in this book, you will be an agent with The New Ideal. Your mission statement should reflect your desire to meet your fiduciary duty by making your client's interest more important than anything else. It should address how you will support their personal decisions even if they conflict with your own.

If it feels appropriate, ask their opinion of the house. Ask what features met their needs and which did not. If it appears that this house simply did not fill their needs, ask whether you can show them some listings on your laptop if they are not already working with an agent. Since you will have your laptop set up and accessible, you can easily input the criteria for the home they are interested in and in minutes have listings that fit their criteria. Tell them you would be willing to meet with them in the next week and show them these properties. You do not want to spend more than a half hour with each prospect. Your main purpose is to sell your client's home, and responding to property-specific inquiries is your primary objective.

Responding to the Offer

You receive a call from a buyer's agent advising that she has an offer on a property you have listed. If she asks to personally present the offer to your client, thank her for the opportunity but respectfully decline. For the reasons set forth in the next chapter, it is not in your client's best interest for the buyer's agent to personally appeal to their emotions.

Don't attempt to convert the buyer's agent to The New Ideal, which discourages sales tactics like the ones the buyer's agent proposes to practice on your sellers. The New Ideal will take hold over time; until it does, this agent is just doing the job as she knows it for her client. Once you have the offer, present it to your clients in person. Don't try to do it over the telephone.

At your office, complete a seller's *net proceeds sheet* based on the purchase price. Also, review your file and prepare a summary of the listing showing how many days it has been on the market and how many offers have been made; compare that to your MLS statistics for average days on the market before sale. You want to assess whether this listing has received its share of the market or whether there is more yet to come. If you are past the average days on the market, the offer should be considered more seriously since this listing has reached its peak.

The **net proceeds sheet** helps the seller understand what their closing costs will be and how much they will net from the sale. It deducts loan payoff, commission, and other estimated closing costs from the sales price.

A **counteroffer** is a response to an offer that changes or adds some terms.

Chapter 20 describes in detail the written agency disclosures you have made to your client and the terms of the offer that will be of the greatest importance to them. Use it as a guide as you review the offer with your clients. Have an extra copy of the buyer's offer for all clients and yourself to review. Go through each and every term and the significance of each to your client. If you are now representing both parties to the transaction, you should amend your agency disclosure that describes whether you are acting on behalf of the buyer only or on behalf of both the buyer and seller.

If there is a term your client is not comfortable with, prepare a *counteroffer*. You should respond to all offers since you have an interested buyer in hand. It makes sense to work with that buyer in arriving at mutually agreeable terms if you can. Any term can be changed. There is no downside to making a counteroffer because the seller can always accept a different offer anytime before the counteroffer is accepted.

Handling Multiple Offers

If you're in a fast market, you must be prepared to encounter and respond to multiple offers. Value is one thing, but in a fast market of rapidly appreciating property where there's just not enough to go around, value has little relation to what an interested buyer is willing to pay. This is the concept of supply and demand at its extreme. When there is little supply but high demand, value becomes quite relative. In such a market, knowing how to handle multiple offers is essential to giving your clients the full representation they are due.

If this type of market beckons to you, meet it with a good plan in place. There's nothing like a good bidding war to get the old adrenaline going. You've got to plan for it and work it to make the most out of this ideal situation. First, set a date for all offers to be submitted and specify the date on your listing with the MLS. If the market is hot and the property is attractive, make sure the word gets out telling agents to submit their client's *highest and best* offer because you are expecting quite a bit of competition. Review all offers before responding to any. After this process has played itself out, you should have the best offer the market will bear.

Now you are ready to accept an offer. You can always accept the others in backup positions in case the first contract falls out of escrow for some reason. It takes skill and experience to handle a bidding war effectively. In my area, the bidding war process can result in offers $200,000 and more above fair market value. If this ideal market presents itself to you and you do not yet have the experience to artfully bring the process through its stages, bring in another agent who does. It is well worth having a capable team on hand to allow this process to render the maximum possible reward for both you and your clients.

Facilitating the Transaction to Closing

As the seller's agent, your main job after an offer is accepted is to facilitate seller disclosures and monitor the buyer's performance. Once disclosures are made, your job is to ensure that the buyer removes his contingencies in a timely manner. It is always best to prepare your seller for later bargaining when the buyer removes his physical inspection contingency. It is at this juncture that the seller should be prepared for yet another negotiation since the buyer sometimes conditions contingency removal on a seller credit to address required repairs.

You want to continually track all steps of the transaction to ensure continued progression toward closing. Although the loan contingency is not your client's, you want to stay in close contact with the buyer's agent to ensure that the loan is progressing toward closing. About a week before closing make sure the settlement statement addressed in Chapter 20 is correct and the lender documents are in or at least ordered.

Make sure that all closing documentation has been prepared and no other documents are required. A buyer surprise or a title company surprise is a seller surprise. The only way to increase the odds of the transaction closing without problems is by staying on top of each stage of the transaction, whether it requires action on your part or not.

FYI!
The old way of handling contingencies was to do everything you could to get the contingency removed. A step closer to closing was the primary goal. In your new professional role according to The New Ideal, your only sales script is, "What is the best possible action for my client?" For example, if the buyer wants your client to credit back an amount that doesn't make sense to the seller, support your client in terminating the purchase agreement. There's no fancy footwork to do, just support your client's decision.

Dealing with a Stale Listing

A listing gets stale if it stays on the market without moving longer than other comparable properties. A home gets its most exposure in its first few weeks on the market. Upon obtaining the listing, you began marketing it directly to potential buyers and to other agents who may bring in buyers. You submitted the home to the MLS, announced it in your office, held a broker's tour, contacted your potential buyer list and agents who may have waiting buyers, held open houses, and submitted advertisements to the local newspaper. Your listing enjoyed its wave of marketing without receiving an offer.

A listing becomes stale for three reasons:

- It is overpriced.
- It has condition problems.
- The market is slow.

If other properties within your listing's price range are moving, the property is the problem, not the market. Your listing is either overpriced or it suffers from a condition problem. If it is overpriced, take it off the market for a time and pop it back on the market at a lower price, or just reduce the price without taking it off the market. Depending on your choice, it will either be shown as a new listing again or a price reduction, and will be priced more in line with the market. You will want to set up another broker's open house if the price has come down enough, because there is a whole new buyer's market to which it will appeal the second time around.

If your clients refuse to come down on the listing price, suggest that they provide a buyer incentive such as *seller financing*, *lease-option*, or *equity sharing*. They need to increase their market by offering an advantage to compensate for the higher than market price. If they refuse an incentive, either release them from their listing agreement with the permission of your office or don't renew their listing when it expires.

If the property itself has condition problems, take it off the market, address the problems, and then reintroduce it to its market with a facelift. If the property has access problems, shows poorly, or needs repair, take steps to address these problems. Sometimes a property just needs minor reconstruction or clearing out of clutter and sprucing up. Taking these steps can make a big difference in how the market responds to your listing. Once conditions have been addressed, put the listing back on the market advising that it has been cleared or renovated. It will come out as a new listing and if the conditions are adequately addressed, it will now receive its market.

def•i•ni•tion

With **seller financing**, the seller agrees to make a loan to a buyer who may not otherwise qualify for a loan or who wants to avoid lender loan costs.

A **lease option** allows the buyer to occupy the property with a right to buy it at a later date. It allows a buyer who is not ready to purchase to occupy the property, have a right to purchase it, and to get ready to purchase it.

Through **seller equity sharing** the seller stays on title for a percentage interest in the property (usually to the extent of the down payment or a portion of it), the buyer does not have to come up with the down payment (or portion of it the seller leaves in), and the seller cashes out the remainder of his interest with the new loan proceeds and receives the amount of his retained equity and his percentage of appreciation at the end of term (often five to seven years). This is an ideal way for a principal residence seller to reduce his tax basis and begin an investment portfolio since his ownership interest becomes his investment property.

Overpricing a listing is like gambling with a valuable asset. If you are very lucky, you might snag a buyer at a price higher than the property's value. Then, you are faced with the buyer discovering his mistake and backing out during the contingency period. If your luck holds and the buyer releases his contingencies, the problem then becomes one of lender appraisal since the property will most likely fail to justify the sale price. If you are not so lucky, your listing will sit, get stale, get a reputation as a house that is impossible to sell, and leave buyers wondering what is wrong with it.

Always remember that if the price is low enough, its market will come. In other words, a low enough price will cure any problem. You can only rely on market comparables if your property is in comparable condition to other similar properties. If it is not, the price must be reduced to bring it its market.

Reporting to Your Clients

The first complaint clients have about agents is the pressure tactics they use. Second is the lack of contact. Once you have a client's listing, frequent, consistent contact is essential. Always keep in mind that you are in the business for more than making the commission at the end of the road. You are here to benefit your clients throughout their transaction, making it the best possible experience for both of you. Treat them like family and they will treat you the same.

Most often your seller also needs to buy another property. In fact, the National Association of Realtors reports that 84 percent of repeat homebuyers nationwide sold

Agent to Agent

Sellers decide if they want to accept offers contingent upon finding a new home. Buyers also can make offers contingent upon selling their home.

their previous home at the same time they purchased their new home. These two transactions therefore should occur in tandem as much as possible. The seller needs to know what is going on even if nothing is going on. They want to know they are on your mind.

Although the commission you will make should never be a gauge of the services you will give to a client, it is a consideration. These clients are significant contributors to your financial support. Why not give them everything you've got to give? If you have nothing to report, tell them so every few days.

Take advantage of the simplicity of e-mail communication. The vast majority of your clients have e-mail. They may not check it consistently, but if you tell them you will keep them advised in this manner, they will. As you update their listing, change their marketing materials, or advertise their property, e-mail a copy to your client. They will feel in the loop and well served. Clients who were reluctant or adamantly opposed to using e-mail as a supplemental communication method often overcome their hesitancies when they see its usefulness.

The Least You Need to Know

- Use a professional stager to give a property its optimum eye-appeal in order to be sold quickly and at its highest price.

- The MLS listing will include a date for the broker's open house and the open house for the public.

- Use the open house to market your services as well as the property itself.

- You should understand the contract terms and be prepared to discuss each with your client when an offer is made.

- Present a purchase offer in person if at all possible.

19

Representing the Buyer

In This Chapter

- Qualifying a prospective buyer
- Making your presentation to a buyer
- Touring properties with buyers
- The offer, the counteroffer, and where you go from here
- Taking the transaction through closing

This chapter is about representing the buyer. It begins with a buyer prospect whom you qualify for readiness to purchase. When your prospect is qualified, you deliver your buyer presentation. This presentation does not result in a signed agreement with your buyer, the way it did with the seller, but it does establish your relationship as this buyer's agent. After the two of you commit to the job at hand, you begin the process of touring properties and ultimately making an offer to purchase.

Later in this chapter, we look at the most important offer terms and how they should be handled with your client. Some states have forms that define transaction terms. This form can be a useful tool for explaining terms to your clients. Opening escrow is the next step, followed by performance of the all-important loan and physical inspection contingencies. At closing, you want to be with your client when he confronts the huge stack of documents to sign.

Qualifying the Buyer

Before you start searching for listings and driving prospects around to tour properties, you want to qualify them, just as you do your sellers. Showing properties to clients takes a lot of time and energy. Before you make this investment, you want to determine whether your potential clients are ready or close to ready to buy, both emotionally and financially.

Agent to Agent _____

In the spirit of generosity and cooperation, you may choose to do some MLS prospecting for nonqualified clients. This would consist of giving them some property listings that fit their criteria. The chances are, when these people are more motivated, they will come back to you both because you were sharp enough to know they weren't ready and kind enough to share listings with them anyway.

Here is a checklist of issues to discuss with prospective buyers in order to qualify them:

1. How long have you been looking for a property and how many properties have you seen? Have you searched properties for sale online? How many?

2. Do you have a preapproval letter from a lender? (If the answer is no, the buyer will need to get that prior to shopping for a new home.)

3. Are you a first-time buyer?

4. Have you worked with other agents in looking for a home? If yes, have you already connected with an agent you feel comfortable with to help you find the home of your dreams?

5. If you own a home, when do you plan to sell it? Have you listed it? Have you interviewed agents to list it?

6. (If they own a home) Do you intend to find a home you want before you put your home on the market? If so, how do you intend to handle a situation where you need to close on the new home before your existing home sells? Have you discussed a *bridge loan* with your lender?

7. What is the biggest obstacle to finding the property you want?

8. What is wrong with the homes you have seen thus far?

9. What qualities do you feel are important in the agent you will choose to represent your interests?

10. If you find a home through my services, are you willing to place the listing of your home with me if you are pleased with my services?

11. If we were to find the perfect home today, are you ready to make an offer?

It is only through discussing the previous set of issues that you can know your prospect's level of motivation. It makes no sense to cart people around to properties for sale if they are not ready to sign on the dotted line, or at least, if they are not reasonably close to buying.

def•i•ni•tion

A **bridge loan** is a short-term loan made in expectation of permanent longer-term loan. Also known as a swing loan.

Cave!

Each step in a transaction is very important. Missing one can break the contract due to the time constraints. So share this with your potential clients, understand it, and develop a method of tracking and following up to keep everything on schedule.

Presenting to the Buyer

After you have qualified the buyer, you will prepare your buyer package, which should include:

- A sample listing

- A sample preapproval letter

- Your office and personal bio and mission statement

- Your most recent newsletter

- List of transaction steps and standards

- Transaction management sample transaction if you use a transaction management program

Review a Sample Listing

Print out a full-color buyer's listing from the multiple listing service as an example of how a property is listed. Point out the categories and explain how you use specific criteria under each of these to select properties that match their needs. For example, show them a sample three-bedroom, two-bath home with a pool. If they desire each of those characteristics, this property will show up as a match in your search of the MLS. This illustration shows them that the more specific they are in their criteria, the more likely a matching property will fit their needs.

Cave!

Potential clients may want to work with several agents at once. Unless you feel confident that you can be the first to show them a property and that they will honor that service, decline to spend your time and effort on them. You can explain this to them in a sensitive way, but ask for an exclusive opportunity if they want your dedicated attention.

On your computer show them how a search is performed and how you are alerted when a property match occurs. As I've mentioned before, agents are far too guarded with the MLS. Clients are highly interested in this service that is off limits to them and appreciate your introducing them to how it works. There's nothing in the MLS rules prohibiting client review as long as you are the one doing the showing and do not show clients the confidential remarks. Now with IDX/MLS we can feature current MLS listings in a client-ready format on our websites and clients can search current listings themselves in real time.

Review Their Loan Approval Status

If your prospects do not yet have *loan preapproval*, advise them that this will be the first step on their home-buying agenda. Only with that in their possession will they be taken to look at properties. No buyer offer is seriously considered without a preapproval letter. The preapproval process will also tell them the loan amount for which they can qualify. With this important financial step taken in advance, they can focus on finding the right property within their budget instead of finding a property they are uncertain they can afford.

def•i•ni•tion

Loan preapproval is different from prequalification. In pre-approval, the lender actually gives loan approval subject to qualifying the property the buyer later chooses. Prequalification is different. It does not confer actual loan approval.

Include Your Bio and Mission Statement

Clients want to know who you are almost as much as what you will do for them. They are interviewing you for the important job of helping them buy their valued asset. Include a mission statement that distinguishes your services from the rest of the pack.

Include information about the company you work for, but keep it to a minimum if you personally have an impressive listing history to show. If not, include the company's listing and sales statistics, but also include information about yourself.

If you do have an impressive history, list current and past listings. Include client contact information (if those clients have given you permission). Attach letters your clients have written thanking you for your help.

Include Your Newsletter

Include your most recent newsletter with your buyer package. Some agents have a mailer covering a variety of topics. If you have one tailored to the steps in a transaction or the services you will provide to the buyer, include that also. If you give free seminars, include your schedule.

List of Transaction Steps and Standards

Have a list of the standard transaction steps, what will be expected of the buyers during the transaction, and which transaction fees are customarily paid by the buyer. Even if the buyers have purchased many times before, it always comes as a surprise to realize just how complicated the real estate transaction is. Most people purchased real estate when the transaction was far less cumbersome. This list helps buyers understand the course their purchase will travel and the need to have an agent by their side who really understands the process and will protect their interests. The agent who explains the process simply and straightforwardly stands out to them. This step will also cut down on surprises later if the transaction takes unexpected twists and turns.

FYI!

It is a wise idea to interview inspectors long before you need them, and add those who are reliable and professional to your personal referral list. One or two will already be on your Power Team. You will want to review some sample reports, talk to some previous clients, and have assurances of availability and price. You place your reputation on the line every time you make a referral, and yet this is part of your service. So pick a team that will work with you and for you.

When you describe the physical inspection contingency, let them know that you will guide them to inspectors who will assess the condition of the property for them. You will review their experts' reports with them and decide whether a seller credit should be given or if perhaps the transaction should be terminated. Tell them that you will support the right course of action for them, whatever that may be, because you are part of The New Ideal.

Include a Transaction Management Sample

If you use a transaction management program, include a sample transaction so your buyers can see how professionally their transaction will be handled. If your transaction management program is online show them how they also can track the progress of their purchase online. Tell them that statistics show that transactions handled with a transaction management program have a higher incidence of closing than those not so coordinated. Explain to them how all of the professionals who will be involved in their purchase will be able to follow the status of the transaction online. They will be impressed by your professionalism and competence.

Listen to the Buyer

The final step of your buyer meeting is to discuss two primary issues with your potential clients: first, what they want in an agent; and second, what they want in the property they are looking for. Always use your best active-listening skills while at the same time making it perfectly clear that you will find them the home they want within 30 days as long as they are specific about their needs. They have to do their part of the job, which is to know what they need and agree on it. If you have a husband and wife who have different needs tell them to call you later when they are in agreement. Then bid them adieu.

After this presentation has concluded you will know whether you and your prospects are a match. If you are, commit to one another. In most states, there is no formal agreement entered into with the buyer. In some states there is a buyer representation form, but buyers hesitate to sign it and would rather wait to bind the relationship until an offer is made. The commitment at this point is more of a moral one where you agree to help them find the right home and they agree to work with you in doing so.

Touring Buyers

In selecting properties to match your clients' needs, make sure you use the purchase price listed in your clients' loan preapproval letter. Before you tour your clients, make sure you preview properties. There should be no surprises when you arrive at a property; if you have not previewed a property, there will invariably be conditions you are unprepared to address. Do not make this mistake.

At the property, give your clients all the space and time they need to really get a feel for the home. Tour them through and answer any questions they may have, but don't crowd them. Nationwide, the typical search takes eight weeks during which the buyer visits nine homes before they buy. If your buyers are Internet searchers, it takes them only four weeks and six homes.

Agent to Agent

Take your clients in your car with you if at all possible. It makes for much better personal rapport and is far more convenient. You have probably been to the properties you're showing your clients, so you know how to get there. You also want to point out the neighborhood features along the way.

Reporting to Your Client

When you are prospecting for buyers, let them know the results of your daily search. Even if there are no new properties meeting their criteria, report that to them. The only way to keep clients happy is to frequently let them know you are working for them and looking out for their best interests.

FYI!
If you train your clients to receive communication by e-mail, you can automate your MLS program to send them a listing if a new one is found. If there are no matches for a few days, advise them that there are no new properties meeting their requirements. There just is no reason whatsoever to miss checking in with your client at least every few days.

A recent survey by the National Association of Realtors reports that communication is the key to homebuyer satisfaction. The survey states that Internet buyers were contacted by their real estate agent every 4.3 days, while traditional buyers were

FYI!

As reported by the National Association of Realtors, repeat homebuyers needed only four weeks to sell their existing home. More than half of repeat home-buyers began their home search before they placed their existing home on the market.

contacted every 6.5 days. More frequent communication resulted in a higher degree of satisfaction among Internet buyers; 90 percent claimed to be very satisfied with their agent as opposed to 32 percent of traditional buyers. The main reason for Internet buyers' satisfaction was that their agent was "always quick to respond." In contrast, the main reason expressed by traditional buyers for their dissatisfaction was the lack of communication from their agent.

Preparing the Offer

When your clients find a property they are prepared to make an offer on, the old sales trainers tell you to sit them down immediately at the property, pull out the offer you've got hidden in your notepad, and go for it. Don't give 'em a second to start second-guessing themselves. If you do, you'll lose 'em. This is Smoking Gun script No. 44.

The agent with The New Ideal is not pushing his clients to make impulsive decisions. Drive your clients back to your office and prepare the offer in a professional setting. There is no rush other than the normal time consideration in making the offer before someone else does. For those occasions when clients are in their own rush, and in some hot markets there is good reason to be, bring out your technology and let 'er rip. For the agent whose other middle name starts with a C, computer technology is the name of the game. The savvy agent has her laptop and printer stored in her car for just this type of occasion.

The next chapter describes in detail the required written agency disclosures you will make and the terms of the offer that you will now prepare. Use it as a guide as you put your client's offer together. Go through each and every term and the significance of each to your client.

Agent to Agent

Seventy-seven percent of buyers said the Internet shortened the search time for their new home. Internet users tended to be younger and purchase more expensive homes than other homebuyers.

It is entirely possible that your client's offer will be responded to by the sellers with a counteroffer. Always prepare your clients for this possibility so that when a counter is received, they are not unduly disappointed. It is just another step in the purchase process.

Offer Presentation

For agents still practicing salesmanship standards, presenting the offer involves setting the stage for a Hollywood soap opera. Many sales trainers advocate the sales pitch method—you've got to pitch the sellers so you can sell them on your clients. They instruct you to contact the listing agent and ask to present your offer in person to his or her clients. If the listing agent is crazy enough to let you in the client's door, you sit down with the sellers and use every gimmick in the book to try to get them to accept your client's offer. Bring your client's letter of introduction and a nice glossy picture of them. Oh, heck, why not bring a video tape of them and play it for the sellers? Better yet, bring your clients with you and let them crawl!

For the agent with The New Ideal, Hollywood dramatics have no place in the offer presentation process. The sales pitch method is clearly not in the seller's best interest, and both listing and selling agents should refuse to participate in it. The buyer's personal characteristics have nothing to do with whether the seller should accept their offer. The offer and acceptance process is not a social or dramatic engagement; this is a serious business transaction where the sellers should exercise objective judgment based on the terms set forth in the offer.

The Transaction Timeline and Steps

After your client's offer is accepted, you will prepare your *transaction timeline*. Hopefully, you will use a transaction management program, and we encourage you to use the online version. This is also the time when you pull in your transaction coordinator, if you have one. It is now time for you to jump into action on three important fronts:

- ◆ Opening escrow

- ◆ Obtaining the title report

- ◆ Dealing with the contingencies

def•i•ni•tion

A **transaction timeline** takes the terms of the purchase agreement and gives them dates, the most important of which are contingency periods and closing date.

Opening Escrow

The first step taken after an offer is accepted is to open escrow. Typically this step is taken by the buyer's agent. When you open escrow, you submit your client's purchase deposit and provide the escrow officer or closing attorney (depending on the state you are in) with the relevant details relating to this transaction. You don't have to know what to say. The closing professional will ask you a list of questions, and you provide the answers. Other than that, make sure any terms relating to amounts to be paid or credited are related to this professional who will itemize these amounts on the settlement statement.

The closing professional serves as a neutral intermediary facilitating the transaction and ordering title reports and title insurance. This professional takes buyer funds in the form of buyer and lender deposits and distributes them to sellers, lenders, and real estate agents. He gives lenders recorded security instruments and gives buyers deeds. He handles the paper and money exchange required in the real estate purchase and sale process.

Obtaining the Title Report

Within a matter of days of opening escrow the preliminary title report or abstract is received, which your client then has a limited number of days to review and approve. Sometimes this requires attorney scrutiny if there are easements and other conditions which limit the use of the property. If an attorney is not handling the closing, make sure you refer your client to one if there are unusual exceptions on the report. For the first several transactions, show the report to your office manager so you may learn what is unusual and what is not.

FYI!

The title report is the legal biography of the property, so to speak. It has three primary components:

- ◆ The legal description
- ◆ The exceptions
- ◆ Title insurance provisions

The title report is of paramount importance because it describes all legal rights and obligations associated with the property. It can be equated with a person's birth certificate, credit report, and life insurance policy. The legal description describes its physical existence, whereas title exceptions list its credit problems. The title insurance pays off if there is a problem with either of these. Thinking of the title in this common sense way can make title issues simple and straightforward.

Although you should not give legal advice, and interpreting these reports *is* giving legal advice, it is important for you to understand these reports. With a basic understanding of title reports, you can head off any title issues that become apparent through your early review. Even trained professionals tend to run the other way rather than attempt to grasp complex title terminology that sounds like language from another planet. Understanding these reports is actually not complicated after you see them in a practical, logical way.

FYI!

In some states, attorneys are required to serve as the title examiner and closing agent. In other states, the attorney is typically not a part of the transaction. Instead, the title company prepares the title report. In states where transactions do not require attorney involvement, the buyer is left to review a highly technical report that includes legal descriptions and legal information that often are beyond the understanding of most people.

The Legal Description

Each property comes into legal existence through a legal description recorded with the recorder's office of the area where the property is located. Often the property's legal description is expressed by reference to a parcel map such as the following for a client's six-million-dollar home:

> All that certain real property situated in the City of Belvedere, County of Marin, State of California, described as follows:
>
> PARCEL 2, as shown upon that certain map entitled, "Parcel Map, Lands of Fred Flintstone, as described in Volume 3296—Official Records, at Page 282, City of Belvedere, Marin County, California," filed for record March 3, 1980, in Volume 17 of Parcel Maps, at Page 87, Marin County Records. EXCEPTING ANY portion of the above described property along the shore below the line of natural ordinary high tide and also excepting any artificial accretions to said land waterward of said line of natural ordinary high tide.

Each time the property's legal existence is affected, a document is recorded on that property. These documents add to or subtract from the full rights of the property. For instance, an easement against the property subtracts from the property's rights whereas an easement in favor of the property adds to the property's rights. The following is an example of an easement in favor of a property, which becomes part of the property's legal description:

> AN EASEMENT for roadway purposes over the portion of the easement described in Parcel Two in the Deed from Belvedere Land Company to John D. Doe, recorded October 10, 1946, in Book 529 of Official Records, at Page 419, Marin County Records, which lies within the boundaries of Parcel 1, shown upon that certain map entitled, "Parcel Map, Lands of Fred Flintstone,

as described in Volume 3296—Official Records, at Page 282, City of Belvedere, Marin County, California," filed for record March 3, 1980, in Volume 17 of Parcel Maps, at Page 87, Marin County Records.

Exceptions to Title

The title report then lists all exceptions to clear title, meaning all financial obligations for which the property serves as security and all physical constraints that restrict the use of the property. For example, the easement described above in favor of one property will be shown as a title exception for the property burdened by the easement. When there is a loan that the property secures, the loan is recorded on the property as a *mortgage* or *deed of trust*, whichever security instrument is used in your state, and is also listed as a title exception. Think of the original legal description of a property as its birth certificate and the rest of the documents that affect the property as its credit report.

def•i•ni•tion

Mortgages are used in some states while **deeds of trust** are used in others to secure a lender's interest in a property. The promissory note describes the obligation while the mortgage or deed of trust is recorded on title to show the lender's security interest in the property.

Conditions and Restrictions

Title reports sometimes list covenants, conditions, and restrictions (referred to as CC&Rs) that affect the use of the property and may affect its value. Buyers must thoroughly analyze these constraints to determine whether they are willing to live under them. These restrictions can mandate the nature and extent of improvements that can be made, whether the property may be leased out, how many animals the buyers can have (and their sizes and weights), and a long list of other freedom-inhibiting factors.

CC&Rs also can show up unexpectedly on title when there is no condominium or home owner's association. These restrictions most often come into existence when the original developer creates a subdivision. In the subdivision process, each parcel will have conditions recorded on title to allow the properties to legally reciprocate with and conform to one another. Sometimes owners enter into agreements with adjoining owners and record these agreements on title.

Often the seller who failed to analyze his own title report when he purchased is unaware that there are title restrictions. These may come as a complete surprise to the unsuspecting buyer. The educated and prudent agent who understands these title warning signs can alert his buyer to these issues early on.

Obtaining Title Insurance

Title companies and closing attorneys search title to make sure all rights and obligations affecting a property are set forth in one report for the buyer's review. Title insurance is then issued to the buyer and lender, insuring that title confers the ownership rights described in the title report. If a claim is later made that the title report was in error, the title insurer steps in and defends the parties, legally protecting their property interests.

Title insurance has a body of law all of its own, which can benefit your clients if you understand it. Just like any other insurance policy, title insurance policies offer a wide range of coverage. There is basic coverage, extended coverage, gold coverage, platinum coverage, and everything in between.

Some policies provide protection that others do not. The property your client is buying may have unique characteristics that require a special endorsement. For example, if your client is buying a property that was just renovated by the sellers, there may be a potential for *mechanics liens* to be recorded on the property after close of escrow.

Agent to Agent

Basic coverage does not involve a site inspection by the title company, whereas extended coverage may. A site inspection allows the title insurance to provide coverage for more conditions than the basic policy.

def•i•ni•tion

Mechanics liens are recorded liens that contractors and suppliers may record on a property if they have provided services or materials to the property. The property is responsible for the lien amount whether the service was contracted for by the current owner or the prior owner. The assumption is that it benefited the property, so the property is responsible, hence a lien against the property.

Basic title insurance does not ordinarily cover mechanics lien claims without a special endorsement. Your client should be advised to talk to the title insurer about additional coverage. It is only through knowing the types of extra coverage available for title insurance policies, or at least those most customarily used, that you can guide your client to make these important title insurance decisions so they do not become last-minute issues.

Dealing with All-Important Contingencies

Contingencies are conditions that can make the difference between a purchase closing or not. A contract is *conditional* (meaning not yet a binding contract) until its contingencies are released, at which point the contract becomes binding and enforceable. In other words, it's a done deal when the contingencies have all been satisfied or removed. Until then, it is conditional.

def•i•ni•tion

A **conditional** contract is one that has conditions which make the contract nonbinding until the conditions are removed. Most often these conditions are loan or physical inspection contingencies, finding a replacement home, or selling a home. If these conditions are not satisfied, the contract terminates without penalty.

Most contingencies are general; some are finely crafted works of legalese. Some say practicing law while others say practicing real estate. The most typical contingencies are the loan and the physical inspection contingencies. You have to plan ahead for these contingencies, carefully monitoring the progress of steps being taken to satisfy these conditions. Until the buyer receives full loan approval from their lender and releases the inspection contingency, the contract is just that: contingent.

The Physical Inspection Contingency

The physical inspection contingency can be a hair-raising experience for you and your client. It takes a lot to perform a medical checkup on a property in a brief timeframe. The condition of the property—all the way from its soil to its roof and then out to its boundaries—requires assessment in order to determine if the property is worth what is being paid. In addition, its feasibility and legality must be analyzed. The feasibility relates to the use that legal zoning allows. Legality is the term that refers to whether improvements have been performed with the correct permits and according to building codes.

During this contingency period the sellers (and the agents in some states) also make their written disclosures of the property's conditions, covered in the next chapter, and often provide the buyer with a pest inspection report. These reports should be carefully analyzed by the buyers and their consultants. Most buyers have a pest control (often ordered by the seller), home, and sometimes roof inspection performed. Others also require a soil inspection, structural inspection, and survey. In most states, these inspections are made at the buyer's expense, with the exception of a seller-provided pest report which is often paid for by the seller.

All purchases should include a trip to the local building inspection department to assess the property's zoning and legality. Your client must confirm that all required permits were obtained when improvements were made to the property and that the use of the property conforms to the zoning requirements. In some localities, a city inspection report detailing these matters is a condition of sale. Although the seller's disclosures should detail these conditions, the buyer is prudent to make his own independent analysis because the seller may be unaware of some requirements and less than forthcoming as to others.

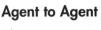

Agent to Agent

There are conventions in each area about who pays for these inspections and mandated local inspections. In some locations, the costs are split; in others, the buyer or seller pays for the inspections. Your office manager will be able to assist you with the customary arrangement for your locale.

Generally, the buyer has a short timeframe within which to complete these inspections. Assume that you are representing the buyers who have 15 days to remove their physical inspection contingency. Get them set up for general building inspections immediately. When the market is busy it often takes a week to 10 days for these professionals to conduct their inspections, and then they must produce a written report. Often recommended repairs need to be analyzed and seller credits need to be negotiated, which may involve hiring a contractor to provide a professional estimate for work to be done.

Fifteen days is therefore a very short period, but the seller wants this period to be brief because this is the contingency when some transactions fall out of contract. Because marketability of the seller's property is impaired during the time a contract is contingent, it is in the best interest of the seller for the inspection contingency to be as brief as possible. It therefore behooves you to move forward with setting up inspections immediately.

Agent to Agent

If you have an inspector or two on your Power Team, offer these names as possible service providers. There is a difference between providing names to select from and choosing the inspector for your client—whenever possible you want to provide options rather than dictating specific providers. Hopefully you have done a good job qualifying the members of your Power Team, and they will do a quality job for your client.

Allow your clients to choose their own inspectors. If they ask you for recommendations, and they will, give them a few to choose from. I have handled more than one lawsuit by the buyer against her agent because the buyer was unhappy with the inspector's services—and the inspector was referred by the real estate agent. The arm of liability swings wide in real estate transactions because of agency relationships that weave in and around the transaction.

The physical inspection contingency is ready to be released only after the inspections of the buyer's choice are performed, the legal analysis has taken place, and the buyer is satisfied with all evaluations. If, based on these many analyses, the buyer feels a credit should be made to the purchase price, this is the time to negotiate its amount. It is during this stage that some contracts terminate because the seller does not want to give the credit the buyer desires, or the buyer decides against purchasing because of facts that come to light during inspection.

The Loan Contingency

The loan contingency is another time-sensitive step. Because the loan can hold up a transaction, make sure you continually check in with the loan broker to ensure that the loan is on track for full *loan approval*. The *loan contingency* typically consists of two stages—preapproval and full approval. Historically, buyer *prequalification* was sufficient as stage one. Times have changed. The modern buyer should be *preapproved* for the loan, not prequalified, either at the time the offer is made or within a few days of its acceptance.

def•i•ni•tion

Loan approval is the full and final process whereby the lender approves of the loan and the property that will secure it.

Loan contingency is the period during which the buyer obtains loan approval. The buyer makes the offer contingent upon obtaining the loan described in the offer. The loan contingency often expires 30 days prior to closing.

In **prequalification,** the lender takes the potential buyer's application and prequalifies them for a loan based on the information provided, but undertakes no confirmation of the buyer's information, as it does in **preapproval.**

After a preapproval letter has issued, loan approval is no longer considered much of a contingency because the buyers are already approved for the loan. The only thing left to approve is the property, which depends on its appraisal and a review of the contract. Typically, neither of these factors presents a problem, but you should continually monitor the loan. Track the date for full loan approval and continue your monitoring thereafter because lenders are famous for last-minute preparation of hundreds of pages of documents requiring review and signing by the buyer. Don't let a last-minute lender spoil the transaction you have taken such care to maintain in a balanced, stress-free manner.

FYI!

A lender takes the potential buyer's application and prequalifies them for a loan based on the information provided, but undertakes no confirmation of the buyer's information. In the preapproval process the lender takes all the confirmation steps it would for full loan approval with the exception of appraisal of the property (because the property has not yet been located). With preapproval, the buyers have already been approved for the type of loan they describe in their offer. Only stage two of loan approval, qualification of the property, remains. Stage two rarely presents a problem as long as there are comparables to confirm the property's value.

Closing

About a week before closing make sure the settlement statement addressed in the next chapter is correct and the lender documents are in or at least ordered. For the buyer, signing closing documents can be a nightmare. If it were not for the loan documents, closing would be rather simple. The loan documents are sometimes a full inch thick and require numerous signatures. If you want to really understand them, it takes more than an advanced degree.

Because of this, it is important for someone who can explain the closing documents in a clear, concise way to accompany your buyer to the closing. For the buyer side of the transaction, the professional team may consist of one or more of your Power Team members. Both your escrow professional and the mortgage broker are well qualified to undertake this task. Because you are the

Agent to Agent

A gift such as that recommended in the referral stream system is a good idea to cement the relationship after the close is complete and the buyers have taken possession of their new property. After all, you have earned a nice commission and have become a trusted advisor to these people.

person who has been by your client's side every step of the way, you should also be at their side when they sign the closing documents. It is part of good service and caring about your clients.

The Least You Need to Know

◆ Your time is important, so qualify the client first.

◆ Know the steps required to make an offer and counteroffer, and understand the complexities in any contract.

◆ Understanding the title report can make you a real asset to your client and can head off any potential title issues early on.

◆ Stay on top of the loan and physical inspection contingencies.

◆ Attend escrow signing with your clients as a matter of professionalism and integrity.

Chapter 20

Using the Transaction Documents

In This Chapter

- ◆ Using a transaction management program integrated with standard contract forms

- ◆ Defining the agency roles you will encounter in a transaction

- ◆ The important terms of the listing agreement and purchase agreement

- ◆ The many required seller disclosures and agent disclosures

- ◆ Agent duties regarding conducting their own inspections

In your prelicensing curriculum and on your exam, the agency relationships and contract documents that will form the basis of your business were covered in part. But these principles are very difficult to grasp without a working foundation. Most licensees just memorize the material without really understanding how these key fundamentals apply to real-life transactions.

Some offices will train you extensively in their sales procedures, legal principles, and contract forms, whereas some will barely touch on these subjects. It is only through working with real transactions that true understanding arises. Although this book can't give you that, it comes close. This chapter introduces you to the transaction forms and how to achieve the most success when working with them.

A Transaction Management Model

In Chapter 12, I discussed the benefits of using a transaction management system and standardized real estate forms. Take a moment to glance back at that information. I would like to take a moment and briefly review that information.

Now that we have transaction management programs and standard real estate forms, there is no reason not to use them and integrate them together. For the most part across the United States, we use ZipForms (www.ZipForm.com) and WINForms (www.WINForms.com) in California, both available online and as product downloads. These standard forms now integrate with transaction management software, such as Relay Online Transaction Management (www.rebt.com) to simplify transaction documentation and management. With the use of these standardized tools an amazingly complex transaction becomes almost cookie-cutter simple. I encourage you to utilize these tools and use them online in your practice.

The Primary Documents

The documents that will become part of your life for your foreseeable future are ...

FYI!
Your escrow officer or other closing professional is the best person to step you through the intricacies of settlement statements. These statements can simplify complicated calculations and itemizations and step you through any problem areas.

- ◆ The listing agreement by which your sellers will employ you.

- ◆ The agency disclosure that advises the parties of their agency relationship with you.

- ◆ The purchase agreement.

- ◆ The seller disclosures and agent disclosures.

- ◆ The closing settlement statement.

The Listing Agreement

The listing agreement is the favorite document of agents. It is the contract that gives you the right to sell your client's property and to earn a commission for doing so.

Generally, the exclusive right-to-sell listing agreement appoints you as the exclusive agent to sell the property. You earn a commission if the property sells during the term of the listing even if someone else sells it. Sometimes other types of listing agreements are used, but most often you will use the exclusive right to sell.

The most important terms in these agreements are as follows:

- The price the property will be listed for

- The term of the listing

- The amount of commission you will earn

FYI!
Although commissions are entirely negotiable, they are often …
◆ 10 percent for raw land.
◆ 6 percent for residential and commercial property.

Listing Price

The listing price should be determined by your comparative market analysis (CMA). Often sellers feel their homes are worth more than what the comparables indicate. If you and your client disagree on price, the discrepancy needs to be resolved. In the beginning you will probably want to take any listing, but when you become seasoned you will realize that servicing an overpriced listing is a headache you really don't need. If your seller won't budge, it might be best not to sign him up.

Listing Term

The term of the listing is how long the listing will last. The agent wants a long term and the client wants a short term. If your clients have not worked with you before, they want assurance that you will perform before they give you a long listing term. You can't really blame them, can you?

You will come across sellers who are unhappy with their listing agent's services, but they're stuck in contract for a term that needs to run. Many real estate firms will not let a seller out of a contract based on dissatisfaction with the agent's services. They insist on expiration of the term before the listing is terminated.

Depending on the market, three months could be a listing period that will give you enough time to fully market the listing. If so, agree to a three month period which can be extended if your client is satisfied with your services. The New Ideal presents a new level of trust and integrity where pressure is no longer the name of the game. Instead, give clients a lot of breathing room and they will come back again and again.

The listing agreement also often includes a protection period, which is often 90 days after expiration of the listing. During the protection period, the agent earns a commission if the seller enters into a contract with buyers the agent dealt with during the listing period.

Commission

The commission to be paid on sale also is described in the listing agreement. Although commission standards are observed by agents within a given office, commissions are negotiable. They are not set by law and the agent is given the duty to advise a client of this fact. At the same time, your office probably requires that you charge a certain set commission. It is confusing to advise your client that commissions are negotiable and in the next breath tell them your commission has to be a certain percentage. However, this is what must be done.

Cave!

Many listing agreements have a bolded notice to sellers that commissions are not set by law and are negotiable.

Agency Disclosures

As a real estate agent, you have an agency relationship with your client. You are their advisor, and as such you are in a fiduciary relationship with them, meaning you are acting on their behalf in a relationship where you have a duty of trust and loyalty to them.

Agency relationships form the basis of an enormous amount of lawsuits in our already congested court system, primarily because they lend themselves to almost unlimited obligation by the agent. It is therefore vital for you to know the extent of the obligations you are required to perform for your client once you enter into this relationship.

Real estate agency relationships are a constant source of ever-changing legal definition, and you should be aware as definitions continue to change. This can only be done if you continually obtain education in this highly relevant area of the law. Given the magnitude of roles the real estate agent plays in a typical transaction, there is always a fine line to walk between illegally practicing another profession, rendering the service you are required to as your client's agent, and going the extra mile to take care of your client in the most thorough way you can.

FYI!

A sample agency disclosure in California describes the duties of the agent *to his or her client* as a fiduciary duty of utmost care, integrity, honesty, and loyalty. To the other party not a client, the agent has these duties:

- ◆ Diligent exercise of reasonable skill and care
- ◆ A duty of honest and fair dealing
- ◆ A duty to disclose all known facts materially affecting the value and desirability of the property that are not known to, or within the diligent attention and observation of, the parties

---

You need to know exactly when to keep going and when to stop dead in your tracks. For instance, when reviewing the title report or the seller's disclosures, when do you step over the line and begin practicing law without a license? When discussing the tax ramifications of your client's purchase or sale, when do you step over the line of legal liability into the bailiwick of the tax professional? If you do not want to wear lawsuits as a shadow, you must be able to make this distinction as part of your second nature.

Whose Agent Are You?

There was a song by The Who that was popular in the 1970s called "Who Are You?" I suggest the new agent play a variation of this song called "Whose Agent Are You?" whenever signing an offer. When you begin your representation of any client, you must advise your client whom you represent and obtain your client's written acknowledgment. In most states, an agent cannot act as a dual agent (representing both sides of a transaction) without written consent of all clients. In law this situation is a conflict of interest; in real estate it is described as dual agency. In other states, dual agency is prohibited, having been replaced by designated brokerage or transaction brokerage.

The agency disclosure form legally describes the type of agency you are performing for your client or clients. It is up to the agent to indicate on this form which option relates to the particular agency. Some of the options are as follows:

- ◆ Seller's agent
- ◆ Buyer's agent
- ◆ Disclosed dual agent
- ◆ Designated agent

The agency disclosure form explains the duties associated with each type of agency relationship. This form is signed by your client during your very first contact with them. If your agency relationship changes at any time during a transaction, you must then issue a new agency disclosure defining your new agency relationship.

Dreaded Dual Agency

Dual agency occurs when the same office represents both parties in a transaction. Some states prohibit an agent from acting as a dual agent while other states allow dual agency but call it something else, such as designated or transactional agency. Even if dual agency is permitted by law, there are many different ways real estate offices respond to fulfilling this precarious role.

Some offices will not allow one agent to represent both sides in a transaction as they believe that although dual agency is not illegal, it is asking for trouble. In those situations, the office manager appoints another agent in the office to act as agent for one of the parties to the transaction. The office itself is acting as a dual agent since the office is brokering both sides of the transaction, but when separate agents are designated to represent the clients, potential problems are significantly reduced.

FYI!
A sample agency disclosure in California describes the duties of the *dual agent* to both buyer and seller as:

- A fiduciary duty of utmost care, integrity, honesty, and loyalty.
- Diligent exercise of reasonable skill and care.
- A duty of honest and fair dealing.
- A duty to disclose all known facts materially affecting the value and desirability of the property that are not known to, or within the diligent attention and observation of, the parties.

The Purchase Agreement

The second most important agreement you will use is the purchase agreement. It is the successor to what used to be called the deposit receipt, and in some states purchase agreements are still called deposit receipts. Before we became a society requiring seven-page purchase agreements, we used deposit receipts of less than a page. Even the one-pager was successor to the good old-fashioned handshake, which today means, "How do you do?" where before it meant, "I stake my life on it."

More often than I would like to admit, agents do not completely understand the forms they use and therefore do not understand the obligations required of them and their clients. A thorough reading and understanding of the purchase agreement you use is absolutely essential. In fact, study it so well you know it verbatim.

If another office is the selling office (the office that brings in the buyer), their contract will be used in the transaction. The contract used is decided on by the office representing the buyer. Therefore you also want to be intimately familiar with any other contract forms that are typically used in the area where you practice. If you do not thoroughly understand the purchase agreement, there is no way your client can.

After you feel you can almost repeat verbatim and give a legal course in the purchase agreement your office uses, sit down with the office manager or a mentor you have chosen. Step through the discussion you should have with your clients as they are signing these forms and making their choices. The purchase agreement sets up significant legal consequences and includes numerous legal choices. You should be able to concisely and articulately explain each provision to your client while conversing intelligently with them about their specific situation.

Cave!

Some purchase agreements protect the agent by stating, "Both parties acknowledge they have not relied on any statements of the real estate agents which are not expressed in this document."

Understanding the Terms

There is an art to stepping through legal forms with a client. There is one way to do it if your client is the buyer and a very different way to do it if you are representing the seller. You should understand which terms are in the contract for whose benefit. You should know what is standard and what is not. You should be aware of other terms that may arise in the purchase or sale transaction. These other terms are only gleaned through experience, which a beginning agent does not have. This is a good time to ask for some guidance from your support team.

If you cannot get this training from your office, find your own training. There are unlimited resources from which to choose. Hire a consultant or an attorney. Go online. Take a real estate course. Go to your local board and review its educational resources. This is essential training. Once you really understand these documents, engage in some phantom transactions. Have your

Agent to Agent

In some states, mediation, arbitration, liquidated damages, and other legal-oriented provisions must be stated in bold lettering and initialed immediately below the provision.

mentor or office manager assign purchases of properties listed on the MLS. These transactions should have differing variables, so that you can experience different buying and selling scenarios.

Prepare the purchase documents and the rest of the documents for these illustrative transactions. Get to the point where you know each term verbatim so that when you are completing these forms with your clients you are knowledgeable. You will need to guide and advise clients as you determine the terms for their transaction, and you will be unable to effectively do this if your face is stuck in the contract trying to decipher it.

For your first few transactions, do what makes you feel most comfortable. You might want to talk with your clients, get an understanding of the terms of their offer, and then complete the offer in private. This way you can really focus on getting the terms right without looking like you don't know what you're doing. When you present the offer to your clients you will have thought out and chosen their options and will be prepared to discuss the terms with them.

Dealing with Legal Terminology

When it comes time to explain legal terminology such as mediation, arbitration, or liquidated damages, have a preprinted definition of these terms for your client's review. I review about 200 transactions a year. More often than I would like to admit, buyers do not choose binding arbitration because agents tell them not to. Agents should not be instructing clients, especially with regard to such important legal decisions. Agents should provide clients with a preprinted definition of arbitration and leave it to clients to decide or consult with their attorney.

The very best way to handle these decisions is to make your clients aware of them before they are in the offer stage. Give your buyers a copy of the transaction definitions so they may consider these important issues in advance so they may be prepared to make their own important legal choices when the time comes.

> **Agent to Agent**
>
> Some states have developed forms describing important transaction terms. If your state has, use this form in defining terms for your client. If your state has not developed this form and your office does not have one of their own, you should prepare a document that defines the important terms.

The Terms of the Purchase Agreement

The following are the most important terms that should be considered by buyers and sellers:

◆ **Purchase price.** The buyer wants to offer his best price, keeping in mind that if it is a seller's market, he may not get the house he wants if the price is not high enough. The seller should consider when he should counter seeking a higher price than the buyer has offered or accept the price offered for the sake of being in contract.

◆ **Deposits.** Many states use 3 percent of the purchase price as the norm for an initial deposit and increased deposit on a home. The *initial* deposit is paid when the offer is accepted and is often 1 percent of the purchase price. The *increased* deposit is most often tied to buyer's release of contingencies and represents the rest of the preclosing deposit. The seller wants to see the buyer put up a high deposit while the buyer wants to put up as little as possible. Thus, they generally follow the norm.

◆ **Loan contingency.** A preapproval letter conforming to the terms of the loan described should either accompany the offer or be submitted within a few days of acceptance of the offer. Make sure the financing terms specified are terms the buyer is willing to accept and that his or her loan conforms to what the market offers. The seller does not want his property tied up in contract only to see the buyer terminate the contract because he is unable to get the loan described. The timing for release of the loan contingency is important to both the buyer and seller. The seller wants to see the loan contingency released as soon as possible so he knows he's in a binding contract that cannot be cancelled. The lenders usually won't lock a loan for longer than 30 days without extra fees. Thus, the norm for release of loan contingency is 30 days before escrow is to close.

◆ **Physical inspection contingency.** The seller wants to see this contingency removed as soon as possible in order to move one step closer to making the contract unconditional. He also wants to get past the negotiation which sometimes accompanies the buyer's release of this contingency. The buyer, on the other hand, wants to have enough time to perform all

Agent to Agent

The usual time for an inspection contingency is 15 days. The usual time for expiration of a loan contingency is 30 days before closing. This may vary by locale and the needs of the parties.

the property inspections required, obtain estimates for any repairs required, and negotiate with the seller for a credit to purchase price if necessary. Most contracts try to keep this inspection period to 15 days.

◆ **Purchase of home contingency**. Should sellers counter the buyer's offer with a purchase of home contingency making finding a new home a condition of the sale of their home? Or, should they just build in a rent-back period so they can rent back from the buyers if they have not found their new home or are not ready to close on it by the time this escrow closes?

◆ **Sale of home contingency.** You will have discussions with your buyer clients about whether their offer should include a contingency making the sale of their home a condition of their purchase offer. In a strong seller market, an offer with this type of contingency will have less chance of being accepted. Generally it takes less time to sell a house than to locate and buy one, so as long as their offer to purchase has a closing date that accounts for sale of their home, they probably should not include this contingency.

◆ **Closing date.** The best way to analyze the timing of an offer is to prepare your transaction timeline by matching up the contract terms with a calendar. Transaction management programs make this job simple. Calendaring specific dates also provides a reality check for both the buyer and seller. Make sure the closing date works for your clients. They may have some needs for an extended closing, a quick closing, or a rent-back situation.

◆ **Liquidated damages**. Some purchase agreements contain liquidated damages provisions. In most states, if the parties agree to liquidated damages, the amount of damages available to the seller against the buyer who fails to close after releasing contingencies is fixed by the amount agreed to. This provision should be carefully evaluated by both the buyer and seller. This is one provision where a legal definition of exactly what liquidated damages are and the effect they have when a party defaults is absolutely necessary.

def•i•ni•tion

Mediation is a settlement process that precedes legal proceedings that is often agreed to in the purchase agreement.

Binding arbitration is a legal process that replaces the court system if the parties so agree in writing.

◆ **Mediation-arbitration.** Have a legal definition of exactly what *mediation* and *binding arbitration* are and how these choices affect the parties' rights if one party needs to sue the other.

◆ **Additional terms** can be the most difficult to understand and have the most legal significance. Review these carefully and pull in an attorney if needed.

Seller Disclosures

The seller's duty is to advise the buyer of conditions that materially affect the value and desirability of the property to the buyer. This is the legal definition. How does a seller judge what is material or desirable to a buyer he has not met? Most states have seller disclosure statements that attempt to elicit seller information bearing on these issues.

Many areas also have a supplement to the seller disclosure form calling for more information than what is called for on the standard seller disclosure statement. One question that often appears on the supplemental form is, "Is there any other condition that affects the value and desirability of the property to the buyer?" This is the catch-all that causes the seller to fulfill his disclosure duty and often creates liability for a seller who responds honestly to the rest of the questions but fails to include something that should be described in response to this question.

The problem with the process is that our seller clients need guidance in completing these forms. Failure to disclose is the most common reason buyers sue sellers and their agents. Yet agents are often advised by their offices to stay away from advising their clients on disclosures because this would constitute the illegal practice of law. The end result is the agent often hands her clients the disclosure forms and says, "Complete these and return them to me." End of story. Actually, the story doesn't end there; it often ends in litigation where both the seller and agent are parties.

> **Cave!**
>
> In some states, including California, agents are required to perform a visual inspection of the property and report written findings on the seller disclosure forms.

There is a better way. It would be a simple matter for each office to have legal counsel prepare a one-page instruction sheet for sellers to use when completing their very important disclosures.

Agent Inspection and Disclosures

Real estate agents have always been responsible for faithfully representing the known conditions of a property. There is now a growing trend across the country to require agents to actually *inspect* a property for visible defects and to *disclose* the results of their inspections to buyers. In some states already, both the agent for the buyer and the seller must undertake a visual inspection and report findings on a disclosure form.

In California for example, the agent's visual inspection duty extends to conditions within improvements on the property and on its grounds, as well as environmental conditions. Agents walk around with a "red flags" checklist performing visual inspections that previously were the job of the licensed inspector. Soon this may be the standard nationwide.

In these states where the duty of inspection is being shifted to the agent, there is a balancing act that must be done to fulfill the agent's duty of inspection while taking care not to hold himself or herself out as an expert. There is also an art to completing the agent disclosure form in a way that achieves these dual purposes. Make sure you fully understand the agent inspection and disclosure laws of your state by discussing this very important subject with your office manager or your state real estate association.

The Settlement Statement

The settlement statement reflects each amount charged or credited to the parties in the transaction. It is your obligation to make sure the terms of the purchase agreement are carried out in this statement. Call a week ahead of closing and ask for an estimated settlement statement. This will cause the closing professional to finalize the details of the transaction and complete anything not yet finished. You want to monitor the settlement statement to ensure that all transaction obligations have been expressed correctly. Is the buyer warranty shown as paid by the seller? Are the transaction fees prorated as described in the purchase agreement? Is any credit to the buyer correctly stated? Are there prorations for expenses between buyer and seller in accordance with the closing date? Is your commission calculated correctly?

The Least You Need to Know

- ◆ You should be fluent in the real estate transaction forms used in your area.

- ◆ The agency relationship is an obligation that needs to be fully understood by you and your client.

- ◆ The listing agreement is a contract between the sellers of a property and the office that will represent them.

- ◆ The purchase agreement is complex and involves contingencies and terms that you should thoroughly understand.

- ◆ Disclosures are mandated by law to be made by the sellers and sometimes their agents to describe conditions that may materially affect the value and desirability of the property.

Part 6

Becoming a Top Dog

Top Dogs adopt creative ways to stand out in their fields, the most popular of which are through cutting-edge strategies, giving and getting support, staging listings, and cultivating future income streams.

Top Dogs have lead generating destination websites that are rich with promotional content and valuable tools. They seek specialized training and professional designations in order to provide the most skilled and best services possible. You'll see why Top Dogs stage listings and pay for this service and you'll learn that Top Dogs also treat their businesses as a conduit for investment deals, always on the lookout for future income streams.

Chapter 21

Cutting-Edge Top Dogs

In This Chapter

- ◆ Making lead generating your first priority
- ◆ Having a lead generating website and providing special value on it
- ◆ Embracing technology with a bricks-and-clicks business model
- ◆ Obtaining specialized training and professional designations
- ◆ Networking to earn community respect and popularity

The Top Dog is a particular breed whose ears point and tail wags when opportunity appears. Top Dogs spring into action when they sense advantage, and in so doing emerge as the top movers and shakers in the real estate sales field. This chapter and the rest of this book describe some of the tools and strategies agents use to achieve admission to this unique breed we call the Top Dog.

Real estate sales can earn its top producers a robust income, and this is borne out by NAR's survey showing that top agents nationwide earn a median gross income of $177,400. In high-value areas like California, where the median home price is twice the national median, the median income for Top Dogs is also doubled. But it is not income alone that defines an agent as a Top Dog. There are many other factors, which are explored throughout these remaining chapters.

The Top Dog's Motivation

What motivates the Top Dog? A study of these unique real estate professionals indicates that they are motivated partially by financial reward and partially by a deep desire for professional and personal challenge. Top Dogs say that when they take their place in real estate, they know they have found their calling, at which point they move ahead with confidence and determination. These are some of the steps they take:

- They have a lead generating website that responds to existing clients and draws new clientele.

- They incorporate technology fully into their business.

- They specialize in a particular market.

- They obtain professional designations and training.

- They practice according to The New Ideal.

- They further develop their personal and professional power.

> **FYI!**
>
> Real estate generates about one third of the U.S. gross domestic product and creates jobs for over nine million Americans.

- They get support from assistants and advisors.

- They get support from a spiritual practice.

- They stage their listings.

- They build a referral stream system.

- They build future income streams.

We've discussed some of these topics already. This chapter focuses on website development, specializing, and obtaining professional designations and training.

Lead Generation Is the Top Priority

Your secret to long-term success, even when you are a millionaire, is to understand that lead generation is not optional. It is the foundation of your business and no matter how successful you become, you must always make it your first priority and personally administer it. Top Dogs have done this for their entire careers. Not only has lead generation been a top priority, it is the first thing the Top Dog does every day. They make sure their lead-generating systems are in place doing their job, and if that means making phone calls, they pick up the phone and work the system.

As technology has begun to automate marketing and lead generation, Top Dogs upgrade their high-tech tools to capture these valuable markets. They realize that marketing is an ever-changing job. Now that clients often come through the Internet door, they make sure their business plan changes to capture this valuable client base. Top Dogs know they cannot remain stagnant; they must incorporate ever-changing real estate models, especially when lead generation is concerned.

Tops Dogs, therefore, incorporate many of the options in the lead generating model described in Chapter 13. They are always testing new systems and innovating their business models. They do not wait for their offices to suggest change. They know they are entrepreneurial small business owners and it is incumbent upon them to have an entrepreneurial state of mind, always moving toward systems that work better and easier.

Destination Websites

According to the National Association of Realtors, 77 percent of home-buyers use the Internet as an information source in buying a home. And 21 percent find their agents through an Internet search. Another survey conducted by the NAR shows that buyers who use the Internet are also among the most desirable clients, because compared to non-Internet buyers, they …

- Spend 20–50 percent more on their homes.

- Close their deals in half the time of the average buyer.

- Are more likely to use an agent to buy or sell property.

Hearing these statistics, the Top Dog is on full alert, so much so that the vast majority of Top Dogs have their own destination websites to attract Internet buyers and sellers.

> **FYI!**
>
> Use of computers by agents now approaches 100 percent, with the majority using portable laptops. E-mail is used by 94 percent of agents while 85 percent use digital cameras. Use of PDAs is on the rise and the majority of agents now use five or more technology-based products.

Catering to Internet Clients

Before the Internet became popular as a way to find information, products, and services, buyers followed traditional methods of home searching: they drove around to look for homes for sale, they used newspaper ads to direct them to properties, and they ultimately hired an agent referred by a friend or family member to find them a home. Internet buyers for the most part discard traditional means and use the Internet to find both properties for sale and agents to represent them. Convenience and information accessibility is often their determining factor when choosing an agent.

Statistics show that on the average, Internet buyers visit six websites to find an agent and eight sites to look at property listings. When they do select an agent, they are motivated and ready to buy. This is the dream client we all hope for and the client the Top Dog sets his aim to secure through being one of the six or eight websites the Internet buyer searches.

A familiar term to all real estate agents is farming. Farming is considered the most effective tool for cultivating and identifying prospective clients. The disadvantage to traditional farming is that it takes a lot of effort and expense over a long period of time to capture your market.

FYI!
The brass tacks of a farming campaign are obtaining a targeted mailing list of about 250, designing and producing a well-designed mailer, composing hand-written notes, affixing labels and postage, sorting, and making trips to the post office. These mailing campaigns must be repeated on a consistent basis at least quarterly. This type of traditional farming is a lot of work, but the master marketing model incorporates it because it can provide good returns.

The answer for the Top Dog is to do reverse farming. Let your clients come to you via a lead generating destination website on the Internet. With traditional farming you decide what your specialty is, pinpoint 250 people who would be interested in your specialty, and bombard them with your mailer over and over and over. In Internet farming, you decide what your specialty is and put up a website that responds to an Internet search for that specialty—and they find you over and over and over.

Can you imagine having a market that delivers your message worldwide 24 hours a day, 7 days a week, 365 days of the year, while you sleep, while you lie on the beach in Hawaii, while you take in a movie? Your website is a 24/7 marketing resource of the most unlimited potential as well as a 24/7 resource for your existing clientele. According to a survey by the National Association of Realtors, nearly 90 percent of adults nationwide are online. This fact combined with continuous message delivery makes website marketing a number-one priority for Top Dogs. They lead the pack by making their business model one of bricks and clicks, offering impressive offices for client in-person contact and an enviable Internet presence for cyberspace clientele.

This edition of the book includes a new topic, a multimedia lead generation model (Chapter 13), which incorporates many Top Dog marketing features and adds a few they will now adopt. Top Dogs and aspiring Top Dogs should carefully review this chapter.

Defining a Specialty that Caters to Keyword Search

The secret to Internet farming is to create a specialty that caters to keyword search. For instance, "Back Bay Boston Mass homes for sale buyer's agent" is sufficiently specific for an Internet buyer who is looking for a home in the Back Bay of Boston and wants to be represented by a buyer's agent to locate an agent whose website uses matching keywords. Through a successful web presence, Top Dogs are able to attract any target viewer by making sure their website keywords draw the market they want.

How do you achieve this goal? Identify a small, focused group to target and make that your specialty. Or tackle this the other way around. Take your specialty, if you already have one, and create keywords associated with it, then break those words down into a smaller, more identifiable market. Be the client you want, sit at the computer, and input the description this Internet buyer or seller would use to describe your services.

> **FYI!**
>
> A seller may not search for homes for sale in a certain area. They may instead do a search for "real estate agents in Phoenix, Arizona." Follow the same process you did as the Internet searcher, but this time be the Internet seller.

It could be "retirement homes in a gated community in Sarasota Springs, Florida" or "golf course homes in Palm Desert, California" or "first time buyer homes (your area)," "lake homes in Sheridan Beach, Indiana," or "stock market investments to real estate market" (this is our Top Dog in Chapter 24). You want to make sure your site will come up in the top ten of the keyword search for both buyers and sellers. For the seller, you may need to also include keywords that attract sellers if they differ from your buyer specialty. Sometimes it takes paying an Internet search engine to achieve top ranking. Only you will be able to determine if this is the best option for you.

> **Cave!**
>
> Don't give in to the urge to forego keyword analysis. Most people do that and do not enjoy the Internet traffic that could conceivably replace the need to prospect for clients.

It is only through acting as the Internet consumer that you will target the right keywords to drive traffic in your direction. This is not the job for your website provider.

Only you can identify the market you want. The company that provides your website will have tools to assist you in completing this important step. If your intention is to be amongst the Top Dogs, take the following steps when key wording your website:

 ◆ Identify your specialty with such specificity that you will come up under the top ten of a keyword search for both buyers and sellers.

 ◆ Make sure the website provider you choose provides a way for you to key in these keywords.

Using Your Site as a Destination Point

Top Dogs make their sites a destination point, not only for those who use the right keywords but for their home base. "Build it and they will come" was meant for website marketing. When they come, as they will, Top Dogs give them a reason to stay. They treat their visitors well and give them what they are after.

For buyers, Top Dogs provide maps of the area, community information, school information, mortgage information, weather reports, a link to obtain their credit report, and access to the listings on the multiple listing service. But they don't stop there. A common mistake agents make is to assume that only buyers are looking at their websites. What about sellers or for sale by owners (FSBOs)? They, too, are part of the Internet generation and an important source of business for you.

def•i•ni•tion

Seller-only services are the single agency representation of the seller only.

Top Dogs attract Internet sellers and FSBOs to their sites by offering a free comparative market analysis, free staging services (addressed in Chapter 23), or *seller-only services* where they represent only the seller, thereby avoiding dual agency representation. If you want to attract sellers in a certain town or area, include detailed information about that community's special characteristics.

As computer and Internet technology has continued to take over the mainstream marketplace, more and more people are using the Internet to assist them in the home buying and selling process. Internet consumers are shopping for products and for services on the Internet. Before they list, many sellers surf the net to determine the value of their homes. In this process, they could easily come across your site if it is indexed optimally, and may very well choose to list with you. A recent survey indicates that 21 percent of Internet consumers choose their agent from Internet searches.

Some Top Dogs also provide concierge services to their clients by providing resources that clients may need to plan their move. Many website providers have followed the lead of the Top Dog by designing websites with pages for relocation that include these types of referrals.

> **FYI!**
>
> Eighty-two percent of listings are placed on the National Association of Realtors website at realtor.com.

E-Mail Productivity and Professionalism

Top Dogs are ready to deliver Internet prospects to their door. Each page of their sites includes an obvious link to send them e-mail. Internet surfers expect an immediate way to get in touch with you to ask about a property or your services. It's your job to make it easy for them to contact you.

You must also respond quickly to these communications. Internet consumers are accustomed to rapid response. If you do not respond in a brief period of time, 15 minutes for instance, they will move on to the next site which is only a click away. Many agents do not make e-mail a high priority. When you have a destination website that has been carefully designed to capture your market, make sure you are set up to respond to it when it comes.

> **FYI!**
>
> Responding to e-mail is where Top Dogs take a leadership role. They have built in ways to respond to contacts while they are in the field through web and voice mail paging.

The Master Marketing Model in Chapter 13 includes tools, such as web pager and 800 voice mail pagers, which will send leads directly to your cell phone from your web site or your 800 call capture system. Top Dogs take advantage of these relay services allowing them to respond to leads "in the moment." When you send or respond to e-mail, whether with Internet prospects or your regular business base, make sure your e-mail includes a full signature and address block. It, too, should be professional looking and include all your identifying information. Setting up a signature file is a simple procedure in every e-mail program. The vast majority of agents do not take advantage of this simple option—these are the very same agents who plaster their names and faces everywhere in every other conceivable manner, yet fail to capitalize on marketing when it comes to e-mail.

Specialized Training and Professional Designations

Another way the Top Dog achieves his status as a peak performer is through specialized training and professional designations. The Top Dog begins his career highly motivated to be the best, continually striving for cutting-edge strategies to tip the scales in his favor. These peak performers are motivated to go the extra mile, and they often believe that specialized training and designations will deliver them to their own personal finish line.

Broker Licensing

In most states there are two levels of real estate agents. The first is an agent or broker associate; the second is a broker. Most people first take the agent's exam and apprentice as an agent for a year or two before taking the broker's exam. Broker licensing is optional, but it is required if you want to work for yourself or employ others.

Top Dogs who obtain their broker's licenses feel they are catapulted to a new level of achievement. They gain a freedom in their newfound ability to work on their own which increases their bargaining power with the company they work for and gives them more of an entrepreneurial frame of mind. Some never leave the company they work with, but their commission split shifts more in their favor. Some start their own offices and either work alone or employ other agents to work for them.

FYI!
In the majority of states, licensees must have two years of full-time agent experience and about 90 hours of additional education in order to obtain broker licensing. This is just an average. Check with your state following the guidelines in Chapters 4 and 5 for more specific information.

In most states, agents may become licensed as brokers if they complete additional educational requirements and a period of time actively working as an agent. Each state differs in its requirements. In most states the broker exam is a full day with a break for lunch. The questions are very similar to those on the agent's exam but cover a broader spectrum of subjects. The broker prelicensing courses and examination preparation are handled by the same companies that prepare agents for licensing, as described in Chapters 4 and 5.

Specialty Training

Some Top Dogs attribute their success in part to the expertise they gain from course instruction. Julie, whom we met in Chapter 3, feels her expertise in understanding tax issues has brought her a broad range of clients she would not have drawn had she not become a tax wiz. Another Top Dog, Eric, believes that the contract law courses he has taken help him to understand contract provisions and contingencies that contribute to his success. Both of these Top Dogs carefully select the courses they take to fulfill their *continuing education* requirements to advance the particular specialty they have identified. Some Top Dogs I regularly deal with specialize in equity sharing and lease options, which gives them yet more ways to put deals together, a clear advantage in the real estate sales field.

Basic tax laws relating to real estate are not difficult to understand. The agent who understands taxation on the sale of a principal residence and on the sale of an investment property takes a leadership stance both among his clients and peers. Of course, you never want to give tax advice to your client, but knowledge of real estate tax laws allows you to converse better with your clientele and direct them to a professional when appropriate.

def•i•ni•tion

Continuing education is required in most states and in Canada to keep your license active. The number of courses required varies greatly between states and provinces.

The current principal residence tax law is simple. It exempts a certain amount of gain depending on whether you are married or not and has time restrictions with respect to residing in the property. That's it. As for exchanging out of an investment property, the tax-free exchange should be understood by every agent, whether residential or commercial. Its rules are also straightforward.

Obtaining Professional Designations

The National Association of Realtors reports that agents holding professional designations have incomes that are significantly higher than those who do not. Most Top Dogs acquire one or more professional designations as they achieve their success. As part of their carefully orchestrated regime to climb the real estate ladder, they achieve financial reward and professional respect far greater than the norm.

Some Top Dogs feel that their designations brought more respect from their clients and peers, which in turn heightened their

FYI!

The National Association of Realtors (www.Realtor.org) offers 15 designations and two certifications. There are other national programs and many state programs in addition. E-Pro is one of the certification programs. This program was featured in Chapter 12 and is recommended by many Top Dogs.

creditability and enhanced their professional development. Some feel that the training and study they undertook to obtain their designations gave them more knowledge and tools to use in their business, thereby increasing their potential. All felt that obtaining professional designations is an important career step to take.

Some designations are conferred by the National Association of Realtors, while some are given at the state and local level. Most of these designations require education, some have experience criteria, and some have tests that must be passed. The following list describes some of the more popular designations obtained by Top Dogs:

CRS (Certified Residential Specialist)—The CRS designation is awarded to agents or brokers who complete advanced training in listing and selling. The CRS designation is the highest professional designation awarded in the residential sales field. Only 9 percent of all agents and brokers hold the CRS designation. The designation has educational and experience requirements that must be met.

def•i•ni•tion

REBAC stands for **Real Estate Buyers Agent Council** of the National Association of Realtors, the national association that confers the ABR (Accredited Buyer Representative) designation. They can be found at www.rebac.net.

FYI!

Research shows that sales agents with the GRI (Graduate REALTOR Institute) designation earn at least 35 percent more than non-GRIs.

ABR (Accredited Buyer Representative)—This designation focuses on all aspects of buyer representation. Designees must complete the *REBAC (Real Estate Buyers Agent Council)* course, pass the test, and provide documentation of buyer agency experience.

GRI (Graduate REALTOR Institute)—Many Top Dogs obtain the GRI designation early in their careers. The GRI program consists of 92 hours of course instruction and is considered by many to be the most comprehensive training program available in the country. GRI is often the first designation agents obtain and becomes the stepping stone to more advanced designations such as the CRS and CCIM.

CCIM (Certified Commercial Investment Member)—CCIMs are recognized experts in commercial real estate brokerage, leasing, asset management valuation, and investment analysis. This is the designation that Jim, our commercial real estate agent from Chapter 3, obtained. There are extensive course and experience requirements for this designation in addition to an examination that must be passed.

CPM (Certified Property Manager)—Top Dogs in the real estate management sector acquire valuable real estate management skills through educational offerings leading to the CPM designation. CPM members have the competitive edge in real estate management.

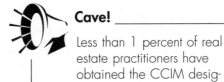

Cave! _____

Less than 1 percent of real estate practitioners have obtained the CCIM designation.

LTG (Leadership Training Graduate)—Some Top Dogs who have leadership roles in their communities have obtained the LTG designation. The course-intensive program consists of a curriculum that focuses on career improvement and individual goal attainment, and is designed to advance leadership skills. Less than 1 percent of real estate professionals have achieved this designation.

Reasons for Success—Community Leadership

You must enjoy associating with and helping a vast variety of people in order to achieve the greatest success in real estate. This is where the Top Dog becomes the leader of the pack.

The vast majority of Top Dogs have become community leaders of sorts. They involve themselves so fully in the community that they become known by a large segment of their communities. They become everyday words that roll off people's tongues whenever real estate is mentioned. They have being a social butterfly down to a science.

The reason for their popularity is not just because they show up. These people are genuinely interested in assisting others. They have earned a reputation for good, honest service. It takes time to earn this type of popularity and reputation, but Top Dogs do. This is the reason Top Dogs are typically older than the rest of us—they have been around for some time earning the respect of their peers and clients.

Watch the Top Dogs in your office or your community. See how they interact with others. Interview them whenever possible. You will find they are likeable, generous people willing to extend themselves whenever possible. They have also been out moving and shaking and have made networking a priority in their lives.

The Rest of the Reasons

There were too many factors leading to Top Dog status to include in this one chapter. The following chapters on staging listings, giving and receiving support, and tapping into future income streams must all be considered to grasp the whole picture of our real estate Top Dogs. They are multifaceted professionals and their expertise entails the many aspects described in the following chapters.

The Least You Need to Know

- ◆ Top Dogs follow the bricks-and-clicks business model, utilizing the Internet for lead generation and to promote their listings.

- ◆ Top Dogs regard e-mail correspondence as a top priority to retain Internet-driven prospects and to coordinate with existing clientele.

- ◆ Your website must be well indexed with keywords to be found in an Internet search.

- ◆ A specialty will help build your niche and get you discovered on the Internet.

- ◆ Additional designations will promote your achievements and set you apart from other agents.

Chapter 22

Giving and Getting Support

In This Chapter

- ◆ Performing an entrepreneurial analysis
- ◆ Reviewing the principles of personal and professional power
- ◆ Getting technology support
- ◆ Getting administrative support
- ◆ Obtaining virtual assistance

Top Dogs realize they can't do it alone. They recognize that it is through community and good values that their business and personal lives become rich. They subscribe to the philosophy that abundance results from equal amounts of give and take. When their business signals either a time to grow or a time to give back, they listen with an entrepreneurial ear. They understand that there are different types of support and are able to obtain the appropriate remedy at a given stage. This chapter demonstrates the necessity of adopting an entrepreneurial state of mind from which to consistently fine-tune your business and give it the support it needs.

The Top Dog Plan

As Michael Gerber describes in his book *The E Myth*, the successful small business must achieve and maintain a balance of three essential aspects: the entrepreneur (the visionary), the manager (administrative, practical steps), and the technician (in this context, the real estate professional). Although good values are implicit in any good business plan, many Top Dogs make them a priority by making personal and professional power a fourth ingredient that must also be considered as their businesses mature.

Agent to Agent

Read Michael Gerber's excellent books, *The E Myth* and *The E Myth Revisited*. These books will assist you in setting up your business with an entrepreneurial state of mind.

Top Dogs are wise enough to identify when their business needs to reach its next stage of development. They understand that the signal for growth is also a call for an assessment of their business plan. The difference between the Top Dog and not-so-Top Dog is that the Top Dog performs this essential appraisal before forging ahead to obtain support. The type of support called for depends on which of the four essential business ingredients requires bolstering:

- Is your *personal and professional power* in need of fine tuning?

- Is the call for growth more of an organizational, *administrational* one?

- Does your business plan require an infusion of *entrepreneurial vision*?

- Does the adjustment required involve the real estate *services* you provide?

Top Dogs realize that it takes continual monitoring of these four aspects for their business to achieve optimum success. If one facet gets out of kilter, the business will begin to suffer. The Top Dog is careful to continually observe her business's barometer to ensure that it stays on an even keel.

Hiring a Business Coach

Top Dogs often hire a business coach or consultant to assist them in performing these important business evaluations, especially at the first critical growth stage. This process doesn't necessarily involve a detailed master plan and days of a consultant's time. Your primary goal is to create a forum from which to make this important assessment and to receive support while doing so. A good coach will assist you in making sure that your business vision is realistic, sufficiently comprehensive, and that it matches the support you feel is required.

Now that coaching has become a popular method for entrepreneurs to gain support, you can set up an appointment very similar to a consultation with your financial planner, and hash out your needs in an hour or two. If you have the right business coach, especially one who has a good entrepreneurial vision and a thorough understanding of the real estate business, your decisions will be far better than if you make them on your own.

Agent to Agent

To find a real estate business coach, use those keywords in your Internet search. If you want to sit down with the coach, key in your locale. If you are open to consulting by phone, you can hire someone anywhere.

This initial stage of growth is critical and Top Dogs know that taking time to consult with an advisor and formulate a business plan is time and money well spent. Moving beyond the comfort zone of operating solo is a challenging step to take. Get the help you need to do it so your business will evolve to its full entrepreneurial fruition.

Monitoring Personal and Professional Power

The Top Dog understands that in order for her personal services business to successfully flourish on a long term basis, services must be delivered with a human touch. It is therefore necessary to first conduct an assessment of personal and professional power to ensure that a good measure of passion, humanitarian values, and good ethics are present in her work. To do so, she reviews the seven principles articulated in Chapter 8.

Cave!

Statistics tell that within the first year 40 percent of small businesses fail and within the first five years 80 percent more fail. The E Myth developed by author Michael Gerber is based on the idea that your business is nothing more than a reflection of who you are. If your business is to thrive, you must continually monitor it and take a self inventory at the same time.

Gary Keller and Joe Williams, the founding partners of Keller Williams Realty, are a perfect example of Top Dogs who practice by these principles. In 1983, these two brokers followed a burning desire to succeed by starting their own brokerage. They positively planned for success, and through a practice of good values, specialized training, and cutting-edge business strategies, they persisted to become a new type of real estate provider. With an entrepreneurial state of mind, they continually reached for new ideals, making personal ethics, teamwork, and empowerment strategies part of their business philosophy.

FYI!

The principles of personal and professional power are:

◆ Principle 1: See your work as your passion.

◆ Principle 2: Develop a burning desire to succeed.

◆ Principle 3: Be an independent thinker.

◆ Principle 4: Have a positive attitude.

◆ Principle 5: Be self-disciplined.

◆ Principle 6: Be ethical.

◆ Principle 7: Have good people skills.

The Keller Williams system evolved with a strong mentorship program whereby new agents are coupled with mentors, and when they become seasoned, they mentor others. They also developed a rather innovative profit-sharing program in lieu of traditional broker-agent commission sharing. Both their mentoring and profit sharing programs are examples of giving and receiving as a consistent flow that energizes and vitalizes business. The result has been a win-win approach whereby Keller Williams teams up with their agents in a personally, spiritually, and financially empowering manner.

The result has been a new generation of broker-agent relationships whereby brokers and agents empower one another and mutually share in the profits of their success. Today, Keller Williams is a highly successful, innovative international company with 273 offices and nearly 20,000 agents. Keller Williams's mission statement is now expressed as follows: "To build careers worth having, businesses worth owning, and lives worth living." Their values are described as, "God, family, then business." For more information about their system, read Gary's excellent book, *The Millionaire Real Estate Agent*. It is chock-full of Top Dog tools.

FYI!

M. Scott Peck, the author of the best-selling book, *The Road Less Traveled*, defines the incorporation of more caring values as the process of achieving spiritual competence.

One reason for Keller Williams's success is that their business model is based on the principles of personal and professional power. This type of mutuality of relationship brings a more impassioned, humanitarian quality of service as Keller Williams treats its agents as team members, and its agents in turn treat their buyers and sellers as team members. Their relationships are marked by a passion and human touch that is rarely seen in a business environment, especially in the competitive real estate world. I have personally had an opportunity to meet an office of these agents. The difference between these people and agents with other offices is dramatic, to say the least.

Although a Keller Williams-style enterprise may not be the goal of all Top Dogs, the vision is nevertheless the same. Many Top Dogs are aware that personal and professional power must be the foundation of their business to thrive in a truly impassioned way.

FYI!

Topping the list of the American Dream is owning your own home. Second to this is owning your own business. Because of the small business owner's inability to compete, small business was gobbled up by big business, putting business ownership out of reach for most. Times have changed with recent exponential technological advancement. It is once again possible for the small business to charge ahead as long as technology is its platform. Small business has been given a second chance.

Obtaining Technology Support

Given the importance of technology in the real estate field, the first type of support your business will most likely need is technological support. Top Dogs realize that technology is their ticket to paradise (or at least to Hawaii), yet before forging ahead for a high-tech overhaul, they take a step back to monitor the four aspects of their business in light of the impact technology will have on it.

Technology support comes under the category of both administration and entrepreneurial vision in the small business model. It is necessary for basic business needs, yet for the Top Dog it is at the core of future marketing and planning strategies. Monica, another Top Dog, demonstrates the plan she followed to merge high technology with her platform of skilled service and personal and professional power. She relates her story in her own words:

I realized in the early stages of my career that technology was a major key to success in the real estate sales business. I realized if I used technology wisely, I would be assured of a greater market share. If I did not, I would be out of business in a few years. I bit the bullet, opting for technology. Since I was not particularly technical, I decided that the best use of my time and patience was to hire a technology advisor instead of trying to master technology myself. My local real estate association continually guided me to the latest computer technology, and it seemed like the assortment of high-tech tools was never-ending. It seems like every time I blink, new technology appears.

First the MLS went online. That was an incredible learning curve for me. Then my desk phone became a traveling cell phone and the lock box became computerized. If that wasn't enough, laptop computers began showing up in the field soon followed by even smaller handhelds. Then wireless technology became the craze. Finally, good old reliable cameras became digital, and now my cell phone takes digital pictures. I have been able to keep in step with technology by having a good technology consultant.

Each time new technology becomes available, I hire my consultant to coach me on my purchase options and train me in the use of each device. When I got a laptop and began taking it home and in the field to clients' homes, my consultant showed me how to connect it to the Internet in each of my locations. When I began using a handheld, my consultant coached me on its use and its features. I learned how to synchronize it with my laptop and to download the MLS listings each morning so I could access up-to-date information anywhere in the field.

> **Agent to Agent**
>
> In these high-tech times, there are tons of technology gurus who like to show off their skills for free, especially if the gurus are related to you. Each manufacturer's website also provides free online tools to navigate you through their products. For Palm's personal digital assistant go to www.palm.com to check out their newest models.

When it comes to technology, I make it a part of my own personal skill set, using it in every facet of my business. I open-mindedly make technology my friend, not just something my hired help use. When I hired my first assistant, I pulled in my technology consultant to train her in the various technologies she would be required to use. I continue to hire my consultant on an as-needed basis as I continue to evolve as technology evolves.

I also keep in touch with technology unique to the real estate field by receiving weekly updates from the National Association of Realtors, and one year I served on the technology section of my local association. Each time new programs become available to make our jobs easier, I know about them. I now use standard real estate forms that integrate with an online transaction management program I use. These features have made transaction coordination more of a streamlined process. It used to be overwhelming for me.

Monitor Your Level of Personal Service

Monica and several other Top Dogs stressed the importance of continuing to monitor the personal services aspect of your business as it becomes more and more technology-based. Monica is sensitive to the fact that while technology has its incomparable advantages, bonding with clients and delivering personalized service cannot be overshadowed. She understands that technology and personal service must be sustained in equal balance.

Some of our Top Dogs shared ways they achieve this balance. For instance, Monica supplements her technology-based communications with a personal call to or an in-person meeting with her active clients at least once a week. She also includes a friendly and warm personal touch in her technology-based communications with clients. Her e-mail messages always include a personalized salutation and an endearing closing such as "have a nice day" or "with all the best," and she often includes a brief message that is personal in nature. She uses e-mail as she would converse with clients by phone. No one ever said e-mail communications have to be dry and impersonal.

Another Top Dog who administers his own website brings the personal touch to clients through technology-based concierge services. He creates a page on his website for each new client to provide them with handy resources and transaction information. This isn't exactly the personal touch that comes from pounding the flesh, but clients feel nurtured and cared for by this high-tech customized service. One of the big differences between Top Dogs and not-so-Top Dogs is the Top Dog responds to change proactively and sensitively, always keeping sight of their number one objective—to provide quality personal and professional services to their clientele.

Monitor Your Website Performance

Monica obtained her own website early in her career. It was specially designed for her and was state of the art when she got it. Now it is not. Monica has kept track of website providers and has observed that her website cannot compete with new turnkey sites that are rich in specialized real estate preloaded content and interactive tools. They offer visitors MLS listing searches and mortgage calculators. They give these Internet real estate consumers invaluable real estate news, information, and interest rate updates. These factors alone convinced Monica to trade in her site for an updated model.

Not only do sites today provide more information, but these new sites can generate leads through forms that Internet visitors fill out. When visitors search for a property, their search criteria goes in her e-mail in box and she in turn automates her system to send them listings that match their requirements. Monica says, "These are leads I would have attended 10 networking meetings to locate. And visitors who request a market analysis, too, are the types of leads I would climb mountains to find. Now, I just sit back and watch my website generate focused leads without me 24/7."

Monica is an entrepreneur in her ability to continually evaluate her business and replace old technology when new systems prove their worth.

Administrative Assistance

In addition to technical support, your business will eventually need administrative support. Monica's experiences in obtaining administrative assistance can help you decide how to do the same. About four years ago, when Monica's practice reached about 18 transactions a year, her business reached the critical stage that is encountered by all Top Dogs. It was time to move her business to its next stage by hiring support. Her office had a transaction coordinator, but because there are 15 agents in the office, a 15-way share did not provide the support she needed.

Agent to Agent

Here are some quotes of Top Dogs relating to the subject of getting help and support:

"Before I had an assistant I did not have a life. Having an assistant allows me to have more balance and more options."

"Earning good money and enjoying your work means spending money and getting support. I do both through hiring assistants."

"A secretary saves you time, but an assistant generates income. I hired an assistant and doubled my income in the first year and also freed up my time."

Monica had mixed feelings about hiring someone. On one hand, support would be a welcome relief as it would allow her to give her clients better service and would provide her with much-needed personal time. On the other hand, she had heard so much about the problems employees can cause. She was ambivalent, but decided to move beyond her comfort zone and hire someone.

Part-Time or Full-Time?

Monica felt that she could either split an assistant's time with another agent or hire an assistant on her own. If you find yourself at this crossroad, see whether another agent in your office has an assistant who could work for you part-time; or see whether someone else in the office could use part-time help. Since Monica's business grew at a fast clip, and would probably continue to do so, she decided to hire a full-time assistant with real estate experience.

FYI!

Fifty-two percent of personal assistants to agents are employed part-time and forty-six percent of personal assistants are unlicensed.

Licensed, Unlicensed, and Experienced?

When considering hiring an assistant, a decision that faces all agents is whether to hire a licensed or unlicensed person. The answer to this question will depend on the specific duties you will require of your assistant. If you find that your assistant can help you most by performing activities directly related to listing and selling properties, he or she must be licensed. Some of the duties that can be performed only by a licensed assistant include developing advertising copy, showing properties, explaining a contract or

> ### FYI!
> Agents who share assistants recommend that the assistant work full days for each person, such as Mondays and Wednesdays for one and Tuesdays and Thursdays for the other, alternating Fridays. Working half days for each person poses continuity problems.

other documents to a client, discussing property attributes with a prospect, and conducting an open house. If your assistant will perform only clerical and administrative functions, the assistant will not need to be licensed. Most states also permit unlicensed assistants to access the MLS and lock boxes.

A good candidate for an assistant is a licensed salesperson in your office, relatively new to the business and still struggling. Monica felt that hiring a new agent was only a good short-term solution since the agent would probably reintegrate into his own business after he got the hang of the real estate business. She wanted a long-term solution.

> ### FYI!
> The laws of the real estate licensing body in your state and the policies of your brokerage company will affect who you can hire. From a legal perspective, a license is required by any person who provides information to the general public that could be considered influential in a real estate transaction. For instance, an unlicensed assistant cannot show a client's property or communicate features of a property to consumers.

In Office or Out of Office?

There are factors that will determine the location where your assistant will work. Is there desk space at your office or will you have to accommodate your assistant in your space? Is it important to you that your assistant be considered an independent contractor (IC) instead of an employee? If so, assistants who work out of their homes are more likely to meet IC status than those working out of your office.

FYI!

Independent contractor (IC) status for an assistant is beneficial to you because it avoids the payment of employee benefits that can be costly.

If your personal assistant is an independent contractor, he or she is responsible for all tax obligations. If your assistant is an employee, you are responsible for withholding taxes and for paying various taxes and benefits in addition to the salary you pay. In other words, you will pay more if your assistant is considered your employee. Review the IC requirements described in Chapter 7.

The office where Monica worked did not have space for her assistant, so her assistant would have to share Monica's office space, work out of her own home, or work from Monica's home. Monica opted not to share her office space, nor did she want her assistant to work out of Monica's home. It was also important to Monica that her assistant qualify as an IC, which was another vote in favor of her assistant working out of her own home. Monica's decision was to hire an assistant who could work out of her own home, unsupervised by Monica. (These days another option for agents is to hire a *virtual assistant*, which is discussed later in this chapter.)

Monica also wanted to hire an assistant who had her own equipment so that she didn't have to purchase equipment. Her assistant needed to have a relatively new computer, Internet connection with e-mail, a fax machine, a scanner, and a printer.

The best way to go about hiring an assistant is to first create a job description. Identify exactly what you want your assistant to do. Take the time required to get a good idea of every duty that will be performed by your support professional. Then prepare the following:

- A list of tasks you want your assistant to perform
- A list of skills that will be necessary to get those tasks done

A List of Tasks to be Performed

This is the job description Monica now uses for her assistant:

- Print out daily calendars.
- Process new listings and enter them into the MLS.
- Use your transaction management program to prepare timelines for each pending transaction, calendar all dates, and track them as a transaction coordinator would.

- Track the progress of listings that are not yet in contract.

- Order appraisals and inspections.

- Track loan approval.

- Schedule listing presentations, open houses, closings, and other appointments.

- Prepare listing presentation packages.

- Prepare buyer presentation packages.

- Place advertisements for listings.

- Photograph listings.

- Process referral stream system gifts and mailers.

- Send progress reports to buyers and sellers.

- Coordinate signage and lock boxes for listings.

- Coordinate closing paperwork.

- Synchronize information between computer databases.

- Make transaction changes in the MLS database.

- Prepare CMAs in the MLS database.

- Perform listing searches in the MLS database.

- Prepare correspondence.

- Pay bills, make deposits, and perform all accounting on the computer.

> **FYI!**
>
> The National Association of Realtors' most recent survey shows that agents with personal assistants earn 2.25 times more than agents without. Twenty percent of agents use at least one personal assistant.

Specific Skills

The following is a list of skills an assistant would need to accomplish the tasks listed in the previous section:

- Internet browser knowledge

- E-mail proficiency

- Understanding of database management

- Microsoft Word experience

- Knowledge of accounting and check-writing programs

- Knowledge of PowerPoint for buyer/seller presentations and seminars

- Transaction management program proficiency

- Good people skills for dealing with clients and vendors

- The ability to multitask and prioritize

- Knowledge of MLS database

- Technological savvy

- Pleasantness

- Willingness to pick up and deliver flowers, newsletters, mail, and so on

How to Find an Assistant

Now that you know what skills you need in your assistant, how do you find this person? First, ask your office manager. Check with other agents in your office. Contact agents at other offices. Contact your local association for their referrals. Better yet, hire a certified real estate professional assistant.

FYI!

The National Association of Realtors provides certification to real estate professional assistants (REPA) following a two-day intensive introduction to the real estate business and to the specific ways they can support agents. The following is a partial course description:

- Understand the business of real estate
- Know what MLS is and be familiar with input forms and reports
- Be familiar with local listing and sales forms
- Know how to manage a transaction
- Understand the difference between licensed and unlicensed
- Understand the types of agency representation and disclosures
- Comprehend key marketing concepts
- Be familiar with the level of professionalism and ethics expected of assistants

The best way to find someone who has become assistant-certified in your area is to contact one of the sponsors of this certification program listed on the website of the National Association of Realtors. Contact the sponsor for your location and ask them for rosters of people in your area who have obtained certification.

Another option is to have the assistant you hire complete the two-day certification program. When Monica looked for her assistant, the REPA certification program was not yet in existence. She placed an ad in the local newspaper, which read: "Real estate transaction coordinator needed, full time, e-mail resume to (her e-mail address)."

She received 25 applicants, interviewed five, and hired one. She conducted skills testing on the computer and all office equipment and on phone answering. She tested for proficiency at software use and database management.

Monica's business did progress to its critical next stage as a result of hiring support. After 18 months her production nearly doubled, and Monica cannot imagine working without the support of an assistant. She is personally happier having someone to share her business with and for the first time since she became licensed, she has the freedom to take vacations and enjoy more personal time.

Money and Benefits

A specified salary plus bonus for each transaction closed is the most common way of paying assistants. You may also want to pay a bonus for each referral your assistant brings into the office. You can also pay benefits, such as medical, dental, and retirement benefits if you choose. The more you give, the more long-term allegiance you get. If appropriate, let your assistant know that he or she can move up from an administrative role to an independent agent if he or she chooses.

When you hire your assistant, don't forget to market to his or her sphere of influence and to give your assistant a referral fee for all business that comes in as a result. Monica's assistant's contacts have brought her several new clients, for whom her assistant has received referral fees. The circle of abundance has therefore reached Monica's assistant as well as Monica, as it should.

Agent to Agent

If you do hire employees, as opposed to independent contractors, enlist the help of a payroll service to handle payroll calculation, tax deposits, reporting, and benefits.

Obtaining Virtual Assistance

A virtual assistant is someone you find through the Internet. Virtual assistants can carry out many of the tasks of in-person assistants while performing their work in remote locations. They will primarily communicate with you through e-mail or phone. Virtual assistants have their own high-tech equipment and can give you a wide range of support without ever setting foot in your door. There are now virtual assistant educators providing certification as Real Estate Support Specialists. One is the International Virtual Assistants Association, www.ivaa.org.

Having a virtual assistant is really not much different from having an assistant who works out of his or her home. Because of the growing demand for real estate assistants, virtual assistants have become quite popular for the active real estate pro. You can even hire a virtual transaction coordinator at a flat rate of $300 (for an example, go to www.teamdoubleclick.com).

FYI!

Searching the Internet led me to web pages of a number of real estate support specialists listing the following services:

- Managing your listings
- Coordinating your closings
- Developing your web presence
- Designing polished marketing pieces
- Updating your MLS and database program
- Sending post-closing gifts

You gain several benefits from employing virtual assistants. Virtual assistants expand your hiring options since you have a global pool to choose from, and the competitive prices and services that an unlimited marketplace permits. For example, you might not be able to find a reasonably priced, experienced transaction coordinator in your area. With cyberspace as your hiring platform, you have highly competitive rates to choose from and can select a professional from virtually anywhere, not confined by the traditional barriers of place.

Virtual Assistance Versus Live Assistance

Virtual assistants offer several advantages over an in-office assistant. First, you have no overhead because you do not provide the assistant with space or equipment. Remember, this person is virtual. Second, they are clearly independent contractors who save you the expense of employee taxes and benefits. Third, you can hire virtual assistants on an as-needed, per-project basis. Fourth, they are paid at varying rates depending on the type of service you require, and some services are provided at flat rates. As the Top Dog moves her markets and business communications through cyberspace, virtual assistance can be a cost-efficient and productive way of gaining support.

Agent to Agent

If your virtual or nonvirtual assistant works out of remote locations, you can share information with them as if they have a direct network connection with your computer. With software such as PC Anywhere, they can connect to your computer and share files with you and vice versa. With synchronization software, you can also synchronize your assistant's calendar and contacts database with yours and vice versa. There are many services that provide sync capability, including Yahoo.com, which provides this service free of charge. Then, of course, you can manage your database online and both work off the same database.

Receiving Spiritual Support

Some Top Dogs also pursue spiritual support. They find that real estate and its competitive mindset present a constant challenge to staying aligned with inner values and empowering philosophies. Historically, the business world has very little experience of people living from a conscious, empowered state of mind. There is almost an unwritten assumption that to succeed in the professional world one needs to be ruthless.

Many find that ruthlessness is built into real estate almost more than other professions because of its highly competitive, fast-track environment. As The New Ideal takes hold, benevolence will begin to replace the lack of compassion in the real estate arena. The profession will become more empowered and integrity-based. For now, we still face ruthlessness more than benevolence.

FYI!

M. Scott Peck describes in *The Road Less Traveled*, "As we evolve as individuals, so do we cause our society to evolve. Evolving as individuals, we carry humanity on our backs. And so humanity evolves."

Many Top Dogs realize that while a strong business model is essential to success, humanitarian values and spiritual competence are the seeds to deeper, more everlasting rewards. They sense that their work has meaning in relation to the whole, allowing their work to bring them closer to mankind. They realize that as they evolve personally, so does society.

It is the unique Top Dog that feels, "My work is my life and my life is my work." She feeds a yearning for relationship with the world, allowing her business to become a conduit for the life she wishes to live, a visible manifestation of who she is and what she believes. I understand this type of Top Dog because I am one. My business has always been a major source of my connection to humanity, a place in which I engage mankind with the most earnest of my potential. Our small service businesses can become a place where the world becomes a handy size, where we can have a little piece of humanity for ourselves.

Most people with a humanitarian yearning have a spiritual practice that continually rejuvenates them and their business. Your spiritual practice may be based in gratitude and prayer. Some use a practice of meditation. Others seek religion and its community. Whatever your practice, it can provide a pipeline to a source of increased vitality and a greater sense of welfare and benevolence. It can be the reason why you get up each morning feeling the world just can't get any better.

Giving Support Through Mentorship

Many Top Dogs had mentors who helped in one way or another to guide them along their professional paths. When some Top Dogs reach a certain level of professional achievement, they often recognize the need to give back. The process of giving back adheres to the principles of personal and professional power. Sometimes the Top Dog accomplishes this through community service and involvement; sometimes she mentors other real estate professionals on their own career path.

Mentoring is a tool used to guide and develop someone else's career. If you focus on the seven principles of personal and professional power and coach your protégé on The New Ideal, then both of you will gain immeasurably. You have an abundance of wisdom and experience to share, and an attitude of gratitude to go with it. Your protégé has enthusiasm and fresh ideas to share with you. The synergy between mentor and protégé is an awe-inspiring process that feeds both mentor and protégé great riches and reward. For some Top Dogs, the process of mentoring is their way to express gratitude for things gone well.

The Least You Need to Know

- ◆ The successful small business is a mix of entrepreneurial, managerial, technical, personal, and professional power.

- ◆ With as-needed technology support, you can keep pace with technology and not have to master it yourself.

- ◆ There are many options concerning an assistant, like full time or part time, licensed or unlicensed, local or virtual.

- ◆ Your may want to hire a business coach to help you monitor your business and its growth.

- ◆ A spiritual practice can vitalize your business with humanitarian values.

Staging Your Listings

In This Chapter

- ◆ A look at what a stager does
- ◆ An explanation of curb appeal
- ◆ A lesson in exterior staging
- ◆ A quick course in interior staging
- ◆ A view of why staging is cost effective for you

Another step some Top Dogs take is to stage their listings. They see every single listing as an opportunity to top the market. They analyze the properties they list and have them professionally staged before they are presented to their market. These Top Dogs pay for their own staging, making it part of their listing package. They see it as a cost of doing business and a powerful market advantage. Let's take a closer look at staging and why it has become an important process utilized by some Top Dogs.

The Stage for Home Staging

But first, let's set the stage for the need for home staging. How many times have you visited a property to give a listing presentation and have been greeted by a disorganized mess? The house was fine, its location was excellent, but it was in need of some tender loving care. You wanted to banish the clutter, freshen up the wear and tear, spruce up the landscaping, and give it a brighter overall look. You toyed with the idea of bringing over a cleaning team, suggesting that your clients have a yard sale, or better yet, just rolling in the moving truck early and taking most of it away. But your hands were tied. You serviced the listing as best you could and the property sold for lower than fair market value and took longer to sell.

> **Agent to Agent**
>
> Do a search on the Internet for "home staging," and then confine the search to your locale. You should find a number of home stagers and a description of their services.

Staging Is Finally Taking Hold

Historically, home staging was the privilege of the wealthy. Staging wasn't really something within the province of the everyday homeowner. Times have changed. Staging has emerged as a respected method of increasing the value of a home for sale and reducing the time it stays on the market. Even *Home and Garden Television* now has several shows showing the great financial benefit of staging a house for sale.

> **FYI!**
>
> Nationwide, the typical home-buyer household consists of a married couple aged 39 with a household income of $71,300. This is the homebuyer staging should be geared toward.

> **FYI!**
>
> The typical home seller has owned their home for six years.

It's not just the cluttered property that staging benefits. The staging process can enhance even the most pristine home, increasing its market appeal and value. In California, where staging is most popular, properties can sell for 5–10 percent more than their nonstaged competition. Although it has taken time, staging is beginning to take hold in most major markets across the country. The Top Dog uses it wisely as a way of making listings more attractive and making sellers feel well taken care of.

Convincing Clients to Stage

Staging is a sensitive subject, especially when you are asking your clients to shell out hard bucks to pay for it. But there is an easier way to accomplish this objective. You can have your listing staged with the blessing of your client. In fact, not only will you have your client's blessing, you will be assured of getting their listing and their many referrals in the future.

The first step is to emphasize that the staging you propose has nothing to do with the seller's decorating choices. It is just a marketing process you feel brings sellers more money than they would otherwise receive. The second step is to pay for the staging yourself.

This is how this Top Dog handles the same situation. The Top Dog starts with: "Mr. and Mrs. B, I believe in getting top dollar for the properties that I list, so much so that I provide staging as a part of my listing services. I am such a believer in it, I pick up the cost. Staging has a proven track record of bringing a higher price and a quicker sale than a property that is not staged." Mr. and Mrs. B respond with, "We appreciate it. How can we help?" The Top Dog answers, "The stager will be asking your permission to take a number of steps that result in making homes appeal to a wider range of buyers. Just your cooperation would be appreciated."

Mr. and Mrs. B respond, "Oh sure, whatever we can do. Thanks so much for your help. Will we pay you back when the property sells?" The Top Dog response is, "No, this is part of the service I provide at my cost." Mr. and Mrs. B (to their sphere of influence of 250 people), "Top Dog paid to have our home staged, and it sold in 15 days for more than the house down the street. The home staging process really worked, and Top Dog didn't even allow us to reimburse him. He paid for this service out of his pocket, increased our sales price, and reduced its time on the market." The Bs' sphere of influence: "What was Top Dog's name and number?" Mr. and Mrs. B, "Better yet, go to his website where the services he provides to sellers are listed, and you can view other properties for sale."

Cave!

Make sure the designer you hire has staging experience. Staging is a highly specialized service entailing specific proven steps that make a home more appealing to your typical homebuyer.

What Is Staging?

Staging a home for sale is a two-step process. Step one is to improve the home's curb appeal. Step two is to enhance its interior appeal. Home staging is a type of psychological artistry. Nobody was trained for it. There's no licensing for it. Although stagers employ some elements of interior design, they may not be licensed interior designers. Some in the staging field break down the process further by defining *home styling* as reorganizing and redesigning the home's *existing* elements and decor while *home staging* involves bringing in *new* elements and decor. For purposes of this book, we will just call the process *home staging*.

The intent of staging is to create a favorable first impression from the first vision of the property at street side to the inside entry and throughout the primary rooms through the skillful use of design procedures. Staging a home for sale is actually the opposite of interior design. Interior designers customize a home to the needs and style of its owner; staging is a *depersonalizing* process. The stager neutralizes the home to give it a look that is universally appealing. The process entails wiping the home clean, refreshing it, and furnishing it in a neutral manner so as to make it appeal to the widest possible audience of home buyers.

Home staging is an art form of sorts, which incorporates openness and light while dramatizing entry focal points. The professional stager who has experience staging homes for sale is able to create a home that does not look as if it belongs to someone else. Instead, it looks like a display in a designer showcase. The effect makes buyers want to call it their own. Let's take a closer look at each of these processes involved in home staging, beginning with improving a home's curb appeal.

Adding Curb Appeal

Have you ever watched a show on *Home and Garden Television* called *Curb Appeal*? This excellent show depicts the process of creating curb appeal at its very best. It is no less than miraculous to watch these talented home stagers increase a home's curb appeal.

Exactly what is meant when someone says a home has good curb appeal? Curb appeal is real estate lingo for a house that looks so good on the outside that it says, "Come on in." First impressions are important when it comes to selling homes. Buyers thirsting for their perfect dream home must be greeted with curb appeal in order for a home to reach the top of its market. Curb appeal is an intangible quality that causes buyers to think emotionally instead of logically.

We've all been exposed to good curb appeal. You drive up to a home, and you want to make it your own. It could be the grassy lawn, the English garden and arbor, or the meandering walkway. This home speaks to the potential buyer, who responds, "Yes. This is it. This is the home I have been dreaming of." This is that subtle quality called curb appeal. A home with curb appeal will get the attention of every potential buyer who sees it.

Agent to Agent

The National Association of Realtors reports that good curb appeal is a major contributing factor in the majority of homes sold.

When your client bought his or her home it probably had good curb appeal. But over the course of a long ownership, people just naturally improve the inside of their homes while paying little attention to the outside. When it comes time to sell their home, an ideal opportunity to restore curb appeal comes knocking on the door. Giving a home curb appeal doesn't have to mean major retrofitting. There are eight basic steps home stagers follow:

1. **Landscaping.** Trim, mow, and clear away. Replace flower beds with fresh blooming flowers. Create a small English garden on the way up to the door with a profusion of flowering and wispy plants.

2. **The entryway.** Is the walkway appealing? If not, spruce it up, wash it, paint it, or replace it. If possible, make it meander gently as it delivers buyers to the front door. Do the porch, landing, or stairs need attention? Painting or surfacing can go a long way toward making the exterior entryway more appealing.

3. **The front door.** The front door is a major focal point. Painting or staining it just the right color to anchor entryway features to the house and yard works wonders to revitalize the exterior.

4. **Exterior paint.** Touch up the exterior trim and paint.

5. **Windows.** A good cleaning of all windows and screens will add sparkle to the entire home. Should some trim around the windows be added? Add shutters if they would complement the look. Would awnings enhance the look of the windows?

Cave!

Your stager should have workers who can follow a basic staging system for a reasonable cost. Be sure, however, that you and your stager agree about what is included in "basic staging."

Agent to Agent _____

One method I have used successfully to make the neighborhood more attractive is to offer to spruce up the yards for the immediate neighbors. I have paid to have lawns mowed and debris hauled. I also use this as a door-knocking opportunity to meet the neighbors who have in turn ended up as my future clients. They are always impressed that I stage my listings and pay for this service.

6. **Accessories.** How about an arbor? Would some wrought-iron accessories be a good addition? Is the fence in good shape or should it be repaired and painted? Would simple additions of roof rails, garden rails, or porch railings enhance the look?

7. **Sprucing up.** Open the front curtains and shutters. Replace the welcome mat with a classy decorative one. Clean out the garage and then keep the garage doors closed.

8. **Neighbors.** What do the neighboring properties look like? One thing stagers sometimes miss is the neighbors' yards. You want your neighbors' homes to look as nice as yours. Often, it is worth paying for a little staging on their properties, if they will agree.

Interior Staging

The following are the primary steps involved in interior staging:

1. **Cleaning, repairing, and painting.** A professional cleaning team deep-cleans every surface, window, floor, carpet, nook, and cranny. All odors are eliminated and air fresheners are placed at ideal locations. Cosmetic and functional repairs are made, such as caulking tubs, fixing drippy faucets, repairing sticking doors, and mending fences. A fresh coat of paint is applied to the entryway and primary rooms.

2. **Getting rid of clutter.** Many homes have many more furnishings than they should. One of the objectives of home staging is opening up the home, giving it an inviting, airy flow. This is done by reducing clutter, furnishings, and accessories. The stager will need your client's assistance in storing many of her furnishings and belongings. All it means is early boxing up or clearing out since they will be moving anyway. About half of the contents of closets, shelves, and cabinets should be packed up and moved out of the home entirely. Space needs to be freed up so a buyer can get the feeling of spaciousness.

3. **Depersonalizing.** Your clients are asked to pack up family photographs and personal collections. Buyers need to envision themselves living in the home, and it is hard for them to do so when faced with the seller's personal items. Every room of the home needs to be neutralized to make it attractive to a wide range of buyers. Nothing should distract the buyer or bring his focus to the seller's belongings instead of the house itself.

4. **Open everything up** to increase the flow to the door, through the home, and into its yard. Furnishings are reorganized to maximize the feeling of space and comfort.

> **FYI!**
>
> If you don't already have a stager on your *Power Team*, find one and establish a package that will address basic staging as described in this chapter. It should not cost more than $1,500. There may be add-ons your stager suggests, and your client can decide whether they want to absorb the cost of items beyond the basic staging package.

5. **Decorating and accessorizing.** Once the home is uncluttered, depersonalized, and opened up, the process of decorating takes place. Some of the owner's pieces are brought back in while some rental pieces are used for accessorizing and décor. Rental artwork is sometimes placed throughout, plants are often brought in, and decorative lighting is ideally situated. Stagers have sources to rent anything and everything.

6. **Highlighting focal points.** The stager highlights key features, particularly in entry rooms, such as fireplaces, view windows, and doors. Sometimes new window treatments and mirrors are added for special effect.

7. **Maintaining.** The seller must commit to keeping the home spotless for the time it is on the market. They should leave the home each day believing it will be previewed by its potential buyer that day. They should keep the outside as well maintained as the inside. Fresh-cut flowers are delivered and placed weekly in the home.

Home staging can be done on many different levels, from a thorough cleaning to a remodeling. The more done in the staging process, the better the opportunity to secure a faster sale and a higher sales price.

More advanced staging involving minor remodeling and landscaping should also be considered in conjunction with basic staging. High-end properties frequently justify this expense, which may increase an already high listing price significantly. Remodels are generally aesthetic in nature, like removing an inconvenient wall or redesigning an entryway. Landscaping changes may encompass modifying the flow of the garden or redesigning how the yard relates to the home. Only you and your stager can determine whether the market and the property justify the use of advanced staging. Just know that it is there for the asking.

Staging Is an Investment

Why would the Top Dog want to incur the expense of staging? It doesn't sound like a good way to make money. The reason is that it sets the Top Dog apart from the rest and causes homeowners to want the Top Dog to make the same thing happen to their homes. The Top Dog gets a well-deserved reputation for selling homes faster and at higher prices. He also becomes known for being professional enough to know what steps to take and being willing to pay for the work to make it happen.

A Top Dog recognizes that it takes spending money to make money. This is the Top Dog's thinking. He looks at the time and money he spends to market his business. Sometimes he gets a return; often he doesn't. Most facets involve his time, like the time-intensive prospecting he once had to do. Staging is a direct investment in obtaining a listing and increasing the value of the listed property from which he will make a commission while reducing the time the home will be on the market. It takes none of his time, only that of his stager. He can't really think of a better investment in his business and a more guaranteed return on investment.

> **Agent to Agent**
>
> The agent also knows that his expenses are deductible, and that his commission increases with the increase in selling price. His time is valuable, too, so if he can reduce the listing time, he reduces the effort required for additional open houses and reviewing unacceptable offers.

When you realize that the new market the Top Dog captures with his listing package allows him to reduce or even eliminate time and money spent prospecting, he's made the staging costs back in spades. But the Top Dog doesn't think in nickels and dimes. He knows that operating a profitable business means making investments. With his entrepreneurial state of mind, he recognizes that this is just another investment in a long line of many made to ensure that his business will thrive and stand out from the rest.

Also, understand that the staging you have done should relate to the commission you will earn. You really do not want it to cost much more than 10 percent of what you will net on the sale. If you practice in an area where values are below the median home price, have your stager customize a package that is cost-effective but is still impressive. You will know how to package staging within your marketplace to bring forth the very best result for both you and your client, even if its cost is only a few hundred dollars. It's more a matter of gaining client allegiance because you care enough to contribute to their well-being while at the same time enhancing the appeal of their home. This is certainly a winning combination.

When your stager performs her job, have her also prepare a list of add-ons she recommends and her price associated with each. Quite often, once sellers see the transformation brought about by basic staging, they are willing to go further and absorb the cost of additional work themselves. Sometimes sellers are willing to match the contribution you have made, making the staging result all that much more dramatic.

Some homes require more than the basic package to achieve an optimum staged looked. Since money is often an issue, especially when the seller is moving and often upgrading to a more expensive home, we have a system in place that allows the seller to pay at closing when the house sells. If the extra work is provided by our stager or one of our regular workers, they agree to defer payment until closing. In the unlikely event that the property does not close, the seller signs an agreement to pay within 30 days of expiration of the listing. If the contractor providing the add-on will not defer payment until closing, I advance the payment with my client's agreement to reimburse me.

The Least You Need to Know

- A stager is a professional whose business is to make a property appealing to buyers at sales time.

- Curb appeal is the first impression that every property you list should have.

- The interior of a home should look spacious and airy.

- Most homes have too much clutter and too much furniture and accessories.

- A properly staged home will typically sell quicker and for more money than a similar home without staging.

24

Future Income Streams

In This Chapter

◆ Benefiting from future income streams

◆ Real estate as an investment choice

◆ Invest in real estate without investing money

◆ Putting together creative real estate investments

◆ Packaging your business for future sale

Top Dogs focus on ways to earn income without spending too much time earning that income. Although commission earnings are far better than hourly earnings, they are still tied to your time. If you don't spend the time, you won't receive an income. The same is true for any fee-based service.

Top Dogs also focus on ways to earn profit free of taxation. This means investing in real estate. They have "intuitive antennas" that are always searching for ways to invest in real estate so they can earn profit and exchange out of their investment without being taxed. In this manner, they stockpile earnings tax-free, and if they do cash out without reinvesting, they are taxed at the lower *capital gains tax rates* instead of *ordinary income tax rates*.

def•i•ni•tion

Capital gains tax rates are significantly lower than **ordinary income tax rates**. Capital gain is the difference between what you pay for a property (and the improvements you made) and what you sell it for. This gain is taxed at lower capital gains tax rates. Ordinary income tax rates apply to the money you earn in your work, for example. This tax rate is much higher.

If you start out your real estate career with the intention of creating *future income streams*, you will have a future marked by financial abundance even if you are unable or unwilling to work. You will develop a frame of mind that continually probes for income stream opportunities. This chapter shows you how some Top Dogs accomplish this objective.

Creating Future Income Streams

There are four primary ways of creating future income streams within the real estate sales field:

- Continually investing in real estate
- Turning your commissions into equity interests in clients' properties
- Facilitating stock market investor transitions to the real estate market
- Selling your business

Each of these is discussed in the following sections, but first, we take a look at your personality characteristics to see if you have an investor state of mind. Don't worry; if you don't, you are on your way to one right now.

The *Rich Dad* Books

I highly recommend Robert Kiyosaki's *Rich Dad* books, but most particularly *Cash-flow Quadrant*. He categorizes people as employees, self-employed, business owners, or investors depending on the way they generate income. Employees work for someone else and find security more important than money. The self-employed are their own bosses, rarely delegate, and generally work very hard with their earnings tied to their time. The business owner hires others to do the work while she navigates the ship. Business owners make money that is tied to their time far less than the self-employed.

The last category, and the one we all aspire to reach, is the investor group. This group makes money *with* money, irrespective of the time they put in. When you become an agent, you join the ranks of self-employed, single-handedly taking the bull by the horns, commission by commission. But if you follow the steps in this chapter and in *Cashflow Quadrant*, you will join the right quadrant of the business owner and investor.

Investing in Real Estate Continually

As a real estate professional, you are exposed to deals every day of your life. You're continually in the right place at the right time. The question is, will you take advantage of your setting? Most agents do not.

Start investing in real estate whenever and wherever you can. We've seen the stock market collapse. Real estate has a reliable long-term rate of return, and with its preferred tax treatment, it really can't be beat. The demand for real estate has skyrocketed as investors have transitioned from the stock market to the real estate market.

Although the real estate market has since softened, it still continues to be a preferred investment choice, not only because it is more reliable and consistent than the stock market, but also because investment real estate has more tax benefits than any other investment. You receive investment income and appreciation, but your taxable bill diminishes as you take advantage of *depreciation*, *tax deductions*, *capital gains*, and *tax-free exchange* tax benefits.

def•i•ni•tion

Depreciation is the allocation of the cost of an improvement over the life of the asset in the form of a tax deduction. Other **tax deductions** for investment property are mortgage interest, property taxes, and insurance, to name a few. **Capital gains** tax treatment allows you to be taxed at minimum tax rates on a sale while a **tax-free exchange** defers any tax on gain at a sale as long as you replace your investment property with another.

Begin to see yourself as far more than a person who assists others in acquiring real estate. See yourself as a real estate investor first and foremost and a real estate agent secondarily. Always be on the lookout for a good deal for yourself. Develop an investor state of mind, always ready to do what it takes to acquire and hold on to real estate. It is your ticket to wealth and early retirement. And as a real estate mogul, your financial expertise will benefit not only you but your clients as well. This is how Top Dogs see themselves.

In the beginning, you may only be able to afford bits and pieces of real estate. But you will learn to carve real estate into divisible co-ownership pieces because your financial plan depends on it. You will begin to specialize in a market that sees co-ownership as a valuable way to acquire the most desirable asset, real estate. Your co-ownership model is described for you below. It takes the worry out of owning property with others while you and your co-owners reap the rewards of leveraging investments through the use of combined assets and talents.

Take Commissions as Equity Interests

One way to create an income stream is to transform a potential commission into an interest in your client's property. If you are not a broker, you may not be able to apply this equity conversion to the company's portion of the commission, but you can for your own portion of the commission. In so doing, you also transform the tax laws relating to what you will earn, and you move from the quadrant of the self-employed to the quadrant of the investor.

Cave!

Check with your tax professional regarding criteria that must be met to avoid a finding of imputed income. Imputed income is income that would have been earned and taxed in a certain manner but was changed by an act of the taxpayer.

FYI!

A recent survey by NAR indicates that a growing number of agents have 100 percent commission arrangements with the offices they work for. They still pay fees, but not by commission split. For these agents, they are able to transform all of their commission to equity interests.

Commissions are taxed as ordinary income whereas profits on long-term investment property ownership are taxed as capital gains. For example, $10,000 of the commission is your split. You and your client, the buyer, agree that you will convert your commission to an ownership interest in the property acquired. As a result, you start an automatic future income stream because you will earn an agreed-upon percentage of the property's appreciation and any income it may produce. This procedure is called equity sharing, also more simply known as co-ownership or a joint venture.

It works like this. Had you received your $10,000 commission, you would have earned $10,000 exactly and been taxed at ordinary income tax rates. You did not receive a commission; instead, you made an investment in real estate. As the owner of real estate, taxation is deferred until the real estate is sold, at which time you have the option of exchanging tax-free into another investment property or paying tax at lower capital gains rates. The net result is you have deferred tax on earnings, set up future income streams, and presumably will make a good tax-deferred profit.

Not-so-Top Dogs do things differently. They are famous for not taking advantage of their ideal circumstances. Somebody asks them to keep their commission in a property, and they take offense, responding, "Don't you think I deserve to earn a living? Don't you think I have expenses to pay?" This is self-employed mentality speaking. Top Dogs are different. They enter into the investor quadrant and take advantage of the opportunity to create future income streams. The by-product of *income stream mentality* is that you become financially sophisticated, and both you and your clients benefit from your expertise. You earn respect for your real estate acumen, acting as both agent and financial partner in your client's transactions. Always remember, however, that a potential conflict of interest arises when you become an owner with your client. Detailed, written disclosures are required along with a good measure of integrity.

> **Agent to Agent**
>
> You may wonder how your investment in a client's home can be your *investment* property for tax purposes. Tax treatment depends on *your* tax treatment of your investment, not your co-owner's use of the property as his principal residence. Thus, your ownership interest qualifies as your investment property.

Facilitating Stock Market Investor Transition

Top Dogs are set up to take advantage of ideal economic conditions by specializing in emerging markets. In the current marketplace, the public can no longer count on the stock market as a means to make them rich. Real estate, with its enviable consistent record of performance and beneficial tax treatment, is more attractive than ever. In addition, as long as low-interest mortgage rates continue, real estate leverage is extremely advantageous.

Of course, one key to a ripe real estate market is for mortgage rates to be lower than property appreciation rates. So always gauge your investments by this test. If loan rates start approximating appreciation rates, you might want to hold off on new investments until either rates come down or appreciation goes up.

Cave!

Always make sure you have a detailed agreement with your co-owners that includes any disclosures you may be required to make and all duties and obligations of the co-owners. These agreements all have the same purpose but can have many different names: a joint venture agreement, a co-ownership agreement, or an equity sharing agreement. They are all basically the same thing—more than one person owning a property together.

These conditions provide the ideal setting for Top Dogs to facilitate investments to the real estate market. Your average investor is highly motivated to invest in real estate, yet he does not have the know-how to tap the lucrative real estate investment pot. Top Dogs step in to create a ready marketplace to fill this need. They are able to fit the needs of the investor wanting to acquire an investment property on his own or just a small percentage of a property.

Create Diversification Opportunities

Top Dogs create *stock-size* investments in real estate to satisfy the stock market investor's desire to easily diversify and buy in with small contributions. These bite-size investments also meet the Top Dog's goal of diversifying his own real estate investments and sharing the financial sting of real estate acquisition with others. Investors are accustomed to calling their stockbrokers and saying, "Buy me some Cisco or put me into something with fixed income." Who do they call now? How does your typical investor directly invest in real estate?

Enter stage left, the Top Dog specializing in stock market investor transition. Agents who can help clients invest in bite-size percentages of property ownership are able to scoop up the business stockbrokers had in the 1990s. In fact, a number of stockbrokers have transitioned into real estate sales and are providing this very service, yet now it is under the umbrella of real estate and is called limited partnership interests instead of shares in Cisco. They acquire investment real estate in the name of a limited partnership or limited liability company and offer investors bite-size ownership percentages.

Agent to Agent

To find out more about title holding entities for real estate co-ownership do a search on the Internet for those keywords.

The Top Dog is the person an investor can now call and say, "Put $30,000 into a good, appreciating real estate investment." The Top Dog has a client base of investors and is able to pool them together in real estate investments. In return, the Top Dog receives a percentage of ownership instead of a commission on purchase and again on sale. The following sections show you how this works.

Your Business Plan

Aside from consistent appreciation, real estate is more attractive than the stock market because real estate comes with a set of tax benefits that stock market investments do not enjoy. With real estate, investors can deduct payments made and pay no tax on gains. All you need to do is collect stock-market-weary investors, which is not a hard thing to do. Just put yourself in the middle of any group of thirty-somethings and up. Or stand on a corner with a sign that says, "Real estate investments, $30,000 each." They will come in droves.

Next find the properties into which you will pool your investors. The philosophy is that the investors supply the initial capital and make the payments while you convert your commission, put the deal together, manage the investment, and receive a commensurate ownership interest. You will also receive the listing at sale later, which can again become a commission conversion to tax-free equity.

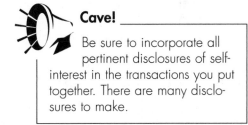

Cave!

Be sure to incorporate all pertinent disclosures of self-interest in the transactions you put together. There are many disclosures to make.

Stock market investor transition is an opportune market for the Top Dog who is willing to work creatively and with income stream mentality.

The More the Merrier

You can make your investment pools as simple or extravagant as you desire. Your investments can be simple single-family homes that are rented out. If you decide to put development projects together, you may want to add additional members to your investment team, and your *Power Team* members are the most likely candidates. The following are categories of professionals that may choose to contribute their time to a project in exchange for a portion of the appreciation at the end:

◆ Attorney for the contract work

◆ Developer for subdivision work

◆ Contractor for property improvement

◆ Engineer for property improvement

- Architect for property design
- Loan broker for contributing commissions earned on loans procured

When the professionals whose services are required to put a development project together contribute their time in exchange for equity, a development project has the best chance of success and profit. Top Dogs cultivate contacts with professionals with similar income stream mentality and have ready teams to put together when a development opportunity comes along.

Use of a Business Entity

You can either use a business entity such as a limited partnership or limited liability company to hold title to these properties or you and your clients can go directly on title. The more investors participating in one property, the more inclined you will be to use a business entity. Lately we have seen a resurgence of *limited partnerships* that were so popular in the 1990s.

def•i•ni•tion

A **limited partnership** consists of one or more general partners and limited partners and is often used as a real estate investment vehicle. Limited partners have no personal liability. This structure provides asset protection.

Before the tax reform of the late 1990s, limited partnerships were a popular method of owning and operating real estate because they allowed limited partners to take tax losses for their investments and to enjoy limited liability. In those days the savvy agent became a general partner in a client's investment and earned a portion of the appreciation in return for his services in pooling investors and managing the investment.

With tax reform, the limited partnership no longer enjoys preferred tax treatment, yet the structure of the limited partnership is ideal for agent-facilitated real estate investing. Whether a limited partnership or limited liability company holds title or the agent and client go on title individually, the intent is the same—the agent takes an ownership interest in lieu of a real estate commission and as compensation for her finder and management services, just as the general partner of the limited partnership did.

Qualified Retirement Fund Investment

Now that your imagination is working, you say, "This would be an incredible venture if investors could use their qualified retirement funds to buy real estate." Since you're wondering, the answer is, "Yes, they can." The one qualification is that if the property is subject to a loan, special rules apply. Retirement funds can be invested in co-owned real estate, as long as the retirement funds are safely segregated in their own ownership interest. The main considerations with retirement funds are as follows:

- ◆ Retirement funds must be transferred to a self-directed retirement account, which means hiring a custodian to take title on behalf of the account owner (see www.pensco.com, for an example).

- ◆ If the property will have a loan, carefully follow the criteria for self-directed retirement accounts.

- ◆ Make sure the retirement account investor's interest is safely expressed as a separate but undivided percentage interest in the property if there is more than one owner of the property.

FYI!

When joining with others owning and operating real estate, liability is always a concern. As part of the service you provide to your investors, you may want to form a limited partnership (LP) or limited liability company (LLC) to hold title to the real estate and appoint yourself the managing member and the investors as passive members. The LLC is similar to the limited partnership but the LLC provides a better shield from liability. With one of these entities in place, you will have the best vehicle to appreciate your new investment, rent it out, and shield yourself and your investors from liability. Have an attorney set up the first company. After that, just follow the same format.

One very popular way of using retirement funds in real estate is to acquire a retirement home. Until your client reaches retirement age, he is not able to use the home for personal or family use, not even for the typical vacation home personal use period. Thus, he rents it out and income is paid to his retirement account. At retirement age, the retirement home is distributed to him. As facilitator of these transactions, you help your clients move their retirement funds to appreciating and tax-preferred real estate, you help them choose their retirement homes, and you manage or facilitate rental of it until they retire.

If we had as many real estate investment brokers as we have stockbrokers, taxpayers would understand that their retirement funds can purchase real estate. Since it is not in the best interest of stockbrokers or retirement fund managers, taxpayers are unaware

def•i•ni•tion

An **exchange intermediary** facilitates an exchange of real estate under IRC section 1031.

that their retirement funds can purchase real estate with the assistance of an account custodian, whose role is very similar to that of the *exchange intermediary*.

FYI!

Go to www.pensco.com for detailed information relating to purchases of real estate with self-directed accounts. They also respond to e-mail inquiry and are knowledgeable and helpful.

To find these custodians, search on the Internet under "self-directed retirement account custodian," and you will find a variety of capable firms that have long, good-standing histories. The custodianship process is simple. The client's retirement funds are signed over to the custodianship of the self-directed account manager. Then the account manager takes title to the designated real estate in the name of the retirement account. There is a fee for this service, just as your stockbroker receives a fee for her service.

Selling Your Business

An important place to look for an income stream is right in your own backyard. Well, not exactly your backyard, but in your business. Every business owner looks to his business for *current* income streams. Every successful entrepreneur looks to her business for *future* income streams. The entrepreneur's mindset is to plan for the future *now* by setting up her business knowing she will sell it when the time is right.

Knowing that you are building something that will live on indefinitely, the administration of your business becomes less mundane and may even border on exciting. Your marketing talent comes to life on behalf of your clients' properties, and your business also becomes the beneficiary of your active imagination. You dream up names to call certain tasks. You begin to assign logos and mottos to your business. You see it as a thriving enterprise because you know it is your nest egg. It is not just a humdrum place where you earn a living until you're 60, and then it's gone. It is your golden egg that will live on perpetually, and earns you a good living now and an early retirement later.

They Are Your Clients

I can hear you say, "How can I sell a business that is part of another business?" You can. The clients are yours; they do not belong to the company you work for. The clients go wherever you go. When you leave this real estate firm, your solid reputation and strong client base go with you.

Many agents obtain their broker's licenses when they reach a certain level of success. Some choose to go work on their own alone while some hire other agents to work for them. Some never leave the firm they're with because they are comfortable with the reputation or the support it provides. Whichever route you follow, your business and your clients are yours. When you sell your business, if you are with a firm and you feel the continued success of your business depends on staying with that firm, you will build in a contingency that the successful purchaser must place their license with the same firm. You should be interested in your business succeeding after its sale because part of the sale price will be paid to you over the next many years.

Cave!

Broker-associate contracts generally do not address ownership of the agent's client list, yet it is prudent to review this agreement with respect to this issue.

Be Entrepreneurial-Minded

Most people are not entrepreneurial-minded. They develop successful businesses and when they retire, the business does too. In other words, they stay in the second quadrant of the self-employed. For Top Dogs, the business lives on and provides an active income stream into the future. Even if your business is a professional service such as real estate, it is a highly marketable business opportunity if you plan it that way from the beginning.

When you retire, you can refer clients to your successor and make money from each referral. To do this, build into the purchase agreement a contingency period to approve of your buyer, so before you commit to a sale you know your successor will continue the business with a similar degree of success and integrity. Stay involved in the transition from yourself to the successful purchaser for a year or two. To ensure successful continuity of your business, it is in your best interest to allow the transition to take place over a well-measured period of time, so your clients and your successor will find a successful rhythm together.

Because your income stream depends on your successor's success, you want to do everything you can to ensure that the purchaser will be successful. Also, you want to

Agent to Agent

The seller services provision of the business opportunity purchase agreement should detail as specifically as possible the extent of the seller's availability in terms of days and hours of days and the types of services the seller will render for the period of time agreed to.

leave your clients with someone who treats them well and will fill your shoes effectively in satisfying their real estate needs.

It might seem early to start thinking about selling your business if you're just starting it up. But income stream mentality should become your state of mind early on, especially in the business formation stage. The time to ready your business for sale is now, not when the goodwill of your business has dwindled and you need to find an income stream. With this state of mind, every function of your business should be set up as a prototype that can be operated by the person or company to whom you sell your business. Everything should be turnkey. Your buyer turns the key and the business operates itself.

Your Business Opportunity Checklist

Here is a checklist of points to consider as you set up your business with an eye toward selling it later:

- **Organize your client database and keep it organized**. You want to be able to show the extent of your client list and a history of your transactions. If you decide to sell ten years from now, you want to have organized and easily ascertainable records that will show all transactions and all clients. *Goodwill*, one of the most important business valuation factors, is based on how long a company has operated as shown by its records.

def•i•ni•tion

Goodwill is the value of the advantages that a business has developed as a result of intangibles such as business name, reputation, and length of operation.

- **Maintain good accounting records**. Part of a business opportunity valuation is to analyze the business's gross and net income and its expenses. Use a good computerized accounting program such as QuickBooks or its equivalent and have computer printouts of all income and expense categories for each year of operation. Have your tax returns clearly labeled and organized for easy review by your purchaser. These records should be produced for at least three years prior to the sale of the business.

- **Have systems in place**. Businesses have more value if the talent responsible for its success is not dependent on a single person, but instead depends on systems incorporated to increase profit. Follow the referral stream system and instruct your buyer in the use of it. The system will have been in place for a period of time showing a reliable rate of return, and all your buyer will need to do is to continue what you have done.

Your future income stream systems, too, should have a proven track record, allowing your buyer to step into the income stream models you have built. Your website and its marketing features are another valuable component of your business. The more self-sustaining systems you incorporate into your business, the more value it will have without you. In fact, if you have sufficient systems in place, you should seriously consider *franchising* your company as opposed to selling it.

> **FYI!**
>
> Often only the prior three years of records are produced to the buyer. However, some buyers want to review longer periods, and the willing seller should be able to produce them.

- **Have competent personnel in place**. If you have a competent staff or assistant to work for your purchaser, your business will better retain its continuity while operation shifts from you to your purchaser.

> **def•i•ni•tion**
>
> **Franchising** is the licensing of others to use your business name and/or business format in return for a fee.

- **Obtain a good lease**. If your business is at a leased location, obtain a favorable long-term, transferable lease before you sell your business. A long-term lease with options for renewal will guarantee the business's location for your purchaser, which will also increase your business' value. It is generally important for purchasers of real estate businesses to stay in the same location where the business operated.

- **Incorporate your business**. Consider incorporating your business if you have not already done so before the sale to your buyer. Incorporated businesses are considered more valuable and more transferable than unincorporated ones.

- **Take back a note**. Consider creative financing by taking back a note as part of the purchase price or receiving a percentage of the profits as they come in. Many times you can get a higher sales price and instill confidence in the buyer if you do so.

- **Offer your services**. Many people stay on with their business for a period of time, perhaps one to two years, to bolster buyer confidence and ease transition problems with your client base. An employment contract with you will benefit you and your purchaser.

◆ **Maintain documentation.** Make sure that you maintain good documentation on every transaction you handle. A buyer has more confidence in a business that is well documented and organized and can show its proven track record.

◆ **Organize and retain your bank statements**. You will need to prove your income and deposits so the buyer can confirm gross and net sales figures.

◆ **Monitor the financial ratio of income to expense.** You will need to provide this information as part of your buyer package.

◆ **When it is time to sell, hire a business broker to list your business.** This professional will prepare a business valuation and suggested listing price just as you would with a comparative market analysis. This valuation is understandably more in depth than the analysis for the sale of a home.

> **Agent to Agent**
>
> If you are with another office when you sell your business, the broker will have your past files for a period of five to seven years after the closing of a transaction. Brokers will cooperate with you in making records available to your buyer pursuant to a confidentiality agreement.

The Least You Need to Know

◆ Your future income stream is the key to your future earnings and gives you freedom from working sooner rather than later.

◆ As an agent, there are opportunities to create future income streams all around you.

◆ You can allow your commission to be converted to an ownership interest in a property.

◆ You can put together investment deals and even use qualified retirement funds of investors to purchase income property and other real estate investments.

◆ Your business can be packaged for sale or for franchise with some careful planning.

Glossary

800 number call-capture service   A toll-free call response service which allows your calls to be serviced 24/7 without you through voice mail information blurbs, fax back, and on-the-spot paging.

access easement   An access easement is the right to use someone else's property for access only.

adverse possession   The acquisition of property through prolonged and unauthorized use of someone else's property.

agency relationship   In real estate, this is a relationship where your client, the principal, is represented by you, the agent, to act on her behalf.

amortization   A process by which you gradually pay off a debt by making periodic payments to the lender.

appraiser   This person's job is to estimate the value of property as of a particular date.

arbitration, binding   A legal process that replaces the court system and the appeal process if the parties so agree in writing.

asset protection   The sheltering of assets from excessive taxation and personal liability by the use of irrevocable trusts, family limited partnerships, house trusts, and limited liability companies, to name a few.

bridge loan   A short-term loan made in expectation of a permanent, longer-term loan. Also known as a swing loan.

broker's open house   This is the property showing for the agent community as opposed to the open house, which is the showing for the public.

campaign-driven contacts database   A contacts database which allows you to program it to automatically send marketing materials by e-mail to targeted prospect groups.

capital gains tax rates   The tax rate you pay when you profit on a long-term real estate investment. This rate is far lower than ordinary income tax rates.

capitalization rates   These represent the relationship between the value of the property and the income it produces.

CC&Rs   *See* covenants, conditions, and restrictions.

closing professional   The escrow agent or closing attorney (depending upon which handles transactions in your state). The closing professional serves as a neutral intermediary facilitating the transaction to closing.

closing statement (a.k.a. settlement statement)   A detailed accounting of buyer and seller debits and credits in the transaction. This is one of the last steps the closing professional performs in a transaction.

community property   A way of holding a title by married persons in states that have community property laws.

community property with right of survivorship   A way of holding a title by married persons in some states that have community property laws, which allows the surviving spouse to receive a deceased spouse's interest without probate.

comparables   Similar properties recently sold, which are located in the same proximity as the subject property.

comparative market analysis (CMA)   A summary of comparable properties in the area that are currently listed, in escrow, have expired, or have sold recently.

conditional contract   A contract that has conditions that make it nonbinding until the conditions are removed.

condominium   A property developed for concurrent ownership where each owner has a separate interest in a unit combined with an undivided interest in the common areas of the property.

contingencies   Conditions that are built into a purchase offer to make it conditional. The offer is conditional until such time as the contingencies are removed. The most common contingencies in the real estate transaction are loans, physical inspections, and reviews of title.

contingency release   A contingency is released either by satisfaction or waiver. There is a specified time period for this to happen.

cooperatives   The ownership of property by a corporation in which each resident owns a percentage share of the corporation, but does not hold title to the property.

counteroffer   A response to an offer that changes or adds terms, such as a change in price or closing date.

covenants, conditions, and restrictions (CC&Rs)   Rules that govern how a property looks and/or is used. They are common with condominiums and multiuse properties, but also sometimes pertain to single-family homes.

deed of trust   A document used in some states, while mortgages are used in others, to secure a lender's interest in a property.

default   This occurs when you do not meet a legal obligation.

depreciation   Allocation of the cost of an improvement over the life of the asset in the form of a tax deduction.

dual agent   An agent who acts for both the seller and the buyer.

E&O insurance   *See* errors and omissions insurance.

easements   Rights to use the property of another person for a specific purpose. Easements are recorded on the title on both the property enjoying the right and the property burdened by the right.

eminent domain   The governmental right to take private property for public use as long as it fairly compensates the owner.

equity   The difference between the value of the property and the loans against it.

equity sharing   A real estate co-ownership strategy whereby one party, the occupier, lives in the property and pays its expenses, while the other party, the investor, puts up the down-payment funds. They share tax deductions and profit. Many other structures are also possible, but this is the most popular.

errors and omissions insurance (E&O insurance)   Insurance that covers you for any claim made against you for your real estate services.

escrow   The independent third party that holds the funds and distributes them according to buyer and seller instructions and processes and prepares the transaction documents. Depending upon your location, escrow is either an escrow company or a closing attorney.

exchange (also known as tax-free exchanges and § 1031 exchange)   Tax-free exchanges, which are also known as 1031 exchanges, allow tax on profits to be deferred for real estate owners selling investment, rental, business, or vacation real estate and investing in other real estate.

exchange intermediary   A professional who facilitates an exchange of real estate property under IRC § 1031.

exclusive right to sell listing agreement   A type of listing agreement between an owner and agent that pays the agent a commission even if the property is sold by someone else during the listing term.

extrovert   A person who directs much of his or her energy to the outer world of people and things. An overwhelming number of real estate sales agents fall into this category.

family limited partnership   A specially designed limited partnership, consisting of one or more general partners and one or more limited partners, which can provide asset protection from personal liability and discount valuation for estate tax purposes.

farm   A prospect-rich group you target and consistently drive marketing materials toward.

fee simple   The highest and most complete ownership one can have in a property.

feng shui   The ancient Chinese science of balancing the elements within the environment. Feng shui means "wind and water."

fiduciary duty   A requirement to act on behalf of your client with the utmost care, integrity, honesty, confidentiality, and loyalty.

floor time   The rotation of agents to respond to inquiries that come from advertisements and signs. These agents get the walk-in traffic and phone calls to the office when no particular agent is requested.

for sale by owner (FSBO)   A property put on market by an owner working without an agent.

foreclosure   To liquidate the property for payment of a debt secured by it.

franchising   The licensing of others to use your business name and/or business format in return for a fee.

goodwill   The value of the advantages that a business has developed as a result of intangibles such as business name, reputation, and length of operation.

grant deed   A deed that transfers title to a property and makes certain title guarantees.

handheld organizer   A minicomputer of sorts that fits in your hand and holds your contacts, MLS database, calendar, and e-mail, referred to in this book generically as a PDA.

home sale/purchase contingencies   Sellers accept offers contingent upon finding a new home. Buyers make offers contingent upon selling their current home.

independent contractor   A worker with the right to direct and control the way he works, including the details of when, where, and how he does his job.

inspection contingency   The right for the buyer to perform inspections he feels necessary to discover the condition of the property. Often this period is 15 days in a fast market.

joint tenancy   A way co-owners hold title in nearly all states if they want a surviving co-owner to receive the deceased co-owner's interest without probate. The co-owners do not have to be married.

lead-generating system   A fairly automated system that captures prospects, usually at an internet intersection, and drives them your way.

lead projector   An analysis that tells you exactly how many leads you need to meet your financial goals.

lease option   Allows the buyer to occupy the property with a right to buy it at a later date.

limited liability company   A company that affords its members limited liability similar to a corporation and pass-through taxation similar to a sole-proprietorship or partnership. It can provide asset protection and discount valuation for estate tax purposes.

limited partnership   A partnership consisting of one or more general partners and limited partners, often used as an investment vehicle. Limited partners have no personal liability. This structure provides asset protection.

liquidated damages agreement   A provision in the purchase agreement where the seller retains the buyer's deposit if the buyer defaults on the purchase.

listing   A contract between broker and owner that gives the broker the right to sell or lease the property.

listing agent The broker who acts for the seller according to the terms of the listing agreement.

listing agreement The contract between the seller and broker, which outlines what the broker will do for the seller and how much the agent will be paid.

living trust A written agreement that appoints a trustee to take charge of assets, thereby sidestepping the probate process at death.

loan approval The full and final process whereby the lender approves of the loan and the property that will secure it.

loan contingency The period during which the buyer obtains loan approval. The loan contingency often expires 30 days prior to closing.

lockbox An attachment to a door that holds the key to that door. Agents have a key to the lockbox so that they can obtain the key to the property on site.

locked in loan The status of a loan when the lender guarantees its rate and terms.

Master Marketing Model A marketing model created for this book which gives you a multimedia system incorporating the most cutting edge forms of advertising into one streamlined 24/7 lead-generating package.

mechanics liens Recorded liens that contractors and suppliers may record on a property if they have provided services or materials to the property.

median home price The price of the home in the middle. Of all the homes sold during a particular period, precisely half sold for more than the median price and half sold for less.

mediation A settlement process that precedes legal proceedings and is often agreed to in the purchase agreement.

metes and bounds A method of identifying a parcel by reference to its boundaries and its shape.

mortgage Used in some states, while deeds of trust are used in others, to secure a lender's interest in a property.

multimedia marketing Lead generating marketing that appeals to many different senses through multiple types of media such as video, audio, print, and graphics.

multiple listing service A database of properties listed for sale and rent within a certain locale.

net proceeds sheet A document that helps sellers understand what their closing costs will be and how much they will net from the sale.

open house   An open house is a set date and time when a home for sale is opened to interested buyers to tour.

option agreement   The right of a buyer to buy a property at a later specified time and price.

passive loss   Loss in excess of income on a rental property.

personal property   Anything on the land that is moveable.

physical inspection contingency   *See* inspection contingency.

preapproval   The lender takes all the confirmation steps it would for full loan approval with the exception of appraisal of the property (since the property has not yet been located).

prequalification   A lender takes the potential buyer's application and prequalifies them for a loan based on the information provided, but undertakes no confirmation of the buyer's information, as it does in preapproval.

property profile   The report a title company provides that includes a property's title vesting, loan, tax information, legal description, and information on surrounding properties.

prorations   The division of a property's expenses between the buyer and seller as of the property's transfer date.

quitclaim deed   A deed that transfers any interest someone has in a property, and contains no warranty of good title.

real property   The land, its rights, and anything attached to it.

recording   The act of entering instruments affecting title to a property in the public record.

referral fee   A fee paid for referral of a client.

section I conditions, pest control report   Conditions that have existing damage.

section II conditions, pest control report   Conditions that do not have existing damage, but if not corrected in the future, they could lead to damage.

self-directed retirement account custodian   A fiduciary who holds retirement funds for a client to be invested pursuant to the client's instructions. These accounts are most commonly used for real estate investments.

self-employment tax   Social Security and Medicare tax paid by self-employed taxpayers on the net income from their trade or business.

self-generating system An automated marketing system that generates leads from actions it takes or responses it draws.

seller financing When the seller agrees to make a loan to a buyer.

seller-only services The single agency representation of the seller only.

selling agent The agent who brings in the successful buyer.

set back A requirement that is established by zoning law or agreement between neighbors as to how far an improvement may be situated from a certain marker.

settlement statement Also known as a closing statement, this is a detailed accounting of buyer and seller debits and credits in the transaction.

sphere of influence The first group you will market to, which should be heavily weighted with current contacts but also include people from the past.

stager A designer or decorator versed in staging properties for sale.

staging A specialized service entailing specific proven steps that make a home for sale more appealing to your typical homebuyer.

survivorship A right whereby a co-owner automatically receives full title without the need for probate when a co-owner dies.

tenants by the entirety The way husband and wife hold title in 27 states if they want the surviving spouse to receive the deceased spouse's interest without probate. It is similar to joint tenancy used in other states.

tenants in common A way for co-owners to own property together without survivorship rights. Their interests pass to their heirs, not to one another when they die.

title company A company that performs a title search to make sure all rights and obligations affecting a property are set forth in one report for the buyer's review.

title insurance A policy guaranteeing that title is clear and the property is legally owned by the seller.

title report The report issued by a title company or closing attorney reporting the condition of title to a property as disclosed by a search of the public record.

transaction coordinator A person who facilitates the steps in a transaction from offer through closing.

transaction management program   A software program, online or offline, that identifies transaction steps and calendar dates for accomplishing them. These programs often integrate transaction forms and are accessible online to any number of transaction participants.

transaction timeline   A timeline that details the dates by which the steps in a transaction must be taken.

trust account   A bank account that holds funds that clients have entrusted to an agent to be used on the client's behalf.

virtual assistant   A support professional providing administrative, creative, or technical services on a contractual basis.

virtual tour   A 360 degree depiction of a property as if it were photographed with a video camera.

warranty deed   A deed that transfers title and guarantees that title is free and clear.

zoning   A governmental regulation regarding the use of a property. For instance, a property may be zoned for use as a single family residence.

Index

A

ABR (Accredited Buyer Representative), 326
accessibility of home offices, 226
accounting software, 175
Active Agent, 174
administrative support
    finding, 340-341
    hiring, 157-158
    in/out of office, 337-338
    licensing, 337
    part-time/full-time, 336
    pay/benefits, 341
    skills, 339-340
    tasks, 338-339
    virtual, 158, 342-343
advanced category agents, 44
advantages of real estate
    emotional, 4-5
    financial, 8-9
adverse possession, 55
advertising
    lead generation, 146-147
    magazine, 197
agencies
    disclosures, 306-307
        including in listing presentations, 265
        type of agent, 307
    dual, 56
    relationships, 56
agents
    demand, 250
    inspections/disclosures, 313
Agent Pro website, 190
amortization, 64

analyzing neighborhoods, 97
appearance, 98
applying to take exams, 60-61
appraisals of properties, 53
appraisers
    daily life, 40-42
    disadvantages, 42
    personality types, 21-22
    rewards, 42
approval of loans, 300
architecture courses, 106
assessments, 53
asset protection, 251
assistants. *See* administrative support
associations
    expenses, 205
    joining, 75, 93-94
    local, 75
attitude for exam-taking, 67-68
availability
    Power Team members, 127
    time management, 154

B

backing up data, 222-223
bank accounts, 101
Barron-Tieger, Barbara, 12
being on-call, 155
benefits for assistants, 341
bios
    buyer packages, 289
    listing presentations, 262
birthday cards, 238
boundaries with clients, 155-156

bridge loans, 287
brokerage
    federal laws, 57
    listings, 56
    option agreements, 56
    principles, 55-56
    property management, 57
    sales contracts, 56
brokers
    licensing, 324
    open houses, 261, 274-275
building
    field offices, 227
    home offices, 223-224
    niches, 25-26
    vehicle offices, 227
businesses
    building
        bank accounts, 101
        construction/architecture courses, 106
        continuing education, 107-108
        expenses, 102-104
        image, 97-100
        insurance, 106
        joining associations, 93-94
        lead generation, 92
        MLS, 94-95
        neighborhood analysis, 97
        office training support, 91-92
        packaging, 105-106
        retirement accounts, 104-105
        specialty training, 108

tax preparations, 101-102
technology, 100-101
touring houses, 96
coaches, 330-331
entities, 364
ideals, 78-79
opportunities, 35, 368-370
plans, 363
reputations, 81
buyers
gifts, 236
greeting, 278
listening to, 290
qualifying, 286-287
representing
closings, 301
communication, 291
contingencies, 298-301
listening to buyers, 290
opening escrow, 293
packages, 287-290
preparing offers, 292
presenting offers, 293
qualifying, 286-287
title reports, 294-297
transaction timelines, 293
touring, 291

C

calendaring systems, 219-221
Canadian National Association of Realtors website, 95
capital gains tax rates, 358
capitalization rates, 18
career transitions, 6-7
cars
image, 98-99
insurance, 106
categories
agents, 44
contacts database

birthday cards, 238
buyer gifts, 236
e-mail newsletters, 232-235
gift certificates for referrals, 235
holiday cards, 237
nice to have met you cards, 236
seller gifts, 236
snail mail newsletters, 232-235
catering to Internet clients, 319-321
CC&Rs (covenants, conditions, and restrictions), 51, 296
CCIM (Certified Commercial Investment Member), 34, 326
cell phones, 168
Certified Property Manager (CPM), 327
Certified Residential Specialist (CRS), 326
Charpics Technologies website, 236
check-writing software, 175
clear titles, 55
clients
boundaries, 155-156
inquisition, 258
listening to, 264-265
loyalty, 366-367
rejection, 266
respecting their decisions, 250-252
supporting, 253
closed escrows required, 206
closings
buyer representation, 301
dates, 312
facilitating, 281
procedures, 55
professionals, 160

CMA (comparative market analysis), 263
commercial sales
daily life, 34-36
personality types, 18-19
commercial transformations of home offices, 225-226
commissions, 306
as equity interests, 360-361
gross required, 206
splits, 30, 201
common interest developments, 50-51
communication
buyers, 291
sellers, 283-284
community leadership, 327
community property, 49-50
companies. *See* businesses
comparative market analysis (CMA), 263
competitor relationships, 254-255
computers
calendaring, 219-221
file organization, 221-222
multitaskers, 217
terminal exams, 65
training, 181
condemnation, 52
conditional contracts, 298
condominiums, 20, 51
ConnecTel, 191
connectivity software, 180
construction courses, 106
contact management
databases, 194-195
software, 173-174
contacts databases, 138
inputting data, 238-239
meeting people, 230-231
organizing, 231
processing, 240-241

setting up
    birthday cards, 238
    buyer gifts, 236
    e-mail newsletters, 232-235
    gift certificates for referrals, 235
    holiday cards, 237
    nice to have met you cards, 236
    seller gifts, 236
    snail mail newsletters, 232-235
contingencies, 19, 298
    inspection, 31, 159
    loan, 33, 159, 300-301, 311
    physical inspection, 298-300, 311
    purchase of home, 312
    releases, 220
    sale of home, 312
    title, 159
continuing education, 107-108, 324-325
contracts
    conditional, 298
    sales, 56
converting leads to appointments, 210
cooperatives, 51
costs of newsletters, 234
counteroffers, 280
courses
    continuing education, 107-108
    prelicensing, 45-47
covenants, conditions, and restrictions (CC&Rs), 51, 296
CPM (Certified Property Manager), 327
CRS (Certified Residential Specialist), 326
curb appeal, 350-352
current market trends, 261

D

databases
    contacts
        inputting data, 238-239
        meeting people, 230-231
        organizing, 231
        processing, 240-241
        setting up, 232-238
    portable, 218
    synchronizing, 165
deeds, 54-55
deeds of trusts, 296
defaulting on properties, 54
demand for agents, 250
deposits, 311
desire to succeed, 112-113
digital cameras, 169
digital signautres, 171
disadvantages
    appraisers, 42
    commercial sales, 36
    mortgage brokers, 38
    property managers, 40
    residential sales, 33
disclosures, 313
diversification opportunities, 362-363
documents, 304-305
drip campaigns, 195
dropping hard-sells, 249
dual agency, 308
dual agents, 56

E

e-fax website, 170
e-mail
    efficiency, 323
    newsletters
        choosing, 233-234
        database category, 232
        frequency, 234
        personalizing, 235
E-Pro certification, 182

easements, 51
editing software, 178
education. *See also* training
    architecture, 106
    computer training, 181
    construction, 106
    continuing, 107-108, 324-325
    office training/support, 79-81
    prelicensing
        courses, 45-47
        exemptions, 44-45
        state requirements, 46
    reality training, 90-91
    specialty training, 108
eminent domain, 52
emotional rewards, 4-5
entrepreneurial, 367-368
entry category agents, 44
equipment for home offices, 225
equity, 51
equity sharing, 26
errors and omissions insurance, 106
escrow, 160
    opening, 293
    closed, 206
estimated closing statements, 160
ethics, 118, 129
exams
    applying to take, 60-61
    attitude, 67-68
    computer terminals, 65
    content, 62
    focus, 62
    pencil and paper, 65
    preparation courses, 64
    preparations, 60
    procedures, 61-62
    simulating, 65
    strategies, 66-70
    topics, 63

Excel, 172
exchanges, 36
   intermediary, 365
   tax-free, 53
exclusive right to sell, 56
expenses, 203
   associations, 205
   deducting, 102-104
   insurance, 204
   marketing, 204-205
   MLS fees, 205
   office fees, 204
   technology equipment, 205
   transaction coordination, 205
   wireless services, 204
expired listings, 149
extroverts, 13

F

family-limited partnerships, 251
fax machines, 170
federal laws, 57
feelers, 14-15
fee simple, 48
FHA (Federal Housing Administration), 54
fiduciary duty, 80, 246
field multitasking, 218-219
field offices, 227
fields
   choosing, 22-23
   researching, 23-24
file attachment software, 177
finances
   commissions, 306
      as equity interests, 360-361
      gross required, 206
      splits, 30, 201
   expenses
      associations, 205
      deducting, 102-104

insurance, 204
      marketing, 204-205
      MLS fees, 205
      office fees, 204
      technology equipment, 205
      transaction coordination, 205
      wireless services, 204
   office agreements, 82
   rewards, 8-9
financing, 53-54
floor time, 7
foreclosures, 54
free seminars, 145-146
frequency of newsletters, 234
FSBOs (For Sale by Owners), 148-149
full time administrative assistance, 336
furnishings for home offices, 226
future income streams
   business checklist, 368-370
   business entities, 364
   client loyalty, 366-367
   commissions as equity interests, 360-361
   diversification opportunities, 362-363
   entrepreneurial, 367-368
   investing continually, 359-360
   retirement funds, 364-366
   Rich Dad books, 358
   selling businesses, 366
   stock market investor transitions, 361-362

G

gifts
   certificates for referrals, 235
   processing, 240

Goodwill, 368
governmental limitations, 52
grant deeds, 55
greeting buyers, 278
GRI (Graduate REALTOR Institute), 326
gross commissions required, 206
gross sales required, 206

H

hard-sells, 249
hardware
   cell phones, 168
   digital cameras, 169
   fax machines, 170
   laptops, 166-168
   PDAs, 169
   printers, 170
   scanners, 171
   suggested, 165-166
hierarchy, 7-8
high-maintenance people (HMP), 155-156
high-tech systems, 165
high-tech lead generation, 190-191
Hill, Napoleon, 111
hiring
   assistants, 157-158
   business coaches, 330-331
HMP (high-maintenance people), 155-156
holding titles, 49-50
holiday cards, 237
home offices
   building, 223
   commercial transformations, 225-226
   transformations, 224
home staging, 348
   convincing clients, 349
   curb appeal, 350-352
   interior, 352-354

as investments, 354-355
overview, 350
home tours, 96
hosting
    broker open houses,
        274-275
    public open houses,
        275-278

I

IDX-Pro, 190
iHOUSE website, 144
in-person networking, 139
independent contractors, 76
independent thinking, 114
in office assistants, 337-338
inspection contingencies, 31,
    159
insurance
    business management, 106
    expenses, 204
    titles, 55, 297
interior staging, 352-354
International Virtual
    Assistants Association, 342
Internet
    access software, 178-179
    clients, 319-321
    farming
        catering to clients,
            319-321
        sites as destination
            points, 322-323
        specialties catering to
            keyword searches,
            321-322
    service providers (ISPs),
        179
interviewing offices, 75, 85-86
introverts, 13
intuitives, 14
ISPs (Internet service provid-
    ers), 179

J-K

joint tenancy, 49
judgers, 15-16

kidnapping the kids, 248
Kiyosaki, Robert, 358

L

land description, 52
laptops, 166-168
Leadership Training Graduate
    (LTG), 327
lead generation
    advertising, 146-147
    buyers or sellers, 209-210
    contacts databases, 138
    converting to appoint-
        ments, 210
    finding leads, 136-137
    free seminars, 145-146
    Lead Projector. *See* Lead
        Projector
    Master Marketing Model.
        See Master Marketing
        Model
    networking, 139-141
    from offices, 83
    past clients, 145
    potential markets, 134-135
    prospecting, 147-149
    required, 207
    specializing, 150-151
    sphere of influence,
        138-139
    survival, 135-136
    Top Dogs, 318-319
    website, 142-144
Lead Projector, 200
    amount of leads, 200
    applying, 208-209
    closed escrows required,
        206

commission splits, 201
    expenses, 203-205
    gross commissions
        required, 206
    gross income desired, 203
    gross sales required, 206
    leads required, 207
    listing appointments
        required, 207
    listings required, 207
    median home prices, 201
    net income desired, 203
    results, 201-203
lease options, 283
legal descriptions of titles, 295
liability insurance, 106
licensing
    assistants, 337
    brokers, 324
    exams. *See* exams
    prelicensing
        courses, 45-47
        exemptions, 44-45
        state requirements, 46
    state requirements, 5, 46
liens, 297
limited-liability companies,
    251
limited partnerships, 364
liquidated damages agree-
    ment, 312
listening
    buyers, 290
    clients, 264-265
listings, 56
    agents, 272
    agreements, 265, 304-305
    appointments required, 207
    packages, 260-261
    presentations, 259
        agency disclosures, 265
        bios, 262
        comparative market
            analysis, 263
        current market trends,
            261

listing agreements, 265
listing packages, 260-261
marketing plan, 261-262
net sheet samples, 264
newsletters, 263
technology, 266
testimonials, 263
transaction management
   samples, 264
promoting on websites, 144
required, 207
sample buyer, 288
staging, 348
   convincing clients, 349
   curb appeal, 350-352
   interior, 352-354
   as investments, 354-355
   overview, 350
stale, 282-283
terms, 305
loans
   approval, 300
   contingencies, 33, 159,
      300-301, 311
   FHA, 54
   preapprovals, 288-300
   preqaulifications, 300
   types, 53
   VA, 54
local associations, 75
lockboxes, 93
LTG (Leadership Training
   Graduate), 327
Lumbleu, John, 229

M

magazine advertising, 197
managing
   businesses
      bank accounts, 101
      expenses, 102-104
      insurance, 106
      packaging, 105-106

retirement accounts,
   104-105
tax preparations,
   101-102
technology, 100-101
contact databases, 194-195
time
   availability, 154
   being on-call, 155
   client boundaries,
      155-156
   closing professionals,
      160
   hiring assistants,
      157-158
   loan/inspection
      contingencies, 159
   partnerships, 158
   peer pressure, 156
   title contingencies, 159
transactions, 205
marketing
   expenses, 204
   farms, 141
   image, 100
   Lead Projector. See Lead
      Projector
   leads
      advertising, 146-147
      contacts databases, 138
      finding, 136-137
      free seminars, 145-146
      marketing to neighbor-
         hoods, 141-142
      networking, 139-141
      past clients, 145
      prospecting, 147-149
      specializing, 150-151
      sphere of influence,
         138-139
      website, 142-144
listing presentations,
   261-262

Master Marketing Model.
   See Master Marketing
   Model
neighborhoods, 141-142
supplies, 205
website, 142-144
MarketReach, 190
Master Marketing Model
   24/7 self generating, 191
   800 call-capture system,
      195-196
   contact management
      database, 194-195
   defined, 188
   high-tech, 190-191
   lead generating, 137
   magazine advertising, 197
   mental attitude, 189
   networking, 198-200
   overview, 187
   secret, 188-189
   web-based paging, 195
   website, 192-193
mastermind training, 80
Master Property Manager
   (MPM), 39
mechanics liens, 297
meeting people, 230-231
mentorship, 344
metes and bounds, 52
Microsoft Office, 172
MLS (multiple listing service),
   81
   fees, 205
   listing homes on, 274
   software, 179
   viewing, 94-95
mortgage brokers
   daily life, 37-38
   disadvantages, 38
   personality types, 19-20
   rewards, 38
mortgages, 54
motivating
   Power Team members, 129
   Top Dogs, 318

MPM (Master Property Manager), 39
multiple listing service. *See* MLS
multiple offers, 280-281

N

National Association of Realtors
 technology updates, 182
 website, 92, 95
neighborhoods
 analyzing, 97
 marketing, 141-142
net proceeds sheets, 280
net sheets, 264
networking
 following passions, 141
 in-person, 139
 joining organizations, 139
 lead generation, 139-141
 Master Marketing Model, 198-200
 positive style, 140
New Ideal, The
 agent demand, 250
 client support, 253
 dropping hard-sells, 249
 fiduciary duty, 246
 relationships with competitors, 254-255
 replacing sales scripts, 253-254
 respecting client decisions, 250-252
 sales scripts, 247-248
 transforming the profession, 248
newsletters
 choices, 233-234
 contacts, 232
 costs, 234
 frequency, 234

including in buyer packages, 289
including in listing presentations, 263
personalizing, 235
niches, 25-26
NTHMYs (nice to have met you cards), 236

O

offers
 counteroffers, 280
 multiple, 280-281
 preparing, 292
 presenting, 293
 responding to, 279-280
office managers, 82-83
offices
 choosing
  company ideals, 78-79
  company reputations, 81
  financial agreements, 82
  interviewing, 85-86
  leads, 83
  office managers, 82-83
  recognition, 84-85
  support, 83-84
  teamwork, 83-84
  training/support, 79-81
  work space, 84
 fees, 204
 field, 227
 home. *See* home offices
 image, 99
 interviewing, 75
 relationships with, 76-77
 vehicle, 227
office suite software, 172-173
on-call, 155
online universities, 80
open houses
 brokers, 261, 274-275
 public, 275-278
 staging, 32

opening escrow, 293
option agreements, 56
ordinary income tax rates, 358
organizations, 139
Outlook, 172
out of office assistants, 337-338

P

packaging
 businesses, 105-106
 listings, 260-261
Palm Treo 650, 169
Palm website, 334
paper files, 222
paperless organization, 216
partnerships
 choosing, 123-124
 time management, 158
part time administrative assistance, 336
passions, 111-112
 finding, 24
 following, 141
paying assistants, 341
PC Anywhere, 181
PDAs (personal data assistants), 169
peer pressure, 156
pencil and paper exams, 65
people skills, 119, 129
perceivers, 15-16
Personality Type, 12-13
 appraisers, 21-22
 commercial sales, 18-19
 extroverts/introverts, 13
 judgers/perceivers, 15-16
 mortgage brokers, 19-20
 property managers, 20
 residential sales, 16-18
 sensors/intuitives, 14
 thinkers/feelers, 14-15
 website, 16

personalizing newsletters, 235
photo management software, 178
physical inspection contingencies, 298-300, 311
planning websites, 144
portable databases, 218
positive attitudes, 68, 115-116
potential markets, 134-135
PowerPoint, 172
Power Team
    availability, 127
    choosing, 122-123
        agent partnering, 123-124
        professional stagers, 125
    commitment, 127
    finding members, 126
    integrity/ethics, 129
    motivation, 129
    people skills, 129
    personal/professional power, 128
    quality control, 130
    quality of services, 128
    transaction control, 130
preapprovals, 288, 300
prelicensing
    courses, 45-47
    exemptions, 44-45
    state requirements, 46
preparation courses, 64
preparing
    exams, 60
    offers, 292
prequalifications of loans, 300
presenting
    bios, 262
    to buyers, 287
        bios, 289
        loan approval status, 288
        newsletters, 289
        sample listings, 288
        transaction management samples, 290
        transaction steps, 289

comparative market analysis, 263
current market trends, 261
disclosures, 265
listings, 259
    agreements, 265
    packages, 260-261
marketing plan, 261-262
net sheet samples, 264
newsletters, 263
offers, 293
technology, 266
testimonials, 263
transaction management samples, 264
primary documents, 304
principles of power, 110, 120
    desire to succeed, 112-113
    ethics, 118
    independent thinkers, 114
    passion for work, 111-112
    people skills, 119
    positive attitude, 115-116
    self-discipline, 116-117
principles of real estate
    brokerage, 55
        agencies, 56
        federal laws, 57
        listings, 56
        option agreements, 56
        property management, 57
        sales contracts, 56
    closing procedures, 55
    financing, 53-54
    real property and ownership
        common interest developments, 50-51
        governmental limitations, 52
        holding titles, 49-50
        land description, 52
        property restrictions, 51-52

real property rights, 48-49
transfer of ownership, 54
valuation of property, 53
printers, 170
printing calendars, 220-221
professional designations, 325-327
professional staging, 125, 272
promoting listings, 144
properties
    defaulting on, 54
    foreclosures, 54
    management
        daily life, 39-40
        principles, 57
    marketability assessment, 272-273
    personal, 48
    profiles, 149
    real, 48
    real property and ownership
        common interest developments, 50-51
        governmental limitations, 52
        holding titles, 49-50
        land description, 52
        property restrictions, 51-52
        real property rights, 48-49
    restrictions, 51-52
    rights, 48-49
    valuation, 53
property managers, 20, 40
prorations, 64
prospecting
    expired listings, 149
    FSBOs, 148-149
    matching, 274
    philosophy, 147
public open houses, 275-276
    greeting buyers, 278

step-by-step process, 276-278
purchase agreements, 308-309
    legal terminology, 310
    terms, 309-312
purchase offers, 19
purchase of home
    contingency, 312

Q

qualifications, 5-6
qualifying
    buyers, 286-287
    sellers, 258-259
quality control, 130
quality of services, 128
quitclaim deeds, 55

R

rates, 18
real estate principles
    brokerage, 55
        agencies, 56
        federal laws, 57
        listings, 56
        option agreements, 56
        property management, 57
        sales contracts, 56
    closing procedures, 55
    financing
        foreclosures, 54
        loans, 53
        mortgages, 54
    real property and
    ownership
        common interest
            developments, 50-51
        governmental limita-
            tions, 52
        holding titles, 49-50
        land description, 52

    property restrictions, 51-52
    real property rights, 48-49
    transfer of ownership, 54
    valuation of property, 53
Real Estate Professional
    Assistant Certification
    (REPA), 157, 340
reality training, 90-91
real property and ownership
    common interest develop-
        ments, 50-51
    governmental limitations, 52
    holding titles, 49-50
    land description, 52
    property restrictions, 51-52
    real property rights, 48-49
recognition in offices, 84-85
recording deeds, 55
referral stream system
    categories, 232
    gifts, 240
    inputting data, 238-239
    meeting people, 230-231
    organization, 231
    philosophy, 242
    reviewing, 241-242
    setting up
        birthday cards, 238
        buyer gifts, 236
        e-mail newsletters, 232-235
        gift certificates for referrals, 235
        holiday cards, 237
        nice to have met you cards, 236
        seller gifts, 236
        snail mail newsletters, 232-235
    snail mail, 240-241
    tips, 243

rejection, 266
relationships
    agencies, 56
    competitors, 254-255
    offices, 76-77
Relay Online Transaction
    Management website, 176
REPA (Real Estate
    Professional Assistant
    Certification), 157, 340
replacing sales scripts, 253-254
reporting to
    buyers, 291
    sellers, 283-284
reputations of companies, 81
researching fields, 23-24
residential sales
    daily life, 28-33
        appeal, 30
        character traits, 33
        counseling clients, 31
        disadvantages, 33
        end of day, 33
        offers, 31
        open houses, 32
        personality types, 33
        rewards, 33
    personality types, 16-18
respecting clients decisions, 250-252
responding to offers, 279-280
retirement accounts, 104-105
retirement funds, 364-366
reviewing referral stream
    system, 241-242
rewards
    appraisers, 42
    commercial sales, 36
    emotional, 4-5
    financial, 8-9
    mortgage brokers, 38
    property managers, 40
    residential sales, 33

S

sale of home contingency, 312
sales
  contracts, 56
  New Ideal, The
    agent demand, 250
    client support, 253
    dropping hard-sells, 249
    fiduciary duty, 246
    relationships with
      competitors, 254-255
    replacing sales scripts,
      253-254
    respecting client deci-
      sions, 250-252
    sales scripts, 247-248
    transforming the
      profession, 248
  scripts
    recognizing, 247-248
    replacing, 253-254
samples
  buyer listings, 288
  net sheets, 264
scanners, 171
scanning software, 178, 239
security software, 179-180
self-discipline, 116-117
self-employment tax, 102
self generating model, 191
sellers
  disclosures, 313
  equity sharing, 283
  financing, 283
  gifts, 236
  qualifying, 258-259
  representing
    broker's open houses,
      274-275
    communication, 283-284
    evaluating properties,
      272-273
    greeting buyers, 278
    listing on MLS, 274

    multiple offers, 280-281
    professional staging, 272
    public open houses,
      275-278
    responding to offers,
      279-280
    stale listings, 282-283
    transaction to closings,
      281
selling businesses, 366
sensors, 14
set-back requirements, 273
settlement statements, 314
seven principles of power, 110,
  120
  desire to succeed, 112-113
  ethics, 118
  independent thinkers, 114
  passion for work, 111-112
  people skills, 119
  positive attitude, 115-116
  self-discipline, 116-117
shadowing, 80
simulating exams, 65
snail mail
  newsletters
    choosing, 233-234
    costs, 234
    database category, 232
    frequency, 234
    personalizing, 235
  processing, 240-241
software, 171-172
  accounting/check-writing,
    175
  connectivity, 180
  contact management,
    173-174
  editing, 178
  file attachments, 177
  Internet access, 178-179
  MLS, 179
  office suites, 172-173
  photo management, 178
  scanning, 178, 239
  security, 179-180

  transaction management,
    176-177
  web-based contact manage-
    ment, 174-175
Sonoma Enterprises website,
  174
specialized training, 108,
  324-325
  broker licensing, 324
  professional designations,
    325-327
specializing, 150-151
sphere of influence, 135,
  138-139
spiritual support, 343-344
staging, 348
  convincing clients, 349
  curb appeal, 350-352
  interior, 352-354
  as investments, 354-355
  open houses, 32
  overview, 350
stale listings, 282-283
state licensing requirements,
  5, 46
stock market investor
  transitions, 361-362
strategies for exam-taking,
  66-70
supplies, 205
support
  administrative
    finding, 340-341
    hiring, 157-158
    in/out of office, 337-338
    licensing, 337
    part-time/full-time, 336
    pay/benefits, 341
    skills, 339-340
    tasks, 338-339
    virtual, 158, 342-343
  business coaches, 330-331
  clients, 253
  mentors, 344
  offices, 79-84

personal/professional
    power, 331-333
professional, 331-333
spiritual, 343-344
technology, 333-335
survivorship, 49
synchronizing
    data, 181-182, 222-223
    databases, 165

T

task lists, 220
tax-free exchanges, 53
taxes, 53
tax preparations, 101-102
Team Double-Click, 177
teamwork in offices, 83-84
technology, 164
    business management,
        100-101
    cell phones, 168
    computer training, 181
    digital cameras, 169
    digital signatures, 171
    expenses, 205
    fax machines, 170
    high-tech systems, 165
    laptops, 166-168
    listing presentations, 266
    NAR, 182
    organization
        backing up data,
            222-223
        calendaring, 219-221
        computer files, 221-222
        computer multitaskers,
            217
        field multitasking,
            218-219
        paperless, 216
        portable databases, 218
        synchronizing data,
            222-223

PDAs, 169
printers, 170
scanners, 171
software, 171-172
    accounting/check-
        writing, 175
    connectivity, 180
    contact management,
        173-174
    file attachments, 177
    Internet access, 178-179
    MLS, 179
    office suites, 172-173
    photo management, 178
    scanning/editing, 178
    security, 179-180
    transaction management,
        176-177
    web-based contact
        management, 174-175
    suggested hardware,
        165-166
    support, 333-335
    synchronization, 165,
        181-182
tenants, 49-50
testimonials for listing
    presentations, 263
thinkers, 14-15
Tieger, Paul, 12
time management
    availability, 154
    being on-call, 155
    client boundaries, 155-156
    closing professionals, 160
    hiring assistants, 157-158
    loan/inspection contingen-
        cies, 159
    partnerships, 158
    peer pressure, 156
    title contingencies, 159
titles
    clear, 55
    contingencies, 159
    holding, 49-50

insurance, 55
reports, 55, 294-295
    covenants/conditions/
        restrictions, 296
    exceptions, 296
    insurance, 297
    legal description, 295
Top Dogs
    business checklist, 368-370
    community leadership, 327
    destination websites, 319
        catering to Internet
            clients, 319-321
        as destination points,
            322-323
        specialties catering to
            keyword searches,
            321-322
    e-mail efficiency, 323
    future income streams. *See*
        future income streams
    lead generation, 318-319
    motivation, 318
    specialized training,
        324-327
    staging listings, 348
        convincing clients, 349
        curb appeal, 350-352
        interior, 352-354
        as investments, 354-355
        overview, 350
    support
        administrative. *See*
            administrative support
        business coaches,
            330-331
        mentors, 344
        personal/professional
            power, 331-333
        spiritual, 343-344
        technology, 333-335
touring
    buyers, 291
    houses, 96

training. *See also* education
  offices, 79-81
  reality, 90-91
  specialized, 324-327
transactions
  facilitating, 281
  including samples in listing
   presentations, 264
  management
   agency disclosures,
    306-307
   agent inspections/
    disclosures, 313
   commissions, 306
   control, 130
   dual agency, 308
   expenses, 205
   listing, 304-305
   primary documents, 304
   purchase agreements,
    308-312
   seller disclosures, 313
   settlement statements,
    314
   software, 176-177
  samples, 290
  steps and standards, 289
  timelines, 293
transfer of ownership, 54
transforming the profession,
 248
transitioning careers, 6-7

U–V

VA (Veterans Administration)
 loans, 54
valuation of property, 53
vehicle offices, 227
viewing MLS, 94-95
virtual assistants, 158, 342-343
virtual tours, 274
VREO, Inc. website, 167

W

warranty deeds, 55
web-based contact manage-
 ment, 174-175
web-based paging, 189-190,
 195
Wi-Fi, 167
WINForms, 177
wireless service expenses, 204
Word, 172
work space, 84
WWAN (wireless wide-area
 network), 167

X–Y–Z

ZipForms, 177
zoning, 18